A POLITICAL EDUCATION

JUSTICE, POWER, AND POLITICS

The Justice, Power, and Politics series publishes new works in history that explore the myriad struggles for justice, battles for power, and shifts in politics that have shaped the United States over time. Through the lenses of justice, power, and politics, the series seeks to broaden scholarly debates about America's past as well as to inform public discussions about its future.

More information on the series, including a complete list of books published, is available at http://justicepowerandpolitics.com/.

A POLITICAL EDUCATION

Black Politics and Education Reform

in Chicago since the 1960s

ELIZABETH TODD-BRELAND

THE UNIVERSITY OF NORTH CAROLINA PRESS
Chapel Hill

This book was published with the assistance of the
William R. Kenan Jr. Fund
of the University of North Carolina Press.

Set in Quadraat types by Tseng Information Systems, Inc.
The University of North Carolina Press has been a member of the
Green Press Initiative since 2003.

Permission to reprint an excerpt from "Why I Go Hungry for Dyett"
in https://ajustchicago.org/2015/08/why-i-go-hungry-for-dyett/ granted by
Dr. Monique Redeaux-Smith.

Cover photos: Karen Lewis during 2012 Chicago teacher's strike
(Jason Wambsgans/ChicagoTribune/TNS); Chicago skyline (CPC_02_D_00733_005,
Chicago Photographic Collection, University of Illinois at Chicago Library)

Library of Congress Cataloging-in-Publication Data
Names: Todd-Breland, Elizabeth, author.
Title: A political education : black politics and education reform
in Chicago since the 1960s / Elizabeth Todd-Breland.
Other titles: Justice, power, and politics.
Description: Chapel Hill : The University of North Carolina Press, [2018] | Series:
Justice, power, and politics | Includes bibliographical references and index.
Identifiers: LCCN 2018016248| ISBN 9781469646572 (cloth : alk. paper) |
ISBN 9781469646589 (pbk : alk. paper) | ISBN 9781469646596 (ebook)
Subjects: LCSH: Strikes and lockouts—Teachers—Illinois—Chicago. |
African Americans—Political activity—Illinois—Chicago. |
Educational change—Illinois—Chicago.
Classification: LCC LB2844.47.U62 I558 2018 | DDC 331.88/1137110977311—dc23
LC record available at https://lccn.loc.gov/2018016248

To my parents,

Saralee Todd and Reginald Todd,

and

the many parents, students,

and educators

whose struggle for a better world

inspired this book

CONTENTS

MAPS AND ILLUSTRATIONS

Maps

Illustrations

ABBREVIATIONS AND ACRONYMS
IN THE TEXT

BYP 100	Black Youth Project 100
CAPTS	Community, Administration, Parents, Teachers, and Students decision-making model
CBUC	Chicago Black United Communities
CCCO	Coordinating Council of Community Organizations
CIBI	Council of Independent Black Institutions
CORE	Congress of Racial Equality
CPS	Chicago Public Schools
CTU	Chicago Teachers Union
CUL	Chicago Urban League
ESAA	Emergency School Aid Act
ESEA	Elementary and Secondary Education Act
FLY	Fearless Leading by the Youth
FTB	full-time basis substitute
HEW	U.S. Department of Health, Education, and Welfare
HPKCC	Hyde Park–Kenwood Community Conference
IPE	Institute of Positive Education
LSC	Local School Council
NAACP	National Association for the Advancement of Colored People
NCDC	New Concept Development Center
PCC	Parent Community Council
PCER	People's Coalition for Education Reform
P.O.W.E.R.	People Organized for Welfare and Employment Rights
PURE	Parents United for Responsible Education
PUSH	People United to Save [later Serve] Humanity (Operation PUSH)
SCLC	Southern Christian Leadership Conference
SNCC	Student Nonviolent Coordinating Committee
TWO	The Woodlawn Organization
UIC	University of Illinois at Chicago
WCB	Woodlawn Community Board
WESP	Woodlawn Experimental Schools Project

A POLITICAL EDUCATION

INTRODUCTION

For seven days in September 2012, the Chicago Teachers Union (CTU) shut down the City of Chicago. Of the CTU's more than 26,000 members, almost 90 percent had voted to authorize the strike. Thousands of striking teachers, community activists, parents, students, and supporters flooded the streets in protest. A sea of red shirts surrounded City Hall and Chicago Public Schools (CPS) headquarters.

In a city known for its long history of residential segregation, it was an incredibly diverse group: people of color and White folks, women—lots of women!—and men, young teachers and older veteran teachers. Teachers and parents marched while pushing strollers and holding little ones' hands. Together they chanted: "Lies and tricks will not divide, Parents and Teachers side by side!"[1] Led by Karen Lewis, CTU president and a veteran Black educator, the teachers on strike in Chicago mirrored the core of the Democratic Party's electoral base, a racially diverse, traditionally Democratic group of middle-class public sector workers. These were the people who show up to the polls and vote. Were it not for the picket signs attacking Chicago's Democratic mayor Rahm Emanuel, one could easily mistake the assembled group for attendees at a rally for Barack Obama's presidential reelection campaign. But impressive as the sea of red shirts may have been, a year later the carcasses of nearly fifty shuttered schools in predominantly Black and Latinx neighborhoods were just as striking.

The year that started with the city's first teachers' strike in a quarter century ended with the largest intentional mass closure of public schools in U.S. history. The leaders who shaped these bookend events represented starkly different political traditions. Karen Lewis drew upon sustained community organizing efforts in the city's predominantly Black and Latinx communities. The striking teachers and their supporters were both protesting the anti-union privatization policies of the local Democratic administration and calling for resources to address the enduring structural inequities that relegated Black and Latinx students to separate and unequal schools. Chicago mayor Rahm Emanuel, a former investment banker, congressman, and presidential aide to Bill Clinton and Barack Obama, insisted that the logic of corporate reorganization and the market necessitated school closures to remedy the struggling system. These colliding political currents were the product of enduring and unresolved struggles over urban racial politics and education reform.

A Political Education: Black Politics and Education Reform in Chicago since the 1960s recovers and exposes this history. This book analyzes Black education reformers' community-based strategies to improve education beginning during the 1960s and shows how these efforts clashed with a burgeoning neoliberal educational apparatus during the late twentieth century. The historic 2012 CTU strike and the massive school closures that followed laid bare the ruptures resulting from this painful collision.

Black education organizing presents an opportunity to examine the possibilities and constraints of neoliberalism as a conceptual frame for the period since the fiscal crises of the 1970s. Though neoliberalism at times seems to encompass everything and nothing, here it describes the significant economic restructuring that has shaped life since the 1970s, with roots stretching back decades earlier. Naomi Klein uses the term "corporatism" to describe the many features that characterize these shifts in the "Global North": the transition from an industrial economy to a service economy, the rise of finance capitalism, and the intensified consolidation of money and power by a small group of political and corporate elites. In this political and economic realignment, crises real and imagined pave the way for dramatic economic and social restructuring based on "the policy trinity—the elimination of the public sphere, total liberation for corporations and skeletal social spending." This economic restructuring profoundly impacted the realm of education where corporate and political elites have projected a perpetual state of educational crisis—of funding, achievement, and pedagogy—to justify the transfer of public funds to private entities, attacks on teacher unions, divestment from funding universally accessible high-quality public education, and the embrace of market-based competition and choice by private sector actors, state officials, and corporate education reformers. This era of neoliberalism affected the context in which the actors in this book operated.[2]

A Political Education is the story of Black activists, educators, parents, and students who navigated, challenged, and contributed to the urban political and educational landscape from mid-twentieth-century civil rights struggles through the more recent corporate reorganization of the public sphere. However, this history must also be understood in relation to Black urbanites' varied political responses to successive invocations of the "urban crisis." The struggle for school desegregation was a hallmark of mid-twentieth-century civil rights struggles, but as deindustrialization and "White flight" left behind city school systems with Black majorities, by the late 1960s many within urban communities found desegregation impractical and undesirable. Ideological conflicts emerged within Black communities about how best to respond, and Black education reformers generated a host of different local community-based responses to the "urban crisis" and the reorganization of the welfare state. These efforts eventually collided with, and contributed to, the proprietary decentralization plans of corporate education reformers who came to see urban education as a new frontier for capital investment.

RETHINKING URBAN AMERICA SINCE THE 1960S

Urban historians have outlined the formal political culture, spatial dynamics, and economic forces that led to a period of "urban crisis" after World War II in northern and western U.S. cities. Social scientists and historians often portray the period after the late 1960s as an era of urban demobilization and civic disengagement or chronicle the triumph of conservatism, the rise of the New Right, and suburban politics. Together, these narratives highlight the power of deindustrialization and "White flight" in reconfiguring metropolitan space and stripping cities of their tax base, as the population of non-White—most often Black—residents increased proportionally. However, this rendering of the "urban crisis" can also leave the impression that cities of this era were wastelands of Black poverty, pathology, crime, and decline where Black residents were too disenfranchised or focused on survival to be politically engaged. Similarly, analyses of the rise of the New Right often disregard the histories of cities and African Americans as meaningful political actors.[3]

To be sure, a rightward political turn during the mid- to late twentieth century produced budget cuts, rollbacks in public services and civil rights gains, and electoral shifts. However, when we focus solely on the rise of modern conservatism, the antecedents of the "Reagan revolution," the dominance of finance capitalism and the "Walmartizing" of the U.S. economy, and the sociopolitical significance of suburbs and Whiteness, Black political organizing and activism become invisible.[4] Narratives that fixate on urban decline and the rise of the right do not adequately account for the range of political activity in urban Black communities since the 1960s. While massive national grassroots Black Freedom movements declined in the late 1960s and early 1970s, the localized struggles that undergirded Civil Rights and Black Power movements continued in communities across the country.[5]

Struggles for school reform reveal that far from demobilizing, Black political activity shifted to new terrain. Black struggles for school reform since the 1960s embraced both continuities and contradictions in political organizing strategies and ideological understandings of education and Black politics, as Black people with diverse political perspectives and strategies worked to put their ideas into action. A *Political Education* presents a different picture of Black politics and Black communities by focusing on the politics of African Americans who continued to live in cities during this period of "urban crisis." Not overcome by apathy or nihilism, Black Chicagoans continued to organize to improve education for Black children in public schools, community and civic organizations, and independent institutions.

Contemporary activists, journalists, and politicians claim that education is "the Civil Rights issue of our time."[6] But struggles for education as a civil right are certainly not new. Informed by educational policy studies, I approach political organizing as a window into the dynamic interplay between schools and communities.[7] Drawing from social scientists' interrogations of intraracial class relations and politics, I employ a historical methodological and conceptual approach to the study of urban life, Black politics, and the "urban crisis."[8] The research for this project took place over nearly ten years, and I used materials from many archival collections, including the papers of community organizations and political officials, activists' and educators' personal papers, and Board of Education and government documents and reports, in order to uncover historical connections and disconnections in Black political struggles from the 1960s through the present. I was also fortunate to have the opportunity to conduct oral history interviews with more than two dozen people actively involved in this history. These interviews often led me to new information, sources, and avenues of inquiry that were otherwise obscured in archives and the official historical record. Both a social and intellectual history, A *Political Education* contextualizes the actions and ideologies of Black Chicagoans who challenged the existing racial order in urban politics and education reform.

As Black Power politics permeated Black neighborhoods in the 1960s and 1970s, community-based groups sought to achieve control of the institutions in their neighborhoods. The language, symbols, and politics of Black Power, emphasizing racial pride, Black empowerment, and self-determination, resonated with many African Americans.[9] Attending to the politics of the educators and administrators who fought for Black self-determination within and outside public school systems provides a unique framework for interpreting Black Power.

Coinciding with more forceful demands for Black self-determination from grassroots organizations, a series of urban uprisings took place during the mid- to late 1960s, including in Chicago, in response to long-standing racial injustices in housing, employment, policing, and education. These events alarmed government leaders and the broader White public, as they came on the heels of major federal Civil Rights legislative gains with the passage of the 1964 Civil Rights Act and the 1965 Voting Rights Act. These uprisings, along with sustained community organizing efforts, increased the sense of urgency behind the War on Poverty programs initiated by President Lyndon B. Johnson's administration to address the sources of urban poverty, substandard housing, and a lack of quality educational and employment opportunities. Black community organizers—including many of the historical actors in the following pages—seized on this moment to obtain federal funding to support their own visions of political change and empowerment through local education projects.[10]

A Political Education focuses on the role of continued Black protest, community-based activism, and insurgent politics in the urban North in what some call the Long Civil Rights Movement. The chronological, ideological, and geographic boundaries of the Civil Rights and Black Power movements seem ever expanding.[11] Education struggles were—and are—vital to the Civil Rights Movement, Black Power Movement, and the production of our contemporary political landscape.

EDUCATION AS A SITE OF STRUGGLE

Education holds a distinctive place in the national imagination. The right to a public education is a uniquely enduring part of the U.S. democratic social contract. As a primary institution through which families come into direct contact with the state on a daily basis, public schools are neither solely authoritarian state-controlled bureaucratic political spaces nor solely community spaces. The contested meanings and purposes of education make schools key sites of conflict and mediation of the everyday aspirations and challenges that people experience within their communities. As such, schools and education struggles allow us to trace the boundaries of U.S. democracy and changes in the relationship between citizens and the state.

The 1954 *Brown v. Board of Education* decision looms large in popular understandings of Black struggles for educational equity. However, the *Brown* decision—which notably stated that "separate educational facilities were inherently unequal"—was not a moment of resolution but instead initiated a new period of contestation over strategies for racial justice and equity.[12] The desegregation policies that were actually implemented in response to *Brown* prefigure the contemporary triumph of neoliberal "diversity" over equity and racial justice.

Desegregation has not been the only, or even the most dominant, strategy that Black people pursued to achieve educational equity and liberation. Within African American communities, education has occupied a place of heightened importance because of linkages between education and freedom: from struggles for literacy by enslaved people and Black northerners' coupling of school integration and citizenship claims during the antebellum era, to challenges in finding schooling to meet the needs of freed people, to Civil Rights era linkages between literacy, education, and liberation.[13] Based on an ethic of self-reliance and self-determination, Black southerners established their own schools across the South in the years after emancipation. During Reconstruction, formerly enslaved women and men also worked with northern benevolent and missionary societies, Republican officials, and the Freedmen's Bureau to fight for universal public education.[14] During the early twentieth century, African Americans embraced a variety of approaches to improve Black education, including Black nationalist and Pan-Africanist appeals to racial unity, separatism, and non-Eurocentric curricula; democratic-socialists' positioning of schools as sites to challenge an unjust U.S. political economic order; Christian humanists' support for a classical liberal education; and progressive-liberalism in the tradition of Carter G. Woodson.[15] Mid-twentieth-century civil rights protests for school desegregation emerged as part of this longer history of diverse Black educational struggles for freedom and justice. During the 1960s and 1970s, Black education reformers drew on the legacies of these older Black education traditions to develop new political organizing strategies focused on quality education rather than desegregation.

I intentionally refer to the Black actors who animate this history as Black "education reformers" to reclaim the term from its popular association. In the early twenty-first century, predominantly White business leaders, education management companies, corporate-style charter school operators, philanthropists, and big-city mayors have come to dominate the discourse on education policy reform so much that they have become synonymous with the phrase "education reform." In their discourse, Black communities are places that need to be reformed, not places that generate reformers. This erases the much longer history of education organizing led by Black parents, teachers, students, activists, and community organizations. In this context, I am not using the term "reformer" as a counter to "revolutionary" but simply as a general descriptor of someone pursuing societal change. Indeed, in a White supremacist society, the pursuit of a quality education by Black people that reinforces their inherent dignity can be a revolutionary act in and of itself.[16] In calling these historical actors "Black education reformers," I am insisting that Black urbanites' education organizing and political engagement was—and is—central to the politics of cities, education reform, and U.S. history and democracy.

For African Americans, the impact of deindustrialization was particularly painful. African Americans were already often the last hired and first fired, but Black unemployment rates increased with the decline of low-skilled, relatively higher-paying industrial work in cities. In the postwar period, as urban manufacturing plants closed across the Northeast and Midwest, Black urban workers were left to face a labor market constricted by discrimination and a spatial mismatch between their location in the city core and expanding job opportunities in racially exclusionary suburbs and the growing "Sunbelt" economies in the southern and western U.S. states. The impact of this restructuring accelerated during the 1970s. In Chicago's Cook County, the unemployment rate among African Americans in their prime working years increased dramatically between 1970 and 1990, from 6.4 to 16.5 percent for Black women and from 5.9 to 22.3 percent for Black men, with even higher rates for Black women and men under twenty-five. During the same period, Black family poverty increased by one-third from 22.9 to 30.9 percent. In contrast, while unemployment increased at a higher rate for working-age White men, overall unemployment levels for this group remained significantly lower than those for African Americans, only increasing from 2.2 to 6 percent, while the White family poverty rate only increased marginally from 8.6 to 9.2 percent.[17]

At the same time, Black Chicagoans were gaining access to employment in middle-class public sector jobs—including teaching and other jobs with the Board of Education—in record numbers. Segregation in housing and education meant that, generally, Black teachers taught Black students in schools located within Black communities. The growing Black middle-class teaching and administrative force served a public school student population that was increasingly Black and low-income. Defying narratives of middle-class flight, many of the middle-class Black activists and reformers central to this study— who organized for school integration, community control, and independent Black institutions—remained in the city and continued to work with, and remain connected to, Black poor and working-class communities.

Understanding Black urban communities since the 1960s requires a reconciliation of this simultaneous expansion of the Black middle class and of the Black poor—or the Black "underclass," in the pejorative parlance of "urban crisis" literature.[18] The politics of Black urban education does just this.

In response to the "urban crisis," Black Chicagoans developed political organizing efforts and social networks that included important coalitions between middle-class, working-class, and poor Black women and men. The Black education reformers discussed in the following chapters emerged from the tier of activists, parents, educators, students, and workers located politically and socially "between the powerful and the wider citizenry."[19] Black education struggles included Black parents from across the class spectrum. Poor, working-class, and middle-class Black parents organized desegregation protests, parent councils for community control programs, and citywide parent and community councils for education reform. However, while an economic cross section of Black Chicago participated in education struggles, the interests of the participants were not always the same. Black communities during this period included people born in Chicago and first-generation migrants whose families left the South in search of better opportunities. Black Chicagoans' political visions were also informed by age, gender, sexuality, religion, family history, and class background. Intraracial differences led to tensions between traditional Black uplift organizations, working-class Black parent organizations, student protesters, Black teachers, and neighborhood-based community groups. These tensions informed the strange bedfellows that emerged in urban education. Intersecting identities and interests influenced African Americans' pursuit of different education reform strategies and highlight divisions within an imagined singular "Black community" united in racial struggle.[20]

As a study of Black education activism, this is also a book about Black women's activism. The personal narratives and political lives of Black women play a prominent role in the following pages. Black women often did the heavy lifting and tedious work required of political and community organizing, while Black men were recognized as the public face of Black political leadership and activism. This was especially true in the field of education. Teachers were a largely feminized workforce during the latter half of the twentieth century. This was even truer for African Americans. Black women constituted the vast majority of Black teachers and Board of Education employees. Black women, like those highlighted in this book, are often sidelined in accounts of Black politics: working-class single mother and labor organizer Rosie Simpson; veteran education administrator and scholar Barbara Sizemore; educator, engineer, and institution builder Soyini Walton; teacher-activist Lillie Peoples; and Black student protester turned union leader Karen Lewis. These Black women were activists, organizers, educators, and intellectuals who theorized and implemented efforts to improve education for Black children. Their political and intellectual labor powered movements for racial justice and belong at the center of discussions of Black politics, social movements, and education reform locally and nationally.

On the national stage, mid-twentieth-century ideas of racial liberalism helped to expand the state's responsibility for social welfare and dismantle the legal apparatus of Jim Crow; however, in northern and western cities, liberal Democratic Party leaders and their White constituents also stifled Black grassroots politics. Historians have spilled much ink in the effort to determine exactly when and why the New Deal labor-liberal coalition crumbled sometime between World War II and the rise of Ronald Reagan.[21] That is not my project. If anything, I hope to deromanticize ideas about the labor-liberal alliance that emerged during the New Deal. This is not to minimize the contributions that interracial coalitions, labor-leftist organizations, and racial liberals made to civil rights struggles. During World War II, the rhetoric of racial liberalism was deployed in the U.S. fight against fascism. In the postwar period, an interracial group of civil rights activists, policymakers, social scientists, and intellectuals promoted a racial liberalism that called for a strong antiracist integrationist state while also espousing anticommunism and understandings of racism that relied on psychological, interpersonal, and individualistic notions of racial prejudice and conflict. It is this version of racial liberalism that the National Association for the Advancement of Colored People (NAACP) legal team mobilized in arguing the 1954 *Brown v. Board of Education* case and that the U.S. Supreme Court adopted to condemn Jim Crow segregation. The Great Society programs of the 1960s continued to espouse a racial liberalism that embraced an activist role for the government in creating societal change—even if government and program officials were often reluctant to implement change without demand. Even while making demands using these notions of racial liberalism, however, African Americans were often critical of the gap between these purported values and their lived realities.[22]

For Black Chicagoans, labor-liberal alliances and an expanded liberal welfare state did not deliver uniformly transcendent gains. Locally, the Cook County Democratic Party—the Chicago Democratic machine—emerged to dominate local politics alongside the New Deal liberal coalition that propelled the Democratic Party into power nationally during the 1930s and remained in power for decades.

Black Chicagoans were junior partners in a Chicago political machine that bound them to constituencies with which they had little in common except a desire for patronage benefits from the machine. Even so, the Democratic machine did produce a unique political infrastructure and power base for Black

Chicagoans to launch campaigns for local, state, and national office. Beyond the machine, Black Chicago generated its own robust grassroots community organizing tradition and Black institutional infrastructure.[23] Forging interracial coalitions could be more fraught. Just as northern African Americans and southern Democrats were a hostile pairing within the New Deal Democratic coalition, in Chicago, White ethnic community and labor leaders and Black Chicagoans were, at times, contentious factions within the local Democratic machine. Black Chicagoans were often excluded from labor unions and—as was the case with the teachers union—forced to fight for full inclusion. Richard J. Daley, machine boss and mayor from 1955 until his death in 1976, was a liberal Democrat who supported civil rights actions to end legal segregation and open access to public accommodations in the South. But he was also the main opponent of Black freedom struggles in Chicago.[24]

The Black organizers, educators, parents, and civic leaders mentioned in the following pages were not necessarily united by philosophies that fit neatly into existing political categories: liberal, conservative, radical, nationalist, or accommodationist. Rather, their organizing suggests the need for a new frame, what I call the *politics of Black achievement*. The four chapters in the first section of the book examine struggles for desegregation, community control, independent Black educational institutions, and Black teacher power as diverse strands of a broader politics of Black educational achievement that developed during the 1960s and 1970s. This particular politics of Black achievement arose in the context of the liberal welfare state's failure to deliver educational equity through desegregation and the proliferation of discourses of Black pathology and inferiority generated by researchers and the state.

While heterogeneous in tactics and ideology, a generation of Black education reformers during the 1960s and 1970s embraced a Black self-determinist politics of Black achievement that forged a political commitment to improving the quality of Black children's education and demonstrating that Black students could achieve whether or not the schools they attended were integrated. This commitment drew on a Black self-determinist critique of the ideas of Black inferiority and pathology embedded in liberal reports and policies (including the *Brown* decision, desegregation plans, and the Coleman and Moynihan reports). This analysis held that even if these reports and related policies argued that the state should address the systemic dispossession of, and underinvestment in, Black communities, these arguments were tainted by ideas of Black pathology, inferiority, and the culture of poverty. Instead, Black education reformers embraced a politics of Black achievement through their pursuit of alternative Black self-determinist strategies for quality education that disrupted ideas of Black inferiority. Desegregation efforts in middle-class communities, community control of schools, the development of independent Black educational institutions, efforts to increase Black representation in the teaching force, demands for funding equalization, and the discourses of supporters of both Black neighborhood schools and charter schools all reflected the politics of Black achievement.

Chapter 1, "The Rise and Fall of the Desegregation Paradigm," analyzes the history of desegregation strategies pursued in Chicago and the processes by which those strategies fell out of favor. The chapter analyzes desegregation demonstrations, mass protests, and citywide committees launched during the 1950s and 1960s by the Coordinating Council of Community Organizations (CCCO), the Chicago Urban League (CUL), and local neighborhood groups. Even during this period of intensive organizing for school desegregation, the slow pace of desegregation and lack of commitment by city officials sowed seeds of ambivalence toward desegregation strategies. Disillusioned with the progress of desegregation, many Black students, parents, educators, and community groups began advocating for alternatives to desegregation, including community control of schools.

Chapter 2, "Community Control," examines the movement for community control that developed in Chicago during the 1960s and 1970s. Students, parents, and community organizations pursued community control of schools through citywide educational conferences, protests, and student boycotts, and in the Woodlawn Experimental Schools Project (WESP), Chicago's experiment with decentralization and community control of schools. Using War on Poverty funds and led by Rev. Arthur Brazier and Barbara Sizemore, WESP brought together historically hostile partners as a joint project between the University of Chicago, CPS, and The Woodlawn Organization (TWO), a Black community-based organization. The War on Poverty is remembered as a moment when government programs expanded dramatically while incorporating more local participation from members of impacted communities into the implementation of these programs. This narrative of the War on Poverty conceals the role of powerful private entities—like the University of Chicago—in publicly funded programs. Originating in a different historical context, WESP was a precursor to national educational trends of semiautonomous school governance and public-private partnerships addressed in the second section of the book. The shift from desegregation to community control was not solely a response to the state's failure to desegregate schools. It also reflected the prominence of a strain of Black political thought that foregrounded Black empowerment and self-governance in efforts to increase Black achievement.

Chapter 3, "Building Independent Black Institutions," focuses on the creation of independent Black educational institutions as another enactment of a Black self-determinist politics of Black achievement. This chapter specifically focuses on the Institute of Positive Education (IPE), an independent Black institution influenced by the Black Power and Black Arts movements. Like the community control advocates of WESP, these Black education reformers were not interested in pursuing integration. However, while WESP worked within the public school system, the architects of IPE rejected the state's ability to provide an adequate education for Black students. Instead, they circumvented the public school system and the financial support of the state by creating an independent school with an African-centered curriculum and programming based in a Black community. By bypassing the state-run education system, the educators and operators of independent Black institutions worked within a set of political possibilities and constraints different from those of organizations that sought engagement with the state. Concerns about IPE's scale and financial viability foreshadow the organization's move to open charter schools, as discussed in Chapter 6.

Chapter 4, "Teacher Power: Black Teachers and the Politics of Representation," examines the growth in Black representation among public sector employees of the Board of Education, from an insurgent group of educators in the 1960s through the establishment of the middle-class base of the coalition that elected Harold Washington as the first Black mayor of Chicago in 1983. Black educators in traditional public schools were on the front lines of efforts to transform Black education and city politics. In the late 1960s, Black public school teachers—frustrated with the inadequate conditions in schools serving Black children and their marginalized role in the CTU—protested the union and even considered creating an alternative Black teachers' union. By the 1980s, internal and external pressures on the union resulted in a significant increase in the proportion of Black teachers and the election of Jacqueline Vaughn as the first African American and woman president of the CTU in 1984. This chapter analyzes the interplay of race and gender in Black women educators' professional and community lives and activism. In the context of deindustrialization and the rise of lower-wage jobs in the service sector, Black teachers served as anchors of communities, caretakers of children, and a relatively stable Black urban middle class through their employment in the public sector. Black educators transformed Black communities and Black political power in the city. Understanding this history is even more urgent given the recent political attacks on public school teachers and public sector employees nationally, which have had a disproportionately negative impact on African Americans.

Chapter 5, "Chicago School Reform: Harold Washington and a New Era of Decentralization," analyzes the racial politics of Mayor Harold Washington's election, his education summit, and the supporters and critics of the 1988 Chicago School Reform Act. Harold Washington's election as the first Black mayor of Chicago in 1983 was heralded by many as the ultimate attainment of Black Power and the success of the local Black Freedom Movement. His electoral victory was grounded in the previous decades' ideological ferment and years of grassroots struggle by Black organizers fighting for integration, community control, and Black empowerment.[25] While historians have largely considered the 1980s as a product of the political triumph of conservatism and the "Reagan revolution," in Chicago a Black-led, urban, antimachine, progressive coalitional politics led to Washington's electoral victory.[26] The disparate programmatic and ideological camps detailed in previous chapters (desegregation activists, community control organizers, founders of independent Black institutions, Black educators) staked claims on Mayor Washington and his political organization. The politics of Washington's education reform summits, however, exposed the fractures within this political coalition. The interracial and intraracial struggles over school reform in Chicago during the 1980s revealed the tensions between a politics of racial representation and a politics of progressive transformation and prefigured the increased privatization of public education in the decades that followed.

Chapter 6, "Corporate School Reform: Magnets, Charters, and the Neoliberal Educational Order," traces how the models for education generated by local community-based Black education organizers in previous decades collided with, and contributed to, neoliberal models of school choice, competition, and privatization. I situate Chicago's education reform policies of the 1980s and 1990s within national debates about the utility of the "Effective Schools" model, shifts to mayoral control of schools, and the proliferation of magnet schools and charter schools. As was the case historically, Black Chicagoans did not respond monolithically to neoliberal educational and political models. Black parents of varying class backgrounds flocked to magnet schools and charter schools. Black teachers in traditional public schools questioned the implications of privatization for hard-fought political and professional gains. Meanwhile, new debates emerged over issues of funding equalization, parent and community involvement in schools, accountability measures, and the value of neighborhood schools. This chapter discusses points of historical continuity and discontinuity in the transition from urban education reform models seeking equity to models promoting market-based "school choice."

The book's epilogue considers the local and national political implications of this history for our contemporary moment. Both contemporary proponents and opponents of "school choice" policies have used language and practices reminiscent of Black education reformers of the past to frame their arguments. Social justice–oriented ideas of self-determination and localism generated within a different political context have been repurposed as modalities of neoliberalization. Moreover, the expansion of private interests in public schools has challenged the role of public entities in the future of urban education altogether.[27] Beginning in the mid-1990s, Chicago mayor Richard M. Daley, only to be outdone in the 2010s by Rahm Emanuel, ushered in corporate education reform and "school choice" plans that expanded charter schools and "turned around" or closed more than 150 public schools, including the mass closure of schools in 2013.[28] The embrace of corporate-style neoliberal education reform policies locally and nationally has been a bipartisan affair, with the Clinton, George W. Bush, Obama, and Donald Trump administrations proposing various policies premised on market-based principles of competition, privatization, charter school expansion, and a reliance on standardized testing. While Chicago has produced many of these policies, the city also produced strident resistance movements against these efforts. The epilogue considers the enduring challenges in public education and urban politics and the dynamic new cohort of activists and organizers proposing alternative visions of educational, economic, and racial liberation and justice.

Focusing on local actors to tell a story that has pressing national implications, A Political Education reveals Chicago as a center for the production of Black politics and national education reform policies. Political scientist Frederick Harris called Chicago "the political capital of Black America." Chicago produced an inordinate number of Black elected officials during the twentieth century. These politicians not only were important locally but also had a major impact on national politics. Chicago is the adopted home of America's first Black president, Barack Obama. The independent Black politics that developed during the mid-1960s in Chicago and continued in various forms beyond then paved the way for Obama's electoral victory in 2008. The city's Black electoral political infrastructure has been matched by an equally formidable grassroots political organizing tradition in the city. The narrative arc of Obama's political career—from community organizer on the South Side of Chicago to U.S. president—again catapulted Chicago to the center of national political and policy discussions. Obama's appointment of former CPS chief and Mayor Richard M.

Daley appointee Arne Duncan as the U.S. secretary of education further elevated Chicago's corporate-style education reform policies as a model for education reform efforts nationally.[29]

Struggles for racial justice in Chicago also reveal broader national trends in the historical collision between community-based responses to urban decline and the rise of neoliberalism. In recent years, Chicago has become ground zero in the battle between corporate capital and community-based organizing for racial and economic justice. The city's 2012 teachers' strike and the historic school closings in 2013 highlight the disjuncture between discourses of postracial politics and the lived realities of racial inequality. As such, the history laid out in the following pages informs contemporary debates over urban inequality, U.S. democracy, and the dismantling of public education nationally. These debates call into question the very viability and future of public institutions. Will a small corporate elite backed by municipal governments take over public institutions? Will insurgent community-based movements reorient policy debates toward demands for racial and economic justice? These policies and debates are the product of a history shaped by Black struggles for education in Chicago.

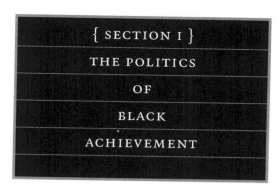

{ SECTION I }

THE POLITICS

OF

BLACK

ACHIEVEMENT

THE RISE AND FALL OF THE

DESEGREGATION PARADIGM

Between World War I and 1970, 7 million Black migrants traveled from the South to the North as part of the Great Migration. Rosie Simpson's family was among them. Leaving behind racial terror and limited opportunities in the South, they sought better social and economic opportunities in Chicago's famed Black Metropolis. However, when Simpson and her family arrived in Chicago in the 1940s, instead of a gilded land of opportunity, they encountered harsh winters and cramped living conditions in a rundown building in the heart of the South Side's Black Belt. Black families like Simpson's were crowded into this densely populated community by housing segregation, employment discrimination, and racist policies that limited African Americans' opportunities for financial and geographic mobility.[1]

Since the late nineteenth century, Chicago has ranked among the most segregated cities in the nation. As Chicago's Black population increased by fivefold between 1910 and 1940, federal and local real estate and banking policies increasingly restricted African Americans into contiguous Black neighborhoods on the South Side and a growing group of racially concentrated neighborhoods on the West Side. Neighborhood schooling policies upheld the link between schools and residential housing patterns, ensuring the maintenance of segregation.[2]

Yet those living in Chicago's Black communities found that segregation also encouraged congregation, the development of Black institutions, and a unique sense of kinship in Black neighborhoods.[3] Rosie Simpson was born in Louisiana in 1930, the second of seven children. In Chicago, Simpson's mother taught Sunday school and cooked huge amounts of food to feed all of the children who were around her home at mealtimes. This made Simpson's apartment the hangout spot for kids on her block and shaped her sense of responsibility for the well-being of her broader community. Black Chicago's segregation also led to the establishment of more formal institutional spaces for intraracial congregation, including the South Side's Wendell Phillips High School, the first predominantly Black high school in Chicago.[4]

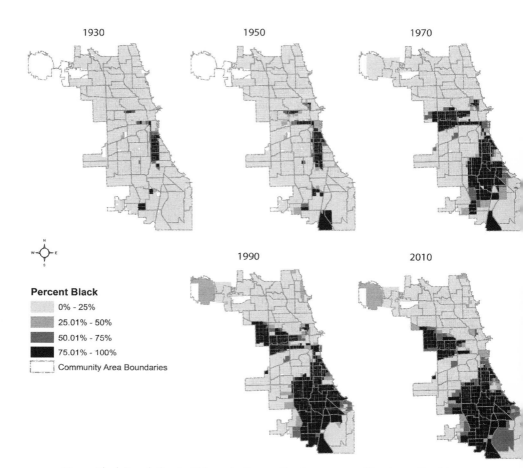

1930 1950 1970

1990 2010

Percent Black

0% - 25%
25.01% - 50%
50.01% - 75%
75.01% - 100%
Community Area Boundaries

Map 1. Black Population in Chicago by Census Tract, 1930–2010 (Courtesy of José Acosta-Córdova, University of Illinois at Chicago, Institute for Research on Race and Public Policy)

Phillips held a revered space in the consciousness of Chicago's Black community and produced a number of prominent Black artists, intellectuals, and community leaders. Beginning in 1927, Phillips was led by Maudelle Bousfield, the first Black public school principal in CPS, who set high academic and social standards for her students. Across the country, Black high schools and their staff anchored Black communities. A number of Black students from Phillips went on to gain national and international acclaim, including Sam Cooke, Dinah Washington, Nat "King" Cole, Gwendolyn Brooks, Herbie Hancock, and Johnson Products founder George E. Johnson. Like Rosie Simpson, many of Phillips's famed students were also southern migrants to Chicago. Attending Phillips heightened Simpson's sense of racial pride and her belief

THE POLITICS OF BLACK ACHIEVEMENT

in the importance of education, even though she never graduated from the school. At age fifteen she lied about her age and dropped out of high school for a job in the Chicago stockyards.[5]

During World War II, Black women like Simpson seized upon expanding job opportunities in industry and factory work nationally. Meatpacking was a centerpiece of Chicago's industrial economy. Early in the twentieth century, racist policies denied Black workers employment in meatpacking or relegated them to the most dangerous tasks. Black women, if hired at all, were assigned to the least desirable positions in the plants for less pay than Whites and men. By the time Simpson entered the packinghouses in the 1940s, the number of Black women working in meatpacking had increased dramatically. Years of protest, and labor shortages during World War II, created employment opportunities in the packinghouses for previously excluded and marginalized workers. During the war, 40 percent of the workers in Chicago's meatpacking plants were Black and one-fifth were women.[6] Inspired by workers who organized for integrated departments and equal pay, Simpson became more involved in the union and was elected union steward. The United Packinghouse Workers of America Local 347 had an active antidiscrimination department, providing Simpson a means of fighting against the intersecting racial and gender inequities of the stockyards. Chicago's packinghouse unions produced a number of Black women civil rights leaders and served as a launching point for struggles against racial and gender discrimination in the workplace and in the community.[7]

Through the union, Simpson entered a broader activist network in Black Chicago. Increasingly active in local politics, she monitored polling places, knocked on doors, and worked with the local NAACP. She met Black activists in Chicago's labor, arts, and civil rights communities who mentored her and nurtured her political development beyond the union, including United Autoworkers and NAACP leader Willoughby Abner, author Frank London Brown, musician Oscar Brown Jr., and educator Timuel Black. Simpson ultimately lost her job in the stockyards as deindustrialization shuttered packinghouses beginning in the 1950s.[8] But she continued to use the political vision and organizing skills that she developed in the union as a leader in education struggles.

In 1963, Simpson started organizing Black parents in response to the poor treatment and conditions that their children faced in Englewood schools. Formerly a majority-White community, by the 1960s Englewood was transitioning into a majority-Black neighborhood as African Americans pushed south and west, beyond the confines of the Black Belt.[9] Like many schools in Chicago's Black neighborhoods, Englewood's Yale Elementary School was overcrowded. In 1962, more than three dozen Black elementary schools exceeded the district's 1,200-student "maximum size." Yet the Chicago Board of Education refused to grant Black students access to open seats in nearby under-enrolled White schools. Instead, Yale administrators informed parents that a new school building would be established in the former Goodwill Industries building. Simpson was appalled. The Goodwill building, located next to active railroad tracks, was abandoned and dangerous. Parents feared that hanging wires and debris inside the building would create hazardous conditions for students.[10]

In February 1963, Simpson organized other outraged parents to boycott and picket the school and set up freedom schools in local churches for students to attend during the boycott. In response, the Board of Education backed down from their initial plan to send students to the abandoned Goodwill building. Not long after this initial victory, while attending a Board of Education meeting, Simpson learned about the board's new plan to build a campus of mobile classrooms to relieve overcrowding. Again, the board planned to avoid desegregation by denying Black students access to open spaces in White schools. This time, Simpson mounted an even larger direct-action campaign. She was elected president of the 71st and Stewart Committee, a newly assembled group of local Black parents in Englewood. The committee demanded the desegregation of CPS schools and created a human barrier to block bulldozers sent to build the portable classrooms.[11]

Simpson's fight to desegregate CPS was grounded in a demand for equal education for Black children. Simpson believed that African Americans should "have the same rights as any other group of people." To claim those rights, she pursued school desegregation as a tool to achieve "equal education." In reflecting back on her struggles for desegregation, Simpson noted that "equal opportunity was what we were fighting for, even though we talked about integration. I think they took that as meaning that we wanted to go to school with White kids, and they would automatically learn, which was not true. We were talking equal opportunity."[12]

Black freedom struggles nationally were rife with tensions over the meaning and implications of desegregation. Should racial integration be a goal in its own right? Should obtaining more funding and resources for Black institutions be the primary goal for organizers? Who benefits and who bears the burden of mandated busing plans? In Chicago during the 1960s, CCCO, the CUL, and local neighborhood groups like Rosie Simpson's 71st and Stewart Committee launched local demonstrations, mass protests, and citywide coalitions to desegregate schools.

Yet, as this chapter will demonstrate, the mid-twentieth-century desegregation movements that arose to address overcrowding and improve Black schooling in Chicago ultimately gave way to alternative strategies. In 1966, a column in the *Chicago Defender* lamented the protracted pace of change: "The gains in the racial field have been minimal. Despite the broad sweep of the Supreme Court's 1954 desegregation ruling, in an overwhelming number of Southern school districts and many in the North, integration is yet a token observance after eleven years."[13] Failed efforts to integrate schools and communities ultimately made organizers like Rosie Simpson wary. Although desegregation remained a moral imperative and an important tactical strategy for many, these efforts were primarily concerned with gaining access to resources rather than seeking racial intermingling of students for its own sake. As a result, many Black education reformers would ultimately abandon desegregation in favor of Black self-determinist strategies.

BLACK AMBIVALENCE ABOUT DESEGREGATION

Black communities had debated the merits of desegregation long before the 1954 *Brown v. Board of Education* Supreme Court decision came down.[14] Nevertheless, desegregation would become a key strategy as battles to enforce *Brown* played out in federal courtrooms, statehouses, and local communities across the South. The passage and enforcement of the 1964 Civil Rights Act allowed the federal government to withhold funds from districts that refused to desegregate and to file suit against districts that violated desegregation mandates. These interventions by the federal government, alongside grassroots movements and court challenges, eventually made southern schools among the most desegregated schools in the nation.[15]

Building on judicial victories in southern states, local and national civil rights organizations worked to desegregate schools in the North and the West. Though many northern and western cities had discarded local laws that required school segregation, they still demonstrated extreme levels of residential segregation—the result of a history of restrictive covenants and sanctioned redlining. Segregation in housing was also policed by neighborhood groups, White racial violence, discriminatory real estate practices, and public housing policies that further segregated residents. Since most public schools assigned attendance areas based on a neighborhood schooling model, segregation in schooling was very closely tied to these patterns of residential segregation.[16]

Activists, civil rights organizations, and community groups fought back. In 1974, with the *Milliken v. Bradley* ruling in Detroit, the Supreme Court significantly constrained possibilities for metropolitan remedies that included urban/suburban desegregation plans. Nonetheless, the fight for the desegregation of schools persisted. In Chicago, a dedicated group of desegregation advocates, including members of the CUL, fought for desegregation into the 1980s.[17]

Yet even at the height of mid-twentieth-century civil rights struggles to desegregate public accommodations, many African Americans across the country expressed ambivalence about integration. Black people clearly opposed the way that segregation was used as a tool to stigmatize them and constrain their liberties and access to opportunities.[18] However, opposition to the ills of segregation did not always map onto an ideological commitment to integration. In the period leading up to the *Brown* case, the NAACP had to work hard to convince Black parents that integration was a better route to achieving quality education than demanding equal resources and facilities for Black schools. In a 1955 poll of Black southerners, only 53 percent of respondents approved of the *Brown* ruling. They questioned whether desegregating schools actually had the potential to significantly dismantle ideologies of White supremacy or deliver racial justice. Others worried that desegregation would require assimilation into White culture.[19]

African Americans also worried that school desegregation would eliminate the jobs and status of Black educators and undermine the contributions of Black schools. In 1955, renowned Black poet Langston Hughes expressed his concern for the fate of Black teachers in a *Chicago Defender* column titled "The Dilemma of the Negro Teacher Facing Desegregation." He warned that desegregation "should not be permitted to bring about major or widespread dislocations and difficulties for the thousands of citizens of color whose profession is teaching." Hughes suggested, as former NAACP leader W. E. B. Du Bois had in the 1930s, that any push for desegregation must be coupled with strengthening Black institutions. African Americans like Hughes doubted that a struggle solely against segregation could eliminate structural political, economic, and social constraints on Black life. Desegregation was one strategy among many to achieve equity.[20]

BLACK CHICAGOANS' EARLY STRUGGLES
IN CHICAGO PUBLIC SCHOOLS

During the first half of the twentieth century, as was the case nationally, Black education struggles in Chicago prioritized the fight for equal resources and facilities for Black schools, rather than desegregation.[21] Many Black parents and educators, including Phillips High School principal Maudelle Bousfield, suggested that improving and expanding school facilities within Black communities was the best remedy for the poor physical conditions and overcrowding in Black schools where students attended school on half-day shifts to accommodate overcrowding. By 1940, all of Chicago's double-shift schools were located in Black communities. Black Chicagoans pursued education equalization through the courts, protests by Black uplift organizations, direct-action campaigns, and appeals to White advocates.[22]

Real change, however, seemed impossible without political power, and African Americans, while granted token representation, played a subordinate role in the White-dominated Chicago Democratic machine. During the Great Depression in the 1930s, the local Cook County Democratic Party—what became the Chicago Democratic machine—took control of Chicago politics at the same time that the party took control nationally with the election of President Franklin Roosevelt. The machine mobilized an electoral coalition of White ethnic, labor, working-class, Catholic, and Black support and solidified its power through patronage. In the ensuing years, expanding federal funds for social services, infrastructure, and public works programs funneled an array of new resources to the city. The machine's vast network of party committeemen, aldermen, ward leaders, and precinct captains organized the city block-by-block and used these resources to dole out political favors, government jobs, and city services in exchange for loyalty and electoral support of machine candidates. Under Mayor Richard J. Daley (first elected in 1955, and the Chicago machine's greatest orchestrator) the machine expanded its strength at the state and national levels by maintaining strong voting blocs in the Illinois state legislature and the U.S. Congress.[23]

Daley's White ethnic base kept him in office, but he also maintained significant support from Chicago's Black communities, particularly poor African American wards where residents sought whatever favors, jobs, services, and assistance in navigating the city bureaucracy that machine operatives might provide. The growth of the Black population in the city from a second major wave of southern migration around World War II had made Black Chicagoans an increasingly important voting bloc. So the machine supported token Black political representation, provided that these officials toed the machine line and worked to consolidate the party's power.[24]

The machine also structured politics within Chicago's schools. Chicago never had a representative elected school board. Instead, the mayor appointed the school board. In 1946, in the wake of public outcry over corruption scandals in the schools, then-mayor Democrat Edward Kelly created what would become Chicago's Advisory Commission on School Board Nominations to take "political influence" out of the schools. This commission developed a list of names from which the mayor would appoint school board members. However, the commission itself was still appointed by the mayor, and its recommendations were extralegal and nonbinding.[25]

The mayor's appointed school board also hired the superintendent of schools. CPS superintendent Benjamin Willis, appointed in 1953, became a major target of desegregation protests. Almost all constituencies other than Black Chicagoans considered Willis an excellent superintendent. As a school administrator of the Progressive tradition, Willis stressed expertise and professionalism, increased teachers' salaries, hired more professional support staff for schools, and built many new schools. His leadership, however, rarely benefited Black students. On racial matters, Willis embraced color blindness, claiming that since the school system did not keep track of racial statistics, he was in no position to comment on accusations of race-based inequities in the schools. By willfully ignoring student racial demographics, color-blind policies—then as now—produce and perpetuate racially discriminatory policies and educational inequities.[26]

Willis opposed integration using the thinly veiled racist rhetoric of a color-blind commitment to neighborhood schools. Yet according to a 1958 investigation in the NAACP's *Crisis* magazine, CPS schools were actually even more segregated than the city as a whole. Segregated housing alone could not explain such a high degree of school segregation. In reality, school board policies actively heightened school segregation by manipulating school assignment policies, meticulously districting attendance areas along racial lines, creating barriers to student transfers, and building new schools to maintain this separation. Notwithstanding the North's regionally specific modes of enforcement, Willis's invocation of the sanctity of neighborhood schools echoed the rhetoric used by segregationist White southerners to circumvent court-ordered mandates to desegregate schools.[27]

Willis's opposition to integration and his denials of racial disparities perpetuated systemwide racial inequality. Across the country, public schools were funded by a mix of local, state, and federal funds levied through taxes. Despite mandating a "foundational level" of funding and periodic efforts at "equalization," at no time since the 1850s has the state of Illinois provided the majority of local school districts' funds. Instead, local property taxes have served as the primary source of school districts' funding. In 1964 nearly 75 percent of CPS's revenue came from local taxes, with state aid and federal aid accounting for 22 percent and less than 2 percent of total revenues, respectively.[28] Pushed by protests and court challenges, in 1963 the Illinois legislature required CPS to begin collecting statistics on the racial makeup of the student body and the teaching staff in city schools. A study conducted that year by University of Chicago education professor Robert Havighurst found that while many of the city's schools demonstrated achievement in the high or middle ranges, three-quarters of the lowest-performing schools were in Black neighborhoods and at schools that were at least 80 percent Black.[29] Predominantly Black schools also had fewer full-time teachers, more substitutes, and more new teachers with less formal training. When the large class sizes and overall attendance numbers at predominantly Black schools were factored in, per-pupil spending on Black children was only two-thirds of that spent on children in predominantly White schools.[30] CPS systematically assigned Black children to poorer-quality schools that were overcrowded and inequitably and inadequately funded.

With protests for civil rights and racial equality intensifying nationwide, Chicagoans mobilized to protest against inequities in the city's public schools.

PROTEST POLITICS: CIVIL RIGHTS AND PUBLIC EDUCATION IN CHICAGO

The full energies of civil rights struggles erupted in Chicago in the 1960s. Organizations and local residents increasingly protested injustices within the school system, and Black mothers were on the front lines. Rosie Simpson may have first developed her political consciousness on the packinghouse floor, but she came into her own in the summer of 1963 as an organizer launching protests against the makeshift mobile classrooms dubbed "Willis Wagons." Like Simpson, Luberda Bailey, another Black mother in Englewood, organized an anti–Willis Wagon demonstration in 1963 at Guggenheim School, declaring, "We don't want mobile units. . . . They only put mobile units in Negro neighborhoods." Bailey pointed out that there were open seats nearby in a predominantly White elementary school. However, Black students were prevented from transferring. Instead, Willis and the Board of Education attempted to build a school campus made up of more than two dozen mobile classrooms, near 73rd and Lowe Avenue in Englewood, to serve several hundred Black children. By lying down in the mud and rain, obstructing bulldozers prepped to install Willis Wagons at this site, Simpson and her fellow protesters were laying the foundation for a citywide mass movement.[31]

Young civil rights activists, the police, and media flocked to the protest site at 73rd and Lowe. In July, activists from the Congress of Racial Equality (CORE) had organized weeklong sit-ins and hunger strikes at the Chicago Board of Education, demanding desegregation and an end to the gerrymandering and redistricting that maintained segregated schools, overcrowding, and poor facilities in Black neighborhoods.[32] In August, young Black and White activists from CORE and Chicago Area Friends of the Student Nonviolent Coordinating Committee (SNCC) joined the local Black parents blocking construction equipment at 73rd and Lowe. As the protest continued, more adults and young people from the surrounding neighborhood also joined the demonstration. Dozens were arrested. Parents and young activists ramped up their protests by collecting garbage from around the neighborhood and dumping it on the proposed construction site to cause delays. As the demonstration went on, the police became more antagonistic and violent toward the protesters, provoking and beating many protesters before arresting them.[33]

To growing audiences, Rosie Simpson and the other protesters made the case that the mobile units perpetuated segregation. Twelve days into the protest, Simpson reiterated her commitment to keep the protest going: "We are going to let Chicago and the whole world know we are tired of inferior education for our children." Simpson's labor connections got the United Automobile Workers union to provide bail money for protesters. Black comedian and actor Dick Gregory and his wife, Lillian Gregory, stood shoulder to shoulder with protesting parents. Dick Gregory was arrested along with parents and young protesters, drawing even more media attention to the protest.[34]

Though Mayor Daley generally refrained from commenting on school matters, he broke his silence on the growing school conflicts in response to escalating protests. In response to demonstrations in front of the homes of Willis, Daley, and Board of Education president Clair Roddewig, Daley held an August press conference where he blamed the media: "Without publicity, the demonstrators would stop this tomorrow." He also claimed that the protests were led by a small group of "outside agitators" and "irresponsible people," who lacked "decency" by demonstrating at officials' homes.[35]

In response, Rosie Simpson pressured the mayor into taking a face-to-face meeting with her on August 20, 1963. To prove that the protests were homegrown, Simpson brought a petition signed by 1,300 local parents. Simpson asserted that "a municipal government responsive to the wishes of its constituency should heed our demands for removal of these segregation-maintaining devices." While Daley did not concede, the encounter hardened Simpson's resolve, setting the stage for citywide boycotts later in the fall organized by CCCO.[36]

During the early 1960s, CCCO emerged as the primary coalition of the Chicago Freedom Movement and civil rights protests in Chicago. An alliance of Black community and civil rights organizations, Black professional organizations, and interracial councils and religious groups, CCCO attempted to centralize the energies of groups dispersed across the city. The public face of CCCO was dominated by men like Rev. Arthur Brazier of TWO, Chicago Area Friends of SNCC co-chair Lawrence Landry, and educator Al Raby. However, Rosie Simpson was also active in CCCO, and the organization included many groups that were propelled and sustained by the work of women from all over the city, including, Brenetta Howell-Barrett, Rev. Addie Wyatt, Sylvia Fischer, Nancy Jefferson, Fannie Rushing, and Faith Rich, among others.[37]

Black women are often erased from histories of civil rights efforts that promoted Black male clergy and other "race men" to leadership positions. As in SCLC, SNCC, and the Civil Rights Movement more broadly, women like Rosie Simpson performed the intellectual and physical work of maintaining organizations by assuming roles at the grassroots and local levels while being excluded from the highest ranks of leadership. This is particularly notable in education struggles where Black mothers and Black women educators were often at the forefront. Black "activist mothers" and Black women educators who "assumed a mother-like role" took on "the mantle of motherhood" as a source of empowerment to organize and advocate on behalf of the children in their community.[38]

CCCO's massive school boycotts were part of a national wave of organizing that demanded quality education for Black students. In Chicago, on October 22, 1963, almost 225,000 students (nearly half of all CPS students) stayed home from school in the Freedom Day boycott. Southern civil rights struggles had been intensifying: it was five months after police used fire hoses and dogs to attack Black children marching in Birmingham, Alabama; four months after a White supremacist assassinated NAACP leader Medgar Evers in Jackson, Mississippi; two months after the March on Washington for Jobs and Freedom; and a month after the bombing of the 16th Street Baptist Church in Birmingham killed four little Black girls. In this environment, the October 1963 school boycott in Chicago also drew national attention. The protesters demanded the integration of CPS students and staff, removal of Willis and others in his administration, publication of reports on school attendance and conditions, and improved school facilities, among other things.[39]

While local circumstances and specific foes differed, Black communities across the country were organizing to address problems of separate and unequal schools. In January 1964, representatives from CCCO traveled to New York City to meet with approximately thirty civil rights leaders from primarily northern and midwestern cities to build support for a multicity boycott effort the next month. During February, hundreds of thousands of students boy-

WHY WE MARCH

WE MARCH TO SECURE QUALITY EDUCATION AND A BETTER LIFE FOR ALL THE CHILDREN OF CHICAGO.

"Why We March" pamphlet advertising 1963 CCCO schools boycott (Chicago Urban League Records, University of Illinois at Chicago Library, CULR_04_0121_1414_001)

cotted schools across several cities, including a second Freedom Day boycott in Chicago.[40] In June 1965, school protesters in Chicago blocked traffic on Lake Shore Drive, and over 250 people were arrested, making it one of the largest mass arrests of the Civil Rights era.[41]

These citywide demonstrations made connections between citizenship, equality, and resources. In the 1963 Freedom Day boycott, Black students chanted, "Two, four, six, eight, we don't want to segregate!" Protesters insisted that "every child should have an equal opportunity to get a good education." Marchers exclaimed, "We want quality in education and this is the main reason that we are marching today" and chanted, "What do we want? Books! When? Now!"[42] These activists clearly understood desegregation as a strategy to garner greater resources and access to opportunities for Black children.

During the summer of 1965, CCCO continued to pursue these ends through the courts, mounting a legal assault on CPS. The coalition complained that CPS was operating a discriminatory system in violation of Title VI, section 601, of the Federal Civil Rights Act of 1964 because "the education offered Chicago's Negro children is not only separate from, but inferior to that offered

THE POLITICS OF BLACK ACHIEVEMENT

white children."[43] This complaint to the U.S. Department of Health, Education, and Welfare (HEW) successfully froze federal funds earmarked for Chicago's schools. However, after Mayor Daley, a powerful force in the Democratic Party nationally, met personally with Democratic president Lyndon Johnson, the funds were released. Instead, an HEW undersecretary negotiated a compromise with the Chicago Board of Education, calling for additional committees and reports to assess discrimination but making few tangible changes.[44]

The efforts of civil rights organizations, Black parents, students, and community members were ultimately quashed by the local and national political power and connections of Chicago's mayor, with the backing of the White business establishment. Just before the Freedom Day boycott in 1963, business leaders, including members of the prominent Chicago Commercial Club, published a letter to Mayor Daley in the *Chicago Tribune* pledging their support for and admiration of Superintendent Willis. In coming decades, business leaders would increasingly weigh in publicly in school matters, but during this period they, too, largely deferred to the mayor and his powerful patronage machine.[45] For Black organizers, the disappointment of these setbacks revived underlying doubts about the effectiveness and value of desegregation.

THE CHICAGO URBAN LEAGUE AND THE CONTINUED FIGHT FOR DESEGREGATION

Not all civil rights organizations and leaders abandoned the desegregation mantle. In Chicago, the CUL kept the issue of school desegregation alive from the 1960s through the 1980s, while the majority of Black communities in Chicago remained highly segregated and largely residentially isolated from non-Black communities.[46] The CUL was incorporated with an interracial leadership in 1917 to help Black migrants adjust to the city. In the 1950s, the CUL was shut down and forced to restructure after White CUL supporters labeled the organization's Black executive director Sidney Williams a radical for forcefully confronting White racist violence and employment discrimination. The CUL was reconstituted in 1956, and moving forward its new leadership, including new Black executive director Edwin "Bill" Berry, would reflect the more conciliatory politics of the organization's board members and financial backers.[47] The CUL's longevity as an important institution in Black Chicago, its commitment to integration as a principle, its prolonged struggle for desegregation, and the space that the organization occupied between Black communities and the larger political power structure in the city offer a crucial view of changing attitudes toward desegregating schools and intraracial class politics.

For the CUL, integration was more than just a strategy; it was a moral imperative for improving the quality of education for Black students. In a 1977 position paper, CUL leaders explained that "we endorse and support the principle of racial integration as a worthy goal to be pursued in its own right. It is necessary as an immediate correction of the current isolation of Black pupils in the system, and as a first step toward improving the scholastic achievement of many school children who are now performing most poorly."[48] The CUL's commitment to integration reflected the politics of its middle-class professional members, who prided themselves on serving the Black community while maintaining close ties with an interracial group of business and political leaders in the city. These dual commitments shaped the organization's posture: formally outside the school system yet invested in mediating between the established political authorities who governed the schools and Black students educated within them.[49]

The CUL's social work orientation and commitment to racial cooperation were also informed by the assimilationist theories of the University of Chicago's "Chicago school" of sociology, intercultural education, and cultural pluralism. The ideas of Black and White social scientists and educators from these traditions—including Kenneth and Mamie Clark, Rachel DuBois, Isidor Chein, Robert Coles, and Alvin Poussaint—influenced the psychological framing of the arguments made in the *Brown* case as well as intergroup dynamics in direct-action civil rights organizations during the early 1960s. Historian Daryl Scott has argued that these cultural pluralists reflected currents of postwar racial liberalism in their rejection of nationalism, ethnocentrism, and class analyses. They embraced a therapeutic and interpersonal understanding of race relations, approaching racism and prejudice as diseases that afflicted individuals, requiring a strong antiracist integrationist state to ease intergroup relations. Even when CUL leaders directly challenged structural inequality, they remained committed to middle-class sensibilities of respectability, developing programs that embraced an interpersonal approach to easing race relations, nurturing a Black middle class, and disciplining the Black working class and poor.[50]

The heterogeneity of the Black community in Chicago produced dramatically different engagements and responses. The brokering work of the CUL could be viewed by some as banal moderate politics. However, it was exactly the organization's intermediary status that uniquely positioned the Black middle-class professionals of the CUL to broker and negotiate between the educational bureaucracy and community interests. School desegregation became a central part of the CUL's work in this arena.

THE POLITICS OF BLACK ACHIEVEMENT

As of the 1950s and early 1960s, desegregating schools in Chicago was not just a progressive but, in some circles, a radical position. The CUL was relatively late to the desegregation battle; but the organization did support groups that more assertively demanded desegregation in schools, and it eventually became a supporter of the CCCO demonstrations and other policies to desegregate schools. Throughout the 1960s, the CUL kept up a careful balancing act: supporting the burgeoning efforts to desegregate schools put forth by local civil rights groups in the Chicago Freedom Movement while appeasing the interests and maintaining the backing of White business and industrial leaders.[51]

The bureaucratic research-and-report-driven CUL was less threatening in a climate where more militant groups were waging direct-action protests, sit-ins, and boycotts. Rather than engaging in mass movement politics, the CUL conducted research and created reports on conditions in Black communities. To maintain its tax-exempt status, the CUL did not engage in direct lobbying on legislative issues, though it did highlight the policy implications of its reports.[52] These reports fueled more confrontational direct-action groups. For example, to dramatize the findings of a CUL report on the disparity between under-enrolled White classrooms and overcrowded Black schools on double shifts, TWO sent "truth squads" of local mothers into White schools. These women documented the significant number of open seats in these schools.[53]

In the 1960s the CUL's leadership was both criticized and lauded by different segments of Chicago's Black activist community. In May 1964, just a few months after the Freedom Day school boycotts, Black journalist, editor, and political pundit Chuck Stone contended that the CUL and Bill Berry "cannot sit in on the planning councils of the direct actionists and the demonstrators and simultaneously seek the financial aid of conservative [White] businessmen. No man can serve two masters." Other activists credited Berry and the CUL with funding their activist work. As a working-class single mother, Rosie Simpson was able to earn an income to support her family as a community organizer working on projects funded by the CUL. She recalled that the CUL provided support for more militant groups "behind the scenes," so as not to compromise the CUL's funding and political standing among White Chicagoans. She reasoned that the CUL "wouldn't have been able to get the money that they got if they had been public. So they played that dual role."[54]

At other moments, Berry and CUL leaders were more blunt in expressing their class biases and politics of accommodation. In 1967 Berry explained to an interracial audience, "There are as many different kinds and classes of Negroes as there are of White people."[55] Several years later Berry further articulated

Rosie Simpson (*second from left*) with CUL community services director Marion Henley and CUL executive director Bill Berry (ca. 1968) (Chicago Urban League Records, University of Illinois at Chicago Library, CULR_04_0200_2270_001)

his paternalistic views on distinct roles for people based on their class standing. With the caveat that he was "an authority on poor people having been one of them most of my life," Berry argued that poor people should not be on the boards of organizations because they did not meet the "ready, willing, and able test" necessary for fundraising and this type of leadership: "I do believe that we should learn from the poor their needs and aspirations. I do know that there are many places for the poor . . . to serve on committees, councils, and in consultative roles. But it is both foolish and unfair to place them in the embarrassing position of serving in a role which is destined for humiliating failure. I am totally in favor of the poor. . . . I so favor them that I recommend that we raise money from those who have it, to run programs to reduce and seek to eliminate poverty. If we succeed then the poor will no longer be poor."[56] An accommodationist orientation was also evident in Berry's and the CUL's self-conscious positioning vis-à-vis the emerging Black Power Movement in 1967: "I don't believe in Black Power. I don't believe in White Power. I believe in Shared Power."[57]

By serving as a mediating force and focusing on research, education, and legislation, the CUL preserved its association with White funders while still

THE POLITICS OF BLACK ACHIEVEMENT

staking a place in movements for racial equality in Chicago.[58] This class-conscious politics of moderation and mediation would come to characterize the CUL's work under Berry. However, while support for school integration had become a firm part of the CUL's institutional mission by 1967, across the city African Americans and Whites were questioning the feasibility and desirability of desegregation in the context of a society increasingly stratified by race and class.

Desegregation and "White Flight"

By the late 1960s there was growing concern at the national and local levels about the implications of "White flight" for the viability of school integration. Between 1950 and 1970, Chicago's White population decreased by nearly 30 percent. White residents who left the city for homes in the suburbs, aided by government subsidies, accounted for much of this loss. However, as historian Amanda Seligman argues, this was a more protracted, contested, and block-by-block process than the term "flight" suggests. Whites in Chicago fought Black residential mobility with violence, legal action, political protest, and selective cooperation in order to slow residential racial transition. While some White Chicagoans moved to the suburbs during this period, others avoided desegregation by moving from racially transitioning neighborhoods on the South Side and West Side into all-White "bungalow belt" neighborhoods on the Far Northwest and Southwest Sides. Over the course of the 1960s, these White communities would become the core of Mayor Daley's Chicago Democratic machine as Black support for Daley weakened. African Americans never became a majority of the population in Chicago as they did in "Chocolate Cities" like Detroit, Newark, and Washington, D.C. Between 1950 and 1970, Chicago's White population decreased by 29 percent, compared with Newark (54 percent), St. Louis (48 percent), and Detroit (46 percent). Chicago retained a larger proportion of White residents than these other cities experiencing "White flight" because of Daley's perceived political protection of White "bungalow belt" residents—preserving all-White neighborhoods by building the "second ghetto" that confined many African Americans to segregated public housing in all-Black neighborhoods and by opposing school desegregation plans. However, while Whites may not have fled the city across the board, they certainly did flee the public schools.[59]

Looking back, we can easily forget that education officials and reformers of the 1960s were not anticipating that White students would leave the public schools in as large numbers as they did over the next several decades. White students left the city's schools at a far more dramatic pace than initially predicted in the late 1960s. A report presented to the Chicago Board of Education in 1967 projected that CPS's White population would decrease from 41.5 percent to 34.7 percent by 1980. However, by 1980, Whites actually accounted for only 19 percent of CPS students, with African Americans making up 61 percent of the CPS student population. While not all moved out of the city, White families overwhelmingly took their children out of the city's public schools. By the 1990s, two-thirds of White children in Chicago attended private schools.[60] It is striking how contemporaries in the 1960s so drastically underestimated Whites' flight out of public schools.

These inaccurate demographic projections left school officials, desegregation planners, and education organizers unprepared to navigate the realities of a school system that featured a super "majority minority" population and a tiny White population. It thus makes sense that during the 1960s, groups of African Americans and Whites were preparing for what they expected to be an inevitable process of school integration. In this environment, creating programs to ease the desegregation process seemed vital.

At the same time, Black popular support for school desegregation was waning nationally. In 1967 Hamilton Bims, an associate editor at *Ebony* magazine, posited that Whites' continued unwillingness to accept and respect African Americans meant that integration was not feasible and "must await the day that Whites show a greater understanding of, and a greater respect for Negro American civilization . . . and are willing to receive from it as well as give to it." Charles H. Good, a teacher at Chicago's Calumet High School, reinforced the idea that it was not the primary duty of Black people to ingratiate themselves to White people: "No Negro should try to be acceptable to the White man." Black elected officials like Terry Francis of the San Francisco Board of Supervisors pointed out the perceived inadequacies of desegregation even for those committed to integration: "Though necessary, desegregation is obviously not enough anywhere."[61]

Activists like Rosie Simpson also pivoted from struggles for desegregation to struggles for community control during the late 1960s. In reflecting back, Simpson saw this shift in tactics as a logical progression: "I didn't have any problems with community control because I thought if we controlled our own communities, then we could control the jobs and the educational system in our community. That was one way of making sure that our children got a decent education, so I didn't have a problem . . . when we changed over to that." This tactical shift, however, did not preclude activists and organizers from working with organizations with different political approaches. Simpson, for example, worked as an organizer for TWO in its efforts to develop community control of schools and for the CUL in its work to promote desegregation.[62] Despite Black communities' increasing frustrations with the implementation and implications of desegregation policies, the CUL maintained its commitment to school integration into the 1970s and 1980s, but its ideological and programmatic loyalties would be tested as it pursued school integration in an increasingly racially and class stratified school system.

The ESAA Project: Class, Integration, and Cross-Cultural Interaction

In the 1970s the CUL pursued its integrationist ideology and programming in the middle-class schools and neighborhoods of Beverly Hills and Morgan Park.[63] In 1973 the CUL received federal funds from the Emergency School Aid Act (ESAA) to sponsor programs to ease racial tensions in the Beverly Hills–Morgan Park community, particularly within schools in the Morgan Park High School attendance area. ESAA funds, distributed by HEW, were aimed at "reducing minority group isolation and problems incident to that isolation in public schools."[64] The CUL's ESAA Project was designed to increase interracial and intercultural exchange and understanding between the longtime predominantly White residents, students, teachers, and parents living in the middle-class Beverly Hills–Morgan Park community and new Black middle-class and working-class residents moving into the community and attending local schools.[65] This scenario presented an opportunity for the CUL to demonstrate that integration could work to the benefit of all. For the CUL, school integration was not only about giving African Americans access to quality education; it was also about class-based ideas of interracial interaction—social and cultural encounters that would prepare young African Americans to succeed in the desegregated white-collar offices and boardrooms of the future.

The CUL pushed on with the ESAA Project in an effort to prove the merits and viability of integrated middle-class schools and communities. The Beverly Hills–Morgan Park community was stable, upwardly mobile, middle class, and located on the outskirts of the city away from the concentrated poverty that constrained Black communities closer to the city core. The community was atypical of most communities where Black Chicagoans lived, but these characteristics also made the Black students of Beverly Hills–Morgan Park ideal candidates to become models of the Black professionals, socialized in interracial environments, that the CUL sought to cultivate. CUL project coordinator Marian Gamble recruited Black and White students, parents, and community members to participate in drama and art classes, tutoring and college preparatory programs, film festivals, lectures, and workshops on conflict resolution. The ESAA Project started a ministerial alliance of White and Black ministers,

Rev. Jeremiah Wright, pastor of Trinity United Church of Christ, speaks at an ESAA school-community forum, "To Change or Not to Change? . . . That Is the Question," hosted at Morgan Park Presbyterian Church, 1974 (Chicago Urban League Records, University of Illinois at Chicago Library, CULR_04_0139_1672_043)

created a "How To" booklet to allow parents to evaluate the quality and effectiveness of their children's schools, and hosted school and community forums on race relations for students, parents, and community members. At the close of the 1975 fiscal year, the ESAA Project had serviced over 3,500 students and 5,000 adults in the Beverly Hills–Morgan Park community.[66] The ideals that guided the ESAA Project were influenced by postwar notions of therapeutic cultural pluralism but also prefigured emerging ideas that foregrounded diversity and multiculturalism rather than equity and reparations for past wrongs.

The CUL believed that by proactively working to establish communication between racial groups, it could ease the desegregation process in Chicago and avoid the violence that often accompanied desegregation in other parts of the country—most notably in Boston, where images of antibusing White mob violence were broadcast on national television in 1974. Chicagoans working to desegregate schools in their own city were very cognizant of the racial violence that accompanied desegregation in Boston. CUL education director Judson Hixson believed that an approach to desegregation based on cross-cultural communication, embraced by Chicago's Citizens Coalition on Desegregation, would produce different results: "Communication and understanding may very well eliminate some of the kinds of problems Boston had."[67] The CUL held up the example of the ESAA Project in Beverly Hills–Morgan Park as the

THE POLITICS OF BLACK ACHIEVEMENT

Participants in the 1974 ESAA community forum discussion "Quality Education—Fact or Fiction?" hosted by Beth Eden Baptist Church: (left to right) Franklin McCallie (Morgan Park High School, crisis intervention specialist); Marian Gamble (CUL ESAA coordinator); Dr. Edgar Epps (Chicago Board of Education member); Patricia O'Hern (Chicago Region PTA, school education chairman); Thomas Burke (Morgan Park High School, principal); William Farrow (Commonwealth Edison Co., manager of industrial relations); and (back) Samuel McCurties (Chicago Teachers Union, field representative) (Chicago Urban League Records, University of Illinois at Chicago Library, CULR_04_0139_1672_002)

exemplar of how a race relations approach focused on cultural understanding and communication could ease racial tensions and facilitate peaceful desegregation.

The CUL leveraged its work from the ESAA Project to build citywide coalitions in support of desegregation.[68] In the 1970s the Chicago school board was under pressure by the state and the federal government to create a comprehensive desegregation plan or face sanctions.[69] City officials responded by creating the City-Wide Advisory Committee of elected officials, school board members, parents, students, business leaders, and other concerned citizens charged with crafting a plan to desegregate the CPS student body. In 1976 the CUL helped to found the interracial Citizens Coalition on Desegregation to funnel ideas to the City-Wide Advisory Committee. Over the course of several months the coalition grew to include members of more than thirty-five groups representing Chicago's Black, Latinx, White, and other minority communities.[70]

After initially gaining traction, the CUL's desegregation plan was dealt a devastating blow. The desegregation plan developed by the City-Wide Advisory Committee included many elements of the CUL's Citizens Coalition on Desegregation proposals: voluntary transfers, mandated integration in an expanded pool of magnet and specialty schools, and mandatory busing and transfers if integration was not achieved voluntarily. But the Board of Education reworked the committee's proposal, and CPS superintendent Joseph Hannon released the watered-down "Access to Excellence: Recommendations for Equalizing Educational Opportunity" plan in April 1978, removing the only part of the plan with the strength of enforcement: the ability to use mandatory busing and transfer policies to force desegregation. The CUL and other Black community groups denounced the fact that magnet schools for "high achievers" were the only schools mandated to achieve racial integration in the plan. In a 1979 letter to the president of the Board of Education, then CUL executive director James Compton blasted what we would now call "school choice": "Access to Excellence . . . may have *some* merit for *some* students; but it does little for the majority of Black and minority students who, for the most part remain in their enclaves of exclusion untouched by the efforts aimed at other students in other parts of the city." [71]

In the wake of the stunning rejection of desegregation in the "Access to Excellence" plan, the CUL reassessed its strategies. By the mid-1980s, the CUL shifted its energies from desegregation to funding equalization. In doing so, the CUL finally came to the conclusion that many other Black organizations had already arrived at in the late 1960s and early 1970s. Desegregation was no longer feasible, and Black community organizations must now try to address the specific needs of their own communities as they were: segregated Black communities with segregated Black schools. Many Black Chicagoans, however, had made the turn away from desegregation decades earlier. Years before the CUL finally abandoned desegregation strategies, controversy over busing Black students to desegregate schools exposed African Americans' growing ambivalence toward desegregation strategies.

QUALITY EDUCATION, DISCOURSES OF BLACK INFERIORITY, AND THE BATTLE OVER BUSING

In cities with extreme residential segregation like Chicago and Boston, proposed busing plans butted against communities' expressed desires for neighborhood schools. White northerners who mobilized to oppose busing often made arguments similar to those of White southerners involved in cam-

THE POLITICS OF BLACK ACHIEVEMENT

paigns of massive resistance. Like White community groups across the country, groups of White parents in Chicago opposed busing through formal political channels, with mob intimidation, and through direct attacks on Black students. Busing plans in Chicago, however, were also unpopular with many Black parents and community members who believed that limited one-way busing plans put an unfair burden on Black students, reinforced ideas of Black inferiority, and ignored the majority of Black students who would remain behind in Black communities in substandard, under-resourced schools.[72]

In January 1967, the U.S. Office of Education issued concerns over the continued level of segregation among CPS staff and students. This move by the federal government was influenced by CCCO's 1965 complaint to HEW charging that CPS's policies violated the Federal Civil Rights Act of 1964. As a result, in 1968, CPS superintendent Willis's replacement, James Redmond, and a group of consultants put together a desegregation plan that included provisions for limited busing. In response to concerns by White politicians and civic leaders that Whites would leave the public schools en masse if the school board pursued comprehensive desegregation policies, the Redmond Plan, as the desegregation plan became known, was pretty tepid. The plan did not put forth any dramatic plans for widespread desegregation. It did, however, propose a limited busing program that would move a small proportion of Black students from overcrowded Black schools to under-enrolled White schools.[73] The Redmond Plan emerged at a time when African Americans and Whites across the city were questioning the feasibility and desirability of desegregation.

The limited busing plan proposed to bus a few hundred Black students from overcrowded predominantly Black elementary schools in South Shore (on the South Side) and Austin (on the West Side) to White schools on the Far South Side and Northwest Side, respectively. Between 1960 and 1970, southeastern sections of the Austin neighborhood experienced more rapid racial transition, as Black residents moved into the community and White residents moved out. Even before Black residents arrived, this part of Austin had a larger concentration of lower-income White residents. Many of the new Black residents with school-aged children were also working class or poor. Like other schools in growing Black communities, elementary schools in this part of Austin experienced a swell in student enrollment and a rapid racial transition, with schools like Spencer Elementary and May Elementary transitioning from more than 80 percent White students to more than 80 percent Black students within four years. The resulting overcrowded Black schools became sending schools in Redmond's busing plan. The receiving schools for Black students from Austin were located in White working-class and middle-class neighborhoods on the Northwest Side. On the South Side there was more socioeconomic and, to some extent, racial diversity in the predominantly Black sending schools from South Shore and in the predominantly White receiving schools in South Chicago. In these communities a considerable group of Black and White residents had achieved middle-class status working as government employees and in manufacturing jobs on the Southeast Side of the city.[74]

The Redmond Plan was met by vehement protest from White parents in the sections of the city slated to receive bused Black students, particularly on the Northwest Side. In January 1968, thousands of White parents, many of them mothers from White neighborhoods on the Northwest Side, marched and protested at a Board of Education meeting in opposition to busing. These White parents argued that busing threatened the idea of the neighborhood school and thus infringed on their individual liberties. An editorial in the *Chicago Tribune* reinforced this view, calling the busing plan an "attack on the concept of the neighborhood school," set on "rezoning families and residential groups out of their home neighborhoods and into alien ones."[75] William M. Zachacki, a state representative from the Northwest Side, indicated that schools in his community were "against all busing and all integration."[76] As it had been with former CPS superintendent Willis, White parents' use of the defense of neighborhood schools tactic to reject busing was implicitly racist.

Ideologies of Black inferiority and White fears of Black residential encroachment fueled White opposition to busing. White parents mobilized ideologies of Black inferiority by arguing that their White children would suffer by being educated alongside what they characterized as culturally deprived Black children. A 1968 statement by the Catholic Interracial Council in favor of busing stated that "strong forces in the White, middle class receiving communities are openly expressing their disrespect for and rejection of innocent Negro children."[77] In arguing that the limited busing plan would help to stabilize racially transitioning neighborhoods, White Board of Education members also revealed their racial prejudices. As board member John D. Carey warned, "Whites are fleeing the city and I don't want Chicago to become a Negro city. ... We must do something to hold the Whites in the city."[78]

Moderate White voices in the busing debate were often overshadowed by boisterous White crowds that organized against busing at public forums and at schools. Chicago's Catholic Cardinal John Cody came out in support of the Redmond busing plan, calling the need to facilitate racial stabilization and integration "a moral issue." In response, a group of antibusing Catholic parents staged a protest in front of the cardinal's home, where they "burned him

THE POLITICS OF BLACK ACHIEVEMENT

in effigy."[79] The first elementary-aged Black students to be bused were met by White picketers and bomb threats, but these demonstrations eventually subsided, as the limited nature of the program did not significantly impact or desegregate White schools in the receiving communities. Ultimately, only a few hundred Black students were bused to previously all-White schools in a voluntary one-way busing plan.[80]

The implicit assumptions of Black cultural deprivation, deficit, and inferiority that undergirded White antidesegregation sentiments were bolstered during this time by liberal social science and government studies of Black families and communities. Notably, U.S. assistant secretary of labor Daniel Patrick Moynihan's 1965 report *The Negro Family: The Case for National Action*, known as the Moynihan Report, portrayed Black communities as pathological by intertwining critiques of historical discrimination and inequality with denunciations of Black families and Black culture in order to explain conditions in disadvantaged Black communities.[81] In relation to schools, this critique blamed Black mothers and families for Black "inner city" students' educational struggles. In a 1967 *Chicago Tribune* article on CPS students' low test scores, principals identified the reasons for these low scores: "poor home experiences, family mobility, hunger, and a lack of enough experienced teachers." When asked to elaborate, they quickly focused on "inner city" Black mothers who received public assistance as the source of many problems: "inner city" students were culturally deprived because "homes aren't oriented toward education," students were coming to school hungry because "mother cannot manage her money," and students suffered from residential mobility because "mothers with their children duck out of tenements during the night to avoid paying rent."[82]

On the ground, the lives of poor and working-class Black mothers reflected the structural constraints of racism and a deindustrializing economy, rather than alleged inherent pathology. Rosie Simpson was a single Black mother and welfare recipient, and her participation in education struggles directly challenged the pathological portrayal of Black mothers in the Moynihan Report and the broader public sphere. Simpson, like many Black parents, cared very deeply about her children's education. She organized to improve educational opportunities for Black children in a climate where her family's educational, employment, and economic prospects were deteriorating. Simpson dropped out of high school in the 1940s because there were jobs available in the packinghouses. By the mid-1960s, blue-collar and manufacturing employment in Chicago was already declining and would continue to do so more dramatically throughout the following decades.

This economic decline particularly impacted Black workers, who became increasingly more concentrated than Whites in the manufacturing sector between 1950 and 1970. In 1954, Chicago's manufacturers employed almost 500,000 production workers. By 1982, city manufacturers employed only 162,000 blue-collar workers. Deindustrialization, including the loss of manufacturing, trade jobs, and related industries, also led to greater racial inequality in income and employment rates. The impacts of this economic restructuring contributed to increases in Black unemployment, poverty, and reliance on public assistance programs.[83] Rather than address the structural changes in the economy that shaped the lives of Black families like Rosie Simpson's, policymakers and the broader public shifted attention to the alleged pathology of Black women and families as a primary cause of urban Black poverty.

Black leaders nationally responded stridently to the invocations of Black pathology in the Moynihan Report. In 1966, Chicagoan and National Urban League executive director Whitney Young Jr. criticized the report as misleading. Articles and editorials in the *Chicago Defender* lamented that the report gave "the impression that the Negro people have a patent on immorality."[84] In 1965, CORE national director James Farmer surmised, "It has been the fatal error of American society for 300 years to ultimately blame the roots of poverty and violence in the Negro community upon Negroes themselves. I felt that the Civil Rights and Voting laws indicated that we were rid of this kind of straw-man logic, but here it is again, in its most vicious form, handing the racists a respectable new weapon and insulting the intelligence of Black men and women everywhere." Farmer went on to argue that the report gave elected officials a license to divert time and resources away from antidiscrimination and antipoverty programs and onto musings about Black pathology.[85]

Black communities were becoming increasingly weary and wary of the liberal welfare state's failure to deliver educational equity and of discourses of Black pathology and inferiority generated by researchers and the state. With continued urban economic decline, the impact of poor-quality schooling for Black children became even more profound. The blue-collar unionized job prospects that were available for Rosie Simpson in the 1940s without graduating high school would not be readily available for Black students in the late 1960s. The public education afforded to poor Black children did not provide the necessary skills for a changing economy or affirm their culture or self-worth. For many Black parents, busing did not seem like a solution that would significantly address these larger problems.

While Black parents and community leaders worried about the hostility their children would face from the communities surrounding all-White schools, they also worried about the hostility their children might face from racist teachers and scripts of Black inferiority deployed in the classroom. They questioned the logic of busing a few Black students to under-enrolled White schools without a comprehensive plan for improving the deteriorating schools in Black neighborhoods for the majority that remained.[86] Barbara Sizemore, a veteran Black CPS teacher and principal, argued that the one-way busing of Black children into White neighborhoods to desegregate schools implied Black inferiority. This position reflected her ambivalence toward desegregation as a method of improving Black academic achievement: "To bus only the Negro children into White schools would be just another way of saying that Black is bad or inferior. We have already had too much of that. If Black children are to be bused, then White children should also be bused. I don't believe in segregation, but neither do I believe in teaching inferiority."[87] For Sizemore, the implications of these ideas of Black inferiority extended beyond the classroom and echoed the ideas of Black pathology and cultural deprivation prominent in broader public discourse during the period. One-way busing implied that there was something inherently inferior about the schools in Black communities beyond under-resourcing and overcrowding and, by extension, something wrong with Black people, their culture, and their communities as well.

Other Black parents reappropriated the argument about cultural deprivation and turned it on its head by applying it to White children. Mrs. Chatman Wailes, a Black parent from Bryn Mawr Elementary, one of the sending schools in South Shore, argued that, in fact, one-way busing deprived White students: "In this desegregated school the White pupil is deprived because he is constantly being given the misconception that he is better because of his color. We, the Concerned Parents of Bryn Mawr, will settle for no less than a system where quality education is maintained, not just to keep White children in Bryn Mawr School but to provide equal educational opportunities for all children."[88] Even Black parents in the Austin neighborhood who supported the busing plan were primarily interested in busing as a means to escape the intensifying overcrowding in their neighborhood schools, rather than based on an ideological commitment to racial integration.[89]

The busing debate in Chicago became another episode that led Black parents, educators, and community organizers to question whether desegregation was the best strategy for quality education and Black achievement. The limited nature of the desegregation busing plan foreshadowed the city's limited approach to desegregating magnet and selective enrollment schools in the 1970s and 1980s, another approach that resulted in the desegregation of a

Rosie Simpson leading an organizing meeting with Concerned Parents of Parker High School (ca. 1970) (Chicago Urban League Records, University of Illinois at Chicago Library, CULR_04_0207_2332_001)

few schools without a comprehensive plan for the majority of Black students who continued to attend segregated, inequitably resourced schools in predominantly Black neighborhoods. The busing plans further convinced many of the city's Black education reformers that desegregation plans placed unfair burdens on Black families. Black parents were also understandably skeptical about the busing plan because the Chicago Board of Education, which had historically mistreated Black students, proposed it. Many of these parents pushed, instead, to shift the focus of education reform toward improving schools within their own communities through increased community control of schools.[90]

Seasoned desegregation activists like Rosie Simpson did not interpret the tactical turn from desegregation to community control as an affront to her organizing work earlier in the decade. For Simpson, the movement for school desegregation was always primarily about access to resources and equitable educational opportunities for Black Chicagoans. She supported the movement for community control of schools because she perceived the movement for community control to be aligned with these same goals.[91] Like many Black education reformers, Rosie Simpson was committed to pursuing quality education for Black children, whether their schools were desegregated or not.

THE POLITICS OF BLACK ACHIEVEMENT

COMMUNITY CONTROL

Like so many Black women who became teachers, activists, and community leaders, Barbara Ann Sizemore (née Laffoon) was raised by a family of educators. She was born in 1927 in Terre Haute, Indiana, and her early educational experiences exposed her to the racial inequities in education as well as environments that nurtured Black achievement. Attending segregated Booker T. Washington Elementary School, she encountered Black teachers who were skilled educators, community-engaged advocates, and models of excellence. She fondly remembered her time at Washington as "the best school experience" of her life. In contrast, Sizemore and her peers were automatically tracked into classes for lower-performing students at the integrated Sarah Scott Junior High School in Terre Haute and at Evanston Township High School when her family later moved to Evanston, Illinois, a suburb north of Chicago. In 1944, Sizemore attended Northwestern University with a scholarship to study Latin and classics at a time when Black students were barred from living on campus. Years before Black college students galvanized around Black Power and fought for community control and Black studies programs in the 1960s, Sizemore participated in student-led protests for racial equality on Northwestern's campus. She began her teaching career in CPS in 1950.[1]

Early in her career, Sizemore developed the pedagogical tools that she would later use to demonstrate that Black students could achieve at high levels in all-Black educational settings. At her first full-time teaching post at Shoop Elementary School in the Morgan Park neighborhood on the Far South Side of Chicago, Sizemore learned from Ella Mae Cunningham, a veteran Black teacher, the importance of setting high standards, instilling students' pride in their cultural heritage, and crafting innovative learning materials for students with differing abilities. Sizemore taught for thirteen years at predominantly Black elementary schools on the South Side of Chicago before becoming principal at Anton Dvorak Elementary School in 1963.[2]

Dvorak was an all-Black school located in the North Lawndale community on the West Side of Chicago. At the time, North Lawndale was a densely populated lower-income Black community and a major settlement destination for

Barbara Sizemore (*row 2, second from right*) with her students at Dvorak Elementary School, 1964 (James S. Parker Collection, University of Illinois at Chicago Library, JPCC_01_0058_0577_0022)

more recent southern Black migrants. Like many Black schools in Chicago, Dvorak was overcrowded. By 1965 the school enrolled more than 1,400 Black students in a school building with only 34 classrooms.[3] To address these problems and racial inequities more broadly, civil rights groups in Chicago and across the country demanded desegregation. In October 1963—the fall of Sizemore's first year as principal at Dvorak—a quarter of a million CPS students joined in the Freedom Day boycotts for school desegregation. As was the case in many all-Black schools, approximately 98 percent of Dvorak students participated in the boycott.[4] Yet Sizemore found little support from school desegregation advocates for helping students succeed at Dvorak. She supported diagnosing students' skill mastery, incorporating phonics into reading instruction, and conducting continuous staff development activities. She reorganized students from kindergarten through eighth grade into only three grade levels—kindergarten, primary, and intermediary—organizing students by subject and ability level within these groupings. During Sizemore's first two years as principal, students' reading test scores at Dvorak increased dramatically. Yet Sizemore recalled that "integrationists saw my new racially isolated

THE POLITICS OF BLACK ACHIEVEMENT

school as a disaster about to happen and told me that my children didn't have a snowball's chance in hell for success."[5]

Sizemore had long been wary of integrationists' implicit claims that Black children needed to attend school with White children in order to receive a quality education. Though Sizemore praised *Brown v. Board*'s overturning of Jim Crow laws, as an educator and product of all-Black and integrated schools, she lamented its implication that all-Black facilities were intrinsically bad or inferior. Throughout her career, Sizemore insisted that the logic behind *Brown* was flawed: "'Separate educational facilities are inherently unequal.' Inherent means existing in someone or something as a permanent and inseparable element, quality or attribute, innate. According to this doctrine, separation inferred inherent inferiority for Black students, but did not acknowledge that this also inferred inherent superiority for Whites. . . . Clearly, no integration model can exist with White supremacy intact. And any strategies for rectification of the condition will require some surrender of privileges and advantages which accrue because one is White."[6] Sizemore's own challenging experiences as a student, teacher, and later as a parent of children in integrated schools informed her belief that desegregation was not a "magic bullet" that would deliver racial equity and Black educational success.[7]

Sizemore used her students' progress at Dvorak to argue that Black children could excel in all-Black schools. In her memoir, Sizemore recounts failed attempts to highlight her successes at Dvorak to movement leaders, including Rev. Jesse Jackson and Dr. Martin Luther King Jr. In an environment where civil rights politics and notions of justice were closely associated with the fight for school desegregation, Sizemore's promotion of Black achievement at segregated Dvorak fell on deaf ears. She was pejoratively labeled "Aunt JeBarbara" and accused of defending the racist policies of CPS superintendent Willis.[8]

By the end of the 1960s, however, many Black Chicagoans came to reject desegregation tactics. They increasingly embraced strategies that centered on Black self-determination, including community control—the idea that African Americans should control the institutions that operate in their neighborhoods. Rev. Arthur Brazier—an influential Black pastor, community organizer, and leader of TWO—was instrumental in creating Chicago's experiment with community control, WESP. In 1969 he recruited Sizemore to serve as director. A convener of CCCO and the Chicago Freedom Movement, Brazier had worked in interracial coalitions alongside organizers like Rosie Simpson to demand the firing of Superintendent Willis and the desegregation of public schools. Yet after years of frustration with stalled progress and perpetual resistance, Brazier became increasingly wary of desegregation as a strategy, shifting instead to demands for community control of schools.[9]

There was no singular Black politics on the ground in Chicago during the 1960s. Likewise, there was no consensus in Black communities on the best strategy or tactics to improve Black education. Nevertheless, a generation of Black education reformers during the 1960s and 1970s forged a self-determinist political commitment to demonstrating that Black students could achieve at high levels, whether in all-Black or integrated educational settings. I call this pursuit of alternative Black self-determinist strategies for quality education that disrupted ideas of Black inferiority the *politics of Black achievement*. Community control—where local Black communities would control the resources, programming, and decision-making in the schools in their neighborhoods—was a prominent strand of a broader politics of Black achievement articulated and put into practice during this era.

This politics of Black achievement developed in the context of the liberal welfare state's failure to deliver educational equity through desegregation as well as the proliferation of discourses of Black pathology and inferiority. It reflected Black education reformers' wariness and weariness of racial liberalism, even as they continued to position education as a crucial space for rejecting Black inferiority and demonstrating Black achievement. The politics of Black achievement was not, however, solely a response to the state's failure to desegregate schools or primarily concerned with "proving" African Americans' abilities to a White audience. It was a self-determinist ideology that drew on historical strains of Black political thought that foregrounded Black empowerment and self-governance in efforts to achieve racial justice. Black education reformers like Sizemore, who had always been wary of desegregation, and Brazier, who shifted from desegregation strategies to community control, embraced the self-determinist politics of Black achievement while pursuing quality education for Black students, regardless of whether they attended all-Black or integrated schools.

The community control ideologies and strategies developed in Chicago during the 1960s and 1970s are the subject of this chapter. Students, parents, and community organizations pursued community control of schools through citywide educational conferences, through protests and student boycotts, and through WESP, Chicago's experiment with decentralization and community control of schools. Led by Brazier and Sizemore, WESP used War on Poverty funding to implement community control in several public schools on the South Side of Chicago. WESP brought together historically hostile partners, as a joint project between TWO (a Black community-based organization), CPS, and the University of Chicago. Originating in a different historical context, WESP was a forerunner of the strange bedfellows that coalesced in later decades around the national educational trends of semiautonomous school governance and public-private partnerships addressed in Chapters 5 and 6.

Black Chicagoans' development and implementation of community control reveals the opportunities and limitations of transforming Black public schooling from *within* the system. Both Brazier and Sizemore—situated within different institutional contexts with distinctive personal, political, and professional histories—came to the conclusion that community control was the best means to increase Black educational achievement, build self-confident Black communities, and help Black children "lead a more meaningful life in a democracy" for themselves and "all mankind."[10] Their ideological evolutions illustrate how African Americans came to embrace community control and a self-determinist politics of Black achievement in the late 1960s. This history of community control reveals both a significant political sea change in Black communities and established authorities' unwillingness to truly cede political power and control to Black communities.

COMMUNITY CONTROL

By the late 1960s many Black education reformers were turning away from desegregation to embrace community control. Beginning in the 1970s, even Derrick Bell, a civil rights lawyer and scholar who had litigated many school desegregation cases, questioned whether desegregation alone could deliver quality education for Black students and whether court orders alone could remedy inequality.[11] Rather than shuffling the demographics of bodies in schools, Black education reformers looked to improve the *quality* of the schools that Black students actually attended. Many of the schools they actually attended were highly segregated and predominantly Black. This included schools like Dvorak, where Barbara Sizemore created an environment for Black educational achievement before other activists had fully embraced community control.[12] Community control was at once both a specific alternative to school desegregation and part of a broader Black political project for Black self-determination and liberation, of which education was just one—albeit a very important—piece. Historian Joy Williamson-Lott argues that the Black radical and nationalist proposals of community control advocates prompted fear and apprehension in conservatives and liberals because community control challenged traditional structures of authority and arguments for desegregation.[13]

The ideological distinction between a politics of desegregation and a politics of community control centered on differing views of who wielded the power to create change in schools. Proponents of desegregation argued that as long as Black and White children attended separate segregated schools, Black children would never be granted educational opportunities equal to those of their White counterparts. They sought changes from boards of education and government officials, the bodies that they saw wielding the power to transform the material conditions and allocation of resources to schools. While not ignoring resource disparities, proponents of community control argued that the power to improve Black educational achievement already existed within Black communities in the collective energies of community members, administrators, teachers, parents, and students who believed that Black students could succeed academically in predominantly Black schools in Black communities.

During the 1960s, the tensions between desegregation and community control played out not only between activists and educators but also in research studies and reports on educational inequality. In 1966, James Coleman, a White sociologist from Johns Hopkins University, and a team of researchers published *Equality of Educational Opportunity*, better known as the Coleman Report. Commissioned by the U.S. Congress, Coleman's research team surveyed approximately 600,000 students, 60,000 teachers, and thousands of school administrators at 4,000 schools across the nation during the fall of 1965. The researchers compiled data about school programs and facilities, as well as information about the race, background, and educational experiences of students and educators. These surveys, along with standardized tests, were used to measure racial segregation, student achievement, and student access to educational opportunities. Published a year after the controversial Moynihan Report on Black families, the Coleman Report was the second-most-expensive social science research project ever conducted at its time of publication.[14]

As with Moynihan's report on the Black family, Coleman's study and proposed solutions blended economic analyses with criticisms of Black culture and families. The Coleman Report argued that schools exacerbated existing "deficiencies" that originated in poor students' home lives and families, and that schools could do very little to transcend these academic deficits: "For most minority groups, then, and most particularly the Negro, schools provide no opportunity at all for them to overcome this initial deficiency; in fact, they fall farther behind the White majority in the development of several skills which are critical to making a living and participating in modern society. Whatever may be the combination of non-school factors—poverty, community attitudes, low educational level of parents—which put minority children

THE POLITICS OF BLACK ACHIEVEMENT

at a disadvantage in verbal and nonverbal skills when they enter first grade, the fact is the schools have not overcome it."[15] Coleman framed these deficits as symptoms of poverty and the culture of poor Black families: "Altogether, the sources of inequality of educational opportunity life [sic] first in the home itself and the cultural influences immediately surrounding the home; then they lie in the schools' ineffectiveness to free achievement from the impact of the home and in the schools' culture which perpetuates the social influences of the home and its environs."[16]

Coleman acknowledged that the most important way to improve poor students' academic achievement levels was to provide direct financial assistance to poor families, yet he downplayed the benefits of increased funding, resources, and compensatory education programs for poor students. "It's not a solution to pour money into improvement of the physical plants, books, teaching aids of schools attended by educationally disadvantaged students." Rather than offering a collaborative model for working with poor Black families, he proposed extending the school day and starting schooling for children at a younger age as a way to "replace [the] family environment with educational life." For many, the takeaway from the report was that schools alone did not have the capacity to improve the achievement levels of poor Black children.[17]

The Coleman Report was criticized from multiple directions. Prominent social scientists and education scholars questioned the validity of the report's methodology.[18] Other education scholars countered its findings, arguing that schools were discrete systems that could improve achievement regardless of other mitigating factors. This latter group of researchers and educators, including some supporters of community control, were increasingly interested in finding ways to improve the achievement of poor Black students within the predominantly segregated schools that they continued to attend.[19]

Community control advocates were tired of reports authored by White researchers and liberal policymakers that coupled indictments of systemic inequality with claims of deficits, deprivation, and pathology in Black people, families, and culture. They particularly objected to the Coleman Report's assertion that sending Black children to school with middle-class White children would have a greater impact on Black achievement than would improving the resources and quality of all-Black schools. Coleman argued that Black student achievement improved when Black students from homes "without much educational strength" were exposed to White middle-class students from homes that were "strongly and effectively supportive of education."[20] Coleman advocated for "more White middle-class teachers and students" in Black neighborhood schools to "reduce the social and racial intensity" and improve Black student achievement. Community control advocates repudiated the idea that proximity to Whites was a prerequisite for Black student success and rejected the intimation that all-Black spaces were inherently inferior.[21]

Community control efforts were implemented in communities across the country, but one of the most intense struggles over community control that reverberated on the national stage took place when an experimental community-controlled school district was created in the predominantly Black Ocean Hill–Brownsville section of Brooklyn, New York. In 1968, the Ocean Hill–Brownsville experiment with community control of schools descended into a power struggle between the largely White and Jewish leadership of the New York City teachers' union and Black teachers, administrators, and community members. Historians have used the Ocean Hill–Brownsville crisis to make broader claims about the political impact of community control efforts, in particular, emphasizing the ways that community control challenged the tenuous interracial alliances of postwar racial liberalism that supported movements for desegregation.[22] However, foregrounding intraracial politics rather than Black-White conflict and focusing on how community control struggles vied for legitimacy in other parts of the country reveal a different set of dynamics.

In the 1960s and 1970s, community control of schools was a prominent strand of a broader politics of Black achievement seeking alternative models for Black education grounded in Black Power era ideals of self-determination. In 1968, M. Lee Montgomery, a cofounder of the National Association of African-American Educators, argued that Black Power "provided the impetus for tremendous pressures on educational systems." He saw community control as an uprising: "In Philadelphia, Pittsburgh, Chicago, and New York, students, teachers, and parents are in open rebellion. We want to control our schools, say the parents. We want to decide what kind of curriculum will be in our schools, say the students. It's our right, it's our responsibility." In 1967, Leslie Campbell (later Jitu Weusi), a Black educator, activist, and community control leader in New York, argued that to "further the goals of black power," Black teachers must transform schools into "tools to shape and mold our communities." In 1969, Dr. Norma Jean Anderson, a Black psychologist and cofounder of the National Association of African-American Educators, noted that Black teachers wanted to control "what you teach in the classroom structure, but also the policy that is set for the education of your children." She argued that because of rampant segregation, "we [Black teachers] have our own schools anyway—all they lack is control."[23]

In the early stages of planning for Chicago's experiment with community control of schools in the Woodlawn neighborhood, project staff traveled to Washington, D.C., and New York City to learn from the experimental educational programs already under way.[24] Community control in Chicago, however, developed out of the unique local history of previous Black struggles for racial justice against the Chicago Democratic machine. In the late 1960s, community control was embraced by an intergenerational group of Black Chicagoans, with Black youth taking on a prominent role in these struggles.

1968: UPRISINGS AND BLACK STUDENT PROTEST

Black youth were on the front lines of civil rights struggles across the country. They attended and taught in Freedom Schools in Mississippi in 1964. They guided the direction of organizing in local chapters of SNCC, CORE, and many other community-based groups.[25] And in the late 1960s, they propelled the rise of the Black Power Movement, including student movements for Black self-determination and community control.

Amidst this profusion of youth organizing, hundreds of urban uprisings took place in Black communities across the country. Significant uprisings—also characterized as "civil disorders," "ghetto upheavals," "urban rebellions," and "riots"—occurred in Harlem and Rochester (1964), Watts (1965), Newark (1967), Detroit (1967), and hundreds of other Black communities during the "long hot summers" of the mid- to late 1960s. The fires and property damage of these uprisings left scars of blight and continued disinvestment that plague many Black communities to this day. President Lyndon Johnson ordered the National Advisory Commission on Civil Disorders—better known as the Kerner Commission—to study the uprisings. Published on March 1, 1968, the Kerner Commission Report recommended $30 billion in government funding for income assistance, jobs, housing, and schools. Just over a month after the report was released, in response to the murder of Dr. King on April 4, 1968, another massive round of uprisings erupted across the nation, including in Chicago. As with the uprisings detailed in the Kerner Commission Report, King's death ignited the powder keg of Black America's frustrations with racially discriminatory policies and persistent inequities in housing, employment, policing, and education.[26]

King had ties to Chicago's civil rights community. Two years earlier, in 1966, King moved into an apartment on the West Side of Chicago, just blocks from Dvorak Elementary. In Chicago, King and SCLC worked with local organizers in campaigns to end slums and promote open housing. SCLC selected Chicago as a northern site to test its nonviolent direct-action strategies, in part because of Chicago organizers' history of mobilizing mass protests against the city's segregated school system. Upon hearing of King's assassination, Black high school students in the city organized memorial services, protests, and school walkouts. A concerted minority of young demonstrators and adults also looted shops and burned down stores on the West Side.[27]

Mayor Daley's bellicose reaction to the uprisings after King's death further strained his relationship with Chicago's Black communities. Calling in thousands of Illinois National Guard, army troops, and police, Daley infamously instructed the chief of police to "shoot to kill any arsonist" and "shoot to maim" looters. These directives enraged many Black Chicagoans while endearing the mayor to segments of his White ethnic supporters who were issuing barely veiled racist calls for "law and order."[28]

When the smoke cleared, more than two miles of the central commercial corridor centered on West Madison Street, and other Black neighborhoods on the West Side, were destroyed. White-owned stores were particularly targeted, but the fires that started at individual shops engulfed dozens of city blocks. The uprisings displaced hundreds of people from their homes and caused millions of dollars in property damage.[29] Four months later, in August 1968, police again clashed with citizens as anti–Vietnam War protesters from across the country descended on Chicago while the city hosted the Democratic National Convention. Nearly 83 million people watched on the national news as Chicago police beat largely White, middle-class, college-aged protesters. Black Chicagoans resented the media's concern for the state-sanctioned brutality meted out to White antiwar protesters on the lakefront and downtown without similar concern for residents in the city's Black communities where police brutality and repression had become routine.[30] On the heels of these uprisings, Black high school students in Chicago organized school boycotts in the fall of 1968.

Unlike earlier protests that had demanded desegregation, Black high school students' citywide protests in October 1968 called for Black self-determination and community control over public schooling. Students organized the boycotts through student-led Black Power organizations, school clubs, and community groups. The student group Black Students for Defense passed out handbills to their peers advertising a series of Monday protests: "No School Monday Solidarity Day for Liberation . . . Black schools need to be improved all around. We all know this. You can show your determination by boycotting your school on Monday October 14. Black determination shall not be crushed!!" An estimated 35,000 students participated in the first citywide "Liberation Mon-

Black student walkouts at
Austin High School, 1968
(John Chuckman)

day" boycott on October 14. The students' demands included mandatory Black history courses, more Black administrators, removal of principals and teachers they deemed racist, quality technical and vocational education, relevant military training, repairs to school buildings, insurance for athletes, use of educational radio and television, and more homework. CPS superintendent Redmond responded to the students in a press conference with promises to meet some of the students' demands. The students were not appeased, staging another boycott a week later.[31]

Black students in local community colleges, universities, and radical community organizations also supported high school students' protests for community control and curricular changes. Black college students connected community-based struggles to protests for educational change at Crane Junior College (now Malcolm X College), Woodrow Wilson Junior College (now Kennedy-King College), Roosevelt University, University of Illinois Circle Campus (now University of Illinois at Chicago [UIC]), Northeastern Illinois University, Chicago State University, and Northwestern University. The protests by Black high school and college students in the late 1960s and early 1970s resulted in the inclusion of Black studies curricula at many schools, changes in teaching faculty at some schools, and an increase in the number of Black administrators.[32]

The 1968 protests provided an opportunity for Black and Latinx students to build solidarity by engaging in parallel and intersecting struggles. Black and Latinx students were staging school walkouts in cities across the country. In 1968, few Latinx students attended public schools in Chicago. Latinx and Black students represented 4 percent and 53 percent, respectively, of the CPS student population. In the Little Village and North Lawndale communities on the West Side, however, Black and Latinx students (primarily students of Mexican descent) attended Harrison High School together. During the fall of 1968, both Black and Latinx students walked out of Harrison. Like Black students, Latinx students demanded greater community control and self-determination within the schools, but in the context of the particular historical oppression faced by Mexican Americans and other Latinxs. In the fall of 1968, Latinx students at Harrison created a Latin American Manifesto demanding more Latinx and bilingual teachers, counselors, and support staff; incorporation of Latin American history and culture into the curriculum; and a soccer team for the school. In subsequent decades, the Latinx population grew exponentially in CPS, and the histories of oppression across marginalized racial groups became increasingly significant in school and city politics.[33]

These struggles were moments of consciousness-raising that impacted the future personal and professional trajectories of many high school and college students. Many young activists, including Illinois Black Panther Party leader Fred Hampton, started as student activists. The politicization of the 1968 school protests made Chicago high schools fertile recruitment ground for the Black Panther Party. Black student demonstrations continued well into the 1970s at a number of high schools.[34] However, not all Black education reformers and civil rights organizations were eager to support community control.

In December 1968, the CUL organized a forum to discuss the pros and cons of community control of schools. Lindblom High School senior Omar Aoki challenged the assembled interracial crowd of more than 500 city leaders and community members for being content to "discuss the issues" while Black students had been in the streets demanding changes in the schools: "We're just wondering why the Urban League is just now coming out and talking about community control . . . when the students were trying to get it a while back. Where were you then? You're kind of late, don't you think? . . . This seminar is a farce and you all know it." Clashes like these, between politicized Black youth and established civil rights leaders, were taking place across the country as Black freedom struggles entered the Black Power era.[35]

Yet many Black educators, parents, and community members joined forces with students in the fight for community control. In the second citywide student demonstration in October 1968, approximately 700 teachers, many of whom participated in Operation Breadbasket's Teachers' Division, joined Black students in boycotting Chicago schools. Barbara Sizemore was among the educators who supported the student protests and was a featured speaker at a large rally supporting the boycotts.[36] By this time, Rev. Arthur Brazier, the leader of TWO and a speaker at the CUL community control forum, was already working to decentralize schools and implement community control

Timuel Black of the Teachers Committee for Quality Education speaking at a June 1969 meeting of the Englewood Community Congress. Black had a long career as an educator, a civil rights and labor activist, a CPS high school teacher, and a professor in Chicago's City Colleges (Chicago Urban League Records, University of Illinois at Chicago Library, CULR_04_0197_2237_012)

through WESP. To connect with community control efforts in other parts of the country, educator Timuel Black and the Teachers Committee for Quality Education convened a workshop in November 1968 with local educators and community members and leaders from community control projects in Harlem and Brooklyn, New York, and Washington, D.C.[37]

Across the country Black Power era community control projects embraced a politics of Black achievement that rejected the racial liberalism of school desegregation efforts. Unsatisfied with the failed promises of desegregation efforts, the movement for community control in Chicago's Woodlawn community during the late 1960s reflected this dynamic. The broad group of Black women and men involved with WESP—educators, parents, youth activists, and rank-and-file members of local community organizations—embraced community control as the best way to improve the quality of education for Black children.

WESP was a federally funded program that operated from 1968 to 1971 in an attempt to implement community control within several schools in the predominantly Black Woodlawn neighborhood on the South Side of Chicago. The strange bedfellows that created WESP prefigured the semiautonomous school governance and public-private partnerships that would become ubiquitous in neoliberal urban education reform efforts in subsequent decades. The project emerged from the conflicting desires of three historically hostile partners: a private institution (University of Chicago), a public government institution (CPS), and a local Black community group (TWO). Spurred by researchers' and policymakers' concerns about educational efficiency and accountability, many large urban school districts were already shifting toward administrative school decentralization. This tendency converged with community control, a movement built by Black educators, parents, and activists who sought to pursue their own self-determinist aims of controlling schools that served Black neighborhoods. The odd alliances that coalesced around efficiency, accountability, privatization, and corporate models that would emerge at the end of the twentieth century are products of the broken promises of earlier education struggles, including the struggle for community control in WESP.[38]

WESP benefited from Great Society and War on Poverty programs—particularly the 1965 Elementary and Secondary Education Act (ESEA)—that injected a new stream of revenue into schools as well as supplemental educational programs for students living in poverty. In 1964, Chicago received less than $4.4 million in federal appropriations (1.4 percent of CPS revenues). Yet by 1966, federal ESEA funds alone brought $23.2 million of new revenue into CPS (6.2 percent of CPS revenues). The 1968 CPS budget projected and expected $66.5 million in federal funds, including ESEA and other federal programs (13.5 percent of the total budget). Bolstered by federal dollars, appropriations from the state of Illinois to CPS also jumped from $559 million in 1965 to $849 million by 1967. While local taxes still brought the majority of revenue into city schools, these increases were meaningful.[39] Across the country Black communities increasingly demanded to control how this growing pool of funds would be spent. While this influx of federal funds and the strategy of community control were not unique to Chicago, the city's distinctive local political culture provided an opportunity to develop a collaborative experiment with community control during the late 1960s and early 1970s in the Woodlawn neighborhood.

Between 1950 and 1960, the residential population of Woodlawn transformed from 86 percent White to nearly 90 percent Black. An initial wave of middle-class Black residents left the overcrowded Black Belt to settle in Woodlawn and were followed by lower-income African Americans as the 1950s progressed. Some of Woodlawn's newer Black residents had previously lived in the Bronzeville area and/or Hyde Park, to the north, but were displaced by government- and university-supported urban renewal projects, derided by critics at the time as "Negro removal" projects. In addition, Woodlawn increasingly became a final destination for the thousands of African American migrants from the South who arrived at the 63rd Street stop of the Illinois Central Railroad.[40]

In a neighborhood of just over one square mile, the residential population ballooned to more than 70,000 residents by 1960. As was the pattern in other overcrowded Black urban neighborhoods, single-family homes and large apartments were converted into efficiency and kitchenette apartments and hotels, and the number of bars, gambling venues, and other "vice" industries expanded to serve more transient populations. When Rev. Arthur Brazier took the helm of the Apostolic Church of God in 1960, these were among the issues worrying his parishioners.[41]

Local clergy organized in response to the deteriorating social and material conditions in Woodlawn, eventually forming TWO and electing Rev. Robert McGee president and Brazier spokesman. Religious leaders courted Saul Alinsky and his Industrial Areas Foundation to work in the Woodlawn community. Once they arrived, Industrial Areas Foundation staff provided neighborhood residents with training and tools to organize and develop community leaders. As block clubs and local civic organizations joined TWO, the group gained legitimacy as a voice for the community. With Brazier as spokesman and later president, TWO would fight encroachment by the University of Chicago, exploitative business practices by White merchants, and overcrowding in Black neighborhood schools.[42]

Between 1960 and 1963, TWO and the University of Chicago engaged in a bitter battle over the university's attempt to claim land in Woodlawn for its South Campus expansion. Black Woodlawn residents feared losing their homes to the university, and for good reason. In the preceding years the university had played a leading role in an urban renewal project that displaced many Black and lower-income White residents from the university's Hyde Park–Kenwood community directly to the north of Woodlawn.[43] After 700 Woodlawn residents protested at City Hall, Mayor Daley was forced to step in and broker a deal. In exchange for the South Campus demolition, the city agreed to replace

Rev. Arthur Brazier, TWO leader, CCCO co-convener, and pastor of the Apostolic Church
of God, speaking at CCCO rally "Power through Direct Action," 1963 (Chicago Urban
League Records, University of Illinois at Chicago Library, CULR_04_0189_2144_001)

deteriorating and abandoned commercial structures between 60th and 63rd
streets on Cottage Grove Avenue with affordable housing for residents displaced by South Campus. However, the wounds and ill will between the university and the Woodlawn community over urban renewal were slow to heal.[44]

But only a few years after the bitter urban renewal battles, TWO and the
university considered joining forces. Brazier helped negotiate areas of consensus to collaborate with the university on a community control plan for Woodlawn schools. This was an indication of the evolving politics of TWO and the
compromises Brazier and leaders of the organization were willing to make in
the name of political expediency. John Hall Fish, a White pastor, scholar, and
TWO participant, described the strategies and ideology of TWO as a "middle
way" between racially liberal integration and Black radicalism, repression and
revolution, politics and culture, planning and participation: "As a community
organization the Alinsky-style Woodlawn Organization represents a middle
way between, on the one hand, the 'accommodative' agencies that seek to as-
similate the alienated into the dominant society by strategies of socialization,
rehabilitation, and therapy and, on the other, the 'revolutionary' groups that

form paracommunities rejecting the values and processes of the dominant society."[45]

The idea of TWO's politics as a "middle way" should not be mistaken as a synonym for "nonconfrontational" or "moderate." Nor should it negate the explicitly Black Power politics of the organization. Brazier and TWO advocated for community-based empowerment while also asserting the right of African Americans to enter and participate equally in mainstream society. They were not primarily interested in maintaining good standing with conventional political, business, or Chicago machine leaders, nor were they interested in advocating for violent revolutionary struggle alongside more radical Black activists. Instead, in Brazier's words, "the Woodlawn Organization has shown that there can be an orderly revolution operating within the framework of American democracy."[46]

TWO forged pragmatic political alliances while staying ideologically committed to self-determination for Woodlawn's Black residents and improving the conditions in the neighborhood. Sometimes this involved collaborating with previous adversaries. This was particularly evident in TWO's shift from advocating for school desegregation to working with the University of Chicago and the Chicago Board of Education for community control of Woodlawn schools. The 1965 struggle over plans for Hyde Park High School accelerated this shift.

In the mid-1960s, community groups put forth plans for how to best address overcrowding at historically high-achieving Hyde Park High School. The Unity Organization was one such group, including University of Chicago professors, the university's Student Woodlawn Area Project, White liberal integration advocates from the Hyde Park neighborhood, and local Parent Teacher Associations. Hyde Park High School was located in the eastern part of Woodlawn, but its attendance area included both the Woodlawn and Hyde Park–Kenwood communities. In its 1965 Unity Plan, the Unity Organization proposed creating a single large state-of-the-art secondary "education park" campus to serve the diverse surrounding South Side communities, with four smaller high schools operating in a new building on an expanded tract of land that included the existing Hyde Park High School.[47]

Community groups across the country and U.S. Commissioner of Education Harold Howe II promoted the education park model as a way to enact desegregation and ensure equal access to educational opportunities. These education parks would include large campuses serving thousands of suburban and urban students, from pre-kindergarten through junior college. Nationally, more than eighty school systems were making plans for some form of

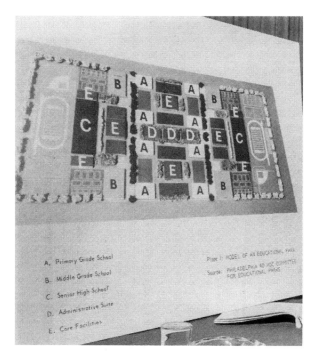

Education park model
(from Philadelphia, Pa.)
used by the Chicago
Urban League (Chicago
Urban League Records,
University of Illinois
at Chicago Library,
CULR_04_0207_2332_004)

A. Primary Grade School
B. Middle Grade School
C. Senior High School
D. Administrative Suite
E. Core Facilities

education park by the winter of 1966. Locally, the CUL proposed that Chicago create more than thirty such racially integrated centers servicing the city and surrounding suburbs. While even Mayor Daley was open to considering some form of education park within the city, CPS superintendent Willis strongly opposed the idea. In Chicago, urban/suburban busing never moved beyond the stage of a proposal.[48]

The Hyde Park–Kenwood Community Conference (HPKCC) opposed the Unity Plan, asserting their desire for a new integrated high school instead. In a June 1965 statement to the Board of Education, the largely middle-class business and civic leaders in the HPKCC stated, "The Hyde Park–Kenwood community is committed to integration." An editorial in the *Hyde Park Herald* reinforced this point, boasting, "We have been able to hold the line so far as the only community with a stable racial balance of approximately 50-50 White and Negro residents." In reality, this idealized integration entailed mechanisms limiting the community's population of African Americans and poor and low-income people through residential displacement and urban renewal projects. By 1965, the Hyde Park High School student population was 89 percent Black and only 9 percent White. According to the HPKCC, only by building a new high school within the more racially diverse Hyde Park–Kenwood

THE POLITICS OF BLACK ACHIEVEMENT

neighborhood could they preserve their integrated community and nurture an integrated high school (see map 2). Without a new high school, they argued, the White student population would continue to decrease because of the rapid population increase in Woodlawn's Black elementary schools. Providing high-caliber educational opportunities for the lower-income Black children of Woodlawn was not a central focus of the HPKCC plan.[49]

TWO leaders, as supporters of the Unity Plan, spoke out against the HPKCC's plan. Rev. Lynward Stevenson, TWO president at the time, articulated this opposition: "To build a separate high school in [Hyde Park–Kenwood] is wrong on two counts: it will pull all the White students out of the present school [Hyde Park High School], leaving it completely segregated. And the best teachers will follow the White students to the new school. We in Woodlawn will be left with a third class school, like so many other ill-conceived Willis schools." Ultimately, Superintendent Willis and the Chicago Board of Education supported the HPKCC plan over the Unity Plan. Kenwood High School accepted its first incoming class of freshmen in 1966 while temporarily housed in a former middle school building. The new Kenwood High School building opened at Blackstone Avenue and Hyde Park Boulevard in the Hyde Park–Kenwood community in September 1969. As a consolation, Woodlawn's Hyde Park High School was promised a multiyear renovation project to modernize school facilities.[50]

Many Unity Plan collaborators were surprised when TWO did not mount significant protests to this decision. But TWO leaders had difficulty mobilizing community support in Woodlawn for the Unity Plan and were skeptical about leading a coalition effort primarily made up of White liberals from the university and Hyde Park–Kenwood community. TWO president Stevenson expressed his disillusionment with the attention paid to the "integrated" middle-class Hyde Park–Kenwood neighborhood and called out "the segregationists" on the Board of Education for "creating an island high school between two Black educational Frankensteins at Forrestville on the north and Hyde Park High on the south. . . . They regard us, who live in Woodlawn, as Black animals in the zoo, to be looked at but not respected, and they want nothing but separation from us." Through this episode it became clear that many Black residents of Woodlawn were no longer invested in the fight to desegregate schools. Instead, they wanted improvements in their community's Black schools.[51]

In 1967, Brazier articulated TWO's evolving perspective on integration: "We aren't forgetting about integration but we aren't waiting for it either. We want quality schools now. It is an insult to tell me that there have to be White kids in

1950

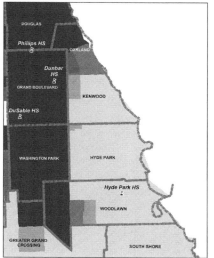

1960

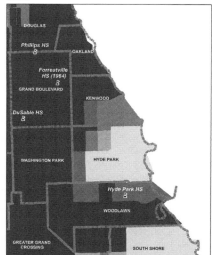

1970

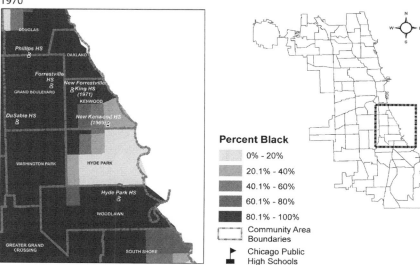

Percent Black

- 0% - 20%
- 20.1% - 40%
- 40.1% - 60%
- 60.1% - 80%
- 80.1% - 100%
- Community Area Boundaries
- Chicago Public High Schools

Map 2. CPS High Schools and Black Population in Selected Community Areas by Census Tract, 1950–1970. The racial demographics of these South Side lakefront communities were changing as proposals emerged during the 1960s for a new Kenwood High School and a new building for Forrestville High School (Courtesy of José Acosta-Córdova, University of Illinois at Chicago, Institute for Research on Race and Public Policy; census tract lines are hidden to increase legibility)

my school before it can be a good school. We want good Black schools now."[52] After collaborating with movements to desegregate schools in the early 1960s, by 1969 Brazier and TWO espoused ideas that resonated with the politics of the Black Power Movement: "Black people must build up their own communities and make them desirable places to live, work, play, and send their children to school. This means encouraging people to remain in their community and helping them to improve the quality of living in it. . . . To build up their own communities black Americans must acquire power. The need is not for slogans or rhetoric, but for mass-based organizations that can develop the kind of power necessary within the Black community to change the domination of White power structures that continue to exploit Black people."[53]

In rhetoric and actions, Brazier and TWO had embraced a politics of Black achievement that pursued Black self-determination through community control. Brazier and TWO sought to empower Black Woodlawn residents by directly challenging traditional forms of governmental and civic authority and power. TWO members also demanded access to and control of the institutional resources and programs held by outside authorities — including the University of Chicago — that operated within their community.

While Brazier was transitioning from support for desegregation campaigns to community control, Sizemore was already implementing Black self-determinist pedagogies and practices at Forrestville High School — the "Black educational Frankenstein" to the north of Hyde Park–Kenwood. Hired as principal of Forrestville High School in 1965, Sizemore took control of an all-Black school with a majority-Black teaching and administrative staff in the low-income Black Grand Boulevard neighborhood (see map 2). Forestville High School shared a building with an elementary school and officially opened in 1964 to relieve overcrowding at nearby DuSable, Phillips, and Dunbar high schools. When the time came to construct a new building for Forrestville High School, one group of teachers at the school wanted it to be built in a location that would encourage integration. Another group of teachers thought it was important for the new school to be built within the Black community. When Sizemore sided with the latter group, conflict broke out into the open.[54]

When CCCO led a desegregation protest at Forrestville in the spring of 1966, a number of Forrestville teachers joined the picketers. The protesting teachers argued for desegregation, while Sizemore and the Forrestville administrators prioritized creating an environment in the all-Black school that fostered Black achievement. While not using the words "community control" explicitly, this was a political struggle between desegregation and community control.[55]

Barbara Sizemore, Forrestville High
School Yearbook, 1968 (Chicago Board of
Education Archives)

Where protesting teachers saw a "culturally deprived neighborhood" sur-rounding Forrestville that deserved greater resources, Sizemore saw a neigh-borhood whose Black students needed curricula that valued students' cultural heritage and teachers who believed that Black students could succeed.[56] Pro-testing teachers argued Black students would never receive the resources nec-essary to succeed until the fates of Forrestville's Black students were linked to the fates of White students. While acknowledging the inequitable distribu-tion of resources, Sizemore countered that desegregation advocates implied Black inferiority when they insisted that Black success could only be obtained alongside White children. Community control advocates wanted more public resources too, but they wanted Black communities to control them.[57]

At Forrestville, Sizemore refined the educational and political philoso-phies she would later implement as director of WESP. She believed that pub-lic schools needed to mobilize the human resources within Black communi-ties and implement culturally relevant curricula and programming. Employing many strategies reminiscent of her own schooling in the 1930s at segregated Booker T. Washington Elementary School in Terre Haute, her administration identified cooperative school culture, student leadership, and racial pride as key elements necessary for Black academic achievement. Social studies teach-ers were provided with an African American-centered curriculum that began by building knowledge of the local Black community surrounding the school. Black faculty members at Northeastern Illinois University's Center for Inner City Studies in 1966 lauded Sizemore as an educator who gave "pupils hope that a better life is possible and belief that it is attainable" and helped "her

THE POLITICS OF BLACK ACHIEVEMENT

students to believe in their own personal worth and to take pride in their heritage."[58]

Sizemore's support for community control, however, alienated some more politically conservative segments of the Black community in Chicago. Writers at the *Chicago Defender*, who in 1966 nominated her for a woman of the year award, by 1968 described Sizemore's politics as too galvanizing and dubbed her a "one-time school principal and Ben Willis ally, gone militant."[59] More conservative members of the Board of Education were also wary of Sizemore's outspoken support of community control and the 1968 Black student protests.[60]

Yet while her stance on community control may have ruffled some feathers, her politics fit well with TWO's ideology. Sizemore and Brazier shared a politics of Black achievement. Both saw links between the implementation of desegregation policies and arguments for Black inferiority. They each argued that public schools needed to mobilize the cultural resources of Black communities and make curricula and programming more culturally relevant to improve education for Black students. Sizemore's concentration on cultivating student leadership and racial pride complemented Brazier's political work to increase racial pride and self-determination in Woodlawn, and in 1969, upon Brazier's recommendation, Sizemore was named WESP director.[61]

The Woodlawn Experimental Schools Project (WESP)

The tenuous alliance that created WESP was forged only after Brazier sent a complaint to the U.S. Office of Education.[62] In 1965 the University of Chicago submitted a proposal for newly available federal ESEA funds to create an experimental school and urban education research laboratory in Woodlawn. The paternalistic undertones of the proposal were made clear in the university's intent to "develop leadership in the Negro community; for it is such indigenous leadership from within that will determine the rate of accommodation of the Negro community to its new legal rights."[63] TWO leaders took offense. The university's purported concern for indigenous leadership in Woodlawn was belied by its failure to seek input from the community's existing leadership. In a May 16, 1966, letter to the university and the U.S. Office of Education, Brazier lambasted the university's approach to the Black residents of Woodlawn: "One cause of alienation and low-self esteem [in "the ghetto"] is being treated like objects, without being respected or consulted by the large bureaucracies that are supposed to be trying to 'help.' . . . Oddly enough, the University may now be trying to study what it may be helping to create—alienation." On this point, Brazier went further: "TWO regards the community as people seeking dignity, justice and self-determination; the University sees the community as a convenient laboratory."[64]

Reviewers at the U.S. Office of Education rejected the university's proposal, stating that the university had failed to get "the cooperation and participation of local community groups"—a condition of many War on Poverty programs. This critique was perceived to be a direct response to Brazier's letter opposing the university's plan. In response, a tripartite relationship developed between the University of Chicago, CPS, and TWO, leading to a revised proposal for what would become WESP.[65]

WESP met the needs of all three invested parties in different ways. The University of Chicago wanted to create schools as urban educational research laboratories. After agreeing to build a new Kenwood High School for the middle-class "integrated" Hyde Park–Kenwood community, CPS was under community pressure to upgrade programming at Hyde Park High School and its feeder elementary schools in Woodlawn. Brazier and TWO leadership wanted to overhaul the educational system to ensure that Black Woodlawn residents had more power over schools and other institutions within the community.[66]

The three parties worked together to create the Woodlawn Community Board (WCB), a quasi–board of education to govern what would become WESP. The twenty-one-member WCB initially included seven Woodlawn representatives appointed by TWO, seven representatives from the University of Chicago, and seven representatives from the Chicago Board of Education. Assessing the communities' needs, WCB staff went to work conducting 164 interviews with teachers, students, parents, and school administrators. Their findings reinforced many things they already suspected: the physical conditions of Woodlawn's schools were poor, academic achievement was low, and there was a great level of distrust between teachers, parents, students, and administrators.[67] The staff concluded that a major overhaul of the social and structural systems in the schools would be necessary.

To start this work, Brazier, CPS district area superintendent Curtis Melnick, and University of Chicago dean Roald Campbell crafted a memorandum of agreement to legally make the WCB the administrator of the planned experimental district. After negotiations with the Board of Education, the resulting language left a great deal of ambiguity as to the power of the WCB over the administration of the schools within the proposed experimental schools project. The agreement required that the experimental district director obtain the advice and "concurrence" of the WCB in all decisions that would be brought to the Board of Education, but it still gave the CPS general superintendent of schools the final authority to "control and manage" the affairs of the schools in the experimental district. The memorandum of agreement was, at best, a good-faith effort at compromise and, at worst, an indicator that the Chicago Board of Education was not willing to cede power.[68] Nevertheless, with the WCB in place, WESP received a $1.35 million grant from the U.S. Office of Education under Title III of the ESEA to begin operating in June 1968.[69]

WESP was made up of three components: a community component, a research component, and an in-school instructional component. The community component was organized and largely administered by TWO and included organizing parents and community members to become more active decision-makers in the schools. Professors and graduate students from the University of Chicago carried out the research component of WESP by testing and evaluating WESP students and the effectiveness of WESP programming. CPS initially led the in-school instructional component of WESP.[70]

WESP set to work on intervention programs at Wadsworth Elementary School and Wadsworth Upper Grade Center and initiated a community-based planning process at Hyde Park High School. The in-school instructional program proved most contentious, as WESP staff had to convince teachers and administrators to actively participate and cooperate with WESP programming. Debates over who had the power to control in-school teaching practices and relationships between teachers, students, and administrators would ultimately lead to challenges to the authority of the WCB. Nevertheless, the WCB and broader Woodlawn community were initially optimistic about the benefits that WESP could provide to the neighborhood.

WESP injected significant resources into the participating schools and community. At Wadsworth Elementary and Wadsworth Upper Grade Center, the additional federal funds more than doubled per-pupil spending at the schools from $546 to $1,262. This funded WESP programs, additional teachers' aides, workshops and training for teachers, community organizing to get more parents involved in the schools, and materials and supplies for students. WESP hired thirty school-community organizers and sixty community teachers and teachers' aides. The in-school WESP staff conducted professional development and training activities for teachers, served as classroom aides to assist teachers and give students more personalized attention, produced curricula, and implemented innovative activities within classrooms. In contrast to the elementary schools, the first year of WESP funding at Hyde Park High School took the form of a planning grant to bring parents, teachers, students, administrators, and community members together to decide what programs they wanted to institute.[71]

While the entire WCB was responsible for running WESP, it quickly became apparent that TWO would lead the community component of the project. Around this time TWO also administered the federally funded Youth Manpower Project that employed local youth in job training and antiviolence programming. The short-lived project's engagement with youth gangs elicited ongoing criticism and targeted attacks by city officials, local media, Chicago police, and members of Congress. As the youth project petered out, former TWO youth project director Anthony Gibbs became the associate director of the community component of WESP. Experienced organizers Sol Ice and Lelia McClelland also helped to recruit and train two dozen Woodlawn residents as WESP school-community organizers. Between 500 and 800 Woodlawn parents became active participants in approximately forty parent councils at Woodlawn public schools. Carrying on the spirit of the youth project, the WESP community component included out-of-school youth who participated in the project in a work-study capacity, youth gang members hired as counselors and mediators, and parents, students, and community members who worked as tutors.[72]

In addition to helping Woodlawn parents become more involved in their children's schools, WESP offered job and volunteer opportunities. In leadership training sessions, parent council members learned about Chicago school law, WCB rules, and Robert's Rules of Order. Parents and community members took on jobs as community organizers, as research assistants, and in WESP classrooms as community teachers, aides, and members of classroom-level problem-solving teams.[73] For the significant proportion of participating parents who were poor and working-class Black women, WESP provided a means of obtaining employment, training, and leadership experience, as well as a stronger voice in their children's education.

Though WCB meetings were initially attended only by a handful of board members and observers, their attendance grew to rival that of citywide Chicago Board of Education meetings. As more and more parents were organized, WCB meetings started to regularly attract 100 to 200 local parents, students, and community members. The meetings were changed from the afternoons to the evenings and moved from the University of Chicago campus to Immanuel Lutheran Church in the heart of Woodlawn at 64th Street and Kenwood Avenue. This was a pragmatic shift to accommodate greater community attendance, but it also symbolized the growing power and influence of the community component of WESP.[74]

In the spring of 1969 the experimental project demonstrated that it could reform itself to be more representative of the interests of the Woodlawn com-

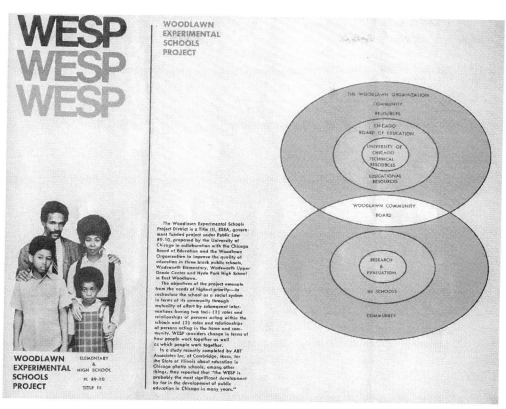

WESP
WESP
WESP

WOODLAWN
EXPERIMENTAL
SCHOOLS
PROJECT

THE WOODLAWN ORGANIZATION
COMMUNITY
RESOURCES
CHICAGO
BOARD OF EDUCATION
UNIVERSITY OF
CHICAGO
TECHNICAL
RESOURCES
EDUCATIONAL
RESOURCES

WOODLAWN COMMUNITY
BOARD

RESEARCH
&
EVALUATION

IN SCHOOLS

COMMUNITY

The Woodlawn Experimental Schools Project District is a Title III, ESEA, government funded project under Public Law 89-10, proposed by the University of Chicago in collaboration with the Chicago Board of Education and the Woodlawn Organization to improve the quality of education in three black public schools, Wadsworth Elementary, Wadsworth Upper Grade Center and Hyde Park High School in East Woodlawn.

The objectives of the project emanate from the needs of highest priority—to restructure the school as a social system in terms of its community through mutuality of effort by subsequent interventions having two foci: (1) roles and relationships of persons acting within the schools and (2) roles and relationships of persons acting in the home and community. WESP considers change in terms of how people work together as well as which people work together.

In a study recently completed by ABT Associates Inc. of Cambridge, Mass, for the State of Illinois about education in Chicago ghetto schools, among other things, they reported that "the WESP is probably the most significant development by far in the development of public education in Chicago in many years."

WOODLAWN   ELEMENTARY
EXPERIMENTAL   &
SCHOOLS   HIGH SCHOOL
PROJECT   PL 89-10
                 TITLE III

WESP brochure (ca. 1970) (Chicago Urban League Records, University of Illinois at Chicago Library, CULR_04_0122_1446_001 and CULR_04_0122_1446_002)

munity. Previously, the majority of WCB board members lived outside Woodlawn, and thirteen members of the twenty-one-member board were White. Black parents, community members, and WESP teachers' aides spoke out at WCB meetings, calling for greater parent and community voice and representation. Responding to these concerns, Brazier helped to negotiate a reconstituted WCB with ten member seats for TWO, four member seats for the University of Chicago, and seven seats for CPS—including two students and four teachers. The new board had eighteen Black members and twelve board members who actually lived in Woodlawn.[75]

WESP planners had identified the schools' primary problem as the breakdown in communication and cooperation between parents, teachers, administrators, and the larger community. The philosophy behind WESP's brand of community control dictated, "If you want to increase academic achievement, you have to first change the system so that those most immediately affected by the educational process have power to influence that process."[76] Changing the conditions in Woodlawn's public schools would require increasing direct parent, student, teacher, and community involvement in school decisions. The first step in building these new relationships required that all invested parties actually come together to meet one another on common ground and collaboratively hash out a plan for what they wanted their new educational system to look like.

During her tenure as director of WESP, Barbara Sizemore fleshed out and implemented the CAPTS (Community, Administrators, Parents, Teachers, and Students) aggregate decision-making model. CAPTS aimed to decentralize power in school-based decision-making while encouraging "mutuality of effort." Each CAPTS constituent group would need to be involved in producing and evaluating school programming, and in theory no one group could hijack the process. In this egalitarian model the work of transforming relationships among CAPTS participants would take place through the negotiation of programming.[77] However, the theory of CAPTS and the actual decision-making processes on the ground became two very different things.

Sizemore became the director of WESP just as the project shifted from being more collaboratively administered—between TWO, the university, and the CPS—to becoming increasingly community driven. By the summer of 1969, the WCB had more representation by African Americans, Woodlawn residents, and TWO members than at any time before. Parent involvement in the schools was at an all-time high. However, simmering tensions between WESP staff, principals, and teachers tested the limits of WESP's and Sizemore's power.

From the time WESP staff members first entered the schools, there was pushback from teachers and administrators. According to John Hall Fish, "Many teachers felt that they were being judged and accused" and saw the WESP community teachers and parents as unqualified "nonprofessionals." On the flipside, WESP staff and parents "felt that some of the teachers were trying to sabotage the project." It was only after WESP staff worked in Wadsworth school for months, bringing resources to the school, leading workshops and trainings, and facilitating group discussions, that trust increased and more of the Wadsworth teachers came to support WESP programming and value the contributions of parents, community teachers, and aides in the schools.[78]

The role of students in WESP at Hyde Park High School also generated controversy. A group of students and teachers leveled complaints against a White teacher, Edward Szkirpan. Students alleged that Szkirpan had betrayed the spirit of the CAPTS model by kicking students out of a meeting where teachers and students were tasked with collectively making plans for the school.

A group of students brought a petition with nearly 700 signatures to a WCB meeting and demanded Szkirpan's removal from Hyde Park High School. Castigating Szkirpan's "flagrant contempt of the Black community," the petition claimed his teaching was "totalitarian, embarrassing, and hostile towards students." WESP staff conducted an investigation and recommended that Hyde Park principal Anna Kolheim put Szkirpan on leave.[79]

Yet this confrontation hinted at the limits of WESP's and WCB's power. Only the Chicago Board of Education had the authority to terminate or transfer personnel. Fearing a showdown, WCB representatives from the University of Chicago and CPS privately worked out a deal with Szkirpan to arrange for his transfer.[80] Similar confrontations would increase in the years that followed.

In April 1970, upon Sizemore's recommendation, the WCB voted that Principal Kolheim should give all teachers a "superior" rating for the year while they worked to create a new CAPTS-informed teacher evaluation process. Kolheim refused to sign off. Once a fellow Black educator-activist and ally to Sizemore, now Kolheim became her adversary in a struggle over authority. Lacking the power to compel the principal, the WCB eventually decided to submit two sets of evaluations: one set by WESP and one set by Kolheim. Teachers responded by boycotting the school for several days in June 1970 and arguing their case to a CPS deputy superintendent.[81] Here, Sizemore's and WESP's lack of authority once again exposed the WCB's limited power within the actual school buildings.

CPS officials challenged Sizemore's authority as well. A central part of Sizemore's vision of community control was the employment of local Black residents in the schools. Although CPS ultimately did not comply with federal standards for faculty desegregation until 1977, in 1969, the federal government was intensifying the push for CPS to desegregate their faculty. Seeing a convenient tool for reasserting control over WESP, CPS claimed that Sizemore's request to hire a virtually all-Black staff violated desegregation mandates, even as CPS was evading these mandates across the city. The board's reluctance to approve any new hires for WESP offered another early indicator that the Board of Education was losing confidence in WESP and in community control as a viable model.[82]

At the same time, fissures within TWO and the community component of WESP threatened the continuation of the project. Brazier stepped down as president of TWO in 1970, leaving behind a vacuum of authority. His replacement was E. Duke McNeil, a lawyer who emphasized cooperation with government agencies, the University of Chicago, and other former adversaries rather than conflict: "The technician replaced the organizer as the key to TWO's operation."[83] TWO's tradition of mass-based organizing faded during its transition from an issue-based "people's organization" to a project-based organization pursuing more commercial ventures. By 1971, TWO had become a community development agency and landlord, managing low-income housing complexes, a grocery store, and a gas station. With TWO in transition, Sizemore's authority in the schools was rendered even more tenuous.[84]

In the spring of 1971, the deteriorating conditions at Hyde Park High School boiled over into a school boycott by students and teachers. After Sizemore implemented a Hyde Park High School senate in accordance with the CAPTS model, teachers and students passed policies to improve security in the school and plan Black cultural events. Principal Kolheim ignored these decisions and gave several popular teachers unsatisfactory evaluations. On Monday, April 5, 1971, in protest of Kolheim's disrespect, students and a group of teachers walked out of Hyde Park High School in protest. For the rest of the week, 1,200 students remained out of school.[85]

While many issues gave rise to this protest, Sizemore saw it as a struggle over who would control Hyde Park High School: "It is my opinion that what's happening at Hyde Park is a struggle for decision making power. . . . The CAPTS (Community—Administration—Parents—Teachers—Students) model is supposed to restructure the social system, and move parents and teachers into decision making positions. I believe that the people should make decisions about the institutions which govern their lives, and this means that the principal will have to give up some of her power."[86] Sizemore faced criticism for allegedly inciting students to protest, and in the wake of unflattering press coverage, CPS area superintendent Melnick removed Sizemore's jurisdiction over Hyde Park High School and put Kolheim on five weeks' sick leave.

In keeping with their shift from "conflict to coexistence," TWO responded pragmatically. As chairman of the WCB, E. Duke McNeil supported returning Kolheim to the school and transferring out the teachers who supposedly incited the walkout. Hyde Park students complained that they were excluded from making their case against Kolheim and for the reinstatement of the teachers at the WCB meeting, in direct defiance of the WESP model. McNeil insisted that the "voice of the community" demanded Kolheim's return.[87] For McNeil, the students were not among the important decision-makers on the matter.

TWO opted to salvage its relationship with the Board of Education and the leadership of Hyde Park High School rather than defend the programs and cooperative decision-making model of Sizemore and WESP. TWO's motivations would face questions in the years that followed. In his July 1974 column for the *Chicago Defender*, Black cultural commentator Lou "Charlie Cherokee" Downings wondered whether McNeil was "a tool of the University of Chicago." He concluded that "some Blacks seem to think he is since he allegedly took over The Woodlawn Organization for ... the expressed purpose of the U of C 'putting down' the Woodlawn Experimental Project" and putting McNeil and the university's concerns "over the educational changes Barbara [Sizemore] wanted to make in the interest of Black children."[88]

Facing a diminishing grassroots base, limited decision-making authority, and damaging interpersonal conflicts, the WESP experiment came to a close in the summer of 1971 when the project's funding was not renewed. Sizemore argued that WESP's power and effectiveness had waned as soon as it was clear that the WCB lacked authority over school restructuring and teacher hiring, firing, and evaluation. In Sizemore's view, the community component of WESP effectively became a patronage organization run by TWO as soon as the WCB was proven powerless. Lacking authority, TWO doled out WESP jobs, hoping to win community support to fight for gains from CPS. While TWO leaders publicly advocated community control and lauded parent turnout at WCB meetings, they also had reservations. Once the WCB became a community forum, TWO had to be accountable to its constituency and could not appear too closely aligned with either the Board of Education or the university. This limited the organization's ability to cut deals.[89]

Sizemore's subject position as a Black woman impacted her power as WESP director. Under Sizemore's leadership, WCB and WESP became more representative of the racial makeup of the community, yet their bargaining power decreased. CPS was less willing to negotiate, compromise, and cede control of its schools to WESP when it was led by Sizemore, a Black woman, than when it was led by her predecessor, Dr. Willard Congreve, a White male professor representing the University of Chicago. The White men from the university and the Board of Education on the original WCB leveraged their social capital to negotiate and garner special favors from the Board of Education and government agencies in ways that Sizemore could not.[90] However, as director, Sizemore was able to capitalize on the collective energies of parents and students to gain community support for WESP in ways that these White men could not.

WESP's greatest success occurred in Wadsworth Elementary School, where parents, teachers, administrators, and WESP leaders cultivated the most consensus. In 1969, during the first year of WESP, only 39 percent of first-grade students at Wadsworth were deemed "ready to read" according to the Metropolitan Readiness Test. In 1971, the final year of the program, 66 percent were deemed "ready to read." Third-graders' reading scores also improved. Sixth-graders demonstrated gains in social studies skills, and eighth-graders demonstrated gains in social studies, arithmetic, and science. WESP programming had the highest impact on the most low-performing students, with reports of greater confidence in their academic abilities and overall self-efficacy.[91]

Though the limitations on Sizemore's power made comprehensive community control of schools in Woodlawn illusory, WESP had a substantial impact. The program gave hundreds of Black parents volunteer and work experience and new skills as classroom and teachers' aides and community organizers. As WESP mobilized Woodlawn parents to become advocates, it challenged the perception that low-income Black parents were uninterested in their children's education. Hundreds of community members actively participated in parent councils and regularly attended WCB meetings. From the fall of 1969 until the end of the program, there were no incidents of violence in the Wadsworth schoolyard. As the WESP final report indicated, violence was curbed through the work of out-of-school youth and gang members hired as counselors. This was community control at its best.[92]

At its worst, however, WESP failed to give Woodlawn residents or local community organizations the power to significantly impact or control the curriculum, staffing, and programming in the schools within their community. The politics on the ground were messy. The Chicago Board of Education was ultimately unwilling to cede power to Sizemore, WESP, or the WCB to create fundamental changes. However, community fissures also played a role in derailing WESP. Though TWO claimed to be an umbrella group representing the interests of all of Woodlawn's residents, the schools and broader community of Woodlawn never spoke in one voice. Disputes sometimes turned potential collaborators into opponents. It was often difficult to reach a consensus while advocating for democratic decision-making powers for a broader range of people within schools. Finally, TWO's transformation from protest organization to project-based service provider and community development organization eroded the organization's grassroots base.

COMMUNITY CONTROL RECONSIDERED

Community control of schools was never fully realized in Chicago. Black education reformers' shift from strategies of desegregation to community control was not merely a reaction to failed attempts at desegregation. Community control was also an important strand of a broader politics of Black achievement. The legacy of the movement continued beyond the protests and projects of the time.

The 1968 school boycotts left a lasting impact on Black students' political consciousness. Student activism has historically provided a unique space for young people to learn the skills of organizing and implement their ideas for societal change. In the 1960s in particular, Black student protests produced an environment for students to push for broader reforms in the education system while also exposing the limitations of students' power.[93]

New sources of federal funding available through the ESEA and other War on Poverty legislation during the 1960s and 1970s generated new opportunities for, and limitations on, community-based education organizing efforts. Because a large proportion of these funds were earmarked for economically disadvantaged children, organizers in poor and working-class Black urban neighborhoods benefited from this influx of federal funds. These were the funds that made WESP possible. Since WESP was forged in the education and justice struggles waged during the 1960s, Sizemore, Brazier, the WESP staff, and parents involved in the project articulated an ideology of community control that emphasized Black empowerment and control over state resources within the Black community.

However, it is important to remember that the impetus for WESP's community control project was a privately controlled and administered proposal crafted by a private institution, the University of Chicago. TWO had to force its way in. The university, despite its nonprofit status, did—and continues to—function as a profit-oriented entity. In the War on Poverty, the state also financed the work of private-driven partnerships.

WESP was a precursor to later trends toward semiautonomous community control in the Chicago School Reform Movement of the 1980s. Precipitated by Mayor Harold Washington's education summits, the 1980s Chicago School Reform Movement brought an unprecedented level of local control to public schools. The ideas of local control institutionalized by the 1980s reform movement included aspects of decentralization, parental involvement, and decision-making advocated by WESP. However, the 1980s reform movement also developed out of a broader citywide coalition of business and civic leaders, educators, parents, and the burgeoning nonprofit advocacy sector.

WESP was also a prelude to the public-private relationships that continued to characterize the public school system decades later. The federal government in the 1960s initially rejected the University of Chicago's proposal to create an educational research center and school. Today, the University of Chicago is home to the Urban Education Institute and Consortium on Chicago School Research and operates four charter schools, including UChicago Charter Woodlawn Campus, initially housed in one of the original WESP schools. While charter schools represent a newer mode of education reform, the coalition partners that helped to create the UChicago Charter Woodlawn Campus were very similar to the partners that created WESP. Chapter 6 will further elaborate on the continuities and discontinuities between these types of reforms. But suffice to say Woodlawn continues to be an experimental community.

By trying to flatten hierarchies and increase the range of people who made decisions within schools, WESP challenged many existing school norms and practices. The politics on the ground within the schools were rife with conflicts over programmatic content and questions of authority, expertise, and inclusion. Community control was a valence of the self-determinist politics of Black achievement that worked to forge change *within* public schools. Another valence of the politics of Black achievement during the same period worked to create Black educational alternatives *outside* the public school system.

BUILDING INDEPENDENT

BLACK INSTITUTIONS

Soyini Walton could not fathom how young Black people could live in Chicago during the 1960s and 1970s and *not* be involved in "The Movement." Immersed in Chicago's Black cultural nationalist community, Walton worked by day as an elementary school teacher at a traditional public school, but before and after work and on the weekends, she volunteered at the Institute of Positive Education (IPE), an African-centered independent Black educational institution. Her work with IPE was all encompassing. She donated half of her pay to the organization for a period of time, met her husband while working with him at IPE, and eventually served as interim director of the organization's New Concept Development Center (NCDC), an independent African-centered school. Her circle of friends included other Black cultural nationalists: visual artists from AfriCOBRA, actors in the Afro-Arts Theater, and young Black writers who met and were mentored in the home of renowned Black poet Gwendolyn Brooks. However, long before Soyini changed her name, hair, and dress in the cultural fervor of the Black Power Movement, her racial and political consciousness was shaped by the politics of her family and young life.[1]

Soyini Walton was born Rochelle Ricks and grew up in the home that her parents owned near Dewey Elementary School, off Garfield Boulevard on the South Side of Chicago. As a child, Walton literally walked to the other side of the tracks to go to school. In 1950, with the train tracks above her head, she crossed under the viaduct near her home to attend kindergarten at predominantly White Dewey Elementary School on 54th Street and Union Avenue. As was the case in other elementary schools located in racially transitioning neighborhoods, Black students were pushed out of Dewey. After leaving Dewey halfway through kindergarten, Walton attended Sherwood Elementary School, an all-Black elementary school also not far from her home. At Sherwood she encountered many of the same conditions that Rosie Simpson and Rev. Arthur Brazier would protest in the years to come. Sherwood ran on a double shift and later received "Willis Wagons"—portable classrooms to accommodate overcrowding while maintaining segregation. Walton's community was disrupted when friends' homes were razed to build the Dan Ryan Expressway, displacing Black residents while further isolating the historic Black Belt's Bronzeville community from the White Bridgeport neighborhood to its west—home of Mayor Richard J. Daley. These types of government actions, along with policies that concentrated public housing in distressed Black communities, would contribute to African Americans' disillusionment with the prospects for desegregation in housing and education. Despite these experiences of displacement and community fracture, Walton built close relationships with friends and neighbors and developed a love for learning and school at Sherwood.[2]

Walton's education continued outside the school building as well. Her father was a janitor at Englewood High School and an avid reader. On the weekends he went to the Wabash Avenue "Colored" YMCA with a group of working-class and middle-class Black men who met to discuss books, history, and politics. Her father came home and taught Soyini, his oldest child, about colonialism and the histories and struggles of oppressed peoples around the world. She recalls that her father's teachings and love of learning greatly influenced her analysis of the world. After Soyini Walton graduated from Englewood's Parker High School in 1963, she enrolled in Chicago Teachers College to pursue a career in teaching.[3]

Teachers College, which shared a campus with Parker High School, served as a springboard for Walton's work building the local institutions that sustained the Black Power Movement. The school was very racially divided, but Walton organized protests with an interracial group of Black and White students to integrate social spaces on campus. Walton graduated from Teachers College in 1966 and started her teaching career at Guggenheim Elementary School only a few years after Luberda Bailey protested against the installment of Willis Wagons at the same school. While teaching, Walton returned to campus for lectures and events. Wilson Junior College, which also shared the campus with Teachers College and Parker, had become a hotbed for Black political activities.

Like many Black activists during the late 1960s, including Brazier and the Black organizers who fought for community control of schools, Walton transitioned away from her previous desegregation activism to embrace the self-determinist ideologies of the Black Power Movement. Walton remembers 1968 as a key year in this transformation. That year Soyini met Black poet and activist Haki Madhubuti (Don L. Lee) at Wilson.[4] Captivated by his intensity and the connections he made between education and Black self-determination, she started volunteering at Haki's independent Black publishing company,

THE POLITICS OF BLACK ACHIEVEMENT

Third World Press, and eventually quit her job to work full time at IPE. For more than a decade she put in the hard daily work of what historian Russell Rickford calls the pragmatic "everyday practices" and "programmatic expression of Black Power."[5] Examining the influences that shaped the development of IPE's African-centered ideology provides insights into the varying currents of Black Power politics operating within Black communities during the 1970s.

Black organizing in the 1970s took many different forms, including the creation of a small but ideologically significant group of Black independent schools and institutions that educated Black youth and families informed by an African-centered worldview. Africa and the African Diaspora were always front and center in the pedagogy and practices of these institutions, which were called Afrikan, Black nationalist, Pan-African, Afrocentric, and African-centered at different moments. This chapter focuses on the ideology, growth, curricula, and prolonged impact of one such institution, IPE, founded during the Black Power era in Chicago. As stated in IPE's NCDC school manual: "Critical thinking, problem solving and application of knowledge in everyday experiences . . . are couched in terms of the cultural, historical, social, and political experiences and needs of African peoples."[6]

The establishment of independent Black educational institutions is another strand of the politics of Black achievement embraced by Black education reformers since the 1960s. Like community control, these independent black educational institutions developed at a time when the U.S. welfare state seemed increasingly incapable of delivering on promises of educational equity. Black education reformers rejected the logic of racial liberalism as government-commissioned social science reports were locating the source of urban problems—including low Black academic attainment—in ideas of inherent Black pathology. In this context, Black education reformers embraced a politics of Black achievement by pursuing alternative Black self-determinist strategies for quality education that disrupted ideas of Black inferiority. Community control articulated this politics of Black achievement by making claims to state resources, reorganizing decision-making power in schools, and empowering local Black communities through Black self-determination in public schools. Articulating another valence of the politics of Black achievement, the architects of independent African-centered educational institutions insisted on independence from the state and the creation of a unique African diasporic subjectivity, curriculum, and worldview that resonated with the cultural currents of the Black Power era.

Translating Black cultural nationalist ideologies into daily practices on the ground was intellectually demanding and labor-intensive work. During a period that is often associated with Black political demobilization and an "urban crisis" that rendered Black residents too disenfranchised or alienated to be politically engaged, IPE members continued to organize, theorize, and build institutions. Some, like Soyini Walton, found liberation in independent African-centered institutions. However, ongoing concerns about IPE's workload requirements, scale, and financial sustainability ultimately contributed to the organization's decision to reengage with the state by opening public charter schools in the 1990s. With remarkable longevity, IPE's ideology, schools, and African-centered curriculum would continue to impact educational practices and shape Black political consciousness for decades.

BLACK POWER, BLACK NATIONALISM,
AND INDEPENDENT SCHOOLS

From the mid-1960s into the 1970s, Black Power movements rose to prominence using language, programs, and symbols that emphasized racial pride, Black empowerment, and self-determination. In the United States, Black Power groups originated in local communities across the country and worked with transnational movements for decolonization and Third World liberation. Black Power both intertwined with and developed separately from earlier civil rights struggles, drawing on a broad and sometimes conflicting set of ideological orientations that included cultural nationalism, Marxism, Black feminism, Pan-Africanism, internationalism, Black capitalism, and socialism. As with the flexible division between desegregation and community control, these ideological distinctions were often fluid. However, over the course of the 1960s and 1970s, significant rifts did emerge — like those between cultural nationalists and Marxists — that fractured Black Power alliances and coalitions and, in the most extreme cases, devolved into violent confrontations between groups.[7]

The politics of Black Power particularly appealed to younger Black Chicagoans. This generation had come of age during the tumult of the 1960s. In Chicago, they had witnessed Mayor Richard J. Daley's rebuff of civil rights organizing, white mobs' vicious response to Martin Luther King Jr.'s open-housing campaign in Chicago, the uprisings after King's assassination, the Chicago Police Department's violent handling of protesters at the Democratic National Convention in 1968, and the law enforcement–led raid and murder of Black Panther Party leaders Fred Hampton and Mark Clark in 1969.[8] Despite struggles for desegregation and new War on Poverty programs, segregated Black neighborhoods seemed to become even more isolated and inadequately resourced over the course of the 1960s. In this climate, Black Chicagoans, young and old, embraced the more defiant posture and politics of Black Power, and a number of new Black Power organizations emerged during the late 1960s and 1970s.

Founded during the Black Power era, IPE emphasized the importance of Black institution building and African-centered education. IPE members operated several institutions and programs in Chicago, including NCDC, their independent African-centered Black private school. IPE argued that the problem for Black people was not the existence of racially isolated Black communities or schools but the racist under-resourcing and systemic neglect of Black communities by the traditional White power structure. IPE did not try to transform Black communities through interracial political collaboration or the racial integration of neighborhoods and schools. Instead the leaders of IPE worked to change the cultural consciousness of Black people as a means of transforming social, political, and economic conditions within their own communities. While the CUL continued to seek to improve public education through desegregation while managing ties with Chicago's White business and political elite, IPE was asking a different question: How do you change the consciousness of a people?

Many independent Black nationalist schools during this period actually developed out of struggles for community control of public schools. In New York City, the Uhuru Sasa Shule, led by Jitu Weusi (Leslie Campbell), emerged in response to the struggles for community control of schools waged by community members and Black educators in Ocean Hill–Brownsville.[9] Hannibal Afrik (Harold Charles), a CPS teacher who led Black teachers' struggles for community control of public schools, founded Shule Ya Watoto, an independent Black educational institution that promoted African-centered education on the West Side of Chicago. These schools rejected desegregation as a means of challenging the existing social and racial order in the United States. Afrik and others argued that "school desegregation as a strategy does not challenge in any fundamental way the cultural and political authority of the ruling elite in the United States over the schooling and education of people of African descent. The African-centered institution-building model . . . clearly does so by seeking power over education and schooling."[10] Through education, these schools sought to challenge the existing racialized social order by generating a new vision for a social order centered on the histories and experiences of Black people.

Independent Black schools were not a new construct. African American churches and communities had established schools since before emancipation. Beginning in the late eighteenth century, Black religious denominations and benevolent societies also established schools for African Americans.[11] While many Black colleges and universities were established by White missionaries during the late nineteenth century, a system of Black-founded private primary and secondary schools operated during the twentieth century—schools like Piney Woods in Mississippi and Universal Negro Improvement Association schools and Nation of Islam schools across the country. Independent, predominantly Black private and parochial schools provided an alternative for parents who did not feel that public schools could address the academic, social, and cultural needs of Black students.[12]

Inspired by Black freedom struggles of the mid-twentieth century, movements for alternative schooling for African Americans during the late 1960s and 1970s offered a vision of society and pedagogy that rejected ideologies of White supremacy and the oppression perceived to permeate traditional public schools.[13] As movement schools, SNCC freedom schools and Black Panther Party schools fostered a new political consciousness among students by adopting curricula and pedagogy that challenged racism and economic inequality in society. These schools positioned education as a central site for generating societal change by acknowledging, and building on, the struggles experienced by Black students and their families.[14] Like independent African-centered schools founded during this period, these schools embraced a self-determinist politics of Black achievement that sought to couple traditional markers of academic attainment (in literacy, mathematics, science, etc.) with transformations in collective Black consciousness, efficacy, and pride.

Seeking alternatives to inadequate public schools during this period, Black parents in Chicago pursued a range of private schooling options. Historian Worth Kamili Hayes identifies this era as part of the "golden age of Black private education," when Black parents enrolled their children in Black private schools to escape the discrimination and racial inequities in CPS. Thousands of Black students attended Black Catholic schools and Nation of Islam schools, as well as secular Black private schools, including the Howalton Day School and Marva Collins's Westside Preparatory School.[15] Like these institutions, IPE was not a traditional state-run institution, so it was allowed a freedom and flexibility to operate semiautonomously outside the rigidity of Chicago formal politics. This contrasted sharply with organizations like the CUL and TWO, which sought some form of engagement with the state. Like IPE, a number of other Black institutions in Chicago during this time framed education as one part of a larger program addressing the holistic well-being of Black youth and communities. These included Centers for New Horizons,

Ujima Family Center, the Kemetic Institute, and Center for Inner City Studies on the South Side, and Shule Ya Watoto on the West Side, as well as more social service–centered groups, including Afro-American Family and Community Services and PRIDE Community Center. Although these institutions were relatively few in number, the collective ideological impact and longevity of many of them was significant.

Unlike other Black private school alternatives in the city, IPE used its political orientation outside the direct control of the state to instruct and raise Black children to embrace a unique African diasporic subjectivity. However, the alternative ideological and educational framework that IPE adopted was not without its set of challenges. Designing a self-consciously Pan-African subjectivity and counternarrative among African Americans born and raised in the United States was, at times, linked with limiting patriarchal norms and the rejection of African American cultural traditions and ideas deemed counter to liberation or too European. Thus, IPE's cadre model and rigid practices both generated an important educational alternative and had the potential to alienate parts of the broader Black community whose consciousness they aimed to correct.

ORIGINS OF IPE AND THE POLITICS OF INDEPENDENT BLACK INSTITUTIONS

According to IPE's founders, independent Black institutions were key to the liberation of Black people. Influenced by the Black Power and Black Arts movements, and drawing on ideas of collective community responsibility and the entrepreneurial traditions of Black capitalism, Black Chicagoans Haki Madhubuti, Carol D. Lee (née Easton, also Safisha Madhubuti),[16] Johari Amini (Jewel C. McLawler, also Jewel C. Latimore), Carolyn Rodgers, and Soyini Walton helped to found several institutions on the South Side of Chicago: Third World Press, one of the oldest independent publishers of Black literature in the country, in 1967; IPE in 1969; and IPE's school, NCDC, in 1972. Within a few years, they bought two storefront spaces for these institutions near 78th Street and Ellis Avenue.[17] They defined independent Black institutions thus: "*Independent*—void of outside control and influence; *Black*—in color, culture and consciousness; *Institution*—a structured program aimed at correcting a deficiency, giving concrete alternatives for our people."[18] The NCDC school was a central vehicle for implementing this mission. As Haki Madhubuti rose to prominence as a Black Arts Movement poet, he further developed the ideology that guided IPE's programming.

The Black Arts Movement was the literary, artistic, cultural, and aesthetic arm of the Black Power Movement. Developing from many of the same political currents that propelled Black Power struggles, it also had roots in artistic traditions honed by Black artists, writers, and performers in the 1930s and postwar bohemian and popular avant-garde arts scenes.[19] As a teenager, Haki Madhubuti found refuge from the ravages of urban poverty that shaped his young life in the work of Richard Wright, Paul Robeson, and W. E. B. Du Bois. From 1962 to 1966, Haki worked as a curator at the Ebony Museum in Chicago (later DuSable Museum of African American History). At the museum, co-founders Margaret Burroughs and Charles Burroughs exposed Haki to a vast library of leftist literature, history, and theory. Prominent Black poet Gwendolyn Brooks mentored Haki and other young writers, helping them articulate a political vision and hone their craft. These artists and intellectuals heightened Haki's awareness of and interest in distinctively Black cultural forms from Africa and the African Diaspora. Along with the powerful speeches of Malcolm X, they provided him with a deeply affirming sense of Black history and Black people in a global context and influenced his emerging Black cultural nationalist beliefs and writings.[20]

Although there were many Black Power groups in the city, Soyini Walton was most invested in Haki Madhubuti's and IPE's cultural nationalist visions of revolution through education, culture, and institution building. Within Black communities at the time, there were multiple groups calling for revolution, but they had different ideas of how the revolution would be achieved. The Black Panthers sought revolution through class struggle, community survival programs, and armed self-defense. The Republic of New Afrika sought land. AfriCOBRA, Ebony Talent Associates, Afro-Arts Theater, and the Organization of Black American Culture sought revolution and transformation through the arts. Others constructed visions of cultural nationalism through personal aesthetics, African dress, or dietary changes. Around the time that Soyini met Haki in 1968, she was also involved with the Afro-Arts Theater. However, Haki's path to revolution ultimately resonated most with Soyini's own interests and training as an educator. Like many of IPE's early members, she was drawn to Haki's dynamic lectures, poems, and discussions of the idea of Black people as a revolutionary people.

For Soyini, IPE's focus on institution building also set it apart from other cultural nationalist groups of the time. She recounted Haki's version of Black nationalism and the path to revolution as having three main tenets: (1) educating our own, (2) publishing our own books, and (3) building institutions.[21] Institution building became a foundational tenet of IPE as an explicitly cultural nationalist organization. While IPE was based in Chicago, its young founders were also part of a larger national network of artists and activists forming independent Black institutions.

IPE's Pan-African cultural nationalist ideology and early programming were influenced by Haki Madhubuti's relationship with prominent Black Arts and Black Power leader Amiri Baraka (LeRoi Jones) and his work in Newark, New Jersey. As part of a larger network of independent Black institutions, IPE staff members and volunteers made trips to Newark to observe and work with Baraka's cultural nationalist institutions. In the early 1970s, IPE leaders saw these institutions as a "visible working model" to inspire the growth of their own young organization. They sought to gain knowledge from the groups in Newark in order to make IPE a model for Black institution building.[22] As poets in the Black Arts Movement, Haki and Amiri Baraka performed together and spoke at college campuses and other venues across the country. Haki was also an important ally in Baraka's political work, electing Black political officials in Newark.[23]

Haki Madhubuti's poetry, work with Baraka, and leadership in the Congress of African People provided a national platform for IPE. As moderate Black politicians, civil rights leaders, and more radical Black nationalist leaders and groups came together in mass Black political conventions during the early 1970s, Amiri Baraka organized the Congress of African People as an umbrella organization to create a Black political party, increase communication among groups, and pool resources. The Congress of African People established branches in more than twenty-five cities, and Haki Madhubuti founded the organization's Chicago branch. However, by the mid-1970s, Haki and Amiri Baraka had become adversaries in the ideological debates between Marxists and Black cultural nationalists that divided the Black Power Movement. Amiri Baraka turned toward a revolutionary Marxist-Leninist-Maoist position, while Haki remained a staunch Black cultural nationalist.[24]

The leaders of IPE believed that it was their responsibility to create institutions that would transform Black culture. While programs and policies would come and go, institutions established a site for longevity that could transcend generations and continue the core work of the founding members for years to come. As Carol Lee, a founder of IPE, explained, the "fundamental thrust was the belief, or the proposition, that in the Black community we needed to develop independent institutions in order to control resources, to control ideas and to inspire political activism in our community."[25] Carol Lee's invocation of "control" here is not necessarily the same control sought by other community control advocates. IPE's political vision did not seek to seize control of state resources but, rather, to create conditions for Black success and consciousness transformation by establishing alternative, independently funded, Black-owned-and-operated institutions in Black communities.

IPE leaders did not trust the government or White private interests to invest in Black communities and public schools. IPE emerged during a period of "urban crisis" in the late 1960s and early 1970s, at the twilight of Great Society and War on Poverty programs and the accompanying public concern for the fate of burning cities after the urban uprisings of the mid- to late 1960s. State and federal dollars were almost always first routed through Mayor Daley's overwhelmingly White Democratic machine. On the South Side, IPE leaders witnessed deindustrialization, economic decline, and underfunded public schools, without effective interventions by government agencies or White corporations.[26] Like other Black nationalist organizations across the country, IPE saw the building of independent Black educational institutions as a means to "supplement the social services that were vanishing from the urban core, a site of massive disinvestment and neglect."[27] Through these institutions, IPE tried to provide a needed educational service to the community and transform the value systems of Black children and their families.

For IPE the importance of African-centered education was understood as part of a larger cultural battle for the minds and consciousness of Black people in America: "In the 1970's the question that is elementary to our predicament is, can we *create* or *re-create* an Afrikan (or Black) mind in a *pre-dominantly European-American setting?*" For the founders of IPE this was not a question to be taken lightly but a matter of life or death by "genocide of the mind."[28] During a period marked by various urban crises, Haki Madhubuti claimed that drugs and prevailing Eurocentric forms of education were the two greatest threats to the survival of Black people. However, from his perspective the former could not be dealt with without first addressing the latter. He argued that many people turned to drugs because of "a lack of *identity, purpose, and direction*"—all areas that he suggested could be strengthened by appropriate African-centered education.[29]

IPE leaders argued that the education necessary to impart identity, purpose, and direction would need to be radically different from the existing public education system. *Planning an Independent Black Education Institution*, a report prepared by a division of the Congress of African People, claimed that more than 99 percent of Black children were educated in "white-controlled" institutions. IPE leaders contended that within these settings, Black people were being indoctrinated with a "spirit of European nationalism." They worried that if Black people did not teach their own, they would be taught by Whites to serve White societal needs and to contribute to their own oppression: "Either a people prepare their youth to be responsible and responsive to their *own needs* as a people or somebody else will teach them to be responsive to somebody else's needs at the detriment of themselves and their people." IPE leaders argued that creating independent Black institutions run by and for Black people could prevent this and create an alternative path for Black educational success and empowerment. IPE and other advocates of African-centered education were "about the business of providing quality education, an African alternative for African children, youth and adults."[30] However, it was not enough to simply state what they were against. IPE needed a positive vision as well.

The work of IPE and the Third World Press was grounded in the directives and philosophies of a Black value system called Kawaida. Developed by Maulana Karenga (Ronald Everett), the Black cultural nationalist leader of the Los Angeles–based US Organization, Kawaida evolved from a quasi-religious philosophy with political undertones into an ideology and guide for living life aimed at creating fundamental societal change. The ideology and program of Kawaida merged African American oratorical, cultural, and political traditions with religious and communal values and rituals derived from a number of African cultures, particularly incorporating many Kiswahili and Zulu words and concepts.[31] This value system merged notions of collective responsibility with Black entrepreneurial traditions.

The Nguzo Saba (Seven Principles) constituted a key component of Kawaida philosophy. The Nguzo Saba outlined the seven guiding principles that should order Black people's lives:

UMOJA—Unity: To strive for and maintain unity in the family, community, nation and race.

KUJICHAGULIA—Self-Determination: To define ourselves, create for ourselves, and speak for ourselves.

UJIMA—Collective Work and Responsibility: To build and maintain our community together and make our brothers' and sisters' problems our problems and to solve them together.

UJAMAA—Cooperative Economics: To build and maintain our own stores, shops and other businesses and to profit from them together.

NIA—Purpose: To make as our collective vocation the building of our community in order to restore our people to their historical greatness.

KUUMBA—Creativity: To do always as much as we can in the way we can in order to leave our community more beautiful and beneficial than we inherited it.

IMANI—Faith: To believe with all our heart in our parents, our teachers, our leaders, our people, and the righteousness and victory of our struggle.[32]

Today millions celebrate these core values in the annual observance of Kwanzaa. Karenga developed Kwanzaa in 1966, modeled after a Zulu harvest festival. Kwanzaa was one of many holidays and practices promoted by Karenga, the US Organization, and other Black cultural nationalist groups in the 1960s and 1970s to provide a cultural alternative for Black Americans and a shared recognition of Black Americans' African cultural roots. During the 1960s and 1970s, observance of Kwanzaa and adherence to the Nguzo Saba was limited to a dedicated subset of Black cultural nationalists.[33] For these nationalists, the Nguzo Saba was more than just a set of named precepts to be acknowledged at celebrations and holidays. They understood the seven principles of the Nguzo Saba as a civic code and blueprint for how Black people should live and interact with one another and the world on a daily basis. This value system became a focal point of the ideological framework and curriculum that African-centered educational institutions produced to transform Black consciousness.

IPE leaders worked to incorporate Kawaida and the values of the Nguzo Saba into daily routines at IPE. Volunteers and staff members adopted African-styled dress, adhered to Kawaida doctrine and the teachings of the Nguzo Saba, and incorporated Swahili words into daily life. Soyini Walton remembers this period as a sort of "second upbringing." These life changes became so deeply ingrained that she "couldn't see any other way. . . . We needed to do these things to actualize Black Power. . . . It was a cultural movement. That's where the term came from, *cultural nationalism*. Because the bent of what we were doing was toward changing our lifestyle and therefore changing our communities and where we lived and how we thought." Walton changed her diet and cut off her hair to start wearing it natural. She and her husband, who also worked for IPE, changed their names from Rochelle and Ronald to Soyini and Chaga. The foundational group in IPE studied and learned these new practices together and incorporated them into their lives.[34]

Collective study—of education, politics, health, and particularly, African history—was central to IPE's mission of cultural transformation. Third World Press published, and IPE study groups read, works by Black historians of Africa and the African Diaspora. Longings for Africa, nations of Africans within the Americas, and Pan-Africanism have historically occupied an important place in the African American imaginary. Black scholar Robin D. G. Kelley reflected back on his early encounters with histories of Africa and the African

Diaspora, similar to those read by IPE members, and their limits: "We looked back in search of a better future. We wanted to find a refuge where 'black people' exercised power, possessed essential knowledge, educated the West, built monuments, slept under the stars on the banks of the Nile, and never had to worry about the police or poverty or arrogant white people questioning our intelligence. Of course this meant conveniently ignoring slave labor, class hierarchies, and women's oppression, and it meant projecting backwards in time a twentieth-century conception of race, but to simply criticize us for myth making or essentialism misses the point. We dreamed the ancient world as a place of freedom, a picture to imagine what we desired and what was possible." Soyini Walton, and other Black cultural nationalists during the 1960s and 1970s, drew upon an amalgamation of traditions, cultural practices, and "Africanisms" from ancient and contemporary African societies to imagine a different future for Black people in America. IPE members aimed to use these ideas to counter what they saw as prevailing Eurocentric miseducation and to articulate a new identity—as Africans in America—for their students and, by extension, the broader Black community.[35]

The Organization Structure, Demands, and Expectations of IPE

While stressing the importance of collectivity and distributive values ideologically and rhetorically, in practice IPE was also a hierarchically structured organization. IPE leadership created and distributed trees, flow charts, and memorandums outlining the specific duties of the organization's leadership, members, staff, volunteers, and schoolchildren. One such chart explained IPE's hierarchy using a pyramid: Baraza Ya Kati (Central Council) at the top, followed by Cadre (the core most committed members of the group), Staff, and Watoto (children). The Baraza Ya Kati handled the upper-level management duties in IPE.[36] The Baraza Ya Kati was responsible for planning the future growth of IPE, making executive decisions, establishing doctrine for the larger organization, acting as the final arbiter for disputes that could not be resolved within the separate men's council or women's council, and enforcing "the democratic constitution of IPE."[37]

Expectations for staff members were demanding. In order to receive minimum-wage pay, IPE staff members were initially expected to work from 7:00 A.M. to 5:00 P.M., six days each week. It was not unusual for IPE staff to work up to sixteen-hour days. IPE staff members who worked full-time jobs somewhere else were required to spend at least ten hours each week working for IPE and to donate a percentage of the income from their full-time jobs to IPE. In alignment with their efforts to create an alternative African-centered culture, U.S. federal and state holidays were not observed. While NCDC students were granted some of these days off, IPE staff members were encouraged, if not expected, to work or attend professional development sessions on the Fourth of July, Memorial Day, Labor Day, Thanksgiving, and Christmas. As an alternative to U.S. holidays, IPE staff observed a number of other holidays celebrating Black heroes and African-derived cultural traditions, including Kwanzaa (end of December through January 1), Saba Saba (July 7), Malcolm X's birthday (May 19), and Marcus Garvey's birthday (August 17). Staff members were also required to attend nutrition classes, staff meetings, "Soul sessions," "Nation Studies," marriage ceremonies, name-change ceremonies, initiation rituals, and other celebrations. Attitude and behavioral standards encouraged staff members to take initiative in leading activities, maintaining an enthusiastic attitude, accepting criticism, acting in their personal lives in ways consistent with the values of IPE, and continuously studying to gain skills that would improve the organization. In the early 1970s, there was a core group of at least forty staff members and volunteers who worked to meet these expectations.[38]

Particularly for cadre leadership, the distinctions between public and private lives tended to collapse. In addition to the general commitments made by all staff members, cadre members were on twenty-four-hour call to serve the needs of IPE. They had to always be "ready to submerge individual preferences to the good of the collective whole."[39] Haki Madhubuti argued that Kawaida provided an alternative to U.S. ideals of individuality and liberalism: "The most damaging value pushed to the 'colonized' people of the world *other than to be white is best* is that of the importance of the 'individual' man over that of the collective body." He suggested that Kawaida provided a cultural platform for ideas of collectivity, socialism, democracy, Pan-Africanism, and liberation, anchored within a cultural context that affirmed Black Americans' identity as Africans in America.[40] This sense of collective responsibility, collective living, and collective work was aligned with the tenets of the Nguzo Saba and IPE's goals of changing the ways that Black people related to one another. However, it was also a grueling lifestyle, and not everyone in IPE appreciated how these values manifested in the day-to-day operations of the organization.

In the early days of IPE, some members resigned in opposition to organizational policies that were intended to create unity. In 1973, Phyllis Franklin resigned from her participation in the Idara Kwa Utu Uke, the women's unit of IPE. In her letter of resignation, she voiced distress over IPE's emphasis on "physical uniformity" in styles, colors, dress, shoes, and hair. She argued that these superficial physical symbols of unity could not serve as substitutes for the actual work of community building. Franklin complained specifically that in planning for trips to Newark, there was more emphasis "placed on what we would wear than what we would do." She claimed that she "was asked more questions about why I wouldn't cut my hair" than about the programming and curriculum that she helped to develop. She expressed opposition to the extended in-group discussions of which titles, preambles, and language should be used to address one another instead of a greater focus on the content of "what we were actually saying." Franklin argued that the uniformity promoted by IPE exacerbated the differences between the group and the larger Black community: "Why create a physical uniformity which may make the group look and feel united with each other, but heighten the differences between the group and the larger Black community?" The entire group was disciplined on the trip to Newark because of Franklin's clothing choices.[41]

IPE leaders dismissed Franklin's concerns. "Uniforms do not heighten differences between one group of Black people and the larger community of Black people; *attitudes* and a lack of meaningful (i.e. speaking to concrete material needs) *activity* isolates both individuals and organized bodies of Afrikans from the larger Afrikan community." The leadership also expressed concern that Franklin's reaction to uniformity in dress and hair reflected her own insecurities about her light complexion, her hair texture, and a lack of "growth and confidence in her Black selfhood." With regard to Franklin's concern over the recognition of her work and time, IPE leadership noted that Franklin had a husband who worked to help support her financially and only one child, while many of the other women in the Idara Kwa Utu Uke were single mothers who worked as much as or more than her. Finally, the leadership stressed that the value system IPE members had sworn to uphold was meant to govern not only the meetings and programmatic work of IPE but every aspect of members' lives.[42] IPE was perhaps more flexible than the most extreme Black cultural nationalist groups, but nevertheless it did not always welcome criticism.

Arguments about guidelines for physical uniformity highlight broader issues around gender roles, patriarchy, and sexism in Black Power organizations. Black cultural nationalists often drew on patriarchal scripts that promoted male leadership, ideas of women's "complementarity" to men, and the coupling of men's adulation of Black women with mechanisms to control Black women. This regulation of women ranged from the type of strict dress and behavior codes that Phyllis Franklin opposed to the maintenance of separate spheres for men and women to the control of reproduction through a condemnation of abortions (often framed as a response to longer histories of forced sterilization) and a host of other practices. While some Black women embraced the male protectionist impulse, others rejected the limitations of these patriarchal practices.[43]

Women in IPE pushed back against sexism and rigid gender norms. In the inner circle of IPE, Sonyini Walton chafed at some of the strict cultural practices and subordinate roles that women were asked to take on. Though IPE was not like other more extreme groups of the era that "overtly said that women had a certain role, and you're seen not heard, . . . somehow that spirit got into our group, too," she recalls. Walton opposed institutional norms that required her to take on a deferential posture in relation to male leaders: "The men would sit and make the big decisions about whether we were going to start doing this or that. I had a problem with that. . . . I felt I had a voice, so I had to write it in a letter." These experiences, coupled with the more informal culture of women serving men, led Walton to write letters of protest to the male leadership and step away from the organization on more than one occasion.[44]

Particularly rigid and patriarchal iterations of cultural nationalism emerged in interactions with IPE's collaborators in Newark. During this time, Amina Baraka, the leader of Newark's African Free School and wife of Amiri Baraka, embraced a doctrine of complementarity and instructed Black women to be subservient to Black men. The conformity and rigidity of the subservient roles required of women in Newark meetings incensed Walton and led her to have "a mini nervous breakdown." She drafted a letter of resignation but ultimately decided to stay involved with IPE. By the mid-1970s, as the Barakas adopted a more class-based analysis of struggle, Amina Baraka came to reject and critique the patriarchy imbued by the strict Kawaida principles she had previously preached to others. While not necessarily becoming self-identified feminists, women in Pan-African nationalist organizations—including IPE—pressed for increased dialogue on gender issues publicly and privately. In response to these protests, Walton recalls, the internal culture of IPE slowly shifted away from stricter patriarchal practices limiting women's decision-making powers.[45] Even so, IPE's leadership remained firm in the requirement that staff members sacrifice their individuality for the needs of the group. While this mandate was often implemented in gendered ways, both women and men on staff had to be willing to significantly reorganize their lives for the work of IPE.

The time, financial, and ideological commitments required of IPE staff severely limited the scope of who might be involved with the organization. Soyini Walton recalls that during the 1970s, she lived communally in an apartment building with several other IPE staff members, their children, and volunteers. While taking care of her infant son, she taught full time at Guggenheim Elementary, donated a large portion of her CPS salary to IPE, and woke up at

4:00 A.M. to put in a few hours at IPE before the CPS school day began. Members of the organization had to integrate their ideology into all aspects of their lives: "What you believe is what you do: lifestyle is the same as ideology."[46] It was up to IPE members to regulate the boundaries of the African-centered philosophies of the organization and decide what did and did not fit within their constructs. Transgressing the tenets and norms of the organization could be perceived as a threat to undermine the credibility of the organization and its ideology. Hence, failing to conform to uniform standards of dress or grooming, as in the case of Phyllis Franklin, became cause for reprimand. It is not surprising, then, that the inner cadre of IPE remained small.

With this core group in place, IPE expanded its programming during the 1970s. In 1976 it opened a new facility at 75th Street and Grove Avenue in the Greater Grand Crossing neighborhood on the South Side. One side of the building housed the NCDC school, and the other side housed Third World Press, publishing operations, and a bookstore. The bookstore became a gathering place where the local Black community could come together to discuss current events and other collective concerns. IPE and Third World Press increased their production of magazines and other publications, seeing the dissemination of ideas within the Black community as central in their struggle. IPE also hosted a series of community workshops on politics, health, and education issues. IPE leaders purchased a farm in Michigan, and their storefront served as a food co-op. These programs and services were open to the public and aimed to engage the broader community. The food co-op and bookstore provided important services in a neighborhood with few options for fresh produce and dedicated spaces for intellectual exchange.[47]

Despite its goal of collectivity and self-sustainability, however, IPE seemed constantly in an unstable financial position. The profit brought in by Third World Press and the other businesses could not cover costs. Ujamaa codes were instituted that required IPE members to contribute a percentage of their income to the organization.[48] Soyini Walton recalls giving half of her CPS teaching paycheck to IPE each month before leaving CPS to work full time for IPE in 1976. IPE's NCDC school charged just enough in tuition to cover costs. But when tuition was not paid or publishing sales slumped, IPE was thrust into a precarious financial position. It eventually had to cut back, selling its Michigan farm. Jabari Mahiri and Jawanza Kunjufu, IPE members who monitored the finances of the organization, expressed their frustration with always having to work financial miracles to keep the organization afloat: "Our business meetings have for the most part involved collectively deciding on which payables seemed most immediate and shifting our resources in such a manner as to avoid economic catastrophe."[49] By 1977, IPE leaders considered pursuing federal funds to support their programming. While committed to financial independence in principle, their initial model of self-sufficiency was proving unsustainable. Looking back, Carol Lee notes that IPE staff endured these difficult financial times by working to make group decisions democratically and forging strong bonds with one another in study groups and dialogue sessions—developing deep platonic and, in some cases, romantic relationships. When IPE opened NCDC in 1972, many of the initial students were the children of IPE staff members.[50]

AN AFRICAN-CENTERED EDUCATION:
THE NEW CONCEPT DEVELOPMENT CENTER (NCDC)

NCDC[51] began as a Saturday school with an African-centered curriculum to counteract the miseducation IPE members saw Black students receiving in public schools. Housed at the original IPE location at 78th Street and Ellis Avenue, NCDC served children from two to twelve years old, holding a morning session from 9:00 A.M. to 12:00 P.M. for toddlers up to age six and an afternoon program from 12:30 to 4:00 P.M. for children ages seven through twelve. A tuition-based school, NCDC charged $2 per child per session or $24 for a full twelve-week session—fees that covered only the most basic expenses of running the school. Volunteers and IPE staff taught children the Nguzo Saba, Black history, reading and mathematics, Swahili, the geography of Africa and the African Diaspora, music and dance, nutrition, and arts and crafts. Children could also attend counseling sessions on Wednesday and Thursday afternoons, where IPE staff worked as tutors and counselors for the children. Partly in response to parental pressure for increased programming, NCDC expanded to a full week program in 1974. Once housed in the new Cottage Grove facility, NCDC operated full-time preschool and elementary school programs, employing eight preschool and elementary school teachers by 1978.[52]

While Haki Madhubuti was the public face and voice of IPE on the national stage, a core group of Black women shaped the intellectual life and led the day-to-day operations of the NCDC school. Haki held a post at Howard University in Washington, D.C., for much of the 1970s and frequently went on speaking tours. Carol Lee served as the director of NCDC for sixteen of its formative years. Soyini Walton also served as director for a period of time when Carol Lee was on maternity leave. Black cultural nationalist groups often drew on patriarchal scripts in ascribing separate spheres of expertise and authority for men and women. This often implicitly reinforced men's superiority, though it also placed women in central command over programs related to child rearing and education. Centrally concerned as IPE was with educating children, this provided opportunities for women's leadership.[53] Haki and Carol were partners in marriage but also partners in developing IPE. Carol Lee was a trained educator and former high school teacher, and it was her idea that IPE create a school in the first place. Her vision, leadership, and work fueled the direction, pedagogy, and curriculum of the NCDC school. Carol Lee, Soyini Walton, and the women who worked at the NCDC school were theorists who performed the intellectual labor of NCDC and IPE, not just the daily operational labor to keep the institution moving—although they did that too.[54]

The curriculum at NCDC was a central tool in IPE's mission of shifting Black consciousness. Over the course of U.S. history, compulsory education has been intimately concerned with creating different types of citizens: Jeffersonian republican citizens, industrious citizens, assimilated citizens, etc. NCDC was engaged in a similar project, molding students into Pan-African transnational citizens through a carefully structured curriculum that aimed to develop "a well rounded individual who is committed to work in the interests of Black people and to defend Black people and who has the necessary skills to carry out these nation building tasks."[55]

Carol Lee and Soyini Walton were very deliberate with their directives for running the school. The preschool curriculum, for children ages three to five, included activities that promoted positive self-image and racial identity, self-discipline, personal advocacy, and pre-mathematics and pre-reading skills. In keeping with their African-centered framework and desire to build a family-like atmosphere at the school, instead of the titles Mrs. and Mr., NCDC teachers were referred to as Mamas and Babas. It was at this young age that NCDC staff first taught the protocols, basic Swahili words, and daily routines that would follow the children through elementary school.[56]

NCDC emphasized discipline and self-control as key elements of education for "nation building." In order to counteract what it perceived as negative constructions of Black identity, NCDC provided a hyperconscious and deliberate set of alternative daily routines. The school handbook meticulously outlined extensive, detailed protocols for punishment, lunch, naptime, forming a line, moving outside the building, etc. The handbook even included two eight-step, detailed protocols with instructions for how girls and boys should use the toilet. The content of these protocols was not too dissimilar from that of any other school's lesson plans for teaching discipline and social skills, but it was filtered through an Afrocentric, Kawaida-influenced lens:

Watoto[children] stands on the taped circle on the floor by holding hands. . . .

Teacher says jambo (hello) watoto.

Watoto respond "jambo sana"

Teacher asks Habari gani watoto?

Watoto responds Njema sante, habari gani (fine thank you)

Teacher then calls each child's name (roll). The child will respond "hapa" (here or present). He/she takes one step forward and a step back into the circle when his/her response is made. Teacher chooses a watoto who has given his/her complete attention (one who has been a good example all morning). . . .

The chosen leader asks watoto to extend their right hand out (fist) and the leader begins the pledge (one line at a time) watotos repeat after the leader.

Everyone sings "Praise the Red, the Black and the Green."[57]

These daily protocols offered IPE members an opportunity to teach new daily routines and ways of relating to one another based on their interpretation of Pan-African traditions.[58] In its quest to transform the cultural consciousness of a people, IPE started with the daily routines of children.

NCDC teachers taught the concepts of the Nguzo Saba and explicitly reinforced the praxis of the seven principles through class assignments and curricular materials. For example, in outlining the language arts curriculum, NCDC teachers stressed that Ujima (collective work and responsibility) and Umoja (unity) should be reinforced by requiring students to help one another to understand the spelling and meaning of vocabulary words and by making the whole group responsible for ensuring that each child accomplished this each week.[59] Teaching materials included Kawaida symbols, jazz compositions, cartoons from the Nation of Islam publication *Muhammad Speaks*, essays and speeches by Marcus Garvey, texts and artwork by Black artists, and pieces written by Haki, Johari Amini, and other IPE members. Similar texts were used in IPE cadre study sessions and "nation studies" classes for community members. These curricular materials produced symbols, mantras, and creeds that were incorporated into the daily protocols of schooling at NCDC.[60]

Often, African-centered education simply meant inserting African history into narratives that would have been Eurocentric at traditional public schools. For elementary-aged children, NCDC teachers taught reading and mathematics, martial arts to promote self-discipline and connections between the mind and body, and lessons on the history, economics, geography, and scientific discovery of civilizations and countries from the African continent. NCDC social studies lessons utilized a timeline of "Tri-Continental Antiquity." The timeline compared the accomplishments and histories of the civilizations of Kemet, Mesopotamia, and Greece. The lesson framed the accomplishments of Kemet—Egyptian civilization—as a part of both African and Black history. This insistence on providing examples of Black and African accomplishments was not typical of the curriculum in many public schools in the 1970s. NCDC teachers and administrators also made this intervention pedagogically by translating the findings of foundational educational texts by Jean Piaget, Maria Montessori, and John Dewey into an African-centered framework. Most of the early NCDC instructors were college educated, but very few had significant experience teaching children. Soyini Walton and Carol Lee were notable exceptions, as both were trained as teachers and had experience working in CPS, although mainly with older children and teenagers. The NCDC staff worked and studied together to bring one another up to speed on teaching practices and pedagogy.[61] NCDC also focused on the importance of science, mathematics, and technology education for Black youth.

Hannibal Afrik, head of Shule Ya Watoto—an African-centered school located on the West Side of Chicago—and an NCDC collaborator, emphasized the importance of science for Black nation building. Afrik had worked as a science teacher in CPS and was a leader of community control efforts at Farragut High School on the West Side of Chicago. In an article titled "Science for Black Survival," Afrik argued that racism had historically excluded African Americans from the pursuit of science, resulting in an "anti-science" "anti-intellectualism" within Black communities. He believed that independent Black schools had a mandate to develop and share with the broader community a Black science curriculum that prepared Black youth to become professionals who could meet Black communities' needs for health care, military preparedness, shelter, protection, and food production: "Society demands greater technological advances and our community demands technicians capable of harnessing scientific knowledge for our liberation." In this same vein, at NCDC Soyini Walton developed models of science education that explicitly incorporated the Black value system embraced by IPE. Afrik and Walton collaborated with Black educators across the country to develop science curricula and a national Black science fair for the Council of Independent Black Institutions (CIBI).[62]

In 1972, NCDC and Shule Ya Watoto were among the founding institutions in CIBI. CIBI was established during the Black Power era as a national network and included independent African-centered schools in New York, Washington,

D.C., Los Angeles, Chicago, the San Francisco Bay Area, New Orleans, and other locations around the country. The Chicago area was well represented in CIBI as a significant source for African-centered educators, curricula, and independent institutions. CIBI held annual conferences, workshops, and gatherings for its members and served as a hub where representatives from independent Black schools across the country shared best practices, collaborated to produce curricula, and facilitated a national science fair with students from member schools. CIBI endured for decades as a network of independent African-centered schools, although NCDC eventually left the network.[63]

Across the country, independent African-centered elementary schools sought to demonstrate Black student achievement through internal assessments and their students' performance on more universally administered standardized tests. But as Carol Lee later explained, Black achievement would not be demonstrated and measured simply through a "trick to raise test scores" but through socializing "young people into being productive citizens who support the development of the communities from which they come . . . competent members of their cultural communities."[64]

As NCDC grew throughout the 1970s, the population of the preschool and elementary school programs increased. To incorporate these new families into the school, NCDC established the NCDC Parent Council, a decision-making body comprised of NCDC parents.[65] NCDC's tuition—$1,240 per year as of 1978—was still a large sum of money for many families who were already struggling financially. Although the Black middle class had grown since the 1960s, in part due to growth in Black employment in the public sector, including teaching, poverty and unemployment in Black Chicago had also become more entrenched due to deindustrialization and economic decline. In response, the Parent Council raised money for families facing hardships.[66]

As the Parent Council grew, it demanded more control over operations, and in the fall of 1977 conflict surfaced. For the first time, a significant group of NCDC parents voiced their concerns with the educational program at NCDC. The parents were concerned about the same issues that many Black parents in the city struggled with, within and outside CPS: teacher qualifications and training, lack of necessary supplies, and quality of curriculum. Parents opposed spending a full month at the beginning of the year on daily protocols before initiating what they perceived to be full-time, content-based academic instruction. Parents questioned where their tuition money was going when classrooms often did not have enough books and paper for all students. Some of the parents also wanted to implement standardized testing to assess what their children were learning and how they stacked up compared to children in other schools.

As with many independent Black educational institutions, NCDC's programming did not extend into high school, and parents wanted to be certain that their students would be socially and academically prepared to attend the upper grades at another private school or a public school. Most urgently, parents claimed that several NCDC teachers did not know how to teach and did not have adequate expertise or teacher training.[67] These concerns echoed the concerns of Black parents at traditional public schools in the city and centered squarely on the quality of education *their* child received and demands for increased accountability from teachers and the school as a whole.

However, unlike their CPS counterparts, the parents at NCDC generally did not question the motives or "political-cultural direction of the school." NCDC parents chose, and paid to send their children to, NCDC largely because of the African-centered curriculum and racially self-affirming culture of the institution. NCDC parents also had direct access to the teachers, principal, and leaders of IPE without having to navigate the dense bureaucracy of a large school system. Within this context, parents demanded that their concerns be discussed and addressed.[68]

Working grueling hours for little pay, a number of NCDC staff members did not appreciate this criticism. In a 1978 letter, a staff member lamented that "we often work a long and tedious work schedule which doesn't allow for too much more to be done when we get home. This depresses me very much." This educator also mentioned looking for additional part-time work, being "not able to save much money" with only an IPE salary. Soyini Walton remembers that her parents thought she had lost her mind when she left her stable job with benefits teaching in CPS to work full time at NCDC in 1976. Staff turnover was a problem, as some of the best teachers left in order to pursue better financial opportunities elsewhere. As Walton put it: "We certainly saw people fall off over the years, lots of people. Falling off, falling out, never to set foot in the place again. I think I quit twice!"[69]

The parents' criticism also challenged staff members' feelings of ownership over and identification with the institution. Staff saw the parents as transient, more concerned with their individual child's education than the broader goals of transforming a collective community consciousness. Haki Madhubuti tried to quell the fears of NCDC staff members: "Yes we built it and it is ours, so let's not be so insecure that the minute a committed concerned force shows an interest in making decisions about their children that we have to view this as a state of war."[70] For years IPE had been run by a small group of individuals who were willing to dedicate their work, lives, families, and finances to the organization. The newer parents' insistence on playing a larger role was a gut-check moment for IPE.

Would IPE continue to operate as a cadre-type group or would the organization allow members of the community to enter the ranks? In October 1977, Soyini Walton called a NCDC staff study session to debate this very question. Staff members were explicitly asked, "What part in decision making will the P.C. [Parent Council] play?" Staff members also debated whether teachers should be chosen based on political consciousness or teaching skill; the definitions of an "elitist private," "community," and "model" school; appropriate NCDC teacher salaries; whether or not to accept private and public grants to fund the school; and why they were not sending their children to public schools.[71]

Ultimately, after consulting with the staff, the NCDC leadership decided that in order to live up to demands of the broader Black community, they would make changes. NCDC staff worked with the curriculum committee of the Parent Council to sort through and select curricular materials. Walton increased in-service training and professional development sessions for new teachers. Parents were recruited to become IPE staff members or to volunteer time and financial aid to the school. Finally, engaged and interested parents were given a stronger role in the administration of the school. NCDC leaders reasoned that giving the parents more authority would increase IPE's visibility, increase the number of people sharing the workload of running the school, and advance IPE's goal of becoming a greater agent of change in Chicago's Black communities. By the 1978 school year, NCDC parents took part in a newly formed Co-coordinating Council. The Co-coordinating Council consisted of a group of three staff members and three parents who collaborated in making schoolwide decisions.

Throughout the 1970s, NCDC continued to grow. By 1982, NCDC served approximately 67 students and their families.[72] While still serving a very small population relative to the size of the Black population in the city, NCDC was able to survive and grow.

IPE/NCDC LEGACY

In many ways IPE's Black Power era stress on the importance of Black institution building was closely aligned with TWO's articulation of Black empowerment through community control. Both groups adhered to a self-determinist

THE POLITICS OF BLACK ACHIEVEMENT

politics of Black achievement, but the implementation of their specific ideologies was quite distinct. Unlike IPE, Brazier and TWO argued that a mass-based community organization was the best vehicle to achieve Black empowerment. This was an important structural, but also ideological, distinction between TWO's community-based mass-membership organizing and IPE's brand of institution building utilizing a smaller cadre structure. TWO sought to empower Black Woodlawn residents by directly challenging traditional forms of governmental and civic authority and power. TWO demanded access to and control of the institutional resources and programs held by state agencies and other external authorities that operated within its community. In contrast, IPE sought to achieve Black liberation using a cadre model to create independent African-centered educational institutions outside traditional governmental forms of political authority. By bypassing the state-run education system, the operators of independent Black institutions worked within a set of political possibilities and constraints different from that of organizations that sought engagement with the state.

However, at times IPE's doctrine limited the ability of the organization to engage with the larger Black community that did not share its worldview. The self-consciously Pan-African subjectivity and counternarrative developed by IPE required the rejection of practices, ideas, and daily routines that could be misconstrued as too European and required an all-encompassing dedication to the ideology of the institution. IPE members' self-positioning as a cultural vanguard of Black liberation and their cadre formation implicitly created distance from the masses of Black people. Harkening back to a longer history of elitism in Black racial uplift traditions, IPE members' self-appointed roles as transformers of consciousness could be interpreted as condescending to those whose minds they deemed necessary of transformation. An IPE leadership flowchart for example, featured the motto "Reach Out and Teach—Pull In Those Reached." By arguing that the existing culture and psyche of Black urban communities was damaged and in need of transformation, IPE unintentionally also provided a language that could be repurposed to support ideas of Black pathology that were already circulating amongst White liberals and conservatives in influential reports like the 1965 Moynihan Report.[73]

Despite these limitations, the tireless work of IPE and NCDC staff members provides an instructive example of the extent to which African Americans were willing to go to create alternatives to the inadequate education provided for Black students in the public school system. IPE staff members often suffered great economic and social hardships in order to continue to support the organization with their time, money, and labor. It was a difficult and precarious position for educators, who were committed to helping Black children achieve, to also feel constrained or burdened by the conditions under which they were required to work. Economic hardship and long working hours could be mentally and emotionally taxing.

For Soyini Walton and other educators who cycled through NCDC, working at IPE ultimately became unsustainable. Walton's difficult decision to leave IPE was shaped by her career ambitions and economic realities. Both Soyini and her husband, Chaga, worked full time at IPE, at NCDC and IPE's printing service Hieroglyphics Inc. But they still could not afford to pursue their dream of buying a house: "We were living on the second floor of my parent's two-flat building. That's the way it was. . . . Then we had a baby. . . . I looked at this and said, 'I can't.'" Walton did not see a viable financial future or career path in IPE that could support her family. She had always been interested in science but was steered away from pursuing it as a career path when she was younger. After the birth of her next child in 1980, Walton left NCDC, went back to school, and became a mechanical engineer. She continued to be involved with NCDC as a parent and as a member of the board of directors. She was deeply committed but left to work a corporate job. While staff may have cycled through NCDC, the institution persisted.[74]

Carol Lee argues that Chicago is unique among other U.S. cities in the longevity of the many African-centered artistic, political, and educational organizations founded there during the Black Power era.[75] Part of NCDC's longevity can be credited to IPE leaders' willingness to adjust to changing political and economic conditions. IPE, while still operating an independent school, filed as a nonprofit organization, increased outside fundraising efforts, and eventually applied for outside grants to support the educational work of the institution. In 1973, Haki Madhubuti took a very strong stand on the necessity of creating an economically self-sufficient institution: "When talking about *independent institutions*, you have to be talking about *independent sources of funding*. The institutions, if they are to maintain their independence and autonomy, must be funded by the people themselves. Once, we step outside of this source, we endanger not only our credibility, but our independence too."[76] IPE tried for years to survive and adhere to this mandate. Staff solicited donations on Black radio programs, sent out contribution mailers to friends of IPE, and held lots of fundraisers. However, after years of operating on the financial brink, IPE was forced to seek outside grants, including utilizing sources of foundational support and government funding. In 1977, Haki submitted a development proposal to IPE staff suggesting that the organization "seek contributions and grants" from Model Cities and other government programs. While tuition remained the main source of funding for CIBI schools, as early as 1973 a quarter of CIBI schools received some funding from the government. Like that of a number of other CIBI schools, IPE's ideology of financial independence ultimately bent to the will of economic necessity.[77]

The debate over funding sources within the independent Black schools community became more heated as some of these institutions began operating charter schools in the 1990s. This debate caused a bitter rift amongst the Black nationalist members of CIBI, including NCDC. Some leaders of CIBI argued that operating a public school—including publicly funded charter schools—compromised the independence of independent nationalist organizations.[78] Carol Lee argued that the money for charter schools was public money, and if White people were going to use it to open schools serving Black youth, the leaders of NCDC should be able to use these same funds to open an African-centered school.[79] For Carol Lee the fundamental issue remained that opening a charter school would allow them to reach exponentially more children. NCDC had scraped along with minimal tuition, but charging any tuition still prohibited some students from attending. While Soyini Walton acknowledged that IPE had always insisted that it was independent and "don't take white folks' money," she also acknowledged that financially the institution was "pretty whipped." She also supported the move to charter schools: "I was for it. We had struggled all that time to make ends meet with tuition, which we couldn't really go up too high because we had just regular working parents. I was for it. I didn't have any problem with it." Opening a charter school was a political risk IPE was willing to take in order to serve more students tuition free.[80]

Charter schools' initial promises of autonomy and innovation meshed with Black cultural nationalists' embrace of Black entrepreneurship. Although critical of both those who turned to Marxism and those who emulated White or "European" cultural forms by pursuing capital accumulation, IPE leaders also embraced entrepreneurship and culturally infused ideas of Black capitalism. IPE's transition to charter schools, discussed more in Chapter 6, is less surprising if understood within historically grounded traditions of Black education and entrepreneurship.[81]

Under the enduring leadership of Carol Lee, NCDC continued to operate and open charter schools during the 1990s and 2000s, including Betty Shabazz International Charter School, Barbara A. Sizemore Academy Charter School, and DuSable Leadership Academy Charter High School. It is noteworthy that IPE chose to name one of its charter schools after Barbara Sizemore, the longtime Black educator and former director of WESP. Sizemore was an influential figure, mentor, and respected elder among Black educators. Her commitment to black self-determination, community control, institution building, and the politics of Black achievement were an inspiration to IPE leaders.[82]

NCDC and IPE's charter schools have served thousands of children over the course of more than four decades. Carol Lee noted that NCDC graduates excelled at some of the most prestigious CPS high schools in the city. IPE teachers and former students have gone on to become educators, artists, professors, youth workers, and other professionals, imparting the gospel of culturally responsive education and Black pride and empowerment to countless others. However, the financial problem of teacher turnover that caused Walton to leave NCDC continued in IPE's charter schools. When Walton returned to serve as principal at Sizemore in 2005, she noticed that she lost "a lot of staff over the years because we can't pay." Despite internal struggles and external political battles with CPS officials, Sizemore has remained open. Today you can still walk into Barbara A. Sizemore Academy on a Monday morning and find elementary school children dressed in African print clothing or red, black, and green uniforms reciting morning rituals in Swahili, being nurtured in a cultural environment quite unlike that of most other schools in the city.[83]

The legacy of Black Power institutions like IPE lives on perhaps most enduringly in the realm of ideas, rather than strictly brick-and-mortar independent schools. IPE and NCDC outlived other nationalist groups of the era in part because they institutionalized the ideas of Black Power and owned several of the physical spaces that housed their institutions. To walk into any Black community and hear African Americans self-identify as "Black" or connected to an African past is a legacy of the societal impact of Black nationalist groups and institutions. In debates about urban education today, race and culture loom large as issues to be addressed in the classroom, at the administrative level, and in research. While Kawaida adherents may still be few and far between, the currency of "culturally relevant" or "culturally responsive" education proposed and practiced by NCDC and other African-centered schools has endured within the education community at large. Carol Lee became an eminent education researcher and professor of education at Northwestern University, and her name has become virtually synonymous with the content and practice of African-centered pedagogy, "cultural modeling," and culturally responsive education nationally.[84] She served as the president of the American Educational Research Association, the premier educational research organization in the United States with a membership of tens of thousands of teachers, researchers, academics, and other practitioners. She continues to be a force in disseminating culturally relevant education practices through her research and work in schools.

Nevertheless, the large majority of the Black student population in Chicago during the 1960s and 1970s never stepped foot in a place like NCDC. For Black families with students in the public schools, the struggle for educational equity overwhelmingly remained in neighborhood schools. While Soyini Walton ultimately left teaching in CPS to pursue an alternative educational vision of Black liberation in IPE's independent African-centered school, most Black teachers remained in the public school system. There, they would simultaneously fight for improvements in schools serving Black students and for recognition, representation, and a greater voice in the teaching force and the teachers' union. These twin struggles transformed Black politics.

{ 4 }

TEACHER POWER

Black Teachers and the Politics of

Representation

Lillie Peoples began her education in a one-room schoolhouse in Camilla, Georgia. It was there that she was inspired to become an educator, admiring the way that her teacher Essie Peterson patiently encouraged the Black students in her classroom. Peoples and her family migrated to Chicago in the 1940s, when she was twelve. She looked forward to moving to the gleaming cosmopolitan North, but Peoples found that the dilapidated housing and crowded neighborhoods and schools in Chicago did not match her expectations. She attended several different schools as her family moved frequently to live with aunts and uncles in communities on the South and West Sides of the city.[1]

Lillie Peoples's educational experiences in Chicago were marred by the low expectations of some of her White teachers who expected her to lag behind academically, even though she was actually better prepared for school than many. She remembers being taught by disengaged White teachers who entered class, wrote page numbers for assignments on the board, and then sat in the corner as Peoples and her fellow students struggled to make it through their work without any assistance. The students at her elementary schools were Black, but the teachers were almost exclusively White. This changed when she attended DuSable and Phillips high schools, prominent Black schools with more Black teachers and administrators. At DuSable and Phillips, Peoples remembers both Black and White teachers stressing discipline but also conveying a genuine sense of caring and holistic support for their students. Unfortunately, this would be an anomalous experience in her education.[2]

In 1953, Peoples enrolled at Chicago Teachers College, ten years before Soyini Walton led civil rights protests as a student at the same college. Peoples was one of only a handful of Black students, and many of the White teachers did not expect Peoples or her Black classmates to finish the program. Peoples graduated, but she did not look back fondly on her time at Teachers College; it

Faculty photograph from Alexandre Dumas Elementary, 1964 (Lillie Peoples, top row, third from left) (Courtesy of Lillie Peoples)

"was hell.... It was one of the most awful experiences I have had in life." Nonetheless, she left with the credentials to start teaching and felt well prepared to lead her own classroom.[3]

The same unjust policies and inequitable resources that shaped Black students' learning conditions impacted Peoples's teaching conditions. In 1960, after a few years teaching at John M. Smyth Elementary School on the West Side, Peoples transferred to teach at Sherwood Elementary School, to be closer to her home on the South Side. In the 1950s, Soyini Walton experienced the chaos of overcrowding and double shifts as a student at Sherwood. Peoples navigated the chaos of operating on a similar shift system as a teacher, struggling to develop meaningful relationships with kids moving in and out of the building several times over the course of the day. In 1963, Peoples was selected to teach fourth grade at the new Alexandre Dumas Elementary School, where she remained until 1985. Dumas was opened to serve the Woodlawn neighborhood's growing Black student population. In 1968, Dumas's teaching staff was 94 percent Black, and all 1,415 of the school's students were Black.[4]

At Dumas, Lillie Peoples became an activist educator and leader, organizing

THE POLITICS OF BLACK ACHIEVEMENT

on behalf of Black teachers and Black students in Woodlawn. When she started teaching at Dumas, Rev. Arthur Brazier and TWO were fighting for school desegregation to increase resources for Woodlawn's children. Peoples organized teachers, parents, and students at Dumas for the 1963 CCCO-led Freedom Day boycott. The vast majority of Dumas students and staff boycotted the school on the day of the protest. Outside Dumas, Peoples started working with a broader group of Black teachers dedicated to improving conditions for Black teachers, students, and communities. She was most actively involved in Teachers' Division of Operation Breadbasket, a branch of SCLC led by Jesse Jackson in Chicago.[5] As a leader in Teachers' Division, Peoples was at the center of Black teachers' political activism during the 1960s and 1970s. These struggles made Black teachers an increasingly important political force in the city. The dramatic increase in the number of African Americans working for CPS during the last third of the twentieth century would not have been possible without the political organizing work of Black teachers like Lillie Peoples.

Even after the first waves of the Great Migration, there were still very few Black teachers in northern and western cities. In 1930, less than 3 percent of teachers in New York, Chicago, and Pittsburgh were Black. In cities where Black teachers made slightly greater inroads into the teaching force, Black teachers were often restricted to teaching in segregated schools and spent years on substitute lists before finding permanent teaching positions. Though there were certainly dedicated White teachers who taught in Black schools, many new White teachers transferred from schools with Black students to schools with White students immediately after the required five months to one year of service on the job. This created higher levels of faculty turnover at Black schools and an environment, much like what Lillie Peoples experienced as a child, where Black students encountered disinterested or blatantly racist White teachers passing time before they could be transferred. As Chicago's Black population continued to grow, the number of Black teachers working in the school system did increase. However, throughout the 1960s, Black teachers encountered racist barriers to certification and were employed at rates disproportionately lower than the proportion of Black students in CPS. By 1968, the CPS student body was nearly 53 percent Black, while the teaching force was still less than 34 percent Black.[6]

Increasingly during the 1960s, Black teachers engaged in dual struggles, advocating for themselves as Black public service workers and on behalf of the predominantly Black students and communities whom they served. African American teachers were active in a range of efforts to improve the quality of education for Black students in CPS and to improve their own standing as

Black teachers within the predominantly White CPS workforce and teachers' union. These diverse efforts included mobilizing for the desegregation of CPS, community control of schools, teacher certification, access to teaching and administrative positions, representation in the CTU, and changing CPS policies and curricula.

This chapter examines how Black educators grew from an insurgent group of teachers in the 1960s into a Black middle-class political base of the coalition that elected Harold Washington as the first Black mayor of Chicago in 1983. In the late 1960s, groups of Black public school teachers—frustrated with the inadequate conditions in schools serving Black children and their marginalized role in the CTU—protested the union and even considered creating an alternative Black teachers' union. These Black educators challenged the racist policies of the CTU and Board of Education while embracing a self-determinist politics of Black achievement that critiqued the failures of racial liberalism. Race and gender shaped Black women educators' professional lives and political activism, as Black women teachers were never adequately recognized for their integral leadership in these movements. By the 1980s, internal and external pressures on the CTU and CPS had forced a significant increase in the proportion of Black teachers in the school system. In 1984 Black teachers outnumbered White teachers in CPS for the first time. Marking the impact of this demographic shift, Jacqueline Vaughn was elected as the first African American and first woman president of the CTU this same year. African Americans' increased representation as CPS employees, and the changing roles of Black teachers within schools and the CTU, transformed Black political power in Chicago.[7]

As public sector workers, Black CPS teachers and staff members transformed schools, city politics, and communities during a period that social scientists have traditionally identified as a time of "urban crisis." Though retellings of this period often focus on the loss of manufacturing jobs in northern urban centers after World War II and the structural racism that isolated Black people within urban ghettos, African Americans in a number of cities—Chicago in particular—were disproportionately reliant on public sector employment to a greater degree than on employment in manufacturing.[8] This chapter seeks to reconsider race, class, labor, and deindustrialization by focusing on the realm of public sector employment, examining how the growing number of Black CPS teachers and staff transformed Black politics in the city as anchors of communities, as caretakers of children, and as a relatively stable Black urban middle class employed in the public sector during an era of deindustrialization.

Black CPS teachers were central to the fight for educational and racial justice in the 1960s, leading organizations, participating in protests, and seeking educational improvements. In 1968, Black student-led boycotts resulted in the inclusion of Black studies curricula at many schools, changes in the composition of teaching faculty, and an increase in the number of Black administrators. While these protests were student led, hundreds of Black teachers, organized by the newly formed Teachers' Division of Operation Breadbasket, risked their jobs by joining the students' protests.[9]

SCLC launched Operation Breadbasket as the economic component of its organizing work in 1962 in Atlanta. Jesse Jackson, a native of South Carolina who had previously worked under Martin Luther King Jr., moved to Chicago to attend seminary and established Chicago's branch of Operation Breadbasket in 1966.[10] After a Saturday morning Operation Breadbasket meeting in Chicago, Jackson called all of the Black teachers in the room together to meet with him. Lillie Peoples was at that meeting and remembers Jackson telling the assembled group that Black teachers needed to organize: "We've got to get organized here, and we've got to be ready for action. I want you, by September, to have organized 500 Black teachers. Every school that has over 12 Black teachers in it, you've got to find a representative in that school, to get information out to the community and start to organize that school and the parents in that school."[11] From that meeting in 1968, Teachers' Division of Operation Breadbasket was born. A core leadership group emerged within Teachers' Division. After a brief stint by Roy Stell, a Black teacher activist within the CTU, David Harrison took over as chairman of Teachers' Division and remained in that post for the majority of the life of the group. Mattie Hopkins was the vice chairman of the group, and Lillie Peoples served as corresponding secretary.[12]

Peoples recalls that as the most senior member of the group, Hopkins brought a sense of history to the group's leadership. Hopkins was a highly regarded educator with a long history in Black education struggles. She earned her bachelor's degree at the Tuskegee Institute in Alabama in 1940 and taught in the South before teaching in CPS beginning in 1951. Hopkins participated in civil rights organizing and protests in the South and in Chicago. She also pursued social justice through her prominent role in the Episcopal Church. Hopkins went on to be appointed to the Board of Education by Chicago's first Black mayor, Harold Washington, in the 1980s.[13] As Mattie Hopkins's institutional leadership highlights, the history of Black teachers' activism is also a history of Black women's activism.

Although often obscured or discounted in debates about education reform, Black women educators had long been powerful activists and organizers in struggles for educational equity and racial justice. There is a rich tradition of prominent Black women teacher activists—including Anna Julia Cooper, Mary MacLeod Bethune, Mary Church Terrell, and Septima Clark—who connected struggles for educational improvements to broader struggles for justice in Black communities. In addition to these prominent Black women educator leaders, Adrienne D. Dixson and Tamara Beauboeuf-Lafontant have documented the ways that Black women teachers also engaged in "everyday" advocacy on behalf of Black children and communities through collective community "othermothering" informed by their Black educator "foremothers." Black women teachers played a central role in mentoring young activists and organizing Black communities intergenerationally. In this context, veteran Black women educators Mattie Hopkins and Barbara Sizemore served as powerful voices shaping the direction of Teachers' Division and grounding the group in the longer history of Black educators' activism.[14]

In the summer of 1968, Teachers' Division organized Black teachers across the city. As the liaison between Teachers' Division and its parent organization, Operation Breadbasket, Hannibal Afrik became the unofficial spokesperson for Teachers' Division. Afrik was a CPS science teacher and organizer at Farragut High School on the West Side. In the fall of 1968, he worked with other Black teachers at Farragut to organize the Farragut Black Teachers Association and release the "Black Manifesto." The document demanded the promotion and appointment of more Black teachers and administrators, an end to overcrowding, utilization of more community-based resources, improvements and renovations in facilities, and Black studies curricula across subject areas. These goals were closely aligned with the demands of the Black students who staged citywide boycotts in October 1968. During these protests, 55 percent of Farragut teachers boycotted the school to support Black students' demands for more community control of schooling, the highest rate of participation by teachers in any high school. Approximately 700 teachers from Teachers' Division supported the demands of the Black students and joined the boycott. Operation Breadbasket's Teachers' Division had organized several hundred Black teachers into an organization that could turn out bodies to put political pressure on individual schools and the Board of Education.[15]

Like many other Black education reformers during the Black Power era, Teachers' Division members embraced a self-determinist politics of Black achievement that focused on determining the role of Black teachers in im-

THE POLITICS OF BLACK ACHIEVEMENT

Students and teachers from Doolittle East Elementary School at the Crispus Attucks Day celebration, March 5, 1969. Attucks, a man of African descent born into slavery in the 1700s, is often described as the first fatality of the American Revolution. Beginning in the 1960s, Chicago's annual Attucks Day celebration aimed to increase the recognition and teaching of Black history. Edward R. Smith, Doolittle teacher, is on the far right, and William Brandon, CUL education specialist, is on the left (Chicago Urban League Records, University of Illinois at Chicago Library, CULR_04_0199_2257_001)

proving Black schools and communities rather than desegregation. In a 1969 position paper, Teachers' Division explained the importance of Black teachers and the group: "Teacher Division of S.C.L.C.'s Operation Breadbasket represents the educational arm of the Black community. Therefore, the primary role of Black teachers is to assist the Black community in achieving full and equal educational opportunities for every Black child. Consequently, Black teachers should exert their total resources in support of our Black students and parents. If the Black schools are to survive white racism and emerge as viable, relevant institutions then Black teachers must remain steadfast in their accountability to the Black community." In calling on Black teachers to transform Black public schools into "viable, relevant institutions," Teachers' Division embraced a self-determinist politics of Black achievement that was more along the lines of the community control movement's vision—advocating for Black studies across the curricula, for equitable funding and facilities improvements for Black schools, and for more Black teachers, administrators,

Educators Lillie Peoples (*front*) and Hannibal Afrik (Harold Charles) participating in an exchange program in West Africa (ca. 1971) (Courtesy of Lillie Peoples)

staff, and contractors—than in line with efforts to create independent Black institutions completely outside the public school system. However, these were fluid boundaries. Carol Lee and Hannibal Afrik were planning independent African-centered institutions at the same time that they worked with Teachers' Division.[16]

In addition to struggles with the city and Board of Education, Teachers' Division also called out the CTU. "The Black community of parents, teachers, and students must attack both heads of a single snake of institutional racism: the Board of Education and the CTU." Teachers' Division identified the need to confront the racism of the Board of Education and the CTU, arguing that the solutions to these problems must be generated by, controlled by, and for the ends defined by Black communities.[17]

The CTU as an organization did not contribute in a meaningful way to civil rights organizing in Chicago. While the American Federation of Teachers was active in national desegregation efforts, many of the union's locals stayed on the sidelines or outright opposed local civil rights organizing. John Fewkes,

THE POLITICS OF BLACK ACHIEVEMENT

the White anticommunist, anti-integrationist president of the CTU, led the organization from 1937 until 1944 and again from 1947 until 1966. Fewkes spoke out against the 1963 and 1964 Freedom Day boycotts and in favor of the continued use of mobile "Willis Wagons" that maintained segregated schools. He was generally a popular leader among the White teachers who constituted a significant majority in the CTU. After Fewkes retired in 1966, John Desmond was elected CTU president.[18]

Desmond condemned the Black students who organized boycotts and walkouts in 1968 and the teachers and communities that supported them. He warned that the "increasing number of disorderly incidents" should be "viewed with alarm" and that calls for more Black teachers and administrators should not be met "under pressures of student disorders or community upheavals."[19] These comments further riled Black teachers' ire toward the union. White members of a group called Teachers for Radical Change in Education also spoke out against Desmond. However, many other White teachers supported Desmond's opposition to Black protests and community control of schools. A 1969 letter to the editor of the *Chicago Union Teacher* outlined the perceived threats that Desmond was responding to: "Teachers are being attacked by community power groups, faculty members and administrators are being shuffled around to 'keep the peace,' standards for professional certification have been greatly diluted, the neighborhood mob leaders have become curriculum experts and consultants."[20]

In trying to divorce community concerns from the concerns of teachers as professionals, Desmond waded into a longer history of tensions within the conflicting identities of teachers' unions. Were teachers' unions professional organizations representing the interests of middle-class professionals, protecting a social status and privileges not granted to other types of workers? Or were teachers' unions workers' organizations, akin to unions of industrial workers, which would fight for better workplace conditions and collective bargaining rights in coalitions with organized labor? As public sector employees, teachers also faced another duality. Were teachers' collective concerns primarily with issues of wages, compensation, and workplace conditions? Or was the teachers' union fundamentally interested in improving schools and communities?

When the American Federation of Teachers was founded in 1916, the union explicitly stated that it was an organization dedicated to improving teachers' wages and benefits *and* improving schools.[21] Over the course of the twentieth century, there have been moments when one side or the other of this duality (wages/benefits vs. improving schools) has been asserted more prominently by different teachers' unions nationally and even in struggles amongst teachers within unions. During the 1960s, Lillie Peoples and the other educators in Operation Breadbasket's Teachers' Division pushed back against teachers' unions, arguing that they could not divorce their concerns as Black teachers from the injustices experienced by Black students and Black communities. Black teachers engaged in dual struggles, advocating for themselves as public service workers and advocating for improvements in the quality of education for the predominantly Black students whom they served as fellow community members. Struggles between Black teachers and teachers' unions peaked at a time when many public sector workers, including teachers, had just recently won collective bargaining rights.

Teachers also won collective bargaining rights at the same time that the economy and the workforce were shifting from the unionized industrial manufacturing sector to the largely nonunionized service sector. During the 1950s, the overall proportion of the workforce that was unionized declined nationally. However, white-collar public sector workers became the fastest-growing sector in the U.S. labor force. The traditional industry-based unions of the AFL-CIO took note. Between 1951 and 1964, government employment at the state and local levels increased by 74 percent, but few of these employees were part of labor unions. In 1961, after a long campaign, including a legally prohibited strike, the United Federation of Teachers in New York City, the nation's largest teaching force, won the right to collective bargaining. At the federal level, President John F. Kennedy issued an executive order in 1962 that allowed federal workers to organize and engage in bargaining. Many state and local governments followed suit, and the number of public sector government workers in unions increased dramatically by the early 1970s. These victories for public sector labor set off a series of campaigns for collective bargaining by American Federation of Teachers locals in cities across the country.[22]

In Chicago, Mayor Richard J. Daley compelled the Board of Education to begin bargaining with the CTU even before official collective bargaining rights were established, in order to court the allegiance of the CTU's White middle-class base and shore up his bulwark against civil rights protests. While the CTU had been in existence since 1937, in the early 1960s the organization did not yet have collective bargaining rights. In 1963, supported by local and national labor organizations, thousands of teachers demanded collective bargaining rights through a CTU petition to the Board of Education.[23] While Mayor Daley saw public sector unionism as a threat to his patronage policies, it was a lesser threat than the growing Civil Rights Movement in the city. At the same time that the CTU was pressing for bargaining rights, CCCO was

THE POLITICS OF BLACK ACHIEVEMENT

organizing the 1963 Freedom Day school boycotts against the segregationist policies of Benjamin Willis, Daley's CPS superintendent. The predominantly White teachers organizing the CTU push for collective bargaining intentionally steered clear of the ongoing civil rights struggles in the schools out of concern that they would alienate the union's White majority base. Daley strategically granted the CTU sole bargaining rights with the Board of Education in 1966 to incorporate the largely White CTU into the Chicago Democratic machine in opposition to civil rights organizing. The CTU's win in securing collective bargaining rights for teachers was a major accomplishment for labor organizing in the city, but the union leadership's tacit collusion with Daley to win these rights and its disregard for civil rights struggles and the problems facing African Americans in city schools caused dissension within the union. As Teachers' Division chair David Harrison explained, Black teachers saw the CTU as "an extension of Mayor Daley and his Irish-Catholic political machine," a political machine that marginalized Black Chicagoans.[24]

In the late 1960s, Black teachers waged major battles against the CTU's lack of attention to the needs of Black students and teachers. By 1969 more than half of CPS students were Black. However, Black teachers only accounted for just over one-third of the teaching force. For years Black teachers were denied positions in schools without a significant majority of Black students. While the law did not sanction these actions, school administrators and many White principals used discretionary hiring practices to limit the schools where Black teachers could work. Black teachers argued that the CTU discriminated against Black members and particularly against Black teachers who participated in civil rights activism. In an effort to combat their marginal place within the CTU, Lillie Peoples, educators in Teachers' Division, and other Black teachers worked within, outside, and against the CTU in a number of different organizations.[25]

In 1966, led by elementary school teacher and CTU delegate Bobby Wright, the Black Teachers Caucus formed as a small group of primarily Black men who used Black Power era patriarchal tropes of manhood to argue for their rights as professionals and community leaders. The Black Teachers Caucus advocated working within the CTU to gain a greater voice for the concerns of Black teachers, improve conditions and resources in predominantly Black schools, and increase Black representation in the teaching force, administration, school board, and CTU leadership.[26] The Black Teachers Caucus supported the Black student boycotts in 1968 and instructed teachers to "either help and advise" the student protesters or "GET OUT OF THE WAY."[27] As with the Black high school students, the Black Teachers Caucus connected the increasing deaths of young Black people fighting in the Vietnam War to issues in the schools: "As long as the United States can spend 72 Million Dollars a year in Viet Nam, they can spend as much as necessary to improve Black schools. That is our money they are spending too. . . . Black People must demand that this country become responsive to our needs or there will be no Peace."[28] Like other Black education reformers, Bobby Wright funneled aggravation with the broken promises of the welfare state into support for community control: "There's really only one demand. That's black control of black schools."[29]

Wright and the Black Teachers Caucus condemned the racism fostered by public institutions and White officials. They also pointed out the failure of "democratic principles" to improve Black communities: "The democratic process was not made for black people and therefore does not work for them."[30] Like many Black Power activists, Wright and the Black Teachers Caucus argued that White liberals' energies would be better spent doing antiracism work in White communities than working in Black communities. In a November 1968 letter to the CTU's *Chicago Union Teacher* newspaper, the Black Teachers Caucus argued, "Every white person who has a job in the Black schools is denying a Black person a job. We cannot afford this. Therefore, the liberal white principals and teachers will leave along with all the rest. If they really want to help then they should go into Gage Park and on the Northwest side and tell those racists they are in favor of Black Self-Determination." By then, the Black Teachers Caucus was advising Black teachers not to renew their CTU memberships or recruit new members to the CTU if the union continued to work against the immediate needs of Black teachers and Black communities.[31]

At the same time that the Black Teachers Caucus leveraged the threat of Black teachers leaving the union, it also pushed Black teachers to become union representatives at their schools. From these positions, the caucus believed that Black teachers could repurpose union resources (school-based union meetings, CTU publications, and citywide events) to push an agenda that supported Black teachers and the Black communities where they taught and lived.[32]

Lillie Peoples's racial and gender politics differed from those of Bobby Wright and the Black Teachers Caucus. Peoples first met Wright during his early days working as a school truancy officer. Like Peoples, Wright was a migrant from the South who became a certified elementary school teacher. Around 1967, Peoples recalls that she reconnected with Wright when one of her younger coworkers at Dumas asked her if she was interested in "becoming Black" and took her to a meeting of Black teachers where Wright outlined his vision for Black self-determination. While Peoples agreed with Wright

THE POLITICS OF BLACK ACHIEVEMENT

on the need for more Black teachers and principals, she was not opposed to having competent White staff work in Black schools. In addition to the racial separatist inclinations of the Black Teachers Caucus, Peoples also felt alienated by the masculinist rhetoric and cadre style of the caucus. While Black women organizers like Ella Baker and Septima Clark had long been critical of the exclusion of women from leadership positions in SCLC (Operation Breadbasket's parent group), Peoples found space for herself and Black women's leadership more broadly in Operation Breadbasket's Teachers' Division, especially through the bold leadership of her friend, mentor, and vice chair of the group, Mattie Hopkins. Hopkins also demanded a role in the Black Teachers Caucus and became the secretary of the organization and one of the few women in the group.[33]

Despite divisions that existed between Black teachers' groups, Black activist educators were often involved in multiple organizations and collaborated in coalitions around the issues facing Black teachers and Black students. One such issue was the fight for certification of full-time basis substitutes (FTBs).

Black teachers made up a disproportionately large number of FTBs. By 1963, FTBs constituted a quarter of the CPS teaching force. By some estimates, 90 percent of FTBs were African American. FTBs were paid less, easier to fire than certified teachers, and barred from full voting rights in the union. FTBs were able to teach because they met the requirements for certification by the state of Illinois, but they were not considered certified in CPS because they had not passed the Chicago Board of Education's certification exam. Many Black teachers argued that this exam explicitly discriminated against African Americans and that the oral part of the exam was used to deny Black teachers certification, much in the way that so-called literacy tests were administered by White officials in the South as a subjective gatekeeping mechanism to prevent African Americans from voting.[34]

Nationally, teacher examinations were often used to deny Black teachers access to teaching jobs or to relegate Black teachers to subordinate status as noncertified or substitute teachers. In the urban North, White liberal officials upheld the use of these teacher examinations as "color-blind" tools. By 1975 New York City, the nation's largest school system, had a district staff that was still less than 13 percent non-White presiding over a student population that was more than 64 percent non-White. During the 1960s and 1970s the city's White liberal school administrators and teachers' union defended the value of "merit based" teacher examinations despite the protestations of Black and Puerto Rican teachers. Nearly two-thirds of New York City teachers, and an even greater proportion of administrators, were Jewish and argued that these meritocratic exams guarded against the racial discrimination, anti-Semitism, and corruption inherent in patronage hiring. In Chicago during the early 1960s, CPS superintendent Willis had used a similar liberal logic of color blindness to argue that CPS should not monitor the school system's racial demographics. Regardless of the motivation for supporting these exams — a White liberalism couched in meritocracy, color blindness, or veiled patronage — the racially discriminatory results were the same. Black teachers were systemically excluded from the teaching force or reduced to the status of FTB.[35]

The politics of Black achievement that informed teachers' advocacy on behalf of their students also informed their advocacy for themselves. In the case of Black teachers' performance on subjective teaching exams, Black teachers asserted their qualifications in the face of claims of Black inferiority in ways that paralleled their advocacy for their students. A Black educator recalled how a White Chicago principal had to vouch for him in order to pass the oral part of the teacher certification exam: "My own ability or whatever meant nothing. Only when a good white man say 'let the nigger in.' . . . I appreciated what he did because he didn't have to do it but he shouldn't have had to do it."[36] The racist presumption of inferiority that was applied to Black students was thus extended to Black adults and educators.

Maintaining the majority of Black teachers in FTB status also provided a mechanism for the Chicago Board of Education to uphold faculty segregation. It excluded most Black teachers from easily requesting transfers, creating an effective barrier that prevented Black teachers from teaching at predominantly White schools. At the same time, CPS officials were able to more easily transfer FTBs to break up groups of teachers participating in civil rights organizing. The White leadership and White majority of the CTU rank and file benefited from Mayor Daley's racial segregation policies and did not address the problems faced by the predominantly Black FTBs.[37]

Black teachers formed the group Concerned FTBs and, beginning in 1967, staged a series of wildcat strikes and "sick-ins," filed petitions, and led demonstrations. Led by James McQuirter, Concerned FTBs included more than 1,000 educators. The CTU leadership responded by warning FTBs to "turn a deaf ear to false leaders who promise them the moon." Concerned FTBs formed a coalition with Teachers' Division and the Black Teachers Caucus to fight for certification against the CTU leadership.[38] These groups leveraged national media attention focused on New York City strikes over the Ocean Hill–Brownsville community control district to advocate for their cause. In October 1968, as the conflict in New York raged and Black students in Chicago staged mass walkouts for community control of public schools, the Black Teachers Caucus warned that "Chicago is going to make New York's school problems look like a Sunday school picnic." By the spring of 1969, there was growing momentum amongst Black teachers, fueled by Teachers' Division, to create a separate Black teachers' union. Even among those who were not invested in a separate Black union, many Black teachers believed that the threat would make for important leverage against the CTU. With tensions between Black teachers and the CTU mounting, the CTU went on strike in May 1969 after union leaders could not get a commitment to fund salary increases from the Board of Education and the state.[39]

The two-day strike in May 1969 was the CTU's first strike since it gained collective bargaining rights, but nearly half of Chicago's Black teachers crossed the picket lines. Black teachers organized against participation in the strike, in a coordinated effort between Operation Breadbasket's Teachers' Division, the Black Teachers Caucus, Concerned FTBs, Teachers Committee for Quality Education, and United Educational Employees. Community control leaders like WESP director Barbara Sizemore also voiced support for the Black strikebreakers. New York City's African-American Teachers Association had crossed picket lines in 1968 in defense of Black self-determination in the Ocean Hill–Brownsville community control experimental school district. While the Black teachers who defied the 1969 strike in Chicago similarly argued for resources and control, the certification issue was their central grievance. Many Black teachers did not have faith in the Board of Education or Desmond and the White CTU leadership: "Desmond has tried to counteract our organizing of black teachers by promising certification for FTB substitute teachers, who are 90 percent black, but we will not be tricked by him. . . . We are urging black teachers to vote 'yes' for the strike and give Desmond enough rope to hang himself. Let him close white schools, but we'll keep the black schools open. And don't any of the white strikers come back looking for their jobs in September." They demanded that FTBs become fully certified.[40]

Black teachers' personal justifications for crossing the picket lines varied. For many teachers, crossing the picket line was meant to signal their commitment to Black students and Black communities, in opposition to the CTU and Board of Education, which they saw as racist and tone deaf. Many Black educators did not see the point of going on strike for increased resources that would not be distributed equally to Black schools. Roy Stell, a CTU activist and early leader in Teachers' Division, blasted White CTU president Desmond for denouncing Black teachers' support for the 1968 student boycotts and FTB strikes and then turning around and expecting Black teachers to support a CTU strike in support of a "racist school system": "We are not against more money for schools ... but we are against exploitation of the black community and black teachers. ... Teachers of Operation Breadbasket will support moves for more money in the school system when the black community decides when we need more money and how it will be spent."[41]

Black teachers crossed picket lines in particularly high numbers in Black communities on the West Side and South Side at all-Black schools like Dumas, where Lillie Peoples organized Black teachers to defy the strike. Approximately 45 percent of Black teachers citywide crossed the picket lines to teach, with some Black schools on the South and West Sides reporting nearly 100 percent attendance. Many of the Black teachers who participated in the CTU strike explained that they only did so because they felt striking would help to improve conditions in and resources for Black schools.[42]

In the months after the strike, the CTU leadership attempted to repair the racial divide within the union by addressing Black teachers' demands for increased presence and power within the union. The contract that CTU members approved after the strike granted teachers a raise and, among other provisions, provided a path to certification for FTBs after three years of successful service. The CTU promised improvements in predominantly Black schools: 750 new teachers were to be recruited and assigned to Black schools, and FTBs were to be granted a path to full-time status and certification without the requirement of an exam. But Teachers' Division was not satisfied and continued to pressure the CTU to preserve Black teachers' jobs, hire more Black teachers and administrators, and create a quicker path to certification for FTBs that was not contingent upon the ratings of sometimes overtly racist school principals.[43] This continued organizing was not in vain, as it kept the pressure on the CTU and Board of Education to create substantive change in the demographics of the teaching force.

BLACK TEACHERS AND THE POLITICS OF REPRESENTATION

Organizing by Black teachers, students, and community groups pressured the Board of Education to hire, certify, and promote more Black teachers, administrators, and staff. Their organizing, along with increasing pressures for faculty desegregation from the federal government, significantly transformed the demographics of CPS employees.[44] In the decade following the 1969 CTU strike, the gross number and proportion of Black teachers, administrators, and CPS employees increased significantly. In 1969, African Americans made up only 34 percent of teachers (7,844 teachers) and 24 percent of the supervisory and administrative staff (377 employees) employed by the Board of Education. However, by 1978, African Americans made up a majority of the total Board of Education workforce. By 1979, African Americans constituted 43 percent (11,068 teachers) of the teaching staff, 39 percent (553 employees) of the administrative staff, and 60 percent (12,460 employees) of the clerical and service support staff in CPS.[45] As these numbers demonstrate, African Americans achieved significant gains in both proportional and gross employment in CPS during the 1970s.

However, into the 1980s, African Americans still continued to occupy a greater percentage of lower-paid service and support staff positions and a disproportionately lower percentage of highly paid administrative positions. In 1979, African Americans made up 67 percent of the lunchroom staff and 71 percent of pupil services staff (including aides, teaching assistants, security personnel, and other support staff) but only 21 percent of legal staff, 20 percent of financial staff, and 30 percent of CPS principals. In 1979, when the CPS student body was approximately 17 percent Latinx, 20 percent White, and 61 percent Black, there still had yet to be a Black general superintendent of CPS.[46] Despite growing representation as CPS employees, in the years immediately following the 1969 strike Black teachers continued to feel the need to organize to advance the interests of Black teachers, students, and communities.

For example, in the wake of the strike, Lillie Peoples continued to organize with Operation Breadbasket's Teachers' Division in opposition to public school security policies that were instituted in the summer of 1969. The security procedures increased police access to schools. Teachers' Division argued that this put Black children in danger by overpolicing and criminalizing Black children in schools and carrying out "repressive actions against Black children with legal sanctions." It was particularly concerned that such measures would be used to persecute politically active Black students and called upon Black teachers to take on the role of "public defenders for Black children."[47]

As with the rise of "law and order" policies across the country, the introduction of police into schools was often connected to local civil rights and Black Power struggles. Beginning in the 1950s, school districts across the country increasingly took disciplinary control out of the hands of educators by centralizing discipline policies. The increased police presence in schools over the following decades disproportionately penalized and criminalized Black and Latinx students, setting the stage for "zero tolerance" policies and a school-to-prison pipeline. The CTU supported increased security in schools. After the distribution of the CPS school security manual in 1969, an article in the *Chicago Union Teacher* declared, "Members of the Chicago Teachers Union have been loud and clear in their fight for security in schools." The debate over security became yet another point of contention between Black educators in Teachers' Division and the predominantly White union.[48]

Teachers' Division also organized against the National Teacher Corps and the Urban Teachers Corps. Decades before Teach for America, these programs brought predominantly White interns and military veterans into urban Black communities to teach and experiment with curricula for "inner city" kids. The interns were paid and given a stipend to cover educational expenses toward master's degrees, funded by the War on Poverty's 1965 Elementary and Secondary Education Act and the Ford Foundation. Teachers' Division objected to the lack of Black representation in all aspects of these programs. Members also found it demeaning that untrained, unqualified White teachers were being assigned to Black schools while African Americans were still being denied the ability to become certified teachers. Teachers' Division suggested that many of the White men who participated were using the program as a way to claim a draft deferment and avoid military participation in the Vietnam War. In a message to the U.S. secretary of HEW, Teachers' Division members emphatically stated their position on the program: "The Teacher Corps represents White colonialism. It must go!"[49]

At the same time that Black teachers were pressuring CPS and the CTU for increased representation and material improvements in schools serving Black children, the federal government was placing pressure on CPS to desegregate its staff. Between 1940 and 1970, the Black population in Chicago grew from 277,731 to 1,102,620, from 8.2 percent to 32.7 percent of the city's total population. With a younger population than the city at large and limited access to private schools, African Americans made up nearly 55 percent of the students in CPS in 1970.[50] The demographics of many schools changed. Black families moved into previously all-White residential areas, and many White Chicagoans moved toward the outer rings of the city and into the suburbs.

These patterns of residential segregation impacted not only students but teachers as well. In 1969, 37 percent of Chicago's public schools had either exclusively White or exclusively Black faculties. Black teachers were concentrated in schools with predominantly Black students. White teachers were more concentrated in schools with predominantly White students. However, there were far more White teachers in schools with predominantly Black students than Black teachers in schools with predominantly White students. Between the 1950s and 1980s, an interracial group of education reformers engaged in multiple attempts to desegregate CPS. While the push for student desegregation had stalled, pressures to desegregate faculty continued. In 1969, the U.S. Department of Justice and HEW demanded that CPS desegregate its teaching force.[51]

Though support for student desegregation was on the wane within Black communities by the late 1960s, support for desegregation of Board of Education employees remained popular. This hinged on a particular understanding of employment desegregation. In this context, desegregation meant *access* and *representation*: gaining access to higher-level administrative positions from which African Americans had previously been excluded and increasing the total number of African Americans employed by the school system. However, these goals were more closely aligned with ideas of self-determination and community control than with desegregation that would integrate Black and White workforces within every school in the city. Black education reformers' understanding of faculty desegregation, based on access rather than integration, did not necessarily match government officials' plans for faculty desegregation. Thus, when the federal government demanded that CPS desegregate its teaching force in 1969, many of the same organizations of Black teachers that had fought for Black access to CPS jobs now actively fought against CPS officials' plan to desegregate the teaching force.[52]

The steering committees of Teachers' Division, Black Teachers Caucus, and Teachers for Quality Education all opposed CPS's plan to desegregate the teaching staff. In July 1969, CPS general superintendent James Redmond and the Board of Education approved a desegregation plan to address the federal government's concerns by hiring more uncertified teachers, providing incentive pay for more experienced teachers to transfer to schools for purposes of desegregation, instituting security improvements at schools, and transferring temporarily certified Black teachers to White schools and temporarily certified White teachers to Black schools.[53]

Black teachers' organizations questioned why faculty desegregation was being pursued while student desegregation had been abandoned. They also pointed out that there was no plan to desegregate the almost exclusively White strata of upper-level administrators. Black educators worried that under the Redmond desegregation plan, even more inexperienced and poor-quality White teachers would be sent to schools with Black students. A 1950s study revealed that teachers who quickly transferred out of "slum" schools after their required terms of service perceived Black and poor students as "difficult to teach, uncontrollable in the sphere of discipline, and morally unacceptable on all scores, from physical cleanliness to the spheres of sex and 'ambition to get ahead.'" The faculty desegregation plan would likely return more teachers with these views back to Black schools while being compensated monetarily for their "sacrifice" in taking these "undesirable" positions.[54]

Black teachers' groups strongly opposed the plan. "We emphatically reject the notion that White teachers coming into Black schools are entitled to 'combat pay.' This suggests that faculties in these schools are inferior and need the 'experience' of White teachers. All this really says is that the same people who fled to the suburbs or the north or southwest areas to escape Black people are being lured back to impose their racist attitudes on the minds of Black children."[55] David Harrison of Teachers' Division went further, suggesting that the move to desegregate the teaching faculty was also an attempt to "break up the unity black teachers are now developing." Lillie Peoples remembers faculty desegregation as an effort to "diffuse the power base" of Black teachers.[56]

Black teachers also feared that they would face a hostile workplace if they were assigned to predominantly White schools located in all-White communities. White residents in several neighborhoods had previously violently attacked Black residents who moved into their communities.[57] Black teachers in Teachers' Division demanded to know "Who will protect Black teachers who are shipped to the same communities that spat on little Black children and tore down the flag because it was at half-mast in memoriam of Dr. M. L. King?" It is within this context that Lillie Peoples and Teachers' Division worked hard to prevent faculty desegregation.[58]

The CTU also opposed the desegregation plan's forced transfers for teachers and incentive pay for teachers who transferred. It argued that these measures undercut seniority and insulted White teachers already working in predominantly Black schools and Black teachers already working in predominantly White schools without "combat pay." Nevertheless, the CTU was willing to compromise, and in 1971, the CTU acquiesced to a new plan that included hiring more Black teachers and assigning and transferring new and newly certified teachers to schools for purposes of desegregation. The plan did not include the forced transfer of senior certified teachers. In tandem with gains precipitated by Black teachers' organizing work, these measures increased the gross number and percentage of Black CPS teachers during the 1970s, but the level of segregation of the faculty did not decrease significantly.[59]

As a result, between 1973 and 1980, the federal government denied ESAA funds to CPS, in large part because of the continued segregation of the school system's teaching and support staff. Toward the end of this period, the U.S. Justice Department expanded these charges further to claim that CPS staff and student assignment policies violated the 1964 Civil Rights Act. In 1977, after years of stalling, drafting, and redrafting new plans, HEW officials approved Chicago's plan to desegregate the CPS teaching force, a plan that included the controversial transferring of certified teachers for the purposes of desegregation.[60]

There were diverse responses among Black and White teachers when the faculty desegregation plan finally came to pass in 1977. Both groups expressed a preference for transferring only the least senior teachers in a school.[61] When some veteran teachers received transfer orders, groups of White students and parents boycotted and picketed schools on the predominantly White Southwest Side, including Bogan and Hubbard high schools. The teacher transfer plans were implemented at the same time as another limited busing plan, compounding outrage over teacher and student desegregation plans. Mary Cvak, a longtime anti-integration White activist in the community near Bogan, used a defense of "neighborhood schools" and the racist language of reverse discrimination and fear of Black encroachment to voice opposition to desegregation: "I moved to what I thought was a white community and I look to live in a white community. . . . Whites are not interested in integrated education. . . . Integration doesn't work. . . . The pressure is always on the Southwest Side and what's left of the white community. It's as if the power structure has decided that we're expendible [sic]. We're the last line, the last place left. As the schools go, so goes the neighborhood." In her Southwest Side community there was little space for more moderate views. As one woman explained anonymously, "If you are middle-of-the-road, you are accused of wanting black children. . . . If you disagree with Mary then you are a 'nigger-lover.'"[62]

While some White teachers tried to contest their transfers in court, other White teachers embraced teaching Black students and the growing population of Latinx students. Daniel Fegan, a White teacher at Harlan High School on the South Side, invoked South Africa's apartheid system in echoing the arguments of Black teachers who did not want racist teachers instructing Black students: "I've worked in an integrated faculty situation for ten years, and I don't want to work with anyone who views this situation with horror. If that teacher wants to stand up for his right to teach only the right/white kind of students, let him transfer to a place where they admire such sentiments—South Africa." Many White teachers accepted their transfers to Black schools without filing court actions. This did not always entail an embrace of the surrounding Black communities, and stories circulated of White teachers scurrying to leave Black neighborhoods as soon as the school day was over.[63]

Though Lillie Peoples and groups of Black teachers and activists had opposed faculty desegregation for years, most Black teachers seemed less dissatisfied with their new assignments than did their White counterparts. Nonetheless, Black teachers at times still faced hostility from parents and the White communities surrounding the schools. Black teachers assigned to predominantly White schools could be just as apt to hurry out of the surrounding White neighborhoods at the end of the school day as their White counterparts teaching in Black communities.[64]

Lillie Peoples and Barbara Sizemore had feared that the type of systemic Black job loss that had accompanied school desegregation in the South would also take place in Chicago. As implemented in the late 1970s, the desegregation plan did not end up leading to massive job losses for Black teachers. However, CPS did use the government's mandate to desegregate as a tool to strategically dismantle community control efforts in Chicago earlier in the decade, as demonstrated by CPS officials' use of arguments for faculty desegregation to rebuff Barbara Sizemore's efforts to hire Black staff for WESP.[65]

After the desegregation measures, the number of Black teachers and staff continued to grow. The 1977 faculty assignment plan required the transfer of several thousand teachers to achieve a racial composition in the faculty at each school that fell within 12.5 percent of the overall racial composition of the teaching force citywide.[66] In 1969, when Black teachers crossed the CTU picket line, they accounted for only 34 percent of the total CPS teaching force. When the faculty desegregation plan was finalized in 1977, the CPS teaching force was 53 percent White, 42 percent Black, 4 percent Latinx, 1 percent Asian or Pacific Islander, and less than 1 percent American Indian. While some teachers were transferred as a result of the desegregation agreement, the total number and proportion of Black teachers working in CPS continued to increase after the agreement. In 1984, for the first time ever, there were more Black certified teachers in CPS than White teachers.[67] As African American teachers increased their presence in the teaching force, they also gained more powerful positions in the CTU. However, this did not always translate into improvements in the quality of education for Black students or produce more radical teachers.

Black Women, Teacher Power, and the Ascent of Jacqueline Vaughn

In 1984, the same year that Black teachers first outnumbered White teachers in CPS, Jacqueline B. Vaughn became the first African American, first woman, and first elementary school teacher to serve as president of the CTU. For Black women educators and veteran organizers like Lillie Peoples, Vaughn's election was a triumphant and hard-earned moment of celebration. Vaughn was born in St. Louis in 1935 and moved with her mother to Chicago when she was two years old. Both of Vaughn's parents passed away when she was a young child, and Mae Alice Bibbs, a teacher, raised Vaughn, encouraging her to become a teacher. Vaughn attended Morgan Park High School on the Far South Side, and like Lillie Peoples and Soyini Walton, she went to Chicago Teachers College before starting her teaching career in CPS in 1956. Vaughn was the head of the special education department at Einstein Elementary School on the South Side and later became a district-level language arts consultant. She worked her way up in the CTU from House of Delegates member in 1957 to union field representative in 1961. She was elected CTU secretary in 1968 and vice president in 1972. Vaughn established a reputation as a confrontational and effective negotiator and leader. This reputation extended beyond Chicago. She was elected a vice president of the national American Federation of Teachers in 1974.[68]

Vaughn also received significant grassroots support from rank-and-file teachers, particularly the growing population of Black women teaching in CPS. When Operation Breadbasket's Teachers' Division was pressuring the CTU to address the concerns of Black teachers and communities, Vaughn would bring the issues raised by Peoples and other Black teachers to the CTU leadership and membership. Peoples remembers how frustrated Vaughn was when Black teachers' concerns were not addressed in the CTU negotiations leading up to the 1969 strike. Although Vaughn's protestations on these issues were not always heeded, Peoples remembered Vaughn as a strong ally for Black teachers within the CTU: "She was inside the union, but she was our spokesperson within the union. She was bringing to the table what we wanted. If she couldn't get it, then we forced them to do it from the outside." Peoples also supported Vaughn because she thought it was important for a Black woman to lead the CTU.[69]

Black women constituted the vast majority of Black teachers and worked hard to elect Vaughn. By 1987, 80 percent of Black teachers were women, compared with 66 percent of White teachers.[70] Black women educator activists such as Lillie Peoples often saw Black men become the public face of the hard work put in behind the scenes by women. In reflecting on this time, Peoples explained:

To be very honest with you, to be a woman meant it got done! This kind of organizing is really a woman's thing. . . . [Women] really carried the movement with men up front. Many times just holding them up or standing them in position and really doing the work, doing the thinking, getting the job done. That was in the era of "Let Black men stand up. Let them be the leader. They haven't had the opportunity." But we always knew it was women who made the difference. . . . We were dealing with it all the time, seeing that it was the women that got the job done in all of these organizations. At some point having to tell the men, "Look. It's over."

Many Black women activists, organizing for education and other causes, echoed this idea that women "got the job done." When Vaughn ran for CTU president, Peoples felt it was her responsibility as a Black woman to organize people to vote for Vaughn. Vaughn had historically supported the concerns of Black teachers and communities and was advocating for smaller class sizes and higher pay—issues that united Black and White teachers. As Peoples recalled, "We knew Jacqui. We saw her capability. That's why we made sure. We wanted her, if any Black emerged in that position, that it be a woman." It took Vaughn's election as president of the CTU in 1984 for Lillie Peoples to finally feel that the CTU represented her.[71]

African Americans' move into leadership positions in the CTU and the Board of Education in the 1970s and 1980s came at a time when the political terrain in the city was shifting, including the relationship between Teachers' Division's parent organization and the CTU. Led by Jesse Jackson, Operation Breadbasket broke from SCLC and became Operation PUSH (People United to Save Humanity) in 1971. Teachers' Division officially came out against the 1971 CTU strike on grounds similar to those of the group's opposition to the 1969 strike. They still identified the CTU and the Board of Education as two "heads of a single snake of institutional racism" and articulated the need for separate Black teachers' groups supporting a self-determinist politics of Black achievement: "Since there is no other organization fighting for the needs of Black children, Black teachers, parents, and students must develop our own bargaining force. To demonstrate our commitment to our students and community, the Teachers' Division will not support the CTU strike and will attempt to educate our students."[72] But by 1973 a rift had developed between segments of the local Chicago-based Teachers' Division and the leadership of Operation PUSH, which had grown to have multiple branches nationwide.

When Lillie Peoples and her allies in Teachers' Division started talking about crossing CTU picket lines again in 1973, PUSH leadership—including Black union leaders—pushed back and officially supported the strike. Prominent Black union leaders, including Rev. Addie Wyatt and Charlie Hayes, held leadership positions in Operation PUSH. Lillie Peoples recalls that some PUSH leaders viewed Teachers' Division as too radical and "anti-union," particularly when it advocated for Black teachers to cross CTU picket lines. Jesse Jackson had insulated Teachers' Division from these criticisms when members crossed

THE POLITICS OF BLACK ACHIEVEMENT

CTU picket lines in protest in 1969 and 1971. But by 1973, PUSH was a larger national organization, and Teachers' Division was no longer the organized force with a large base that it had been a few years earlier. PUSH was working to create stronger bonds with organized labor, including the CTU. As Lillie Peoples remembers it, this conflict led to the expulsion of Teachers' Division from PUSH. She still did cross the CTU picket line in 1973 but with far fewer teachers than in 1969 and without a formal organization to support her. PUSH continued to maintain an Education Division of approximately fifty to sixty educators, parents, and community members who ran tutoring programs and educational programs, but for Lillie Peoples it was the end of an era.[73]

There was a sense that the turbulent days of the 1960s were now a part of history. In the spring 1974 issue of the Chicago African-American Teachers Association newsletter there was a "Where Are They Now?" segment about Black "Chicago Educators of Action" from the 1960s. All of the former teachers listed were men, with the exception of Mattie Hopkins. The majority of these Black men educator activists, including Bobby Wright, Timuel Black, Al Raby, Harold Pates, and Anderson Thompson, were teaching at local colleges and universities or had taken administrative positions in educational institutions, social service agencies, or labor organizations.[74] As had been the case during their days of intensive organizing, the contributions of Black women were once again largely hidden.

Instead of leaving their teaching posts in CPS, many of the Black women teacher-organizers of the 1960s and 1970s continued to teach for decades in local public schools. Peoples loved teaching, but she also noted that of the Black women teachers involved in her education organizing circles, "not one of us out of that core group ever got beyond classroom teaching! ... You do not fight the system and it rewards you." A notable exception was Mattie Hopkins, who was appointed to the Chicago Board of Education, but not until Harold Washington was elected as mayor.[75] As indicated in the newsletter, by the mid-1970s there was a growing sense of distance among Black teachers from the politics and tactics of the 1960s.

Black Teacher Politics and Public Sector Employment in the 1970s

After Mayor Richard J. Daley's death in 1976, Mayors Michael Bilandic and Jane Byrne increasingly turned to business leaders to run the schools. After a severe CPS financial crisis in 1979, the Illinois state legislature ushered in the private School Finance Authority to oversee all CPS budgetary decisions. Many in the Black community saw the all-White School Finance Authority, and broader attempts to decentralize CPS, as a mechanism to strip power away from Black

CPS teachers, administrators, and union leaders.[76] During the 1970s, mainstream civil rights organizations in the city also became more closely aligned with the Chicago business community in an effort to gain access to the levers of power in the city, while interracial business organizations, most prominently Chicago United, increasingly asserted more influence over public schooling in Chicago.[77] In this climate, between the 1970s and 1990s the increasingly Black leadership of the CTU embarked upon the challenging task of representing teachers as both workers and public servants—advocating for higher wages and increased benefits on behalf of teachers as workers and attempting to effect policy changes to improve the schooling of the overwhelmingly low-income Black and Latinx children they served.

Great Society programs, government affirmative action policies, and intensive organizing by African Americans for access to public sector jobs—like Black teachers' activism in Chicago—paved the way for increased Black employment in the public sector and created a growing Black middle class during the 1960s and 1970s. Manufacturing work was neither the singular nor always the most important route to middle-class status for African Americans during this period, as Black Chicagoans were disproportionally concentrated in public sector jobs during the second half of the twentieth century. By 1980, 31 percent of Black women and 23 percent of Black men working in Chicago were employed in the public sector, compared with 12 percent of White women and 11 percent of White men. Increasingly, African Americans entered higher-level managerial positions in the public sector as well, with more than half of all Black managers and professionals working in the public sector by 1980. In Chicago between 1970 and 2000, Black women were more overrepresented and relied more heavily on public sector employment than any other demographic group.[78] Black women teachers, as public sector workers, constituted a stable middle-class population in the city and a political base for the coalition that would elect the city's first Black mayor. The organizing work of Black activist teachers during the 1970s laid the foundation for the Washington campaign in the early 1980s.

Lillie Peoples and Mattie Hopkins continued their community organizing work after the demise of Teachers' Division while also participating more in electoral politics. In the early 1970s, former teacher, integration activist, and CCCO co-chair Al Raby organized the United Teachers of Chicago under the Illinois Education Association. Peoples and Hopkins were not particularly interested in joining the Illinois Education Association, but they were grateful that Raby's institutional affiliation provided them with a physical space to meet and continue the work they started in Teachers' Division. They briefly started a new Black Caucus after Teachers' Division was expelled from Operation PUSH in 1973. Unlike the earlier Black Teachers Caucus, the new Black Caucus was led by four women: Mattie Hopkins, Lillie Peoples, Delores Williams, and Sarah Coggins.[79]

In this new Black Caucus, Peoples and Hopkins tried once again to rally Black teachers around their collective concerns. The organization analyzed local and national education policies, encouraged Black teachers to push back against policies that hurt them and their students, and fought for the interests of Black teachers through and against the National Education Association. While not collaborating directly with IPE or other Black cultural nationalist groups, the Black Caucus did include the ideas of cultural nationalists in its critiques of individualism and by ending its newsletter with an outline of the Nguzo Saba (Seven Principles). Hopkins and Peoples used the Black Caucus to try to convince Black teachers to reject individualism and opportunism and to fight collectively against their common oppression as Black teachers in Black communities.[80]

As the CTU became increasingly Black in the 1970s, it did not necessarily become significantly more radical. Black teachers' politics and positions in the teaching force and the union had changed since the days of the 1969 CTU strike. The certification issue had largely been resolved, and many Black teachers achieved greater seniority and raises. Lillie Peoples believed that Teachers' Division's large base of Black teachers had become too comfortable: "I've gotten certified. I'm moving up. Salary lane. I'm secure. I'm not interested. . . . You could rouse them if they felt personally threatened." But many Black teachers felt a sense of professional progress, not imminent threat. Peoples credits the organizing of the late 1960s and early 1970s—particularly the 1968 Black student boycotts—for the increase in Black principals and administrators. But she also worried that many of these new administrators had not been on the front lines of these struggles or "paid for what they got." She recalls experiences with Black principals who "did not operate the schools any better than the White principals had." Racial representation did not always translate into significant transformations in leadership. At the same time, research, including reports written by Barbara Sizemore, consistently identified strong, culturally competent school and instructional leaders as key drivers of academic improvement and achievement at low-income Black schools.[81]

Nationally, Black educators had also been debating the proper role for Black middle-class professionals in Black freedom struggles. During the late 1960s, Dr. Olivia Pearl Stokes, a Black educator and director of urban education for the National Council of Churches, argued that "educated, well employed, and comfortable" African Americans could take a leadership role in promoting Black self-determinist projects, pointing out structural inequities, and "inject[ing] a sane voice into the mainstream" to "challenge and warn whites who hold power and who embody racist attitudes and methods . . . as a counterbalance to methods of the black revolutionaries and nationalists." While acknowledging differences in methods among African Americans, she maintained that "the black community is probably closer together in its agreement on the need for change in the American social structure than it has ever been. No matter where a diagnostic statement is made among the middle-class Negroes, or among the extremists, there can usually be assent, and hardy support for a commonality of understanding of the dimension of the agony of blacks and poor in America."[82] Conversely, in a 1968 edition of *Forum*, the publication of the Afro-American Teachers Association, Brooklyn educator Jitu Weusi argued, "The Negro professional [including Black teachers] is too secure and comfortable" and "becomes obsessed with the amassing of material wealth and aesthetic comfort. . . . Instead of leadership and direction from the Negro professional, the black masses receive deceit and betrayal." Weusi went further in declaring, "The creation of a schism between the Negro professional and the black masses is the last remaining weapon of the Establishment in its effort to maintain white supremacy."[83] As part of a growing Black public sector workforce, Black teachers sat at the pivot point of these very divergent views of intraracial class dynamics. Political debates emanating from these tensions continued as African Americans made inroads into electoral politics.

Black activist educators now used their organizing expertise to push for changes in electoral politics. Hopkins and Peoples worked on Al Raby's campaign for alderman in 1975. The next year, Peoples worked as coordinator in the South Shore neighborhood for Black U.S. congressman Ralph Metcalfe's 1976 reelection campaign. Metcalfe broke away from Mayor Daley's political machine in 1972 and faced an intense primary battle when Daley intentionally ran a candidate against him. Metcalfe won. Lillie Peoples and other Black organizers built on the antimachine fervor of the Metcalfe campaign to coordinate Harold Washington's first campaign for mayor after Daley's death in 1976. These earlier organizing efforts laid the groundwork for Washington's 1982–83 successful run for mayor.[84]

The influx of African Americans into the teaching force and the highest positions of power in CPS and the CTU changed the balance of political power in the city. The impact of this on Black student achievement was more ambiguous and undercut by stagnant per-pupil spending on CPS students (when adjusted for inflation) that did not keep up with the growing instructional and social support needs of CPS's increasingly low-income student population.[85] Whereas the predominantly White leadership of CPS and the CTU had once been staunch enemies of African Americans fighting for integration and community control in the 1960s, by the 1980s Black educators were increasingly represented at all levels of these organizations. Many formerly insurgent Black activists became important architects of school policies in the 1980s and beyond. Leaders of the original Black Teachers Caucus, Mattie Hopkins and Grady Jordan, who once boldly opposed the CTU leadership's discriminatory policies, later became, respectively, a member of the Board of Education and a CPS high school district superintendent.[86] Hannibal Afrik, a CPS teacher, innovator of African-centered education, founding member of CIBI, leader in Operation Breadbasket's Teachers' Division, and strong supporter of the 1968 student boycotts for community control of schools, was chosen as an early member of Mayor Harold Washington's education summit, which birthed the Chicago School Reform Movement of the 1980s.

Teaching was Lillie Peoples's passion. After leaving Dumas in 1985, she went to teach at Carter G. Woodson School. Named after the father of Black history, the school was located in a low-income Black neighborhood not far from the former Forrestville site where Barbara Sizemore was principal nearly two decades earlier. Peoples put her whole being into her time at Woodson and embedded herself in the life of the community. She petitioned the Chicago Park District to create a park next to the school and did some of the landscaping work herself. When asked to assess her teaching career Peoples gushed:

I loved it. I loved it. I taught some very smart kids, but when I went to Woodson and these kids came out of Washington Park homes, those projects at that time, it was the most rewarding experience of all my years of teaching. Because these children needed the most. Four of us went there at the same time, from Dumas. I took fifth, one had sixth, the other two had eighth grade. It was utter chaos and I heard, "No need to knock yourself out. They come from the projects. They don't care. They ain't gonna do nothing." Blah, blah. I just kept right on working. Within a year's time, that school was just completely turned around. The eighth graders had a cotillion. The fifth graders, the month of February, every week we had some place to go. Went to the museums. Their boundary had been 43rd Street and 47th Street. Just to see how these children blossomed. . . . I said to a friend, "You know your location doesn't determine what your brains are." . . . What I saw in a teacher, that saying, "You can do it," and assisting you to do it and giving you that kind of confidence. I think I was at my best at Woodson. I really do. I know I have the most rewarding feelings about that time. All the places I've been, that was the most rewarding. It was the most difficult. It was a challenge but I really feel rewarded about those years.[87]

Peoples's identity as a Black woman, her profession as a teacher, and her commitment to working in Black schools connected to Black communities were inseparable parts of her identity, approach to teaching, and organizing work. Black teachers matter—in the lives of their students, for their fellow educators, and for Black communities more broadly.[88]

Though Black middle-class CPS employees became an important political constituency supporting the successful 1982–83 campaign for Chicago's first Black mayor, Harold Washington, old intraracial and interracial cleavages would emerge again. Washington's attempted reforms would spur disagreements between nationalists and integrationists, middle-class reformers and working-class parents, and White business leaders and Black community groups, and among the school board, the CTU, and community organizers. Yet Black teachers constituted an important part of the Harold Washington coalition and the political fabric of the city. Washington was forced to be accountable to this constituency in a way that previous political administrations had not.

THE POLITICS OF BLACK ACHIEVEMENT

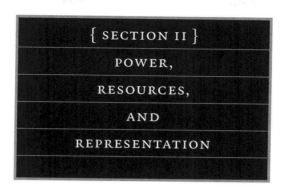

{ SECTION II }

POWER,

RESOURCES,

AND

REPRESENTATION

{ 5 }

CHICAGO SCHOOL REFORM

Harold Washington and a

New Era of Decentralization

During the 1960s and 1970s, Black education activism and organizing emanated from grassroots efforts and operated mainly outside electoral and official political channels out of necessity, as African Americans had been systematically excluded from these spheres.[1] In the 1980s, Harold Washington's campaign for mayor momentarily united this diverse set of Black constituencies. Washington's brief time as mayor provided Black education reformers with meaningful access to formal politics and power in government institutions for the first time, even though the politics of Black achievement that had powered Washington's rise would soon collide with increasingly powerful corporate education reformers.

For many, Harold Washington embodied Black power and Black achievement at the highest level. He would not have won the mayoral election in 1983 without critical support from Chicago's growing Latinx community and a small but significant group of White liberal allies. However, the unprecedented registration and turnout of Black voters formed the foundation for Washington's victory. Occupying the highest political position in the city, Washington was a visible symbol of Black political power and echoed the community control sensibilities of the Black Power Movement by promising access and agency not previously afforded to Black communities. Born in Chicago in 1922, Washington came of age in the social world of Black Chicago's Bronzeville community and its Black institutions (Black public schools, Black political organizations, Black churches). He was the only mayor to attend a CPS high school (DuSable High School) since at least the early twentieth century, and his success—born of Black institutions (including schools)—represented the type of achievement that Black education reformers had insisted could and should be possible for many more Black children.[2]

Black activists, organizers, and educators finally saw an opportunity for inclusion, representation, and power in city politics in the Washington administration after struggling for decades to have their voices heard and demands met by city leaders and a liberal welfare state that betrayed promises of equality. No longer outsiders, under Washington, Black education reformers could now presumably work with, rather than against or around, city officials and institutions to create the conditions for Black achievement. Once Washington became mayor, however, interracial and intraracial contradictions and cleavages that characterized earlier decades reemerged in his attempts to reform CPS, exposing the tensions between a politics of racial representation and a politics of progressive transformation.

These political struggles for power, resources, and representation played out in a city and nation increasingly governed by logics of austerity, with a diminishing tax base, budget cuts, and general economic decline, leading some to wonder whether this new Black political power was a "hollow prize."[3] During the 1980s the meaning of "education reform" became highly contested after Republican president Ronald Reagan's administration released *A Nation at Risk*, a damning report that blamed U.S. public schools for the nation's economic woes. A series of economic crises during the 1970s and 1980s also provided openings for corporate interests to become more involved in providing public services, including public education. As was the case nationally, the mantle of education reform in Chicago was taken up by groups with very different politics and prescriptions for remedying the ills of public schooling: policymakers, teachers and teachers' unions, government leaders, business executives, parents, students, and community groups.[4] At the same time that Black parents and community groups gained new access to governing power in Chicago, corporate interests also took on a more prominent role in school politics, compromising Black political power.

This chapter examines how the disparate constituencies detailed in previous chapters—Civil Rights and Black Power era organizers, community control advocates, founders of independent Black institutions, and Black educators—staked claims in the grassroots political mobilization that propelled Washington into the mayor's office, in Washington's governing coalition, and in his administration's education summit process. The negotiations among competing school reform plans during this period reveal the bipartisan support that was developing for the increased role of corporate interests within public education, locally and nationally.

Harold Washington was not the first Black mayor to preside over a major U.S. city. Following the 1965 Voting Rights Act, the number of Black elected officials increased dramatically, to almost 1,400 in 1970 and almost 5,000 by 1980, mainly in the South and primarily in local posts in places with Black majorities.[5] During the late 1960s and into the 1970s, a range of groups within the Black Freedom Movement in the United States consciously shifted their playing field and tactics from "protest to politics." During this same period a number of U.S. cities achieved Black-majority populations, or were moving toward them, through Black in-migration and White out-migration. These relatively new Black majorities elected Black mayors in Atlanta, Gary, Newark, and Washington, D.C. In Cleveland in 1967 and Los Angeles in 1973, both majority-White cities at the time, Black mayors Carl Stokes and Tom Bradley forged electoral coalitions with Whites en route to the mayor's office.[6]

In Chicago, Harold Washington faced a different set of political challenges. Since the Great Migration, Chicago had claimed one of the largest populations of African Americans of any U.S. city. However, Chicago never became a "Chocolate City" with a Black majority. In 1980, African Americans made up 40 percent of Chicago's population.[7] Washington did not receive much support from Whites, and particularly not from White business leaders and political elites. Washington also faced one of the most enduring political machines in the country.

The White-led Chicago Democratic machine had controlled city politics since the 1930s. As mayor and local Democratic Party chairman since 1955, using patronage and a well-organized machine apparatus, Mayor Richard J. Daley had dominated local politics and exerted significant power at the state and national levels as well. Daley's coalition included a White ethnic base and significant support from Chicago's Black voters. But Daley's opposition to school desegregation, his conflicts with Martin Luther King Jr., his violent responses to urban uprisings, and his complicity in the murders of Black Panthers Fred Hampton and Mark Clark incensed Black Chicagoans. Daley's death in 1976 accelerated Black Chicagoans' revolt against the increasingly conservative and blatantly racist politics of the machine.[8]

Demographic changes in Chicago enabled a different kind of coalition politics by the 1980s. Since World War II, continued in-migration of Black southerners, growing in-migration of people of Latin American descent, and out-migration of Whites shifted the racial composition of the city. Between 1940 and 1980, Chicago's total population only decreased by around 400,000 residents, from approximately 3.4 million to 3 million residents. However, during this same time the White population decreased from 92 percent to just less than 50 percent of the population, and the Black population increased from 8 to 40 percent of city residents. The decade preceding Harold Washington's electoral victory cemented this racial realignment. Between 1970 and 1980, as White Chicagoans continued to move to the suburbs, the White population in Chicago decreased by almost a third (from approximately 2.2 million to 1.5 million people). While the large migrations of African Americans from the South that characterized the preceding decades were over by the 1970s, the city's Black population still grew by approximately 9 percent during the 1970s. In 1980, nearly 1.2 million Chicagoans were Black. While Mexicans and Puerto Ricans had lived in Chicago for generations, between 1970 and 1980 additional waves of migration dramatically increased the Latinx population in Chicago from 247,000 to 423,000 people (from 7 to 14 percent of city residents). In 1980 less than half of Chicago's population was White for the first time since the city was incorporated.[9]

Beginning in the early 1970s, a series of court orders, the Shakman decrees, sought to limit political hiring and patronage. After Daley's death, his successor, Mayor Michael Bilandic, had difficulty mobilizing the machine with the same level of success as "Boss" Daley and was defeated in 1979 by Jane Byrne, a former Daley apprentice running as an antimachine candidate. Not long after assuming office as the first woman mayor in Chicago's history, Byrne reestablished ties with old guard machine leaders. By the time Harold Washington ran for mayor in 1983 against Byrne and Richard M. Daley, the former mayor's son, he was leading an insurgent political force storming the machine's castle. Washington's election symbolized, for many at the time, both the defeat of the Chicago Democratic machine and the ascendance of Black political power.[10]

Harold Washington was by no means a radical politician. For many years he was a reliable soldier in the local Democratic organization. Before entering politics, Washington served in the military and earned an undergraduate degree from Roosevelt University and a law degree from Northwestern University. He practiced law briefly with his father, Roy Washington, who served as a precinct captain in the Third Ward Democratic Party organization. After Roy Washington's death, Harold began his political career firmly within the ranks of the machine. As a precinct captain, Harold Washington was adept at mobilizing get-out-the-vote efforts and delivering his precinct's votes for the machine ticket. His leadership of the ward's Young Democrats and his rising star status in the party citywide caught the eye of the newly elected Mayor Richard J. Daley. However, early in his career, Washington failed to uniformly play the acquiescent role that the machine demanded of its Black members. As a result, Daley withdrew his intention to groom Washington to serve as city prosecutor. Washington still remained loyal to the machine and used its resources, power, and influence to propel his campaigns for the state legislature, where he served in the Illinois House of Representatives from 1965 to 1976 and in the state senate from 1976 to 1980.[11]

During the late 1960s, Washington weighed in on educational issues from his position in the state legislature. He advocated for multicultural and culturally relevant textbooks and curricula, greater state funding for CPS, strategically building new public schools to promote integration, and Black access to vocational training. Washington sponsored a set of resolutions supporting CCCO desegregation demonstrations and against then-superintendent Benjamin Willis. These resolutions were nonbinding and thus allowed Washington to walk the fine line between following his convictions and staying in the good graces of machine leaders. In 1967, Washington supported CPS superintendent Redmond's moderate desegregation plan that provided for voluntary busing of Black students to under-enrolled White schools, creation of magnet schools, expanded modern vocational education, and proposals for integrated secondary education parks, much like the Unity Plan's education park proposal initially supported by Rev. Arthur Brazier and TWO in Woodlawn. Washington also advocated for desegregation of the almost exclusively White Washburne Trade School, one of the major pipelines to union jobs in Chicago. Increasing Black access to the trade school reflected Washington's commitment to ensuring that schools provided preparation for the workplace. When Washington became mayor, connecting CPS high school students to employment opportunities in Chicago's business community was the initial driving force behind his education summit process.[12]

However, while it was important to Washington that Black CPS students receive a quality education and training to join the workforce, he was ambivalent about the role of widespread desegregation in achieving this goal. He had been educated in Black public schools and believed that children could be successful in all-Black schools. While not a Black nationalist, Washington did respect the nationalist critique that demands for integration often implied the inferiority of Black people and Black institutions. Widespread desegregation seemed impractical to Washington, given the declining White student population in CPS. However, he also did not believe that anyone should be barred from attending a school based on race, and thus he supported smaller-scale desegregation efforts that reflected his commitment to equal access to quality education. In his commitment to access and his concerns about implicit suggestions of Black inferiority in desegregation discourses, Washington evoked a politics of Black achievement that echoed the self-determinist community control sensibilities of Brazier, Sizemore, and Peoples. Accordingly, the major thrust of Washington's pleas for equal educational opportunity were directed toward equalizing funding for public schools serving students of color and low-income students, rather than desegregation. He would not step out of the shadow of the machine to propose more assertive educational programs and policies until later in his political career.[13]

Over time, Washington chafed under the pressure to stay loyal to the machine and yearned for an opportunity to govern more independently. Washington reflected back on his frustration as he neared the end of his time in the state legislature: "I didn't know it, but deep down, I was getting ready to get out of the machine. . . . I didn't like the system. I didn't like the way we were pushed around. . . . I looked upon myself as one of the Toms. I didn't have any policymaking position in the Democratic party. . . . I just couldn't live with it anymore."[14] This was not an unfamiliar position for African Americans trying to make political inroads in Chicago. In *Black Power*, Stokely Carmichael and Charles V. Hamilton had warned about the hazards of Black incorporation into existing political machines and the need for new political organizations: "Black visibility is not Black Power. . . . The power must be that of a community, and emanate from there," rather than "being representatives of 'downtown' machines, whatever the cost might be in terms of lost patronage and holiday handouts."[15]

During the 1960s and 1970s, Black leaders in Chicago often felt pinned between serving the best interests of Black students and navigating the city's powerful machine. The leaders who took over TWO in 1970, during conflicts between CPS and WESP, observed firsthand the punitive consequences of attacking established political authorities, when CPS officials demoted Barbara Sizemore and effectively ended WESP. Black teachers also had to struggle against the institutional racism of the machine and the union in order to make inroads into the teaching force. The founders of IPE tried to work outside the established political and educational system to create independent Black institutions, but they eventually opted back in.

Washington ultimately decided that he would no longer operate *within* the machine and would instead work to *defeat* the machine. In 1977, joining other recent Black defectors from the machine, Washington ran and lost in a special mayoral election held to determine Daley's replacement. In the citywide primary, Washington came in third, behind acting mayor Michael Bilandic, who still had the organizational apparatus of the machine backing him. In 1980, Washington ran for U.S. Congress without the support of the local Democratic Party organization, but he won the election because of his popularity amongst the majority-Black constituents in his congressional district.[16]

In the U.S. Congress, Washington found some measure of freedom from the Chicago machine. He gave passionate speeches on the floor of the House of Representatives in opposition to the Republican Reagan administration's attacks on civil rights and voting rights, supply-side "Reaganomics," and cuts in job training and social welfare programs. As a member of the Education and Labor Committee, Washington rallied opposition against Reagan's plan to eliminate the U.S. Department of Education and federal financial aid programs that enabled low-income students, including students in his district, to attend college. An active member in the Congressional Black Caucus, Washington was ranked fifth in anti-Reagan votes by the *Congressional Quarterly*. This strident resistance and the considerable time he spent forging connections with local constituent groups in Chicago during his first term in Congress bolstered his popularity at home. The local Democratic machine, which had now turned against Washington, could not find a legitimate contender to run against him in 1982. Washington was reelected in a landslide victory.[17] Meanwhile, a grassroots movement was materializing in Chicago that would ultimately propel Washington into the mayor's office.

Black Politics and the Movement to Elect Harold Washington

In the late 1970s, Black Chicago was ideologically divided. A solid, diverse, Black cultural nationalist community continued to work through organizations like IPE and other Black Power era groups. In older uplift organizations like the CUL, a segment of the Black middle class and Black elite pursued integration programs by working to build strategic coalitions with White elites to increase African Americans' access to middle-class employment. The Chicago Democratic machine also still claimed the loyalty of a cross section of the Black elite, middle class, working class, and poor who tried to reap the scarce favors, jobs, and benefits that the machine could still deliver. For some, being antimachine, in whatever form that opposition might take, constituted a politics in and of itself. Others were more engaged in local churches, community organizations, arts groups, and block clubs than wedded to any rigidly defined formal political organization or ideology. Finally, having become frustrated with the failures of years of Civil Rights and Black Power efforts to bring tangible changes to the communities they felt crumbling beneath their feet, another group of Black Chicagoans had lost faith in politics—formal electoral, local, machine, cultural, and community based alike.

In this somewhat disjointed environment, the Black electoral revolt against the machine picked up momentum. African Americans voted against the machine by throwing their support behind Jane Byrne for mayor in 1979. Byrne promised to increase Black representation in important city government positions and won fourteen of sixteen Black wards, with particularly large margins in Black middle-class wards where antimachine sentiments had long simmered. Almost immediately after taking office, however, Byrne enraged her Black supporters by reversing her antimachine stance, systematically decreasing Black gains in city politics and aligning herself with Alderman Edward Vrdolyak and other officials associated with the most extreme racist elements of the Democratic Party organization. Some of Byrne's greatest perceived offenses against African Americans took place in the realm of education.[18]

The CPS financial crisis that Mayor Byrne faced in 1979 was set in motion during the later years of the Daley administration. Since the late 1960s, Mayor Daley had presided over budget deficits and mounting debt endemic to many U.S. cities experiencing deindustrialization and a shrinking tax base accelerated by "White flight." While in office, Daley was able to use his political power to pressure state legislators and financiers to allow CPS to borrow more money, refinance outstanding debt, buoy the city's bond rating, and overestimate projected tax revenues. Subsequent mayors were unable to win the same financial favors, and in 1979, banks refused to loan CPS $125 million necessary to operate the school system. Seizing on this dire financial situation as an opportunity, Chicago's business leaders sought a larger role in the schools, asserting a corporate vision for CPS managerial reforms in the interest of workforce development.[19]

In January 1980, Mayor Byrne agreed to a bailout plan privately negotiated by Illinois Republican governor James Thompson and city business leaders, including prominent members of the Chicago Commercial Club, who had been pushing for CPS to implement corporate-style management reforms. The agreement condensed and restructured district and central office staff, eliminated thousands of Board of Education positions, fired the existing Board of Education members, and cut curriculum supports and compensatory education programs that were implemented as part of earlier desegregation efforts. Most notably, the agreement created the Chicago School Finance Authority, a board of five corporate executives who would manage CPS's finances. The influence of business executives significantly increased.[20]

The 1979 CPS budget crisis became a justification for austerity measures. In

1980, officials of the all-White School Finance Authority, appointed by Byrne and Thompson, were charged with overseeing a school system whose student population was 60 percent Black. Under the School Finance Authority's oversight, CPS's increased focus on "management efficiency" and "systemwide reorganization" resulted in a 20 percent cut in the number of Board of Education employees between 1979 and 1981 (from 48,316 to 38,288 employees). These cuts undermined Black employment gains by disproportionately laying off Black staff, particularly administrative staff. While there were deep cuts across the board, Black central and district office staff were cut by 70 percent (from 2,630 to 768 employees), while White central and district office staff only decreased by 53 percent (from 2,783 to 1,299 employees).[21]

Education struggles, particularly surrounding Black representation and leadership in CPS and on the Board of Education, became critical to allying Harold Washington with grassroots Black organizers and elevating his prospects as a mayoral candidate. In 1980, Lutrelle "Lu" Palmer, one of the most vocal leaders in the school board debates, helped to organize Chicago Black United Communities (CBUC), a coalition of more than fifty diverse Black community organizations, including grassroots organizers, church groups, educators, and political organizations. Palmer was an unapologetic Black nationalist, and his newspaper columns and radio show were widely popular. Influenced by his father, a school principal in Newport News, Virginia, Palmer was also dedicated to Black education and worked closely with IPE. Palmer's oft-repeated tag line, "It's enough to make a Negro think Black," reflected his skepticism about the impact of civil rights gains for the masses of Black people and was a call for more militant thinking and action.[22]

The newly created CBUC organized a mass meeting, at which Harold Washington was a featured guest, to advocate for increased Black representation on the Board of Education and oppose Mayor Byrne's plan to back Thomas Ayers for board president. A White former chairman of Commonwealth Edison, Ayers had served on the boards of multiple city institutions, including the CUL and Chicago United, an interracial group of Chicago business and civic leaders that had proposed corporate management strategies for CPS.[23] CBUC filed a suit charging that Ayers lived outside the city limits and was thus ineligible for the Board of Education post. CBUC won the suit, and in May 1980 Byrne's appointed school board selected the Reverend Kenneth Smith as Board of Education president, the first African American to serve as president of the board.[24]

After the racial turmoil over the selection of a school board president, Mayor Byrne chose Dr. Ruth B. Love, a Black woman from Oakland, California, to serve as CPS superintendent in 1981. Though she was the first African

American to hold the post, Love encountered resistance before she even took office. Some Black activists were upset that Love, "an outsider" backed by Chicago United, was selected rather than a local Black Chicagoan, specifically Manford Byrd Jr., who had worked his way up the ranks under previous administrations.[25]

After the long struggle for Black representation and educational leadership, the appointments of Love and Smith seemed empty victories. Because of the newly created School Finance Authority, Love was stripped of the power to manage the school budget, one of the superintendent's main powers. Additionally, after appointing two African Americans to the Board of Education, Byrne replaced two other Black board members with White members who had led protests against school desegregation on the Northwest and Southwest Sides of the city.[26] Harold Washington called a press conference to denounce the appointments of these White board members. Even CUL leaders who still occupied a place at the table within the Byrne administration were outraged. The CUL's James Compton described the appointments as "unconscionable": "Mayor Byrne has once again shown insensitivity to Chicago's Blacks.... To appoint a woman who is ... a known leader of the segregated Bogan community is a slap in the face."[27] This only reinforced African Americans' perception that Byrne was a racist, duplicitous, and disrespectful politician who flagrantly violated her campaign promises, fueling the surge that compelled Harold Washington to run for mayor. Based on CBUC's success mobilizing coalitions with Latinxs and Whites in the school board struggles, the Washington campaign's mayoral electoral coalition was becoming clear: a fairly unified Black base buttressed by significant grassroots Latinx and progressive White support.[28]

The movement to elect Harold Washington for mayor was a coordinated coalition effort that had not been seen since the late 1960s in what historian Jakobi Williams describes as the "original Rainbow Coalition." During that time, on a smaller scale, Black Panther Party members helped to forge a grassroots coalition with Puerto Rican and progressive White organizers to politicize poor and working-class people across the city to fight against police brutality and gentrification and for community-based social services and economic and racial justice. This fledgling coalition faced massive state repression and largely dissipated after Panther leader Fred Hampton's assassination in 1969, but many of the coalition's original participants saw a rebirth of their ideals in the citywide support galvanizing around Washington's run for mayor.[29]

First, Washington had to be convinced. Over the course of a series of mass meetings during 1981 and 1982, CBUC brought together Black community groups, including leaders from the CUL, to create a plan for Black community

Chicago voter registration drive (Chicago Urban League Records, University of Illinois at Chicago Library, CULR_04_0221_2479_001)

empowerment and meaningful representation in formal electoral politics. Lu Palmer and others met with Washington to determine what it would take for him to run for mayor, after Washington spoke at a mass meeting held at Bethel AME Church in July 1982. Washington made clear that he would only consider running for mayor if the assembled community groups could raise $250,000 to $500,000 and register at least 50,000 new voters to demonstrate that his candidacy was viable.[30]

Organizers and volunteers worked across the city to register new voters. Black West Side activist Nancy Jefferson of the Midwest Community Council and White activist Slim Coleman from the Uptown neighborhood on the North Side worked with People Organized for Welfare and Employment Rights (P.O.W.E.R.) to register welfare recipients and public housing residents. Washington's old friend and political ally Renault Robinson, of the Afro-American Patrolmen's League, raised money and garnered financial and advertising support from Edward Gardner, chairman of the Soft Sheen Black hair care empire.

Gardner funded catchy advertising campaigns on Black radio that encouraged voters to "Come Alive October 5!"—the deadline to register to vote. Operation PUSH's Jesse Jackson organized a meeting of over 100 Black church leaders who agreed to put forth measures to register their congregants to vote.[31] Along with CBUC and P.O.W.E.R., other groups such as the People's Movement for Voter Registration, Citizens for Self-Determination, Concerned Young Adults, and Grassroots Youth Organization trained hundreds of people in political education classes and registered 125,000 Black voters, many of whom were residents in some of Chicago's poorest wards. Impressed with the voter registration drives and fundraising, Washington entered the mayoral race in November 1982.[32]

Washington's campaign also benefited from organizing in Chicago's growing Latinx communities, which were poised to break from the machine. The Democratic Party organization had marginalized Puerto Ricans and Mexican Americans on the Near West Side, North Side, and Far South Side historically. Efforts in the 1960s by South Chicago's Tenth Ward Spanish Speaking Democratic Organization to vie for more autonomy from the machine were stifled by local White machine operatives. During the 1960s and 1970s, Latinx activists also worked outside the machine in grassroots organizations like the Young Lords, a Puerto Rican nationalist group, and the predominantly Mexican American Alianza Latino Americana para el Adelanto Social. Among other things, this latter group supported the demands of the Latinx students who boycotted Harrison High School in 1968. In the 1970s, the Young Lords' José "Cha Cha" Jiménez reprised the energy of the original Rainbow Coalition in his failed campaign for alderman.[33] In the early 1980s, the Independent Political Organization of the Near West Side revived Mexican American antimachine politics, led by Rudy Lozano, Lidia Bracamonte, Jesús "Chuy" García, and Linda Coronado. Lozano, Jiménez, and others built support for Harold Washington's progressive antimachine platform in Latinx communities and forged coalitions with African Americans and White liberals.[34]

Managing the tensions between Black nationalists, Black professional middle-class leaders, integrationists, and community-based groups was one of the great successes of the Washington campaign. Washington replaced his initial campaign manager, Renault Robinson, with Black Chicago civil rights leader and CCCO cofounder Al Raby, whose appointment was seen by some as a move by the Washington campaign to expand its appeal to White liberals and a multiracial business and professional elite. Raby moved the campaign headquarters from the South Side to downtown offices closer to media outlets, the headquarters of special interest groups, and other political institutions.[35]

Raby was a former teacher, and his movement-building experience was forged in education struggles. He was a leader of CCCO during the desegregation struggles in the 1960s, and in the 1970s he provided a home base for former Operation Breadbasket Teachers' Division leaders Mattie Hopkins and Lillie Peoples to continue organizing Black teachers. Teachers like Peoples built on their education organizing experience and work with earlier anti-machine candidates to coordinate registration and get-out-the-vote efforts. Soyini Walton, who had left NCDC by the 1980s, canvassed and passed out flyers for the Washington campaign. CTU then–vice president Jacqueline Vaughn harnessed the power of the union to raise money and pack Washington rallies with bodies. Raby sought to mobilize all of these constituencies and to build on the existing grassroots base in Black neighborhoods, while also creating the institutional structures of a formal political campaign. Washington's Black middle-class base was cultivated through grassroots support from churches and strong support amongst Black educators.[36]

The Black nationalist arm of Washington's coalition of supporters, though somewhat marginalized, continued to stay active in the Task Force for Black Political Empowerment. The Task Force was nationalistic in tone and headquartered in the heart of the Black community on the South Side at 47th Street and King Drive. It included individuals and several dozen groups that had previously mobilized grassroots campaigns on school issues, including CBUC, Operation PUSH, Black Methodist Ministers Alliance, Chicago Black United Front, Concerned Young Adults, and the Kenwood-Oakland Community Organization. The Task Force staged protests against Black ministers and churches that supported Byrne or Daley and went on Black radio to attack Washington's opponents for supporting institutional racism. These actions were too politically risky to be associated directly with the formal campaign, but when executed by a "shadow campaign," they could have the desired effect of mobilizing the Black poor and working-class vote without alienating middle-class African Americans and liberal Whites.[37] While there was some dissension between the downtown Raby-led formal political organization and the more militant Task Force, both groups were necessary for Washington's electoral victory.

Chicagoans with divergent political ideologies claimed different stakes in Harold Washington. For Black nationalists, proponents of community control, and a broad segment of folks in Black communities who felt alienated by Chicago's formal political structure, Harold Washington symbolized the promises of transformative Black political power. For an interracial group of integrationists, Harold Washington symbolized the promise of access. For a subset of antimachine, middle-class, racially liberal Whites, Washington symbolized an ideal of diversity and the possibility for governmental reform. For a significant group of Latinxs, Washington symbolized the renewed possibilities of a rainbow coalition, promises of access to city government, and a better option than the machine politicians who had ignored or marginalized them for so many years.[38]

In the primary, Washington won a resounding 79 percent of the Black vote but defeated Jane Byrne by just over 36,000 votes. In the general election, Washington won by a slim margin of less than 49,000 votes, reflecting the scale of the White racist backlash in a city where the Democratic candidate usually cruises to victory over the Republican. In the general election, Washington received 98 percent of the vote in predominantly Black wards. Of his total electoral support, Washington garnered 77 percent of his votes from Black voters, 17 percent from Latinx voters, and 6 percent from White voters.[39] In the end, Washington's support from Whites was dismal, but his overwhelming support by a unified Black community, a significant Latinx vote, and a smaller group of White liberals gave him the win.

For many, Harold Washington—the antimachine Black reformer—seemed to be the personification of Black achievement and Black Power realized. Leon Finney Jr., president of TWO, could hardly contain his excitement. Like many, he saw Washington's win as the culmination of years of Black Chicagoans battling the machine: "I feel an exuberance that can only be directly related to the fact that—for the first time in my life—I feel that I am, you are, we are historical phenomena for all generations to come. . . . You have been the framer of the victory of a 50 year undeclared battle in the city of Chicago."[40] But what would happen when an African American took the helm of power in Chicago?

Washington had tethered together a political coalition with internally contradicting politics. Independent reform-minded antimachine politics were often seen as antithetical to ethnically based group politics. Furthermore, Washington ran on promises of an anticorruption, antimachine government that would be racially representative of the entire city, redistributing resources and power away from the machine and downtown elite to the city's neighborhoods. For example, his economic development plans reversed Daley era downtown development strategies in favor of policies that "balanced growth" between downtown and the neighborhoods, decoupling job creation priorities from real estate development priorities.[41] Yet real estate interests, downtown business elites, and machine loyalists were still embedded in the city's economic and governing structure.

Electoral victory was not enough. As a Black elected official, Washington mobilized masses of Black voters, but as he governed, he also courted the

White corporate and business interests who actually controlled most of the city's economic institutions.[42] Interracial and intraracial divisions between his opponents and among his grassroots, working-class, and middle-class professional supporters continued to percolate within Washington's administration beyond the election. Washington's efforts in the realm of education illustrate this continuing conflict and both the opportunities and the limitations of racial representation ushered in by Chicago's first Black mayor.

MAYOR HAROLD WASHINGTON AND EDUCATION REFORM

In 1983, Harold Washington took control over a city and public school system that had experienced dramatic demographic transformations over several decades. By 1983, approximately 61 percent of CPS students were Black, the growing Latinx population accounted for 21 percent of CPS students, and less than 16 percent of CPS students were White. By 1986, more than two-thirds of CPS students came from low-income families. By the end of the decade, Whites still accounted for 45 percent of the city's population, but of the White families who remained in the city, two-thirds would opt out of the public school system and send their children to private and parochial schools. A significant proportion of Black middle-class families were also relocating to the suburbs, while those who stayed maneuvered to get their students into the city's more racially and economically diverse magnet and selective enrollment public schools.[43]

Black public sector CPS employees, the majority of whom were Black women, formed an important middle-class base in Harold Washington's electoral coalition, and he would have to be accountable to them in crafting his education reform plans. Yet he was beholden to multiple constituencies. Washington's campaign raised expectations among Black parents and families across the city that he would improve schools through sweeping reforms. He also won the loyalty of Black CPS employees, upon whom major reforms would have the most immediate impact. As a mayor preaching the gospel of reform and good government, Washington appealed to the growing educational non-profit and advocacy industry. Washington also wanted to use education as an issue to engage Chicago's business leaders, a group whose support he did not have during the election. He hoped to work with local business leaders to create jobs for CPS graduates. Washington tried to unite these diverse constituencies through an education summit.[44] In his early days as mayor he was cautious not to alienate any of these constituent groups.

During his first term, Washington was constrained by his commitments to the constituencies that elected him and by the contentious "council wars," in which hostile White aldermen obstructed Washington's ability to push initiatives through the city council. Soon after Washington took office, it became clear that many of the remaining city council members who were loyal to the Democratic Party organization had no intention of cooperating with the new Black mayor. Cook County Democratic Party chairman Alderman Edward Vrdolyak organized a group of anti-Washington aldermen dubbed the "Vrdolyak 29" against Washington's supporters in the city council, the "Washington 21." This political divide fell along racial lines. The Vrdolyak 29 included 28 White aldermen and 1 Latinx alderman. The Washington 21 included all 16 Black aldermen and 5 White aldermen who were Washington allies.[45]

This political divide was exacerbated by lingering animosities about the racist tactics and pronouncements by Vrdolyak and many of "the 29" during the mayoral campaign. In addition to supporting the Republican candidate for mayor in the general election, many of the White machine committeemen rallied their constituencies against Washington using racist rhetoric. When speaking to a group of supporters during the primary, Vrdolyak had implored his base to vote against Washington and for Byrne: "It would be the worse [sic] day in the history of Chicago if your candidate, the only viable candidate was not elected. It's a racial thing. Don't kid yourself. I am calling on you to save your city, to save your precinct. We are fighting to keep the city the way it is."[46] Vrdolyak and "the 29" often excluded Black aldermen and White aldermen who supported Washington from important meetings and conspired to strip "the 21" of their leadership positions in the Democratic Party. "The 29" were able to block almost all legislation put forth by Washington and "the 21." However, because "the 29" could not override Washington's veto power, they could not pass legislation either.[47]

The resulting standstill lasted until a court-ordered redistricting of the city's wards, to comply with voting rights laws and ensure "fair representation," mandated new elections in three majority-Black and four Latinx wards. In 1986, Washington picked up two more Black supporters and two Latinx supporters in the council. City council loyalties were now split down the middle, 25-25, with Washington holding the tiebreaking vote. Approaching the election for his second term, Washington was finally able to push appointments and legislation through the council.[48]

Penned in by the confines of a hostile city council, Washington accomplished very little on the educational front during his first term. He issued an executive order to reestablish the Citizen Nomination Committee, a group of community members and civic leaders, to recommend school board nominees. He also replaced CPS superintendent Ruth Love, the first African American to serve as general superintendent, with Manford Byrd Jr., the Black CPS insider who was favored by local Black leaders when Byrne initially chose Love. Washington's lack of progress in implementing meaningful education reforms during the majority of his first term prompted his call for an education summit in the summer of 1986.[49] His second-term election loomed, and he had made little progress on his long-held goal of connecting CPS students with jobs in Chicago industries. A summit might also help reconcile the drastically divergent solutions that different groups proposed to respond to the broad consensus that there were major problems in public education.

Washington's first term played out alongside the response to the Reagan administration's 1983 report *A Nation at Risk: The Imperative for Education Reform.* As reformers and policymakers absorbed the report's denunciation of public schooling and rejection of the previous era's experimental education reforms, the Reagan administration promoted budget cuts, punitive accountability measures, and privatization through school vouchers, tax-credit programs, and market-based competition models. Amid the administration's cuts to domestic discretionary spending, including education funding, the Congressional Budget Office estimated that child poverty increased by nearly 50 percent between 1979 and 1987.[50]

In Chicago, the funding provided for CPS was not keeping up with the needs of students. While the actual funding per pupil in CPS more than quadrupled between 1970 and 1988, from $958 to $4,079, when adjusted for inflation, per-pupil funds were relatively stagnant over the course of this period. However, as was the case nationally during this same period, the number of low-income students in CPS increased.[51] Articles in the CTU's *Chicago Union Teacher* echoed *A Nation at Risk*'s acknowledgment that schools were being called upon to make up for a lack of needed social services. Educators were "routinely called on to provide solutions to personal, social, and political problems that the home and other institutions either will not or cannot resolve." However, in her January 1987 testimony before the U.S. Senate Committee on Labor and Human Resources, CTU president and national American Federation of Teachers vice president Jacqueline Vaughn noted, "In the three years since *A Nation at Risk* was issued [the Reagan] administration has been long on rhetoric and short on money."[52] Schools needed significantly more, not less, funding. The sources and symptoms of child and family poverty would never be resolved through austerity measures and budget cuts to schools and social services.

CPS administrators, the CTU, business leaders, education nonprofit groups, grassroots community organizations, and parents had very different ideas about what types of reforms were needed. Business leaders from Chicago United wanted to decrease the size of the CPS central office and foster competition between schools and new parental choice programs. Groups of parents and community members proposed school-based governance, with varying levels of community and parent control, to make school staffing decisions, direct school budgets, and shape curricula. Academics and education policy organizations also proposed school-based councils alongside "Effective Schools" social and organizational models. The CTU worried that school-based management would undermine collective bargaining rights, but it did support more challenging requirements for students and teachers, new teacher evaluation processes, and decreases in class size to improve schools' teaching and learning environments. While the CTU, CPS administrators, and the majority of parent and community groups insisted that any reforms must be accompanied by increases in education funding, business leaders generally opposed large-scale funding increases.[53] As Washington's education summit evolved, the mayor brought all of these groups to the table to help craft a slate of school reform measures. However, the first meeting of the summit in 1986 only included a select group of upper-level education, civic, business, and union leaders to create partnerships between CPS students and local businesses.

While Chicago did not suffer as badly as its Rust Belt neighbors, deindustrialization did dramatically impact the economic landscape of the city and inform Washington's school reform priorities. Days after Washington was elected mayor in April 1983, *Chicago Tribune* economic reporter R. C. Longworth offered a bleak description of the city that Washington inherited: "The heavy industries on which its entire economy is built are dead or dying. None of the more modern industries—not services nor finance nor high tech—has taken up the slack in wages or jobs or tax base."[54] Between 1972 and 1983, manufacturing jobs in the city decreased by 34 percent. The loss of manufacturing jobs exacerbated racial, economic, and spatial inequality. Black people with a high school diploma or less found it disproportionately more difficult to secure living wage jobs.[55] These problems extended into the schools. Political scientist Wilbur C. Rich argues that while schools had "provided workers with the requisite knowledge and socialization for work in the old economy," they were not equipped to address the shifting workforce needs and rising unemployment that accompanied this period of economic restructuring. In 1985, the overall youth unemployment rate in Chicago was 32 percent. For Black young men ages sixteen to nineteen, the rate was 51 percent. A report prepared by the Washington administration predicted that 43 percent of CPS students entering high school in 1985 would end up dropping out.[56] To address issues in employment and education, Washington convened the education summit in 1986 explicitly "to improve the employability and employment of Chicago's young people."[57]

Current and former CUL leaders played prominent roles in the education summit and informed Washington's approach to education policy reform. Concerned about CPS's high dropout rates and high unemployment rates among students who did graduate, Washington's education summit called on Chicago businesses to commit to hiring CPS students. This approach drew on Washington's longtime efforts to connect Black Chicagoans with pathways to jobs, including his efforts to desegregate Washburne Trade School so that African Americans could gain access to union jobs. Sharing similar concerns, the CUL was historically one of the most prominent forces in the city working to find jobs and forge partnerships between Chicago's business leaders and Black communities. Harold "Hal" Baron, a White former CUL researcher, was Washington's chief policy advisor and proposed the summit's central plan, eventually titled the "Chicago Learning Works Compact." Bill Berry, former CUL leader and a Washington ally, worked to develop a relationship between Washington and Chicago United, the interracial group of city business leaders that had closely counseled Mayor Jane Byrne on education issues. Washington courted Chicago United business executives to participate in the education summit as a group of employers with access to job opportunities.[58] Dr. Gwendolyn Laroche, CUL director of education, was chair of the summit's Community Support Working Group, which created a proposal to increase parent and community participation and decision-making roles in the schools—a precursor to what would eventually become Local School Councils (LSCs).[59]

The Washington administration provided a new environment where current and former CUL leaders could forge business-community partnerships at the highest level of city government. Though previous White mayors were willing to consult with CUL leaders because they were racial brokers with relatively moderate politics, these mayors rarely granted them decision-making roles. In Washington's administration and education summit, current and former CUL leaders became insiders with significant leadership roles, decision-making powers, and the political will of the mayor on their side.

Summit working groups were led by an interracial cross section of Chicago's business and civic elite. Gene Cartwright of Amoco Corporation led a group on hiring policy, Mary LaPorte of the Jane Addams Development Corporation led a group on literacy and job training, Philip C. Adams of Touche Ross & Co. led a group on school improvement goals, Laroche of the CUL led the group on community support, Consuelo Williams of the Chamber of Commerce and Kris Ronnow of Harris Bank led a group on business support options, and Dr. George Ayers, president of Chicago State University, led a group on school and college connections.[60] Each of these working groups drafted plans to reform different aspects of the public schools.

One of the major initiatives to come out of the education summit meetings during 1986 and early 1987 was the Chicago Learning Works Compact. It was based on the 1982 Boston Compact, in which the Boston business community guaranteed full employment for qualified graduates from Boston Public Schools provided that Boston Public Schools could demonstrate progress in decreasing the dropout rate, increasing attendance, improving students' basic skills, and increasing the number of students achieving permanent employment or pursuing postsecondary education upon graduation. Similar programs existed in Pittsburgh and Baltimore. Just as summit subcommittees were starting to meet regularly and draft proposals, Washington's reelection campaign was getting into full swing. Despite explicitly racist attacks, Washington ran again as an antimachine reform candidate and convincingly defeated Byrne and Vrdolyak. Washington's electoral win was based on solid backing from Black communities and more support from Latinxs and Whites than in 1983.[61]

After Washington's electoral victory, the education summit stalled as CPS and the Chicago Partnership for Education Progress (an offshoot of Chicago United) could not come to an agreement on the terms of the Learning Works Compact. What started as a cooperative relationship among summit members slowly began to fall apart under the pressure of disagreement and dissension between Black CPS superintendent Manford Byrd and Peter Willmott, the White CEO of Carson Pirie Scott and chairman of the Chicago Partnership for Education Progress.[62] The Partnership group proposed providing 1,000 jobs for CPS graduates in 1988 and increasing this number to 5,000 within four years, provided that CPS increase math and reading scores to meet the national average in three to five years and decrease the dropout rate to the national average within ten years. Byrd agreed to the Partnership's request for an external audit of the program and to work to meet national standards. However, he rejected the idea that the jobs or CPS's funds should be contingent upon meeting those goals: "I think it is patently unfair to tie employment of a graduate of our high schools to what 7th and 8th graders do.... I agreed that arriving at national norms is a desired goal. I did not see reaching that goal without an infusion of more funds." He also indicated that CPS would need an additional $100 million to meet the goals, requesting that business leaders lobby for these funds in the state capital. Willmott and members of the Partnership were incensed.[63]

Negotiations on the Learning Works Compact reached an impasse. CPS leaders felt that the government and the business community should work to increase funds for the school-to-jobs program; business leaders felt that CPS should engage in corporate restructuring to use its budget more efficiently. Willmott argued that education reform should follow the lead of business by "eliminating layers of administrative management, reprioritizing goals, reducing administrative expenses, and redeploying resources . . . meeting these effectiveness goals with the existing huge resource treasure chest." Byrd sought to protect schools and staff from outside interference while arguing for the increased financial support he believed the schools needed.[64]

The tensions in the summit between business and public sector representatives prefigured the coming move toward privatization. It was certainly not new for business interests to be involved, politically and financially, in public school matters at the municipal level. Since at least the Progressive Era, corporations and public interest groups had proposed contradicting visions of how public education systems should be managed. Even during the supposed era of government largesse during the Great Society, powerful private entities collaborated with the federal government to implement War on Poverty programs. WESP had been one such collaborative project between the University of Chicago, CPS, and TWO. The 1980 School Finance Authority group had allowed White corporate executives to consolidate power over the schools by overseeing CPS's finances and budget decisions. Now the summit's proposed Learning Works Compact provided a template for imposing private business practices on a public entity, allowing business executives to set accountability standards and further transferring management of public services into private hands.[65]

These entanglements between business and public entities in education were taking place alongside experiments in austerity and disinvestment in other parts of the public sector nationally. In addition to restructuring public education, the Reagan administration proposed drastic cuts to social services and considered measures to privatize health care, food aid, housing, transportation, federal credit markets, the U.S. postal service, defense contracting, correctional facilities, and other public services.[66] The Reagan administration defined privatization as "a strategy to shift the production of goods and services from the Government to the private sector in order to reduce Government expenditures and to take advantage of the efficiencies that normally result when services are provided through the competitive marketplace."[67]

Chicago business leaders' calls for assessments and accountability, competition, and choice resonated with the Reagan administration's push for increased private influence and control of public institutions broadly, and public education specifically. Nor were Black school administrators averse to adopting the language of corporate reform. In her first address at a Board of Education meeting in 1981, Chicago's first Black superintendent, Ruth Love, encouraged community participation in school matters while also suggesting that "the school system will be run similar to a major corporation. . . . Employees will have to be accountable for their work and function in a 'product-oriented' manner . . . recognizing that our products are educated students."[68]

While public education had been widely understood to be a nonnegotiable, publicly administered entitlement in previous decades, underinvestment and austerity policies put the future of education in doubt. In her January 1987 congressional testimony, CTU president Vaughn pointed to increasing debates over whether public education would remain a squarely government-funded-and-controlled entitlement. The Reagan administration proposed 33 percent and 29 percent cuts to the Department of Education for the 1983 and 1988 fiscal years, respectively, while proposing various education privatization measures. The U.S. Congress ended up appropriating 55 percent and 45 percent more funds, respectively, than the administration requested for those years. According to Vaughn's testimony, only "because of bipartisan support in the Congress" did a continued affirmation of the need for publicly funded and administered public schools remain, "at a time when the administration actively sought ways to reduce or eliminate most education programs."[69] While there was not yet consensus for a wholesale surrender to the logic of the market, corporate influence and experiments with the privatization of public entities were on the rise.

The 1980s were a seedtime for the corporatized management, assessment, and accountability mechanisms that would guide the next generation of school reform in the 1990s. Although the Chicago Learning Works Compact was never implemented, by the mid-1980s such a scheme could be proposed by business leaders and imagined by Democratic city leaders and school leaders as a baseline plan from which to initiate negotiations. A teachers' strike shifted attention away from the stalled debate, but privatization would return.

Education Summit Reboot: African Americans and 1980s School Reform
The Chicago teachers' strike in the fall of 1987 reignited passions over the urgent need to intervene with swift action to reform CPS. The CTU and CPS were unable to agree on the stipulations of teachers' contracts, instigating the

ninth teachers' strike in eighteen years. The nineteen-day strike closed schools for the first four weeks of the year, keeping 431,000 students out of school.[70] The strike provided an opportunity for parents and community groups to voice their longtime frustrations with CPS and demand a major overhaul of the system. At the close of the strike, CPS and CTU leaders agreed to participate in Mayor Washington's expanded and reconstituted education summit.

Veteran Black education reformers joined a multicultural array of individuals and new groups pressuring the mayor to enact more forceful school reform. Parents United for Responsible Education (PURE), an organization started on the North Side, staged protests and rallies at City Hall. The People's Coalition for Education Reform (PCER) brought together parents and social service agencies from the South Side and West Side to set up freedom schools around the city to educate children during the strike. Former CPS teacher, organizer, and African-centered school director Hannibal Afrik and CUL education director Dr. Gwendolyn Laroche had worked within the initial education summit to push for more community and parental involvement in schools. During the teachers' strike, TWO's Leon Finney, Black educator and organizer Dr. Sokoni Karanja, and others took this struggle to the streets, leading mass rallies to demand community and parent representation in school decision-making and improvements in CPS. A grassroots education reform coalition was developing with significant Black leadership, and Washington's summit would have to respond.[71]

The strike provided the impetus for Mayor Washington to take the lead on school reform. Pressured by parent and community protests, Washington became more directly involved in the final negotiations that ended the strike. CPS and CTU officials could claim few victories when they reached an agreement to end the strike on October 3, 1987. The teachers received a small raise in exchange for cutting 1,700 jobs. In addition, class size was reduced by two students per class in selected Black and Latinx schools. However, as part of the settlement, Washington convinced the CTU and CPS to come to the table to address more far-reaching school reforms as part of his revived education summit.[72]

On October 11, 1987, just eight days after the strike ended, Washington kicked off a reconstituted education summit process, with significantly greater parent and community participation. Over 1,000 education advocates, teachers, parents, students, organizers, and community members attended the event where Washington announced the creation of a Parent Community Council (PCC) that would join the summit group, along with members of the Board of Education, CTU, community and civic organizations, business leaders, and grassroots organizers. An article in the *Chicago Tribune* called the

MAYOR WASHINGTON'S
EDUCATION SUMMIT FORUM
UNIVERSITY OF ILLINOIS AT CHICAGO OCT. 11.1987
"BUILDING NEW PARTNERS IN EDUCATION"

Mayor Washington's Education Summit Forum, October 11, 1987. Harold Washington speaks to a large gathering of parents and community members as part of the reconstituted education summit after the 1987 CTU strike. With him are Frank Gardner (third from left), president of the Chicago Board of Education, and Jacqueline Vaughn, president of the CTU (second from left) (Peter J. Schulz photo; Chicago Public Library, Special Collections and Preservation Division, Harold Washington Archives & Collections, 1987-10-11)

event "the most remarkable gathering to focus on the Chicago public schools in at least 25 years."[73] The reconstituted summit set aside the failed Learning Works Compact and focused on broadly overhauling CPS's structure and the quality of the education that students received. This was reflected in the revived summit's proposed mission statement: "to improve the educational outcomes for all of Chicago's young people," to be determined by both their "educational achievements and their successful employment."[74]

The fifty-four members of the newly formed PCC were chosen from across the city and represented a diverse cross section of parents and community organizations from the city's communities.[75] Black and Latinx parents made up the majority of the parent representatives in the PCC, reflecting the demographics of CPS students. After the PCC held ten open forums across the city to solicit input from local parents and community members on what types of reforms they would like to see enacted in the public schools, Washington granted ten votes to the PCC, making it a powerful force in summit negotia-

POWER, RESOURCES, AND REPRESENTATION

tions. Washington then called on the PCC, CPS, CTU, and Chicago United to create school reform proposals to present and be debated at summit meetings, to form the basis of a comprehensive plan to take to the state legislature.[76]

These plans were made even more urgent in early November 1987 when CPS made national news. President Reagan's Secretary of Education William Bennett declared that Chicago's public schools were the worst in the nation, saying, "There can't be very many more cities that are worse. Chicago is pretty much it." Mayor Washington condemned Bennett's claims, given that the Reagan administration had worked to "dismantle public education in this country." Though CTU president Vaughn defended the excellence of Chicago educators, many students were unquestionably languishing in under-resourced schools, as Washington acknowledged: "We're not proud of this system. We're going to change it."[77] Washington was very clear that he wanted the parents of the PCC to lead this change and during the summit shape the school reform plan that he would present to the state legislature: "What the parents are saying is, they're going to clean it up. I'm with the parents."[78]

This level of parent and community involvement from the neighborhoods would have been unthinkable under previous administrations. But inclusion was a hallmark of Washington's administration. For many, Washington's efforts to reach out and incorporate the city's communities and neighborhood people into the governing process held the promise of transformation and a more racially and economically representative politics.[79]

Harold Washington's sudden and untimely death after a heart attack on November 25, 1987, struck a blow to the education summit process. The new mayor appointed by the city council, Black alderman Eugene Sawyer, kept the summit intact through the summer of 1988, but he did not have the power that Washington had to hold the summit coalition together.[80]

The education summit began to crumble during the winter and spring of 1988. Initially, many summit participants were committed to continuing on the path to school reform in homage to the deceased mayor. Yet while summit participants' commitment to solving problems in CPS did not diminish, it became clear that the bonds that united the summit participants to one another were tenuous. Without Washington's leadership to defuse tensions, personal, ideological, and political conflicts emerged within the diverse summit group.[81]

Representatives of the business community, most of whom were White, wanted to see improvements in the schools, but many others at the summit did not trust them. They were seen as outsiders, not privy to the day-to-day realities of CPS because most of them sent their children to private schools.

Business leaders did, however, have the potential to bring their capital and connections to the summit process, which would be particularly important when the time came to lobby the state legislature in Springfield.[82] Still, the power differentials between Chicago business leaders and Black communities generated moments of open conflict.

The idea of an oversight committee produced one such exchange. Willmott and other White Chicago business leaders suggested the need for an oversight board to monitor and evaluate any decentralization plan. In response to the suggestion of "oversight," all hell broke loose. Willmott did not realize at the time that many of the African Americans at the meeting would interpret the concept with such an intense reaction. The idea of oversight was not explicitly articulated with direct reference to race, but many Black leaders of varying political persuasions at the summit collectively recognized oversight as a racialized concept.[83]

The idea of White Chicago businessmen serving on a CPS oversight board evoked a long history of African Americans being granted the illusion of power before "oversight" took it away. This practice of conferring power with one hand and removing that very power with the other hand was reminiscent of what occurred when Ruth Love was named the first Black superintendent of schools at the same time that the power to manage the budget was taken away by the School Finance Authority, an oversight board. The perils of oversight also harkened back to the push for community control of schools in WESP. When the Woodlawn Community Board became majority Black and tried to make significant changes in Woodlawn schools, CPS leaders refused to grant the board the authority to make substantive changes. White oversight and political control over Black Chicago was an entrenched part of the Chicago Democratic machine that Harold Washington's electoral coalition had resoundingly rejected. Within Chicago's Black communities there was great concern that Black governmental power was again being obstructed—as just recently witnessed during the "council wars."

The suggestion of oversight of CPS or city government by Whites was particularly controversial at a time when the mayor, the general superintendent of CPS, the president of the Chicago Board of Education, and the CTU president were all African Americans. Summit participants James Deanes, a Black parent leader in the PCC, and William Farrow, a Black Board of Education member, were on opposite sides of many issues brought before the summit. However, on the racialized question of oversight, they found common cause and united to defend the legitimacy of Black political power. Both asserted that White elites had neglected CPS and allowed the schools to deteriorate on their watch. They worried that now that African Americans were in positions of authority, White elites wanted to use decentralization with oversight by White business leaders to regain power. Deanes objected that parent and business leaders in the summit had been working together productively "for hours and built this bond, and now you're going to destroy it? Why assume we'll mess it up? Why not assume we'll do fine?"[84] As with the oversight of the School Finance Authority and obstruction of Mayor Washington in the "council wars," this episode demonstrated the constraints that endured even after Black officials acquired positions of political power in a landscape plagued by institutional racism.

The education summit was also riven with intraracial class conflicts, exposing the cracks in the "unified" Black voting bloc that Washington had fused together in his mayoral campaign. The assembled Black summit participants did not share a monolithic politics or ideology motivating their support for reforming schools. In the summit, Black CTU president Vaughn fought fiercely to defend the pay, hours, and seniority status of the teachers she represented. CPS superintendent Manford Byrd Jr., a seasoned Black bureaucrat, defended the actions of CPS upper-level administration against the summit's reform recommendations for decentralization that would take power away from Byrd and other CPS administrators. Parents in the PCC were particularly critical of Byrd and CPS administration. Given the dismal performance of students within the school system, Byrd was not in a strong position to argue against proposed reforms. At times, as in the oversight debate, racial solidarity brought Black parents and CPS and CTU representatives together in defense of a common cause. However, Black parents in the PCC also called the Black middle-class leadership of CPS and the CTU to task and forged alliances with White business representatives against CPS and CTU leaders.[85]

Coretta McFerren, a Black education activist on the PCC with children and grandchildren who attended CPS schools, was among the most vocal forces in the fight for school reform. Part of the PCER group that brought together parents and community groups to protest for school reform during the CTU strike, McFerren was quite critical of CPS administrators whom she perceived to be more protective of their positions than they were interested in improving public schooling: "I do not blame them for the problems with education instituted while we were still being a maid in Miss Ann's house. But we do blame them for perpetuating the problem. As Black administrators in this city at this time, how can they so soon forget where they came from? We expect more of them, because we suffered to allow them to be where they are."[86] Here McFerren argues that racial inclusion and representation in the political process did not necessitate transformative or progressive politics. Black parents like McFerren were fed up with CPS bureaucracy and the excuses for Black underachievement in the schools given by Byrd, Vaughn, and Frank Gardner—all African Americans in authority positions over the schools. McFerren reminded the city's new Black political leadership that their positions were secured by decades of struggle and organizing in Black communities and that these were the communities to which they should be accountable.

Black political power was not necessarily transformative or radical. Political scientist Cedric Johnson contends that since the late 1960s, "insurgent demands for black indigenous control converged with liberal reform initiatives to produce a moderate black political regime and incorporate radical dissent into conventional political channels." Although Johnson specifically referenced post-1960s politics, Black Chicagoans were certainly familiar with this phenomenon vis-à-vis the Democratic machine's Black political operatives who had held Black Chicagoans at bay for decades with promises of patronage rewards. In her call for the city's Black political leadership to be accountable to Black communities in the 1980s, Coretta McFerren reprised Carmichael and Hamilton's charge in the late 1960s that Black power "must be that of a community, and emanate from there."[87] In Harold Washington, Chicago seemed to have a Black mayor who was the product of a community-based movement and who promoted racially and economically redistributive policies. However, Washington's tenuous progressive coalition crumbled after his death, and Black political access to power became increasingly divorced from accountability to a grassroots base and commitment to redistributive policies. Nonetheless, in the waning days of the education summit, McFerren and other parents advocated for a new era of community control and decentralization that would give local parents and communities more power in the schools.

As the spring of 1988 wore on, the PCC's influence ebbed, and conflict emerged over contrasting understandings of what decentralization actually meant. A predominantly White group of consultants from the Northwest Regional Educational Laboratory were hired to evaluate the feedback from PCC open forums that were held with parents in neighborhoods across the city. When PCC representatives reported back on the open forums, they relayed Chicago parents' desires for teachers who could teach children of color and working-class children to become academically successful and for an end to the persistent teacher strikes. When the hired consultants reported on the forums, they interpreted these same parents as indicating that they wanted to take over the school system. The former interpretation would suggest the need for higher academic standards and improved resources and support for curriculum and instruction at CPS schools; the latter interpretation suggested the need to decentralize educational governance and establish LSCs. According to one PCC participant, parents in the PCC never "even wanted to talk about breaking up the system." The PCC ultimately insisted that Black nationalist–leaning consultants from Northeastern Illinois University's Center for Inner City Studies review and synthesize the findings from the community open forums. These moments of racial and class-based misrecognition further eroded participants' faith in the summit process.[88]

Moreover, this episode demonstrates a broader problem of racialized "selective hearing." In explaining this phenomenon, scholars of the criminal justice system argue that, historically, Black communities' "calls for tough sentencing and police protection were paired with calls for full employment, quality education and drug treatment, and criticism of police brutality." In selectively hearing these demands, White policymakers "pointed to Black support for greater punishment and surveillance, without recognizing accompanying demands to redirect power and economic resources to low-income minority communities."[89] A similar phenomenon took place in education struggles. White-dominated nonprofits, business leaders, educational experts, consultants, and policymakers decoupled Black parents' calls for parent decision-making in schools from their accompanying demands for increased funds at the local, state, and federal levels to support multicultural curricula, bilingual education, improved wraparound support services, administrative transparency, and teacher, principal, and parent training programs. PCC parents insisted that the different elements of their plan must not be subdivided: "We have fashioned a report which cannot be disassembled and analyzed in a chart without robbing it of its soul. . . . You must not permit the report of the Parent Community Council to be destroyed by 'experts.'"[90]

With a parallel bill moving through the legislature, some education advocacy groups left the summit. Included in this group of defectors was Don Moore, a White Harold Washington supporter and the leader of the education research and advocacy group Designs for Change. Moore was a major organizer of the Alliance for Better Chicago Schools reform coalition that, beginning in the spring of 1987, ran parallel to the education summit in the state legislature. This group assembled to move a school reform bill through the state legislature and initially included a number of education advocacy groups and coalitions of parents from predominantly White neighborhoods in the city. During the fall and winter of 1987–88, following Washington's death, additional organizations and individuals joined the coalition to push reform legislation at the state level, including Coretta McFerren, Sokoni Karanja,

Benjamin Kendrick of the Marcy-Newberry Association, and Puerto Rican activist Tomas Sanabria of the Network for Youth Services.[91]

Despite the involvement of these prominent activists of color, the Alliance for Better Chicago Schools reform coalition was still perceived by some in the Black community as an effort led by White liberals to decentralize Black political power and strip African Americans of power over education in the city. In 1988, a school reform bill was passed at the state level but without many of the major provisions that Washington had hoped to include. The legislation, for example, did nothing to meaningfully fulfill Washington's initial intention of creating pathways for CPS students to obtain living wage jobs or tie reform measures to guaranteed funding increases for CPS. As with many initiatives from Washington's administration, school reform became another arena in which to wonder what could have been if he had lived.[92]

The 1988 Chicago School Reform Act did deliver an unprecedented degree of control to parents and communities through the creation of LSCs at each school that consisted of parents, teachers, community members, and the principal. LSCs had the ability to hire and fire the principal and power over the school's discretionary funds. Peter Willmott and other business leaders and education advocacy groups argued that LSCs would put pressure on principals to improve the quality of education at individual schools. In LSCs, poor, working-class, and middle-income African Americans and Latinxs obtained more access to decision-making power in their schools than ever before.[93]

However, many Black educational leaders interpreted this new decentralization of CPS in a different way. African Americans who had lived through previous struggles for community control and Black self-determination, including Barbara Sizemore, Conrad Worrill, and Carol Lee, saw the decentralization of the 1988 Chicago School Reform Act as a way to strip power from and undermine the professional authority of principals and CPS and CTU leaders now that more of those leaders were Black. The CUL, Operation PUSH, TWO, and other Black community groups were conspicuously absent from the deliberations that ultimately constructed the Chicago School Reform Act. Reflecting this, education scholar Dorothy Shipps concluded that the 1988 act "was a compromise, bearing the traces of every community interest involved, but deaf to the concerns of those outside the coalition, chiefly Blacks and educators — in many cases, one and the same."[94]

Reflecting back on administrative decentralization efforts in the 1960s, scholars have argued that decentralization coupled with more racial inclusion in administration masked the continued inequitable distribution of resources along racial lines. "School decentralization ... supported minority demands for power without redistributing educational benefits between Whites and Blacks. The institutional critique, coupled with inclusion, legitimized the unequal distribution of resources and the continued separation of the races in the name of transforming the bureaucracy."[95] In the 1980s, Black education reformers and Washington allies similarly insisted that decentralization had to be coupled with increased funding for Chicago's majority-Black and Latinx school system. However, White Chicago business leaders involved in the education summit opposed this. This ideological disagreement signaled yet another split in opinion amongst the participants in the now-defunct education summit group. The 1988 Chicago School Reform Act that passed in the state legislature did not require increased funds for CPS. As a result, a number of Black CPS staff members—stalwarts of Washington's Black middle-class base—were fired.[96]

RECONCILING TWO ERAS OF DECENTRALIZATION

Harold Washington was elected to office by a unified base of support in Chicago's Black communities. As an antimachine candidate running a reformist campaign, he appealed to many Chicagoans who felt marginalized and underserved by the Democratic Party organization that had run the city for almost half of a century. However, for African Americans he also embodied a different sort of promise. He was the personification of Black power and Black achievement, the answer to the unmet potential of the Civil Rights and Black Power movements. In earlier attempts to improve educational opportunities for Black youth in the city, groups and individuals had pursued strategies to desegregate the public schools, sidestep the public school system altogether by creating Black independent schools, and deliver control of schools to Black communities. Ultimately, the goal of each of these strategies was to improve the quality of education and life for Black children in the city. However, the power to actually create fundamental change in Black schooling was often stalled by the entrenched forces of the Chicago Democratic machine. While Washington was able to mobilize the unified support of Chicago's diverse Black constituencies in his 1983 and 1987 electoral victories, governing would prove more difficult.

Washington had to navigate racist obstruction in the city council and manage the divergent interests of groups within his own electoral coalition. The remaining White reactionary machine leaders in the city council prevented Washington from passing legislation and seating appointments for over three years. Once he was able to begin implementing reform, he encountered dissent within his coalition of supporters. Washington's first education summit was stalled because White business leaders and Black CPS superintendent Manford Byrd could not come to an agreement on a school-to-work program. After the 1987 teachers' strike, Washington expanded the scope of his education summit by including prominent business and civic leaders and CTU and CPS representatives, along with parents and representatives of community organizations. Yet conflicts in the summit between CTU and CPS officials, White business elites and African Americans, and Black parents and the Board of Education again exposed the limits of Washington's interracial and intraracial coalitions.

In the leadership vacuum after Washington's death in November 1987, the fissures within the education summit widened. The power of the PCC was marginalized as a parallel school reform movement, organized by education advocacy groups with more White leadership, rerouted Chicago school reform from the city to the state level. The resulting legislation created LSCs and decentralized CPS's power, while a segment of Washington's most loyal supporters, Black middle-class employees of the Board of Education, lost their jobs. Reflecting back on the era, Conrad Worrill speculated that Harold Washington would not have been in favor of LSCs had he lived. He argued that with African Americans occupying all of the most important posts in the school system, he did not think that Washington would have "given away the power."[97] But whom, exactly, was the power given away to? LSCs allowed poor, working-class, and middle-class African Americans and Latinxs more access to decision-making power in their schools than ever before—making good on Washington's initial promises to redistribute power from downtown to Chicagoans living in the city's neighborhoods.

Yet the political context of the movement for local control and decentralization of the schools in the 1980s was distinct from earlier community control efforts. Amidst an influx of federal funding for education projects, particularly in cities, Black community control activists in Chicago in the late 1960s and early 1970s asserted the right to determine how these government resources would be spent. In contrast, during the 1980s the Reagan administration cut back or eliminated funds that supported local school districts and social programs. At the local level, important, and nearly inverse, distinctions were at play as well. In the late 1960s, Black WESP community control organizers tried to wrestle power away from the autocratic operatives of Mayor Richard J. Daley's White-led Democratic machine. In the 1980s, Chicago's first Black mayor initiated the broad-based education summit that accelerated school reform and local control efforts.

The coalitions organizing for community involvement or control through decentralization during these periods were also distinct. In WESP, a coalition of local Black community organizers worked with the University of Chicago and CPS to explicitly design and implement a district-within-a-district under community control. The school reform efforts during the 1980s included a broader interracial coalition of civic leaders, business leaders, the CTU, CPS officials, education advocacy groups, and parents from across the city. Moreover, while WESP failed to deliver sustained community control to Black Woodlawn residents, the Chicago School Reform Act did indeed deliver a significant degree of decision-making power to parents, teachers, and community members at the school level citywide.

It is interesting, then, that many in Chicago's Black communities, and particularly some previous participants in WESP, interpreted the achievement of local control of schools in the 1980s so negatively. The education summit and 1988 Chicago School Reform Act was interpreted by many African Americans to be a project led by White liberal advocates, academics, and business leaders. Black community organizer and educator Sokoni Karanja, who was active in the coalitions that pushed for the Chicago School Reform Act at the state level, ultimately felt that he had become "a token on the leadership for the reorganizing of education in the city."[98] While the 1988 law decentralized CPS authority and distributed new school decision-making powers to Black parents, it was still perceived by some as a paternalistic White-led reform movement that stripped Black school leaders of their power. On the other hand, as WESP became an increasingly Black-led, Black-run endeavor, cooperation from CPS and White political authorities in the city gutted and eventually canceled the funding for WESP.

The devolution of the education summit after Washington's death exposed the limits of Black power when this power relied on the personality and negotiating talent of one individual rather than a more sustainable organizational infrastructure. Ultimately, we will never know whether Harold Washington would have been able to change the course of 1980s Chicago school reform. In the first iteration of the summit, he was unable to force CPS and the business community to come to an agreement on the Learning Works Compact, an issue he was passionate about. However, adherents to divergent and at times conflicting strands of political thought within Black communities also coalesced around Washington's mayoral run in order to elect the first Black mayor of Chicago. Washington had a unique ability to bring together groups of politically diverse and seemingly competing interests and approaches to education reform. However, depending on Washington as the force to manage school reform points to the danger of relying on a single charismatic leader to deliver political power and transformative change for an entire group of people. Washington's own inability to pass any meaningful legislation during the council wars—including any education reform measures—also demonstrates the insidiousness of systemic and institutionalized racism that undercuts the efforts of Black individuals.

During the 1970s and 1980s a new Black governing elite took control of schools in urban districts with Black majorities across the country. Historian Keeanga-Yamahtta Taylor argues that "Black faces in high places," however, did not guarantee improvements in Black communities and often served to direct political and economic gains toward Black elites, to the detriment of poor and working-class Black communities.[99] This new wave of Black urban officials came to power at the same time that federal, state, and local governments were cutting education budgets and cities' tax bases were decreasing as a result of continued White and middle-class flight and the decline of the industrial economy. Chicago had a more diversified economy that allowed the city to navigate this period of economic restructuring more "successfully" than its Rust Belt neighbors like Gary and Detroit. However, Black Chicagoans still disproportionately lost ground in their ability to secure employment and, if employed, experienced declines in their wages and employment conditions.[100] As in other cities, the brief period of Black governance in Chicago did not eliminate these economic and social problems.

When Harold Washington was elected, Chicago was the third-largest city in the country, with a larger school system than any other city where Black leaders presided over a Black majority in the schools. The Black professional class did see expanded opportunities during this period, while Black poor and working-class Chicagoans faced intensifying economic struggles. However, in Chicago this was also a moment when poor and working-class Black parents and community members gained more influence in the schools than at any previous time.

Political scientist Wilbur C. Rich notes that as new insiders to formal politics, Black officials presiding over predominantly Black school systems had to negotiate a shifting set of anxieties: "The old anxiety was that whites would continue to make it difficult for blacks to make school policy through financing and state law. The new anxiety was that black school administrators and leaders would fail to demonstrate any improvement in student performance, creating demand for yet another takeover. The most foreboding fear was that schools under black control might contribute to the economic paralysis of the black underclass."[101] Harold Washington's administration attempted to address this last concern through the education summit. It would be "yet another takeover" in the 1990s, however, building on corporate leaders' increasing influence in school affairs, that further elevated Chicago's school policies to the national stage.

In the 1980s and 1990s Chicago became a leader in two conflicting models of education reform and a bellwether city for school reform efforts nationally. In the late 1980s, under Black political leadership, Chicago embarked on a groundbreaking experiment with decentralization and local control of schools. This moment, however, was short lived. By the mid-1990s a different city leadership, led by a White mayor enacting "pinstripe patronage," gained national acclaim for reversing course and championing recentralization, mayoral control of schools, corporate management practices, and punitive accountability measures.[102] In the 1980s the Black parents and education reformers who participated in Washington's education summit had understandings of what local control and decentralization would mean for Black students and communities that differed from those of the prominent White education advocates who pushed the Chicago School Reform Act through the Illinois state legislature and the business leaders advocating for new standards and private oversight of schools. This form of racial misreading and "selective hearing" surfaced again, locally and nationally, in debates over "school choice," magnet schools, charter schools, and the privatization of public education in the 1990s.

{ 6 }

CORPORATE SCHOOL REFORM

Magnets, Charters, and the

Neoliberal Educational Order

As one of its first actions in the fall of 1989, the newly elected Local School Council at William H. Ray Elementary School unhappily put out an advertisement to replace its principal, Sara Spurlark. The child of educators, Spurlark (née Liston) was born in Winston-Salem, North Carolina, in 1923. After earning her undergraduate degree at the Hampton Institute and a master's degree at the University of Connecticut, she moved to Chicago in 1947 to start a Ph.D. program in biochemistry at the University of Chicago—an impressive feat given the significant racial and gender barriers. After getting married and having three children, Spurlark was hired to teach chemistry at the almost exclusively White Kelly High School in 1955. Years before government mandates for faculty desegregation, Spurlark became one of the first Black teachers integrating the school. Eleven years later, Spurlark transferred to the new Kenwood High School in the Hyde Park–Kenwood community. She was an assistant principal at Kenwood in 1968 when Black students at the school participated in citywide boycotts demanding more Black administrators, among other things. She served as principal at nearby Ray Elementary from 1979 to 1990 before retiring from CPS, though her retirement was in name alone.[1]

For the next fifteen years Spurlark worked in the educational research and advocacy field that had developed rapidly alongside Chicago's rise to national prominence as a model for educational decentralization, for local control, and, soon enough, for corporate reform and privatization. During this time, Spurlark cofounded the University of Chicago's Center for School Improvement, helped to open two charter schools, and served on the Chicago School Finance Authority. Into the 2000s, these types of institutions became symbols of a new era of corporate school reform nationally. Spurlark's entry into these spaces emanated from frustrations with the status quo and the public school system's limited ability to address the challenges facing Black and economically disadvantaged students. However, as a leader at the highest levels in these institutions, Spurlark was an anomaly. She was a veteran Black public school teacher and administrator in an urban education landscape increasingly shaped by White corporate, philanthropic, and foundation leaders.

Local control and decentralization of power in CPS during the late 1980s gave way to corporate-style recentralization in the 1990s, as business and government elites pursued dramatic restructuring schemes involving deregulation, privatization, and devastating reductions in social spending. In Chicago and nationally, a bipartisan group of corporate and political elites embraced the logics of neoliberalism and corporatism in projecting and exploiting perpetual crises in public education—of funding, achievement, and pedagogy—to transfer public funds to private institutions, attack teachers and their unions, and promulgate "school choice" programs.[2]

Though hastened by the financial crises of the 1970s and increased corporate involvement in schools in the 1980s, Chicago elites' embrace of corporatist education policies did not firmly take hold until the Daley administration in the 1990s. Democratic mayor Richard M. Daley's administration diminished the power of LSCs, opened the city's first charter schools, and implemented corporate-style school leadership models. City leaders reorganized CPS using organizational structures and management practices from the for-profit business world while increasingly applying market-based principles of competition, accountability, and privatization to the public education system. Chicago's school reform debates and policies were broadcast and adopted nationally through a number of prominent educators, education reformers, and policymakers, as well as a budding industry of educational research and advocacy organizations that opened in Chicago during the 1980s and 1990s.[3]

Black organizers, educators, and parents navigated, challenged, and at times contributed to the rise of neoliberal politics in the late twentieth and early twenty-first centuries. Black parents of varying class backgrounds took advantage of "school choice" models by vying for spaces in magnet schools and charter schools. Black teachers in traditional public schools witnessed privatization and the corporate reorganization of schools undercut their hard-fought political and professional gains. Meanwhile, new debates emerged over funding equalization, parent and community involvement in schools, accountability measures, and the value of neighborhood schools. While some Black education reformers directly challenged the encroachment of private interests into public domains, others sought to stake a claim on the emerging order.

African Americans' responses to the privatization of public services were largely based in histories that preceded the ascendency of neoliberalism. They reflected past struggles for racial justice and the historical denial of Black self-determination in urban public schools, rather than strong commitments to privatization or corporate logics. As this chapter reveals, the ideas, symbols, and educational practices developed by Black education reformers to create quality education for Black students were remixed by a corporate education reform movement. By obscuring and appropriating the intentions of a Black self-determinist politics of Black achievement in service of a neoliberal political agenda, corporate education reformers positioned urban education as a new market for private investment and capital accumulation. The brief moment, however symbolic, of Black political access and empowerment, local control, and redistribution ushered in by Harold Washington's administration was replaced by a corporate school reform agenda in the 1990s. Black self-determinist ideas of autonomy and achievement now converged with market-based ideas of choice and competition, and Black parents, educators, and community activists were forced to navigate a new political environment to improve education for Black students.

THE RACIAL REALIGNMENT OF SCHOOL REFORM: FROM LOCAL CONTROL TO CORPORATE REFORM

At the close of the 1980s, Chicago schools were a national model for experiments with democratic school governance, local control, and decentralization. The coalitions developed in Mayor Washington's education summit meetings and the Chicago School Reform Movement of the 1980s decentralized elements of CPS administration and increased local control over public schooling through the creation of LSCs. Impressively, approximately 312,000 people voted in the first LSC elections in October 1989, the result of coordinated organizing by community organizations, city officials, and the Board of Education. In LSCs, teachers, parents, and local community members at individual schools were able to manage the school's discretionary budget and hire and fire the principal, among other responsibilities. The new reform legislation also established a School Board Nominating Commission, made up of five mayoral appointees and twenty-three LSC community or parent members selected by their peers, who created lists of candidates from which the mayor must choose new Board of Education members. Sara Spurlark, a member of the commission, applauded this "unique exercise in democracy" and the significance of the commission and LSCs: "Those people who are most interested and involved in schools have the authority to pick the people who make important decisions for all schools. That happens nowhere else in this country." The nation took notice. In the words of an article from the *New York Times* in Octo-

The first LSC members are sworn in at the UIC Pavilion, November 2, 1989
(Photograph by Bill Stamets for *Catalyst Chicago*)

ber 1989, just after the first LSC elections, Chicago school reform "may be the
most sweeping decentralization plan ever attempted in the United States."[4]

However, even before the LSC elections, participants from Washington's
education summit were losing faith. James Deanes, a Black parent from the
West Side and chair of the education summit's PCC, contended that Black
parents were increasingly marginalized after Washington died in November
1987. At the same time, the White leaders of education research and advocacy
groups—particularly G. Alfred "Fred" Hess of the Chicago Panel on Public
School Policy and Finance and Don Moore of Designs for Change—took on disproportionately more power in shaping the 1988 Chicago School Reform Act.
Moore was a dedicated education researcher who advocated for the right of disenfranchised communities to local democracy through LSCs. For his part, Hess
viewed Deanes as part of an encouraging new group of Black parent leaders
rising through grassroots struggles for school reform. Hess saw Deanes and
this group as a challenge to the established Black leadership of organizations
like TWO and the CUL that were "paralyzed by the need to take sides" between
insurgent parents and the newly all-Black officials presiding over the schools
during the 1987 teachers' strike. Deanes disputed this analysis using Black self-
determinist arguments: "I didn't emerge from anything! . . . I was already here.
. . . Fred Hess can't speak for Blacks. . . . He isn't Black. He can't describe Black
leadership. . . . He cannot choose our leaders. We choose our leaders!"[5]

While perhaps not the appropriate messenger, Hess was right that 1980s
Chicago school reform efforts exposed divides among Black activist parents,
teachers, politicians, and established community groups like TWO and the

CUL. The interracial and intraracial tensions witnessed in the education summit process persisted into the actual implementation of decentralization, leaving many Black reformers with lingering mixed feelings.[6]

On one hand, decentralization through LSCs allowed active Black parents to play a significant role in the day-to-day decision-making in their schools. Five years after the 1988 School Reform Act, 40 percent of schools in Chicago had new principals selected by LSCs. LSCs impacted staffing by creating 3,365 new positions using schools' discretionary funds. LSC members also made efforts to transform curricula. Implementing an African-centered education within public schools may not have been viable in the 1970s, but in 1990, for example, Black parent and LSC chair Herman W. Baker Jr. worked to implement an Afrocentric curriculum at Harlan High School on the South Side.[7]

On the other hand, many Black education reformers were upset that the final 1988 Chicago School Reform Act did not include the commitment to sustained increases in state funding for CPS, which they had sought. While parents and community members might have more input, they were still making decisions with inadequate budgets in under-resourced schools. Longtime Black organizer Nancy Jefferson of the Midwest Community Council hyperbolically declared, "School reform in Chicago is the biggest sham that has ever been perpetrated on Black Americans."[8]

Debates over parents' roles in LSCs also exposed class divides. In the education summit, parents like Coretta McFerren had called out Black political officials and school leaders for upholding a status quo that failed poor and working-class Black children and communities. Meanwhile Arthur Turner, a Black Illinois state representative from the West Side, criticized LSCs using the same tired tropes of Black pathology—centered on the failures of Black women/motherhood—that White policymakers and social scientists had used for decades to disenfranchise poor Black people and blame them for their economic conditions: "We're saying, 'Hey, this young girl who's 13 today, whose kid will be in school five years from now—we're telling her that she can run the local schools. She will determine whether the principal is qualified and what the curriculum is.' Mind you, she has already dropped out of school. I didn't think this concept would work in Lawndale/Garfield or any other extremely poor community. In upwardly mobile communities, it has a better chance of working."[9]

Parents, teachers, and community members certainly needed training to perform their functions on LSCs, even more so when corporate and government funds for training were reduced following the first LSC elections. However, this Black elected official's assertion that young Black women and parents living in poverty—including his constituents—were unfit for self-governance undermined visions of community-based participatory democracy and Black self-determination that Black education reformers had proffered in the 1960s and 1970s.[10]

Corporate Reform and Mayoral Control

Amidst continuing strife over the implementation of school reform, Richard M. Daley was elected mayor in 1989, nearly thirteen years after his father had died in office. The younger Daley's electoral coalition differed significantly from Harold Washington's. As sitting Cook County state's attorney, Daley had defeated the incumbent appointed mayor, Eugene Sawyer, along with Black alderman Timothy Evans and Washington's old antagonist Edward Vrdolyak. While Daley ran as a self-proclaimed reform candidate, he was tagged "Son of Boss" by the media and retained strong ties to his father's machine. At this time the city's population was roughly 45 percent White, nearly 40 percent Black, and 20 percent Latinx. In contrast to Washington's coalition of African Americans, a significant group of Latinxs, and a smaller segment of White "lakefront liberals," Daley's electoral victory relied on liberal reform-leaning elements and conservative machine-loyal elements, robust White voter turnout, support from the city's growing Latinx communities, and noticeably few votes from Black Chicagoans. Once in office, Daley further courted Latinx communities by appointing Latinxs to posts in his administration and making appeals to a shared immigrant history between White ethnics and Latinxs. As Latinx voters' electoral loyalty to Daley grew, his limited Black voter support became less consequential.[11]

Daley forged strong ties with Chicago's business community, a constituency that Washington had struggled to incorporate, and Daley rewarded elite business leaders with "pinstripe patronage"—business-friendly public policies and political favoritism. Daley reversed Washington's efforts at redistributing power and development from the downtown elite to the city's neighborhoods. According to education scholar Dorothy Shipps, "Ninety-five percent of new development in the 1990s took place in seven of the city's seventy neighborhoods—those in the Loop and surrounding areas."[12]

Daley's school decisions revived familiar racial controversies. Despite the naming of CUL leader James Compton as interim president of the Board of Education, in Daley's administration the CUL was pushed back into its traditional role as mediator between Chicago's business and governing elites and Black communities. Daley refused to appoint a Black majority to the Board of Education, despite the fact that Black students accounted for nearly 60 percent of CPS students. Daley's appointed school board terminated General Superintendent of Schools Manford Byrd and replaced him with Ted Kimbrough, a Black school administrator from Compton, California. As with Ruth Love's appointment several years earlier, the replacement of Byrd with another Black non-Chicagoan "outsider" generated protests by Jesse Jackson of Operation PUSH and Leon Finney of TWO. However, Byrd was also criticized by many— including Black Chicagoans—for his resistance to making major changes in the schools. By the time Byrd was actually terminated, lots of parents and education advocates were not particularly sorry to see him go.[13]

Many Black education reformers understood Daley's actions as a challenge to one of the crowning achievements of the Washington era: the brief moment when there was simultaneously a Black mayor, a Black general superintendent of CPS, a Black president of the Board of Education, a Black CTU president, and multiple Black under-deputies. Through Black representation in city government, these education reformers saw the potential to shift Black power from Black community-based organizations into the formal political authority of municipal government. Anything that undercut this new authority granted to African Americans in positions of power was seen as threatening.[14] Alex Poinsett, an editor at Ebony magazine, interviewed dozens of Black activists and community leaders, both supporters and critics of Chicago's school reform plans, and cataloged their concerns in May 1990: "Some Black activists fear that current events in the $2.9 billion Chicago school industry may be part of a larger scenario to rid the city of any vestiges of Black political power. Never again a Black mayor, they fear. Never again a Black superintendent, unless he/she is a figurehead. Never again a Black Board president, unless he/she only fronts for other interests. Never again the substantial concentration of power in the hands of Black bureaucrats. And so, as critics charged early on, school reform may turn out to be, at best, 'school deform.'"[15] Daley's increasingly corporate-style school reform policies heightened these linked concerns about racial representation, political power, and the economic potential of public education as an expanding and lucrative "industry" for private interests.

In 1995 the Illinois state legislature passed the Chicago School Reform Amendatory Act that eliminated or blunted many of the 1988 reforms, recentralizing CPS under Mayor Richard M. Daley's control. The Illinois house gained a Republican majority in 1994, riding the national conservative tide that put both the U.S. House and Senate in Republican control two years after Democrat Bill Clinton was elected president. In January 1995, Republican governor Jim Edgar indicated that he would not help CPS close a projected $300 million budget gap: "It's up to the Chicago schools to look internally at ways to cut costs. If they expect to be bailed out by the state, it isn't going to happen. The day of reckoning is coming." As with the budget shortfall in 1979 that paved the way for the School Finance Authority, Republican state lawmakers and business associations seized on this looming financial crisis to push a corporate agenda for the schools. They drafted new education legislation that would implement a corporate management structure and punitive accountability practices in CPS, weaken the teachers' union, and facilitate privatization.[16]

The resulting 1995 legislation gave Mayor Daley unprecedented power over the schools. It eliminated parts of the 1988 Chicago School Reform Act that facilitated direct parent and community input in selecting school board members. This stripped the powers of the School Board Nominating Commission that parents, community members, and appointees, including Sara Spurlark, had used to directly create the pool of potential board members for the first time. Instead, the new legislation charged the mayor with handpicking a new "Reform Board of Trustees." The law eliminated the oversight powers of the School Finance Authority and requirements for a balanced budget, giving Daley and his chosen corporate management team for the schools greater power to borrow from the teachers' pension fund and to decide how to allocate almost all school funds from the state, including some funds previously managed by LSCs. The law also made it easier to outsource school positions and services, eliminate teaching positions, and dramatically limit teachers' ability to strike and bargain over issues beyond wages and benefits. While Daley disagreed with Republican lawmakers about funding, he was not opposed to many of these reforms and cooperated in crafting the final legislation.[17]

While Republicans were more closely associated with unfettered free markets, it was not unprecedented for Democrats and liberal government officials to use the language of business to discuss public education reforms. In 1966, during the Democratic Johnson administration, U.S. Commissioner of Education Harold Howe II promoted the benefits of teacher merit pay, as opposed to pay based on seniority, in a speech to the American Federation of Teachers titled "Education as a Business and Desire." This was not, however, a wholesale endorsement of shifting responsibility for providing education away from the public sector to the private sector. In the same speech Howe acknowledged that the nation has "paid lip service to the importance of universal education … but without demonstrating a corresponding readiness to pay adequately for this service which it proclaims essential." Nonetheless, as detailed later in this chapter, as early as the 1960s and 1970s the seeds for bipartisan acceptance of corporate practices in public education were being sown.[18]

Daley's embrace of corporate management, accountability regimes, and centralized mayoral power over schools demonstrates how bipartisan support for corporate school reform and privatization had crystallized by the 1990s. State Republicans were willing to turn over control of the schools to Daley because they saw him as a nonideological Democrat amenable to Republican policies. Eschewing reformers' visions of decentralization and local control, Daley embraced mayoral control: "Mayors need to set the standards for the community, to give people direction so that they can make a difference. That is why it is important for mayors to be accountable."[19]

Daley oversaw the corporate reorganization of CPS—recentralizing power over schools into the mayor's office, appointing a new "Board of Trustees" (Board of Education) for the schools, privatizing and outsourcing school positions and services, imposing new accountability benchmarks, and implementing a "corporate management team" for the schools with a CEO, CFO, and other business-oriented officers. Daley elevated two loyalists without relevant education experience as the new president of the Reform Board of Trustees (his chief of staff Gerry Chico) and chief executive officer of CPS (his budget director Paul Vallas). With Daley's support, Vallas imposed managerial reforms that required rigid lesson plans, increased reliance on standardized testing, and ended social promotion in CPS schools.[20]

Though not the first U.S. city led by a Democratic mayor to embrace mayoral control, Chicago became a model for the nation. Where Harold Washington had to contend with the Reagan administration's hostile policies toward cities and urban education, Mayor Richard M. Daley had a much cozier relationship with Bill Clinton's administration. A decade after Reagan's education secretary called Chicago's schools the worst in the nation, in the late 1990s President Clinton repeatedly held up Chicago's school reforms under Daley and Vallas as a model for the nation: "I want what is happening in Chicago to happen all over America. . . . What is working in Chicago must blow like a wind of change into every city in every school in America." Despite these national proclamations of success, the mayoral takeover of CPS most punitively impacted poor Black and Latinx CPS students, dramatically tempered the power of LSCs, and challenged teachers' political power.[21]

The Pitfalls of Progress for Black Teachers

Daley's efforts to increase efficiency and cut government costs through privatization particularly impacted Black public sector workers. As mayor, Daley privatized dozens of public services, including janitorial and maintenance services, car towing, parking enforcement, and drug addiction treatment, using outside private contractors.[22] Black employees held a disproportionate number of the positions targeted for privatization. In 1992, prior to gaining mayoral control of schools, Daley laid off 773 city employees, 61 percent of whom were Black. In the schools, cuts in service and support staff, paraprofessional positions, and maintenance workers also disproportionately impacted African Americans. For example, in 1991, 68 percent of lunchroom workers were Black (2,247 Black workers, 82 percent of whom were Black women). By 1996, the number of Black lunchroom workers had been reduced by nearly a quarter. As one Black activist observed, "We have to cut the fat. That sounds good. But when you look, it's evident that they didn't cut fat. They cut Black." While Daley vehemently denied any racial bias, Black workers disproportionately lost their jobs both because of the types of positions that were privatized and due to "last hired, first fired" policies, which disproportionately affected Black workers who had only more recently gained access to jobs because of historically racist employment practices. Couched in a color-blind language of efficiency, these types of practices formed the backbone of persistent institutional racism. At the beginning of Daley's term in 1989, 48 percent of CPS teachers were Black. In 2010, the year before Daley left office, for the first in more than forty years, less than 30 percent of CPS teachers were Black.[23]

The CTU was divided over the mayoral takeover of CPS. Jacqueline Vaughn, the first African American and woman to serve as CTU president, passed away from breast cancer in 1994. Thomas Reece, the CTU's White vice president, took over as president after Vaughn died. Though committed to education, Reece was less confrontational, public oriented, and connected to rank-and-file teachers than Vaughn. Instead of attacking Daley, Reece directed the CTU's ire at the state's Republican governor and legislators: "We should not be sorry that the control of our system has been transferred to City Hall. The mayor of our city cares more about our school system than any of the non-Chicagoans who wrote [the 1995 Amendatory Act]." Reece was willing to negotiate so long as Daley continued to increase teachers' wages and benefits and advocate for CPS teachers at the state level. Daley and his school appointees were likewise willing to work with the CTU to maintain labor peace and consistently increased teacher pay. CTU leadership credited the mayor and his team for easing or working around some of the more punitive parts of the state reform bill and continuing to pressure the state legislature for more school funding.[24]

Despite this rosy outlook, in the ensuing years Daley's and Vallas's reforms stripped teachers, and particularly Black teachers, of much of their professional discretion in the classroom. In the fall of 1996, Vallas designated nearly one-fifth of CPS schools as schools in educational crisis and put them on "probation," largely based on students' test scores. Once the schools were on probation, Vallas could sanction them, dissolve LSCs, require schools to use support services from private consultants, or fire principals, administrators, staff, and teachers, requiring them to reapply for their jobs through a process of school "reconstitution." These positions could then be given to teachers who went through alternative fast-track certification processes or be outsourced to private partners. The new policies directly undercut Black teachers' employment gains of the previous decades. Researchers found that between 1997 and 2010, new teachers hired in Chicago through reconstitution and other "turnaround" models "were more likely to be White, younger, and less experienced," without permanent certifications, than "teachers at the schools before the intervention." In many sanctioned schools, CPS required remaining teachers to use strict "back-to-basics" mandated lesson plans that stifled teachers' freedom and creativity in the classroom. As the majority of schools slated for remediation or on probation were predominantly Black, these policies had the greatest effects on Black students and teachers. These schools were left with the least democratic governance, least teacher autonomy, and least inventive and stimulating curriculum, compounding other forms of disinvestment and disenfranchisement in Black communities.[25]

Black teachers were relatively defenseless, having lost the organizing connections within Black communities that had enabled predecessors like Lillie Peoples to fight back. Peoples blamed this demobilization of Black teachers, in part, for the union's decreased influence and decline in moral authority. During the 1960s and 1970s, Black teachers had organized outside the CTU in multiple groups, such as Operation Breadbasket's Teachers' Division, the Black Teachers Caucus, Concerned FTBs, and Teachers Committee for Quality Education. By organizing themselves as Black workers and on behalf of Black students and Black communities, Black teachers earned the authority to speak for community concerns in addition to issues of wages and benefits. Once they were incorporated into the CTU, Black teachers largely stopped organizing outside the union.[26]

Scholars have suggested that the precarious position and mainstream political incorporation of the Black middle class weakened the transformative potential of Black politics.[27] Thanks to Black teachers' earlier struggles and their eventual incorporation into the CTU, Black educators constituted an important base within the Black middle class. However, Black middle classness was always more materially and socially precarious than White middle classness. Researchers have produced evidence backing colloquial assertions of a "Black tax," the notion that because of White supremacy, Black people have

CUL, CPS, and Merrill Lynch officials celebrate their partnership at a CPS elementary school (ca. late 1980s–early 1990s). Chicago's Democratic political leadership opened the door for corporate leaders to assert more influence over schools through the School Finance Authority, corporate adopt-a-school programs, business leaders' prominent participation in Mayor Washington's education summit, and increasingly, public-private partnerships and the privatization of public services in the 1990s (Chicago Urban League Records, University of Illinois at Chicago Library, CULR_04_0224_2513_003)

to be twice as good or work twice as hard in order to go half as far or get half as much as White people. Historian Andrew Kahrl documents how Black homeowners shouldered "a heavier tax burden (for inferior public services) than whites," through discriminatory overassessment of property taxes in Chicago. White investors and tax buyers reaped million-dollar profits from the property tax delinquencies that resulted from this literal Black tax. The vulnerability of the Black middle class in a society undergoing economic restructuring incentivized middle-class African Americans like teachers to distance themselves from poorer Black communities by physically moving farther away from poverty and disinvestment or by rhetorically distancing themselves using White supremacist discourses to denigrate their Black poor and working-class neighbors and relatives as pathological. The decline in stable job opportunities for Black people in industry and other parts of the private sector made public sector jobs like teaching even more important for Black workers. The increasing economic and social precarity of late-twentieth-century capitalism discouraged Black middle-class teachers from bucking the system and challenging the status quo.[28] According to Lillie Peoples, after Vaughn's death, with no Black radical or progressive teacher-based organizing force outside the union, there was no one to challenge the rise of conciliatory union leaders. Peoples lamented that Black teachers "couldn't see the bigger picture that no matter whether there was a fight imminent, we should always stay organized . . . as a group."[29] The vacuum created as Black teachers withdrew from actively organizing in the communities they served allowed corporate opponents of unions to frame teachers as greedy exploiters of the public sector who were more concerned with collecting paychecks than teaching students. While collaborating with Chicago's emergent corporatist leadership may have initially seemed expedient for the CTU, the neoliberal turn in education proved disastrous for Black teachers, students, and communities.

The corporatized CPS leadership model that emerged in the 1990s increased public-private partnerships, cemented reforms based on "choice," and encouraged the growth of the charter school system. Yet corporate elites and neoconservatives were not the only groups who proposed privatization and alternative organizational management structures for schools.[30] While groups of Black education reformers opposed these measures, some Black education reformers participated. At times, the earlier struggles for desegregation, community control, and Black independent schools had even produced ideas that borrowed from corporate organizational practices. One such example was the "Effective Schools" model.

EFFECTIVE SCHOOLS:
ORGANIZATIONAL MANAGEMENT FOR BLACK ACHIEVEMENT

Ronald Edmonds, a Black educator, scholar, and school district administrator in New York, pioneered the Effective Schools Movement as part of the broader shift away from desegregation in the wake of the 1960s. Previously a desegregation advocate, like many other Black education reformers he eventually lost faith in desegregation strategies. He argued that poor Black children could learn effectively in the predominantly Black schools that they already attended.[31]

The Effective Schools model identified conditions and characteristics that produced Black academic success and sought to replicate them. Its advocates argued that the organizational and social-psychological context of schools could be manipulated to provide an environment in which all students could succeed regardless of family background, race, or socioeconomic status.[32] Edmonds embraced a politics of Black achievement. For him the failure to educate poor children of color was a problem of political will, not a problem of the purported uneducability of students related to the presumed pathology of poor families: "It seems to me, therefore, that what is left of this discussion are three declarative statements: (a) We can, whenever and wherever we choose, successfully teach all children whose schooling is of interest to us; (b) We already know more than we need to do that; and (c) Whether or not we do it must finally depend on how we feel about the fact that we haven't so far."[33]

Edmonds's arguments paralleled those of community control advocate Barbara Sizemore. Sizemore, Edmonds, and a national network of Black education reformers argued that the failure to replicate to scale the practices of schools that produced high levels of Black educational achievement was a problem of collective political will. For Sizemore, this demonstrated U.S. society's lack of concern for Black children and reinforced racist ideas that linked Black inferiority to notions of Black cultural pathology or an innate biological lack of abilities. Like Edmonds, Sizemore researched the conditions and organizational characteristics of schools that produced high levels of Black academic achievement. She implemented a set of principles for Black student achievement in CPS schools—the "structured ten routines." The structured ten routines and Effective Schools correlates were based on similar tenets. The prescriptions for Effective Schools also reflected specific innovations in organizational management practices used in commercial production.[34]

The Effective Schools Movement drew on ideas developed by W. Edwards Deming, who worked to revive the postwar economy of Japan through organizational philosophies that came to be known as Total Quality Management and Statistical Product Control. To increase production and profits, these philosophies require strong organizational leadership to explicitly center all facets of an organization's structure and culture on the product quality. They emphasize efficient production and close attention to consumers' needs and desires, but rather than focusing strictly on outputs, these organizational philosophies involve constant data collection and evaluation of all aspects of the production process and different departments within the organization. After taking root in postwar Japan, these organizational management practices were more fully embraced by U.S. businesses in the 1980s, before informing the Effective Schools model.[35]

Elements of Ronald Edmonds's approach to ensuring the quality of schooling were very similar to Deming's process for ensuring the quality of products. Deming identified fourteen organizational principles of productive organizations; Edmonds identified a similar set of key principles or "correlates" of effective (quality) schools. For example, Edmonds's principles for "Clear and Focused School Mission," "Frequent Monitoring of Student Progress," and strong "Instructional Leadership" mirrored Deming's principles of "constancy of purpose," "constantly analyze all results," and "demonstrate leadership from the top."[36] The Effective Schools correlates addressed issues that were directly under the control of school personnel, just as commercial organizational management principles focused on areas under the control of plant managers.

By focusing primarily on issues under the control of schools, rather than attending to the impacts of structural inequality, poverty, and racism that shaped students' lives inside and outside the schools' walls, Edmonds and Effective Schools advocates rejected the Coleman Report and others that "repudiate urban school reform as an instrument of social equity." Edmonds responded to critics who argued that schools did not have the institutional capacity to overcome class disparities: "While recognizing the importance of family background in developing a child's character, personality, and intelligence, I cannot over emphasize my rejection of the notion that a school is relieved of its instructional obligations when teaching the children of the poor."[37] However, by asserting solutions that required relatively little additional funding and were generally confined within the walls of the schools themselves, rather than linking school issues to larger-scale calls for economic redistribution and racial reparations, Effective Schools–type reforms attracted the interest of policymakers and business interests. The idea that students and their learning outcomes should be treated like commercial products to be monitored, evaluated, and more efficiently produced would gain currency in the coming decades.[38]

The defense-business nexus that produced new ideas for organizational management also influenced Barbara Sizemore's work. Political scientist and U.S. Defense Department policy advisor Graham Allison developed the Organizational Process Model in a study of the Cuban Missile Crisis. Sizemore used the Organizational Process Model to identify the routines that created high-achieving schools, arguing that the "promise of effective schools research" lay in its ability to identify the organizational structures and routines in schools that effectively taught poor Black children and then replicate these practices at schools that were failing.[39]

The Effective Schools Movement permeated national educational policies during the 1980s and 1990s. Particularly in the rush to create education reform plans after the 1983 Nation at Risk report, a growing group of education scholars, organizations, and policymakers looked to Total Quality Management and other private sector approaches. In 1981, Black CPS superintendent Ruth Love's assertion that "educated" students should be the "products" of the school system suggested the growing popularity of this approach to public education reform. Black Democratic U.S. congressman Augustus Hawkins, head of the House Education and Labor Committee, also promoted the Effective Schools model. While Black education reformer Ronald Edmonds was a key developer of the Effective Schools model, the Effective Schools Movement was racially diverse and widely embraced. In 1988 the National Education Association initiated a study that formally merged Deming's principles with the Effective Schools correlates.[40]

In Chicago, a number of researchers and advocacy groups promoted the benefits of Effective Schools strategies. Proponents included Don Moore and Designs for Change and Fred Hess and the Chicago Panel on Public School Policy and Finance. Beginning in the early 1980s, Moore used the Effective Schools correlates to inform his work helping CPS parents to evaluate and shape the education in their children's schools. In 1991, Hess argued that Chicago was "the foremost example of a large urban district that successfully implemented the Effective Schools Process." In the early 1990s, White University of Chicago sociologist and school reform researcher Anthony Bryk took up the mantle of Effective Schools in his suggestions for "five essential supports" to improve student performance. However, when Daley and Vallas assumed control in 1995, Bryk opposed Vallas's changes to CPS curriculum and policy that relied on scripted lesson plans and limited indicators of student learning and school effectiveness. Still, Effective Schools advocates retained significant influence in CPS and a growing number of educational research and advocacy institutions.[41]

An industry of educational research centers, advocacy organizations, watchdog groups, and support services proliferated in Chicago during the 1980s and 1990s. Bryk helped to found the University of Chicago's Center for School Improvement in 1988 and the Consortium on Chicago School Research in 1990. Providing information and reports related to implementation of the 1988 School Reform Act, Chicago developed a robust network of education researchers, advocates, journalists, and new publications, like Linda Lenz's *Catalyst: Voices for Chicago School Reform*, that amplified stories of Chicago school policies and inequities. CTU leaders were wary of what CTU president Reece called a "reform subculture," requiring the constant churning of change to legitimate their research, advocacy work, and employment. Though many of these new groups were sincere, Reece warned teachers that "if a person or a group's livelihood depends on reform," or "if they have a big job or a big grant in mind for themselves, we must be very careful that the brightly colored paper on the gift they're offering doesn't cover an empty box."[42]

The burgeoning educational research and advocacy sector maintained an ambiguous relationship with Chicago's Black communities. The organizations and centers launched from the 1980s school reform era were predominantly White-led, yet they studied Black schools and communities. Sara Spurlark, who founded the Center for School Improvement (later renamed Center for Urban School Improvement) along with Bryk and Sharon Greenberg, was one of the few Black leaders in the upper echelon of these institutions. With partners at the center, Spurlark crafted an ambitious new literacy program in 1993 embracing the ethos of the Effective Schools Movement to improve teachers' instruction and principals' leadership. Through this work, Bryk credited Spurlark with helping the University of Chicago improve its infamously poor relationship with Chicago's Black communities.[43]

Once a leader of Woodlawn's community control efforts, in the 1990s Sizemore returned to Chicago as dean of DePaul University's School of Education and sided with Vallas in his disagreements with White liberal architects of the 1988 Chicago School Reform Act. In WESP, Sizemore had used a community control strategy to restructure power relationships among parents, students, teachers, administrators, and community members. But Sizemore's end game was always increasing Black academic achievement. By the 1990s, it seemed to her that Vallas's plan to recentralize CPS administrative power with a focus on educational gains and accountability was the most appropriate way to achieve that very goal. Over time, however, she came to feel that Vallas spent too much time fighting symptoms—dropouts and poor attendance—instead of addressing what she saw as the root of the problem: the lack of culturally relevant and differentiated curricula and a pedagogy of low expectations for low-income students. For Sizemore, these were the sources of Black academic failure.[44]

It is striking that Sizemore, a community control champion, supported Vallas and opposed the outcomes of Chicago school reform efforts in the 1980s, arguably the most democratic educational process implemented for local control in Chicago's history. During her career Sizemore was alternately perceived as a race-traitor allied with anti-integrationist superintendent Willis, a radical Black Power community control advocate, a militant community-based researcher, and an ally of the corporate reorganization of public schools. Underlying these shifting characterizations, however, Sizemore was consistent in her relentless quest to foster black achievement and demonstrate the fallacy of ideas of Black inferiority.

The processes for identifying the characteristics of effective Black schools and the organizational management principles for Black student achievement developed by Edmonds, Sizemore, Spurlark, and Bryk paralleled corporate reformers' desire to reorganize school management. Although emanating from different histories and motivations, these reformers all found flaws in the Coleman Report's suggestion that schools, as institutions, lacked the capacity to improve the achievement of low-income Black students. Organizationally, they also opposed the Coleman Report's suggestion that students should be evaluated on the end-product educational outcomes they produced. Achievement models derived from corporate organizational models suggested that student progress should be measured at multiple points along the way. To that end, Edmonds and Effective Schools proponents advocated multifaceted modes of assessments, including portfolio-style student work samples, mastery checklists, and teacher-generated tests.[45]

However, much like with the "selective hearing" that decoupled decentralization plans from mandatory school funding increases in the 1980s, Effective Schools practices were rarely implemented as a total package. The stress placed on frequent assessment opened the door for an overuse of standardized tests. Test preparation and administration were becoming a multimillion-dollar industry and a new site for capital investment. At the same time that organizational management strategies modeled after the private sector were gaining traction in the Effective Schools Movement, models of educational equity were giving way to models of "choice" through the proliferation of magnet schools.

MAGNET SCHOOLS: FROM DESEGREGATION TO CHOICE

Magnet schools are public schools that specialize in a particular subject area or mode of instruction. Some might implement Montessori pedagogy; others might specialize in fine arts, world languages, or math and science. Some school districts require students to test into these specialty schools; others grant admission using some form of lottery system. School officials hoped that the unique curricula of these schools would turn them into "magnets" for a racially and economically diverse set of students and encourage desegregation. In urban districts, magnet schools were created to attract and retain White students in city public schools and stem the tide of White students leaving increasingly non-White urban public schools. To this end, magnet schools did not normally require students to live within a specific neighborhood school boundary.[46]

During the 1970s, urban school systems increasingly used magnet schools

POWER, RESOURCES, AND REPRESENTATION

as desegregation tools. The first of these kinds of schools opened in the late 1960s in Tacoma, Washington, and Boston and quickly spread across the country. In 1975, federal courts confirmed that magnet schools could be used to strategically promote desegregation, at the time one of the few desegregation tools still permitted by the courts. By 1991, there were more than 2,400 magnet schools and programs serving more than 1.2 million students in more than 230 school districts across the country.[47]

Magnet schools became a central feature of Chicago's desegregation efforts. The first magnet school in the city, Walt Disney Magnet Elementary School on the North Side, opened in 1969. Disney expanded in 1973 to a large campus designed to serve 2,400 preschool through eighth grade students using a pod structure and educational model without traditional grade levels, much like the nongraded system instituted by Barbara Sizemore at Dvorak school in the early 1960s. Around the same time, Robert A. Black Elementary on the South Side established a magnet program in response to a proposal initially put forth by South Shore community members in 1968. At the high school level, Whitney Young High School on the near West Side opened in the mid-1970s as the first official magnet high school in the city, following Chicago Metropolitan (Metro) High School in 1970 in the Loop. While Metro was not initially called a magnet school, like magnet schools it intentionally drew a diverse racial mix of students from across the city to its experimental "school without walls," city-as-laboratory educational model.[48]

On a much smaller scale, these magnet schools revived the educational park desegregation model that had been championed in the 1960s, though never implemented. At both Disney and Black, the Board of Education provided bus transportation for all students and used quotas to ensure that the racial makeup of the schools matched the demographics of an expanded set of neighborhoods around the schools to promote desegregation. In 1970, groups of White parents from the Mount Greenwood, Ashburn, and Gage Park neighborhoods on the Southwest Side went to the Board of Education to protest magnet schools' use of racial quotas. White parents from these same communities also opposed the limited busing plans that enrolled a small number of Black students in previously all-White neighborhood schools. As with busing, these parents used a defense of the neighborhood school to charge that Robert A. Black Elementary's race-conscious selection process threatened "the civil rights" of White students. Accusations by Whites that racial equity plans impinged on the rights of White students or were forms of "reverse racism" proliferated locally and nationally in the ensuing decades. However, in 1970 these protestations only prompted the board to shift from a language

of "racial quotas" to one of "racial composition" without significantly changing the actual procedures for student selection.[49]

In the late 1970s, school leaders in Chicago embraced magnet schools as
a voluntary means to desegregate schools in opposition to even less popular mandatory student assignment plans. In response to the state of Illinois's
direction to desegregate the CPS student body, Superintendent Joseph Hannon produced the 1978 "Access to Excellence" plan. The plan stressed the creation of more voluntary measures and specialty programs, including magnet
schools, permissive transfers, and "choice" for parents in finding schools to
fit the needs of their students as individuals. Much in the way that charter
schools were initially envisioned years later, a 1973 article in the *Chicago Union
Teacher* suggested that magnet schools would benefit all schools in the system
by acting "as an educational catalyst for the city as a whole. The innovative
programs developed by their faculty members would be shared with faculties
throughout the city." Buying into the mythos of magnets, Hannon believed
that specialty programs and "schools of choice" would both improve educational opportunities and produce voluntary desegregation.[50]

Understandings of educational "choice" changed nationally between the
1950s and the 1990s. Mainstream political support for desegregation plans
shifted to advocacy for "school choice" models. In the immediate post-*Brown*
period, "choice" was associated with policies that allowed White families in
the South to defy the courts' mandate to desegregate. White students in southern public school districts were provided the "freedom of choice" to continue
attending public schools or were granted tuition waivers that allowed them
to attend all-White private schools established as "segregation academies."[51]
In 1955, Milton Friedman, the economic father of modern conservatism, suggested that public monies should fund vouchers that families could use to attend public, private, or religious schools—an unpopular measure at the time.
However, by 1966 business leaders in a U.S. Chamber of Commerce task force
were proposing a voucher-like program to introduce market-based values of
competition into public education.[52]

During the 1970s, public entities increasingly experimented with "choice"
models and education privatization measures. In 1970, under the Nixon administration, the U.S. Office of Economic Opportunity offered funding to
Kansas City, Seattle, San Francisco, and other urban school systems to conduct feasibility tests for an experimental program of publicly funded school
vouchers that could be used for public or private schools. This program was
supported by conservatives but was also directed by White liberal social scientist Christopher Jencks. In 1968, Jencks suggested that public funds should be

used to support independent Black nationalist schools because public schools had failed Black students. Jencks, like Coleman, argued that public schools could not overcome "the whole complex of social arrangements whose cumulative viciousness creates" the Black ghetto. However, in 1970, Jencks's and the U.S. Office of Economic Opportunity's voucher program was still so controversial that almost all of the cities refused to fully participate. Closer to Chicago, in Gary, Indiana, Behavior Research Laboratories of Palo Alto, California, was granted a performance contract to manage and reorganize Gary's public Benjamin Banneker Elementary School.[53]

The president of the Gary Teachers Union met with CTU members and reported that private management of Banneker resulted in teacher layoffs, increased class sizes, and an overreliance on standardized tests to assess student achievement. In the 1970s, CTU leaders condemned performance contracts and the "incursion of 'big business' into the classroom" and called vouchers and tuition tax credits "an all-out attempt . . . to destroy the very fiber from which the American dream is woven—by closing the main means by which the poor achieve upward mobility [public education]." They warned that the funneling of public money to private schools would "mean the loss of teaching jobs in the public schools, and the eventual end to public schools as we have known them."[54]

Long associated with segregationist rhetoric, school choice advocates did not begin to enter the political mainstream until the late 1970s. This transition was aided by the rise of conservative politics nationally on the precipice of the "Reagan Revolution" and broader global economic restructuring.[55] The focus on "choice" and the needs of individual students—including the magnet school model—deflected attention and resources away from the systemic, historically produced inequities that Black education reformers had struggled against for decades. This shift from a focus on structural solutions to individual "choice," from "equity" to "excellence," was reinforced nationally in reform plans that foregrounded school choice as a response to the Reagan administration's 1983 Nation at Risk report. By the early 1980s, more liberal desegregation advocates like sociologist James Coleman (of the 1966 Coleman Report) came to support school choice policies and vouchers, having lost faith in the large bureaucracies of public education. Similarly disillusioned with public schools, some veteran Black education reformers came to support school choice programs.[56]

While seemingly strange bedfellows, self-determinist Black education reformers and conservative and corporatist education reformers shared a wariness of the state that, at times, converged in mutual support for school choice programs in the 1990s. Conservatives' and market-based education reformers' distrust of government was tied to ideologies of small government, deregulation, and the premise that the market is better equipped to address societal problems than the government. In contrast, many Black education reformers' distrust of the government was expressed in a self-determinist politics of Black achievement that was forged in the context of failed state attempts at desegregation and the expanded racially liberal welfare state's failure to ensure educational equity for Black people.[57]

Black activist Howard Fuller's political trajectory is among the most striking convergences between the politics of Black achievement and market-based corporate support for school choice programs in the 1990s. Fuller became a leading advocate for Milwaukee's 1990 first-in-the-country, large-scale school voucher program. The program gave low-income students publicly funded vouchers to pay for tuition at private schools. Fuller had participated in struggles for desegregation in Cleveland in the 1960s, founded an independent Black educational institution in North Carolina in the early 1970s, and later led efforts to preserve a Black Milwaukee high school from being converted into a magnet school to serve more White students. Frustrated by the way that these earlier efforts to reform public schools were thwarted, he embraced school vouchers as a way for Black families to "opt out" of the public school system. Fuller's adoption of the language of "parental choice" in the 1990s incorporated aspects of the language and logic of Black self-determination and parent empowerment used in movements for independent Black schools and community control in the 1960s and 1970s. In supporting vouchers, Fuller and Black Democratic state representative and longtime education activist Polly Williams allied themselves with Wisconsin's Republican governor and voucher advocate Tommy Thompson and other White conservatives and business leaders. Fuller understood this "Unholy Alliance" as a matter of "interest convergence": a "temporary merger of interests that don't necessarily extend beyond parent choice." Thompson and his White corporate allies may have supported vouchers using conservative arguments against government intervention, but Fuller's lack of faith in the public education system was firmly grounded in Black history.[58]

Vouchers, "school choice," Effective Schools, and magnet and charter schools all represent the many different paths Black education reformers explored as they questioned the liberatory capacity of traditionally administered public institutions. For most self-determinist Black education reformers, the endgame remained Black achievement—Black students receiving a quality, equitable, culturally relevant education that prepared them for life. As such,

Fuller was among a small minority of Black education reformers who supported vouchers. Many other Black education reformers vehemently fought against market-based education reforms. In practice, students utilizing school choice policies like vouchers have not performed demonstrably better than students in traditional public schools. In Chicago, vouchers never took hold because of strong opposition by unions and the city's Democratic leadership. However, other "schools of choice"—including magnet schools and charter schools—did gain traction.[59]

In Chicago, the 1978 "Access to Excellence" plan reflected the national shift in school reform discourse from addressing systemic inequities to creating "schools of choice." Criticizing the plan's evasion of comprehensive desegregation actions that would require mandatory student transfers, CUL leaders characterized the plan and magnet schools as "isolated integration" and "elitist by design." E. Toy Fletcher, representing schools in the Black low-income Grand Boulevard neighborhood, argued that the plan would "drain off our best kids" while ignoring Black students with greater instructional and social support needs who would remain in the community's existing under-resourced segregated schools. While programs for "gifted" students existed within CPS since early in the twentieth century and special testing was required for admission into technical high schools such as Lane Technical High School, the number of selective enrollment schools that required testing for admission, as well as other magnet and specialty schools, increased after "Access to Excellence."[60]

The specialty programs and magnet schools for "high achievers" discussed in the "Access to Excellence" plan were mainly based in schools located outside the poorest Black wards in the city. Magnet schools also restricted eligibility for students "awaiting placement in special education classes" or with "special problems in attendance, behavior or health"—all issues disproportionately found in poor Black communities as the result of systemic inequality and institutional racism. A decade earlier, then CUL executive director Bill Berry lamented the 350-year history of systemic Black subjugation in America: from slavery to rural peonage to ghettoization and colonization and, finally, to tokenism. "Access to Excellence" seemed to be the newest tool in the era of Black tokenism.[61]

Nationally, educational "choice" plans created greater racial and economic stratification in public school systems. These emerging choice programs included magnet schools, special curricular programs within schools, and voucher programs. As the children of more affluent families with social, cultural, and economic capital were concentrated in a small set of elite schools, school choice programs created a path for a limited group of African Americans to gain access to higher-quality educational opportunities. Meanwhile, the majority of poor and working-class Black students and students from families with less access to educational resources were consigned to inequitably resourced, underperforming segregated schools. Individual Black success stories challenged long-standing African American traditions of linked fate and collective struggle. With this stratification, the understanding of Black achievement as a collective community endeavor in struggles for desegregation, community control, and independent Black institutions was reoriented.[62]

In 1980, the U.S. Justice Department filed suit against the Chicago Board of Education and the city of Chicago for violating the Fourteenth Amendment by operating a dual school system that segregated students on the basis of race.[63] For the CUL, this suit represented a major victory in its decades-long battle to desegregate CPS schools. To resolve the suit, the federal government and the Chicago Board of Education entered into a consent decree to desegregate as many schools as possible and provide supplementary programming for Black and Latinx schools that remained segregated. The consent decree did not require widespread mandatory reassignments or busing. By 1980, only 17 percent of CPS students were White, with Black and Latinx students accounting for more than 80 percent of CPS students. Privileging the White minority, the Board of Education and the U.S. Justice Department compromised by requiring desegregation so that no school was more than 70 percent White. This agreement did little to reduce racial isolation in predominantly Black and Latinx schools, which remained overwhelmingly segregated.[64] One of the most successful areas of the plan, however, could be seen in the targeted desegregation of the city's most elite selective enrollment and magnet schools.

As a result of the consent decree, magnet and selective enrollment schools grew as targeted desegregation programs used racial quotas to affirmatively ensure racial diversity.[65] To comply with the consent decree, selective enrollment schools had to consider race in pupil admission and assignment policies and ensure that no more than 35 percent of the students in these schools were White.[66] While organizations like the CUL were critical of "Access to Excellence" in 1978, by the 1980s the prospect of comprehensive desegregation and the political will to create quality neighborhood schools seemed more and more remote. In this context, middle-class Black families increasingly took advantage of the "schools of choice" model. Selective enrollment schools became an outlet for the dwindling group of White parents who kept their children in CPS as well as for Black parents looking for opportunities beyond their inequitably resourced neighborhood schools.

Magnet schools and selective enrollment schools served as a new mechanism to segment and stratify the CPS student population by race and class. By the late 1980s, students in Chicago's elite selective enrollment schools were among the most racially diverse and the most high-achieving academically. Students who attended selective enrollment schools were disproportionately "high-achieving," as measured by standardized tests, because earning high scores on separate entrance exams or other standardized tests was required for admission to many of these schools. Students admitted into selective schools tended to come from more affluent families and have parents with higher levels of educational attainment than the larger public school population. While selective schools were positioned as schools of merit, admittance was often more a reflection of students' and families' access to resources than some direct measure of ability or intelligence. As part of plans to impose accountability measures in CPS, corporate leaders in the Chicago Commercial Club supported finding programmatic ways to "sort the kids."[67]

Magnet and selective enrollment schools exacerbated issues of inequality and access for students and teachers. Sara Spurlark never taught or served as an administrator at a magnet or selective enrollment school. In 1980, her school, Ray Elementary, with a student population that was 52 percent Black, 39 percent White, 8 percent Asian, and 1 percent Latinx, was more racially and socioeconomically integrated than most CPS schools. However, even as the leader of a high-performing integrated school, Spurlark still felt that "magnet schools are stealing the best students and the best teachers from us." These concerns about "creaming" persisted in relation to magnets and charter schools. In addition, magnet schools also often had greater access to funds earmarked to enhance "equal educational opportunity." CUL officials lauded these new avenues for Black academic achievement while lamenting the fact that the majority of CPS students were still relegated to highly segregated underserved schools.[68]

Integrated selective enrollment and magnet schools modeled the type of cross-cultural interaction and high academic achievement that the CUL had long argued was necessary to cultivate the next generation of middle-class Black professionals. In the years after the implementation of the desegregation consent decree, the student population in elite selective enrollment high schools was not too different from the population that the CUL worked with in its ESAA race relations programs at Morgan Park High School during the 1970s. Both high school student populations were disproportionately more racially integrated with a more heterogeneous economic class base than the majority of CPS schools. Through the early 2000s, the most elite selective enrollment schools continued to be among the most racially integrated schools in the city through the use of racial quotas in admissions. This would change in 2009, when a judge vacated the desegregation consent decree imposed in 1980. Nonetheless, after their initial opposition to the "Access to Excellence" plan, CUL leaders eventually shifted to claim magnet and selective enrollment schools as sites to continue struggles for desegregation.

The shifting justification for magnet schools, from desegregation to school choice, was framed as a move toward creating "quality" schools of choice. Like CUL leaders, other Black educators and activists involved in earlier Black self-determinist educational movements found spaces to pursue their education work in the growing school choice landscape. Charter schools, in particular, brought together unlikely bedfellows as community-based ideas of Black autonomy converged with market-based ideas of choice and competition in the 1990s and beyond.

THE TANGLED ORIGINS AND EXPECTATIONS OF CHARTER SCHOOLS

The first charter schools opened nationally in the 1990s as the product of seemingly contradictory impulses and interests. Groups of teachers imagined charter schools as teacher-led schools for experimentation and innovation. Community groups saw them as an opportunity to gain more control over the curriculum and culture within schools. Corporate education reformers envisioned a new venue for market-based school reforms.[69] In Chicago and nationally, publicly funded and privately managed charter schools became the most prominent and contested symbol of the shift toward school choice and the privatization of public education.

Albert Shanker, president of the American Federation of Teachers, presented the idea for charter schools in a speech at the National Press Club in 1988, the same year as the passage of the Chicago School Reform Act. As president of New York's United Federation of Teachers, he had strongly opposed community control during 1968 clashes between White teachers and Black educators, parents, and community groups in Ocean Hill–Brownsville. Nevertheless, Shanker remained very popular amongst the predominantly White teaching force in New York City. As the school choice movement gained steam in the 1980s, Shanker proposed charter schools as a public school alternative to voucher programs, which he believed would siphon public school students and resources into private schools.[70]

Shanker, along with education scholar Ray Budde, argued that publicly funded charter schools could be teacher-led innovation laboratories. These schools would allow teachers to partner with parents to try out innovative new teaching methods without some of the stricter regulations binding traditional public schools. Like Effective Schools advocates, Shanker derived inspiration from commercial business management practices, modeling his proposal after practices implemented at a Saturn automotive plant in Tennessee. However, Shanker also imagined charter schools as racially and economically diverse schools that dispensed with some of the more rigid conditions of collective bargaining around curriculum and instruction while still maintaining union representation for teachers. Like the CTU's vision of magnet schools in the early 1970s, charter schools were imagined in the late 1980s as hubs of innovation where educators could try out creative and experimental curricula and programming that would generate best practices to share and replicate at other public schools. In 1991, the state legislature in Minnesota, consulting with Shanker, authorized the creation of the first charter school in the country. However, Shanker quickly became dismayed as market-based education reformers came to dominate the charter movement and use the charter model to undercut teachers' unions.[71]

Liberals and conservatives, Democrats and Republicans, came to embrace market-based urban education reforms through charter schools. Increasingly centrist Democrats saw charter schools as a public alternative to vouchers that might head off more extreme aspects of the school choice movement. The national Democratic Leadership Council—of which Bill Clinton had been chair—supported charter schools, and in 1994 the Clinton administration passed legislation to provide federal dollars for charter schools. This was in line with moves within the national Democratic Party beginning in the 1980s to remake the Democratic Party into a centrist force to compete with Republicans. Democrats would ally themselves with business leaders, advocating for pro-growth policies over redistributive economic policies, taking punitive "law and order" stances that exponentially increased the Black prison population, and increasing appeals to White middle-class voters rather than addressing the demands of racially marginalized groups. On the right, conservatives supported charters as vehicles for ideals of market-based competition and the deregulation of public schools. In 1993, Jeanne Allen of the conservative Heritage Foundation created the Center for Education Reform, a national organization to promote charter schools. Other conservative and liberal foundations and philanthropies followed suit, further swelling the education reform research and advocacy industry.[72]

By the 1990s, corporate investors increasingly treated public education as a

lucr̶ ̶ ̶ ̶ ̶ment. Contracts with school systems, provision
of ̶ ̶ ̶ ̶ ̶ ̶ ̶xtbooks and curricular materials, test-
ir ̶ ̶ ̶ ̶f debt interest, new education
 ̶ ̶ ̶ ̶ ̶ment companies, and
 ̶ ̶ ̶ , and transformations
 ̶ . Scholar Noliwe Rooks
 ̶ractices that profit from
 ̶s could potentially be even
 ̶r example, when students
districts purchased new test
ofit firms; banks could collect
 ̶s to school systems that were
 ̶urchased school buildings at low
price̶ ̶ ̶ ̶ ̶ ̶ ̶ormance or under-enrollment and
redeveloped ̶ ̶ ̶ ̶ ̶ ̶ke a profit; private education management corporations ̶ ̶ ̶ ̶ public funds to "turn around" public
schools that were deemed "fai̶ ̶ ̶ ̶ open new brick-and-mortar or online
schools. Local and national legislation propelled charter school expansion in
Chicago and across the nation.[73]

When the first charter school opened in Chicago in 1997, it was still not clear
the extent to which charter schools would grow and displace neighborhood
public schools, further stratify the student population, or "cream" students
from traditional public schools. During the 1998–99 school year there were
only twelve charter schools in Illinois. Black self-determinist, community-
based groups also opened charter schools, reflecting a history different from
Shanker's idea of teacher-led charters or corporate operators' ideas of market-
based charters. Reminiscent of pro-integration, anti–community control arguments from the past, some liberal education leaders like Shanker opposed
the development of charters with racially and culturally specific missions. The
leaders of IPE, who still operated the independent, African-centered NCDC
school, opened one of these early charter schools in Chicago.[74]

Building on their Black independent school tradition, the founders of IPE
and NCDC opened their first charter school in 1998. As NCDC continued to
operate as a private preschool, the group founded several additional public charter schools, including Betty Shabazz Academy Elementary, DuSable
Leadership Academy High School, and Barbara A. Sizemore Academy Elementary. These charter schools were modeled on the African-centered curriculum and structure of NCDC. Together, these three African-centered char-

ter schools made up the Betty Shabazz International Charter Schools network, a nonprofit charter management organization.[75]

NCDC and Betty Shabazz International Charter Schools founder Carol Lee remained active as an education practitioner in these schools and also became a highly revered education researcher. While working as a teacher and program director at NCDC, Carol Lee earned a Ph.D. from the University of Chicago; she became a professor in the School of Education and Social Policy at Northwestern University in 1991. Carol Lee was not particularly invested in the decentralization reforms implemented in Chicago during the 1980s. However, from her perspective, charters provided an opportunity to gain access to state funds that would allow NCDC to expand its reach and impact. She argued that the money for charters was public money and that Mayor Daley did not care if they flew a red, black, and green flag or taught an African-centered curriculum as long as the school maintained high test scores and the school leaders did not back someone to run against him for mayor. If White people were going to use charters to open schools for Black children in Black communities, Carol Lee saw no reason why the Black leaders of NCDC should not use these same funds to open African-centered schools in Black communities: "We pay taxes. If this [charter schools] is the game in town then we need to get a piece of the action." However, the group's proposal for the Shabazz charter school was initially denied. Their charter was only approved after IPE leaders worked every connection they had in the city and in CPS, including meeting with CPS chief executive officer Paul Vallas personally, to make their case. The Betty Shabazz International Charter Schools are among only a few Black-run charter schools that are operated by almost exclusively Black leadership at the highest levels.[76]

Community activists often characterize charter corporations as White neoliberal efforts to turn a profit by paternalistically educating Black and Latinx urban youth. The Shabazz schools demonstrate the potential for community actors with more radical or progressive politics to claim charters that might otherwise serve corporate interests or reproduce existing race-based inequalities. It is also notable that in 1992, before charter schools even existed, Carol Lee described independent Black educational institutions like NCDC "as 'laboratory' schools for the development of pedagogy and projects that reflect African world views and interests" that were a "worthy model for others [including public schools] to follow." This description is in line with the early intent of charter schools as hubs of innovation and also speaks to IPE's interest in expanding its impact in traditional public schools. In the early 1990s IPE developed the Mary McLeod Bethune Teacher Training Institute that trained CPS teachers to implement African-centered pedagogy and curriculum in their classrooms.[77]

For Carol Lee and the Shabazz charter schools, the much maligned, increasingly corporatized world of public education in the neoliberal age initially provided an opportunity to increase the number of children attending African-centered schools. This decision caused a major rift within the Black nationalist and Pan-Africanist community in CIBI, of which NCDC was a founding member. Even within NCDC, parents and teachers had conflicting opinions on charters. However, Carol Lee continued to make the compelling argument that opening charter schools was a political risk worth taking if they could maintain the integrity of the schools' African-centered curriculum and methods and serve more students without the constraints of tuition.[78]

IPE's transition to charter schools is not entirely surprising if understood within the heterogeneous ideological context of the Black Power Movement that birthed the institution. IPE's notion of independence drew on ideas of collective responsibility and culturally inflected traditions of Black entrepreneurship that gained currency in the Black Power and Black Arts movements of the 1960s and 1970s. IPE's ideas of Black autonomy and cultural transformation for liberation, however, were not centered on an explicitly anticapitalist critique in opposition to privatization. The experiences of IPE leaders, as operators of an independent private school, resonated with the curricular autonomy and entrepreneurial start-up sensibilities promised in early charter schools. However, despite the motivations of IPE leaders and other African-centered and culturally relevant pedagogues, the culturally relevant educational tools and practices incubated in institutions like IPE have been repackaged and deployed in different contexts by market-based corporate education reformers.[79]

The explosive growth of charters in Chicago took off in the 2000s. Republican president George W. Bush's 2002 No Child Left Behind Act, combined with Democratic mayor Richard M. Daley's 2004 Renaissance 2010 plan, opened the floodgates to high-stakes testing, school closings, and the expansion of school choice through new charter schools. Market-based corporate-style charter operators now dominate the charter school landscape, rather than long-standing community institutions promoting racial self-determination like IPE or the teacher-led schools imagined by Shanker. As education scholar Pauline Lipman concluded, "Whatever its progressive origins, the charter school strategy has been exploited and rearticulated to the interests of education entrepreneurs, venture philanthropists, investors, and corporate-style charter school chains."[80]

Charter schools overwhelmingly serve African American and Latinx students, but there are very few charter organizations led by African Americans and Latinxs. In cities like Chicago, there is a colonial veneer to the arrangements by which White people make up the majority of teachers in charter schools and the highest levels of leadership in many charter management organizations, which serve overwhelmingly Black and Latinx children. While in many cases well meaning, these White charter leaders do not live in or have deep connections to the communities served by their schools, yet they receive public funds and get paid to direct the structure, curriculum, and discipline policies in these schools with minimal transparency, public accountability, or requirements for engagement with the communities of color where they operate and where their students live. This lack of representation evokes the very types of colonial Eurocentric ideologies that groups like IPE were founded to combat.

While some Black education reformers involved in earlier education struggles found a place within the charter school movement, many others vigorously opposed the expansion of charter schools. In the 1960s and 1970s, Rosie Simpson organized against "Willis Wagons" and racially discriminatory CPS policies and later worked in movements for community control. However, she condemned the proliferation of charter schools: "I'm against all that. I'm against the charter schools." She argued that charter schools further stratified the schools: "Charter schools are only going to siphon off those who already [made it]." She also contended that charters were a blatant ploy to privatize schools and that the time and resources dedicated to charter schools would be better spent on improving existing neighborhood schools. Teacher-activist Lillie Peoples also railed against the overall quality and lack of accountability in charter schools: "They're not held to the same standards that public schools are. They can suspend, eliminate at will whoever presents a problem to them. I [don't] see that as a solution for education, particularly of the poor and Black and other minority groups. There's nothing about them that I see as elite in terms of you getting a real, quality education."[81]

The observations of these Black education reformers are supported by empirical data. Nationally, students in charter schools have not consistently performed overwhelmingly better than students in traditional public schools in terms of student achievement or life prospects. However, charter schools do disproportionately hire more young White teachers than veteran teachers and teachers of color, cause financial strains for traditional public schools, underserve special needs students, and suspend, expel, and push out Black students at higher rates than traditional public schools.[82] In the Woodlawn community, charter schools became the newest episode in a longer history of education reform projects.

In 1969, Rev. Arthur Brazier, leader of TWO and pastor at Woodlawn's Apostolic Church of God, described living conditions in Woodlawn in his political memoir and call-to-arms for community control, *Black Self-Determination: The Story of the Woodlawn Organization*: "This is Woodlawn, on the central south side of Chicago. . . . It is a neighborhood where streets still hold last winter's salt and last fall's leaves in the gutters, where boarded-up shop windows speak to the residents of the White man's racism, where spray-paint graffiti on buildings and fences remind everyone of the explosive mixture of hope and suppressed rage to be found in every young person who roams the streets."[83] In some ways this was still an apt description of Woodlawn in the early 2000s. Abandoned lots gave way to laundromats and drugstores, liquor stores and check-cashing depots, boarded-up stores and boarded-up homes. After attending the same schools that underserved their parents, many young people had little faith that the public education system would help to improve their material conditions. Youth violence was a much too frequent and tragic part of the community's landscape.

However, some things in Woodlawn had changed since the days of WESP and the community control movement. The University of Chicago significantly expanded its reach south of the Midway Plaisance. In 1964, TWO pressured the university to agree not to expand beyond 61st Street. That agreement remained in place into the early 2000s, though the university's private police force did extend its patrols into parts of the neighborhood. The university spurred housing and commercial redevelopment and new university construction, particularly in the northern part of the community closest to the campus and north of 61st Street. The university also continued to use Woodlawn as a site for educational experimentation. Since the 1960s, Woodlawn experienced multiple waves of reform with TWO leaders' continued involvement in redevelopment and reform plans for the community.

Since the 1970s, the community leaders from TWO who led WESP shepherded multiple redevelopment projects in Woodlawn. As TWO shifted from community organizing to redevelopment, Rev. Arthur Brazier (ordained Bishop Brazier in 1976), along with longtime TWO leader Leon Finney Jr., founded the Woodlawn Community Development Corporation, the Woodlawn Preservation and Investment Corporation, and the Fund for Community Redevelopment and Revitalization. Brazier and Finney led the way for housing and retail redevelopment in East Woodlawn near the site of Brazier's Apostolic Church of God. They also replaced deteriorating housing in East Woodlawn with new and rehabbed single-family homes and condominiums.[84]

Critics accused Brazier and Finney, in their real estate redevelopment ventures, of turning their backs on low-income Woodlawn renters in order to encourage homeownership for Black middle-class residents with ties to the church. While still active in Woodlawn, Finney (Doctor of Ministry, 1990) became pastor at Metropolitan Apostolic Community Church in the South Side's Bronzeville community. Accusations of conflicts of interest escalated as Finney pursued development opportunities while serving as executive director of TWO and holding positions on numerous boards and commissions in Richard M. Daley's administration, including the city planning commission and Chicago Housing Authority. Some in the Black nationalist community claimed that Finney was co-opted by the machine. Despite these critiques, Brazier and Finney remained politically significant figures in Woodlawn and citywide.[85]

The interests of Brazier and Finney in real estate redevelopment in Woodlawn are not necessarily out of line with the philosophies of community control and Black self-determination, which they exhorted in WESP and other TWO initiatives during the 1960s and early 1970s. Brazier supported community control as one of a number of strategies to achieve Black self-determination, but Brazier's end goal was always for African Americans to gain access to mainstream American life. As he wrote in 1969, "The ghetto must find access to the mainstream."[86] In WESP, Brazier and TWO were willing to collaborate with the University of Chicago and CPS to gain control over schools in Woodlawn. Similarly, Brazier and Finney were willing to collaborate with Mayor Richard M. Daley to bring real estate redevelopment to Woodlawn. As leaders of nonprofits, they were constrained by regulations that limited their political activities at the same time that they worked to provide much-needed services for the neighborhood—services that the government was increasingly divesting from and privatizing.

Nonprofits became increasingly important during the latter part of the 1970s as the government rolled back social services previously provided by New Deal and Great Society agencies and programs. Scholar Ruth Wilson Gilmore explains that while nonprofit organizations in the United States have existed since before the nation won its independence, "the third sector"— neither business nor the state—grew dramatically during the 1980s to make up for cuts in public social welfare services, forming what social scientist Jennifer

Wolch called the "shadow state." During the 1980s and more fully during the 1990s under Bill Clinton, Republicans and Democrats, conservatives and liberals, increasingly supported neoliberal ideals that narrowed the "legitimacy of the public sector in the conduct of everyday life" and insisted that the market could most effectively address social problems and that "the withdrawal of the state from certain areas of social welfare provision [would] enhance rather than destroy the lives of those abandoned." Gilmore argues that the nonprofit sector grew under the logic that "where the market fails, the voluntary, non-profit sector can pick up any stray pieces." Sociologist John Arena adds that "nonprofits play a central and crucial role on behalf of political and economic elites, facilitating the often politically difficult job of privatizing" public services, displacing people, and assuming responsibility for "other regressive features of contemporary neoliberalizing cities." Thus, despite many nonprofit workers' desires to help people most in need, as a sector, nonprofits were often positioned to serve functions that delivered more benefits to elites than to comprehensively impact the lives of those abandoned by the state.[87]

Longtime Black activists found the transition into nonprofit management difficult. Arena describes the perils of this shift among Black housing activists in New Orleans: "No longer politically or financially accountable to their grassroots base, the new organizational framework led activists to abandon direct action as their key political weapon for coercing concessions and defending the interests of public housing residents. The political allegiances and financial benefits of the nonprofit model moved these activists into a strategy of insider negotiations that prioritized the profit-making agenda of real estate interests above the housing and other material needs of black public housing residents." TWO's shift away from direct action to insider negotiations was evident in the early 1970s when TWO leaders retreated from supporting Barbara Sizemore and WESP in hope of future negotiations with CPS and the city. This tactical change progressed as Finney and TWO founded community development corporations, became landlords and social service providers, strengthened ties with city political leaders, and operated nonprofit organizations. The education research and advocacy nonprofits that developed from 1980s school reform efforts were less impacted than TWO by the regulations that restricted nonprofits from political engagement, because they were largely disconnected from longer histories of community-based organizing and direct-action protest. For TWO leaders, on the other hand, the rules restricting nonprofits' political activities also limited their ability to engage in the type of explicitly political tactics directed at the state and businesses that had earned the organization community legitimacy from the beginning.[88]

In practice, "the transformation of grassroots activists into nonprofit officials" was more prominent than, and had many of the same pitfalls as, the transition from Black activists to Black elected officials. While certainly still mounting the periodic direct-action campaign, like the protests at the Board of Education during the 1987 teachers' strike, many of the community-based leaders and organizations that were prominent in school protests in the 1960s and 1970s (TWO, Operation PUSH, and the Kenwood-Oakland Community Organization) later became nonprofits, increasingly engaged in backroom negotiations with city leaders, or struggled to find resources and were forced to pursue programming that matched the proclivities of their funders.[89] Despite these limitations, Brazier focused until his last days in 2010 on redeveloping Woodlawn using housing and education as drivers for Black achievement.

Woodlawn continues to serve as a laboratory for new education reform efforts. The University of Chicago, despite its nonprofit status, continues to function as an entity in pursuit of capital accumulation. It is also home to major centers of educational research established by researchers and practitioners like Bryk and Spurlark, particularly the Urban Education Institute, which absorbed the Center for Urban School Improvement and the Consortium on Chicago School Research. Frustrated with the bureaucratic and environmental barriers endemic to CPS, Spurlark concluded that only by developing an alternative to conventional public schooling could she create the conditions for poor Black students to achieve at high levels. In the late 1990s, Spurlark worked with a team at the University of Chicago to open its first charter school, an elementary school in the North Kenwood–Oakland community north of the university. In 2006 the University of Chicago opened its first charter high school — the UChicago Charter School Woodlawn Campus.[90]

While charter schools represented a newer mode of education reform, the coalitional partners that helped to create the UChicago Charter Woodlawn Campus were very similar to the partners that created WESP — the University of Chicago, CPS, and Bishop Arthur Brazier. However, that is largely where the similarities end, as WESP and UChicago Charter Woodlawn Campus had very different orientations to the Woodlawn community. The charter school initially shared a building with Wadsworth Elementary School, one of the original schools targeted for community control by WESP. In the late 1960s, WESP entered Wadsworth as part of a collaborative project between CPS, the University of Chicago, and TWO to restructure social and power relations and provide more community control and decision-making in schools. The relationship between Wadsworth and the UChicago Charter Woodlawn Campus was not similarly collaborative. In 2013, CPS allowed the university's charter school to take over the entire Wadsworth school building, relocating the Wadsworth school staff and students to the building formerly occupied by Dumas school, which CPS had recently closed. This was a top-down decision made by CPS and the university. In contrast, WESP worked to increase the involvement of parents, students, and local community members in school decision-making.

The UChicago Charter School Woodlawn Campus is not a neighborhood school. The school enrolls students based on a lottery system, albeit prioritizing a segment of seats for students from the neighborhood. The school was founded with a twenty-one-member governing board primarily made up of university officials, parents of charter school students, and wealthy philanthropists. In 2016, the University of Chicago broke ground on a new $27.5 million school for the UChicago Charter School Woodlawn Campus on 63rd Street, a block north of the Wadsworth building. The city offered the plot of land, appraised at $755,000, for the new school to the university for $1. In May 2016, a university official indicated that after a series of "community meetings" the more than forty-year ban on university development south of 61st Street was lifted. Longtime Woodlawn resident Ulysses Blakely called the sale of the land for the new charter school building "a giveaway to the University of Chicago." While the University of Chicago passed on purchasing the Wadsworth school building, university representatives indicated that they would like to see the site used for "residential, commercial and retail development." In the meantime, the Wadsworth building would be left empty pending CPS's decision on whether and how to redevelop or sell the site where halls once bustled with multiple generations of Woodlawn's children. Much had been promised to the Woodlawn community in 2006 when the charter school originally opened in the Wadsworth building; the local Black alderman, Willie Cochran, echoed those promises when he argued, in 2016, that the new charter school building would be "a resource that brings benefits for the broader community." However, as a charter school with attendance based on a lottery system, a new building owned by the University of Chicago, and few required mechanisms for accountability to the local neighborhood or the broader public, the nature of these community benefits remains to be seen.[91]

The specific education reforms in Woodlawn had significantly changed in the more than forty years since WESP, but in many ways Woodlawn in the early 2000s remained an experimental community, governed by public-private partnerships, under the oversight of powerful private interests. When Barbara Sizemore directed WESP, she partnered with CPS and the university to pursue quality education using community-based organizing to increase parental and community decision-making in Wadsworth and other Woodlawn schools. WESP ended when CPS and the university curtailed Black community control. In the 2000s and 2010s, the university again flexed its political muscle, co-locating and then taking over Wadsworth with its charter school and displacing teachers and students to the Dumas school building, where Peoples had worked for two decades. Whereas Lillie Peoples organized Black teachers as an educator at Dumas in the 1960s and 1970s, when the UChicago Charter School Woodlawn Campus opened in 2006, there were only two full-time Black classroom teachers on the staff at a school serving an almost all-Black student body. While it would have been difficult for Sizemore and Peoples to foresee the rapid pace of privatization and the musical chairs of school closings that took place in Woodlawn during the 2000s and 2010s, it would not have been difficult for them to imagine Woodlawn as a neighborhood with contested visions of education reform. Woodlawn's Black children certainly deserve a beautiful, state-of-the-art educational facility. Most charter school teachers, regardless of race, are very dedicated to teaching, particularly given that they often work longer hours for less pay than traditional public school teachers. However, as with magnets and selective enrollment schools, charter schools—as "schools of choice"—use the language of community and equal opportunity while reinforcing stratification and restricting access.

EQUITY VS. CHOICE

The increased privatization and corporatization of public schools that developed in the 1990s furthered the shift from reforms based on equity to reforms based on choice. School choice advocates repurposed the Black self-determinist language of collective community control into a proprietary assertion of the right of individual parents to choose between public, private, and public-private hybrid forms of schooling. In this environment, corporate leaders, philanthropic organizations, and education advocacy groups became the spokespersons for education reform in the city, rather than parents, teachers, students, or members of the largely Black and Latinx communities where the majority of CPS students live. School choice advocates argue that imposing market concepts on the governing of public schools will create competition and thus improve the quality of schools. Like many economic models, this model assumes that traditional public schools have the capacity to act as "rational agents." But public institutions—and particularly public schools—

are not, and should not be, idealized rational economic firms driven by a profit motive. Individual public schools in distressed urban public school systems often do not have the resources to compete in such a marketplace.[92]

The proliferation of "schools of choice" and educational models based on market-based competition created greater stratification and inequities within urban school districts. In 1995, before the first charter schools were even opened in Chicago, CTU president Thomas Reece expressed his doubts about "schools of choice" in a plea for more equitable funding for public schools: "If we create a few 'charter,' 'special,' 'academy,' etc. schools and they become wildly successful (whatever that means), we will still have all the rest of the schools with the same problems that they had before. Is there really so great a difference between societal neglect and selective societal neglect?"[93] As veteran Black educator and administrator Barbara Sizemore noted in the early 1970s, in a capitalist competitive marketplace, there "will always be losers. The question is not will there be unemployment, but who will be unemployed?"[94] If public schools are governed by this same logic, some children will win and many more will lose. In the United States the winners are systemically more likely to be White, male, heterosexual, and/or moneyed, and the losers are systemically more likely to be Black or people of color, women, queer, and/or poor. It is inappropriate, unethical, and not in the public's best interest for public schools, as public entities with public missions, to mimic profit-driven firms in this way.

The assumption that schools of choice will share best practices is also flawed. The idea of sharing best practices promotes decontextualized pedagogy and an ahistorical and apolitical approach to school reform anathema to the idea of culturally relevant pedagogy and community control of schools. Even if we presume that it is a good idea to share and implement best practices germinated in schools of choice, the market-based model of corporate reform does not encourage this practice. For example, under the logic of competition, the market encourages charter schools to repackage and sell, or more often franchise, best practice educational models, rather than share best practices with traditional public schools. Ultimately, school choice models encourage further stratification of public schooling. The supposedly "free" market where these decisions are being made is often highly segmented, unequal, and marred by a lack of actual choices.[95]

"Choice" and "accountability" are very attractive terms. What parents would not want choices for their children and for their schools to be held accountable? In pursuit of quality education, many Black parents have rejected the status quo by seeking out charter schools and taking advantage of school choice programs. However, just as Black support for desegregation strategies did not signify a wholehearted belief in the necessity of racial integration, Black families who utilize school choice programs or send their children to charter schools do not necessarily embrace the broader politics of market-based education reform or school choice policies. Despite the lack of community representation, control, and accountability in many charter schools, school choice advocates often invoke the language of parental involvement, civil rights, and community control to market these schools to Black families. Unfortunately, it is rare that poor and working-class Black parents, in particular, ever fully realize the increased control and independence that they often seek through "school choice" options.[96]

Macro-level discussions of neoliberalism do not tell the whole story of urban racial politics and school reform. Neoliberalism both powerfully articulates shifting political and economic dynamics and erases previous historical struggles for racial justice. Responses of Black education organizers to these shifts in political economy were the products of histories that included the development of a politics of Black achievement that preceded the rise of neoliberalism.[97] Sizemore's and Ronald Edmonds's use of corporate organizational models to replicate high-achieving schools for poor Black children was informed by their work in struggles for desegregation and community control. Their ideas reflected a different history and set of motivations from the market-based school choice policies of the conservative Heritage Foundation or the liberal Democratic Leadership Council. When the architects of IPE fought to create charter schools, they were not blindly colluding with an emerging corporatist order but responding to the historical denial of quality education to Black communities and a lack of Black community control of urban public schools.

On the other hand, Black parents, teachers, and community organizations have also mobilized the history, organizing tactics, and language of struggles for desegregation and community control to stridently fight back against the forces of privatization in urban public schools. In 2010 even IPE founder Haki Madhubuti acknowledged that "the charter schools or the private schools or the contract schools, that's not the answer. That is an answer, but it's not the answer. And we run three charters, so it's not the answer. The answer is we've got to deal with these public school issues. . . . You don't have serious people who understand education. And we're not serious about it. So I'm saying that you need billions and billions of dollars."[98]

As the Black organizers in this book have demonstrated, African Americans are a heterogeneous group of people, grounded in particular histories, with diverse interests and shifting, and at times conflicting, political ideologies. Black education reformers in Chicago were incredibly dedicated to ensuring that Black students received a high-quality, equitable education. They pursued a variety of tactics to achieve these ends, including working for desegregation, community control, and independent institution building; organizing Black teachers; infiltrating electoral politics and formal government; and making space for alternative visions of "school choice." These efforts were perpetually challenged and thwarted by the local White Democratic political machine, financial instability, powerful moneyed interests, and entrenched systems of White supremacy and structural inequality. By the close of the twentieth century and in the early twenty-first century, the semantics and ideas of Black education reformers, which had previously been used to advocate for Black students were arrested and superseded by market-based reformers peddling "school choice" policies. These policies commodified Black students as new products and "failing" urban schools as new spaces for capital investment and accumulation, which could generate returns regardless of whether educational quality or student achievement improved. While contemporary privatization models present a different set of challenges, the history of Black education struggles is nothing if not a history of creativity and perseverance. So the struggle continues.

In the fall of 1968, a Black student boycotted Kenwood High School on the South Side of Chicago for several consecutive Mondays. She did not act alone but was part of a movement of tens of thousands of Black students at high schools across the city. These were not spontaneous walkouts. Her father drove her and her friends to and from organizing meetings where the students outlined their demands for more Black teachers and administrators, the incorporation of Black history into the curriculum, and improved facilities at predominantly Black schools in the city. Her parents worried that she would be arrested but encouraged her and supported her activism. Collectively, these boycotts nearly shut down several predominantly Black schools in the city and compelled the superintendent of schools to concede to a number of the students' demands. In 1968 this lone student's voice would not necessarily have stood out among the many young voices of protest in the city. In the 2010s, however, it would be difficult to miss her. This high school student was Karen Lewis (née Jennings), future president of the Chicago Teachers Union and the face and voice of the 2012 Chicago teachers' strike that once again brought the city's education system to a halt and elicited concessions from previously intractable city authorities.[1]

Karen Lewis's political trajectory maps onto much of the history documented in this book. Her parents were Black migrants to Chicago who became CPS teachers. While not on the front lines of Black teacher organizing like Lillie Peoples, her parents participated in CORE and the NAACP and were part of a generation of Black educators who struggled against racist barriers to certification and leveraged the hard-earned benefits of unionization for employment gains. Lewis attended Kenwood, a high school born of desegregation debates during the mid-1960s and founded as an intentionally integrated school. But Lewis's protests at Kenwood in 1968 were for Black Power, not integration. Like the Black architects of community control in WESP and the founders of IPE, Lewis embraced a self-determinist politics of Black achievement in the late 1960s and 1970s. When she first started teaching chemistry in CPS in the 1980s, Lewis admired Harold Washington and CTU president Jacqueline Vaughn as leaders and symbols of Black political power, but she wasn't particularly involved in the union. Lewis's political trajectory underscores the permeability of different Black political ideologies and the importance of understanding Black political perspectives historically, intergenerationally, and relationally, rather than oppositionally and out of context.[2]

Lewis benefited from the earlier struggles of Black teachers, but the bulk of her teaching career during the 1990s and 2000s coincided with the decline in Black teacher organizing. Mayor Richard M. Daley had brokered labor peace with the CTU while stratifying public schooling with new charter, selective enrollment, and magnet schools. Lewis worked at two selective enrollment schools: majority-White Lane Technical High School on the North Side and majority-Black King College Preparatory High School on the South Side. She supported the idea of using magnet and selective enrollment schools to promote integration but also acknowledged the failure of that strategy. In 2008, dismayed by increased privatization and attacks on public education, Lewis started attending reading groups, speaking out at Board of Education meetings, and working to restrict charter school expansion with a new CTU caucus, the Caucus of Rank-and-File Educators. Lewis recalled that working with this group "reminded me of my student activism days in the sixties, so I felt like I was right back to where I started from. It was just like this full circle thing."[3]

As a primary antagonist of the corporatist regime in the city, Lewis's trajectory is firmly situated in Chicago's long history of Black protest politics and community organizing. However, running parallel to this history is the formidable history of more top-down autocratic political and corporate power. For much of the twentieth century, operatives of the Chicago Democratic machine expertly wielded this power. In the 2000s, the old-school politics and political tactics of the machine merged with the strategies of increasingly powerful corporate and philanthropic leaders in service of neoliberal policies. To make sense of our current historical moment, we must understand the longer history that led to the convergence of the politics of Black achievement with the neoliberal order.

Nationally, Republicans and Democrats have come together to support neoliberal education reform policies. These policies encouraged reforms that prioritized competition, privatization, school closings and "turnarounds," charter school expansion, and a reliance on standardized testing. Democratic president Barack Obama, a Chicagoan and the first Black president of the United States, ran on a platform of change in 2008. However, in the realm of education he largely advanced the policies of his predecessors, nationally and locally: Republican president George W. Bush's 2002 No Child Left Behind law at the federal level and Democratic mayor Richard M. Daley's 2004 Renaissance 2010 education reform policies in Chicago. Together these policies opened the door for high-stakes testing, school closings, and the expansion of "school choice" through charter schools. Obama appointed Arne Duncan, CPS CEO and Paul Vallas's successor, to serve as the U.S. secretary of education, further elevating Chicago's corporate-style education policies as a model for education reform efforts nationally. Duncan oversaw Obama's major education initiative, Race to the Top, which mirrored on the national level many of the policies that Daley and Duncan had administered in Chicago. Race to the Top required states to compete for federal education funds and emphasized new standards and accountability measures, charter school expansion, test-based assessment of teachers and schools, and a preference for mayoral control of schools.[4] While Chicago policies and officials contributed to the Obama administration's national political agenda, Obama administration officials also cycled back to Chicago—most significantly Rahm Emanuel, Obama's White House chief of staff.

Buoyed by Obama's blessing, Rahm Emanuel was elected mayor of Chicago in 2011. Emanuel had previously worked as an investment banker, a U.S. congressman representing parts of Chicago's North Side and northern suburbs, and a presidential aide to both Clinton and Obama. He furthered Mayor Daley's Renaissance 2010 plans, embracing corporate education reform and "school choice" plans that opened new charter schools and "turned around," consolidated, or closed more than 150 public schools, including the closure of approximately 50 schools in 2013—at the time the largest intentional mass closure of schools in recent U.S. history.[5]

In engineering the school closures, Emanuel argued that the logic of corporate reorganization and the market necessitated right-sizing measures to remedy the city's failing school system. However, Emanuel and his school officials toggled inconsistently between justifications for closing schools based on under-enrollment or "under-utilization" and closings because of academic underperformance. As had been the case for decades, Black students, parents, and communities were dissatisfied with the status quo in many of their under-resourced neighborhood schools. However, they questioned why the schools had to be closed instead of improved. The CTU and community members also questioned definitions of under-enrollment that assessed full utilization at over thirty students to a classroom.[6] In accounts by city and school officials, the history and policies that displaced and depopulated Black communities and produced under-enrolled schools were erased.

City and school officials' market-based interventions accelerated under-enrollment in Black schools in neighborhoods that were already experiencing population losses as a result of the city's demolition of public housing and broader Plan for Transformation policies. In their 2017 report "Closed by Choice," sociologist Stephanie Farmer and a team of researchers found that "of the 108 new charter schools opened between 2000 and 2015, 62 percent of new charter schools were opened in areas with high population loss of school aged children (25 percent or more). . . . 71 percent of new charter schools opened between 2000 and 2012 were opened within 1.5 miles of the 49 schools that would be closed due to low enrollments in 2013." Thus, despite arguments for under-enrollment, privately managed charter schools were often opened in the same Black communities where traditional public schools were being closed for "under-utilization." The corporate reorganization and increased privatization of CPS impacted both Black and Latinx students in CPS in many ways. However, school closings particularly affected Black students and communities. Between 2001 and 2012, of the tens of thousands of students in the more than 100 schools impacted by school closings, turnarounds, phase-outs, and consolidations, 88 percent were Black. Of the 50 schools closed in 2013, 94 percent had student populations that were majority Black.[7]

In Chicago and nationally, these privatization policies drew support and funding from corporate interests and philanthropists, including the Chicago Commercial Club, the University of Chicago, the Bill and Melinda Gates Foundation, the Walton Family Foundation, the Eli and Edythe Broad Foundation, the American Enterprise Institute, and the Heritage Foundation. These liberal, centrist, and conservative foundations set the agenda for the further privatization of public education as funders of school districts, charter corporations, and politicians' electoral campaigns.[8] However, neoliberalism alone cannot explain the current state of urban racial politics and education reform. Instead, we must also learn from the complex history of Black education struggles.

Education has been a vital site for Black activism, organizing, and politics. In the mid-twentieth century, ideas of racial liberalism helped to expand the state's responsibility for social welfare nationally, challenging the legality of Jim Crow policies in the South. Many Black education reformers pursued desegregation as a means to obtain quality public education for Black children. In Chicago, Black parents, students, CCCO, the CUL, and TWO organized demonstrations and mass boycotts for desegregation and equitable education. Even as they used the language of racial liberalism, African Americans critiqued the gap between these professed values and their lived realities. For Black Chicagoans, the expanded welfare state did not deliver uniform gains, as the White-led Chicago Democratic machine suppressed Black grassroots politics.

In the context of the liberal welfare state's failure to ensure educational equity through desegregation, and the proliferation of discourses of Black pathology and inferiority generated by researchers and the state, a generation of Black education reformers during the 1960s and 1970s embraced a self-determinist politics of Black achievement. The logic of the politics of Black achievement reflected Black education reformers' weariness and wariness of racial liberalism, even as education remained a crucial arena in which to reject Black inferiority and pursue racial justice. Neither simply a response to the failures of desegregation nor solely concerned with "proving" Black students' abilities to a White public, the politics of Black achievement was a self-determinist ideology drawing on historical strains of Black political thought that foregrounded Black empowerment and self-governance. During the late 1960s and 1970s, in struggles for community control, independent Black institutions, and Black teacher organizing, Black Chicagoans embraced a politics of Black achievement committed to improving the quality of Black children's education and demonstrating that Black students could achieve at high levels, regardless of whether they attended all-Black or integrated schools.

This generation of Black education reformers pursued robust visions of quality education for Black children without being wedded to a particular tactic to meet this end. Black education reformers' quest to foster black achievement could encompass a trajectory like that of Bishop Arthur Brazier, who went from leading protests for desegregation to leading a community control project; of IPE leaders who went from operating independent Black educational institutions to finding autonomy in charter schools; or of a champion of community control like Barbara Sizemore, who later collaborated with corporate reformers in the 1990s. The fallout from the broken promises of racial liberalism and the welfare state's failure to provide quality education for Black students, historically, created strange bedfellows—from the tripartite relationship between the University of Chicago, CPS, and TWO that created community control in WESP to the alliances between Black parents and predominantly White business leaders in Mayor Harold Washington's education summit. The strange bedfellows that have coalesced around neoliberal approaches to education reform are a product of these longer histories. Black people both challenged and contributed to this emerging order.

Groups of African Americans did seize on aspects of neoliberal restructuring to pursue their own interests. Political scientists Michael C. Dawson and Megan Ming Francis note that the potential economic and political rewards of neoliberalism have proved particularly attractive to a growing group of Black upper middle-class, technocratic elected officials and corporate elites. These folks often embrace narratives of their individual exceptionalism and triumph over racism through mastery of the free market or a "progressive" Black neo-liberalism that supports some state intervention to alleviate the conditions of the most disadvantaged but still mainly turns to market-based solutions to social problems.[9]

Yet recent scandals and accusations of misconduct in urban public school systems have demonstrated the tenuous position of the Black men and, in particular, women who have participated in the neoliberalization of public education. In school systems across the country, linking student test scores to teacher evaluation and pay has fostered corruption. In the spring of 2015, a group of Black teachers and administrators in Atlanta—the majority of whom were Black women—were sentenced to multiyear prison terms for running a cheating ring. In Chicago, CPS CEO Barbara Byrd Bennett, Mayor Emanuel's selection to oversee and take much of the political heat for the 2013 school closings, was sentenced to more than four years in prison for corruption and ushering in a no-bid CPS contract with her former employer.[10] While these officials' actions were indefensible, it is notable that Black women have borne the brunt of this crackdown as the face of cheating and the excesses of educational privatization. At the same time, the predominantly White corporate, philanthropic, and governmental architects of the corporatist educational reforms that created punitive educational standards and the conditions for corruption continue to profit monetarily and politically from these same policies. The fall of Black neoliberals is also, quoting historian Nathan Connolly, "a testament to what happens when black people act in the interest of capital, and do so without the benefits of capital's greatest privilege—namely whiteness."[11]

Yet the actions and ideas of the Black education reformers in this book also belie totalizing interpretations of neoliberal political economy. While public domains have become increasingly privatized, in this book I have intentionally focused instead on the ways that African Americans in Chicago attempted to "reshape and redefine their worlds" through a range of ideological approaches and programs to improve education for Black students. African Americans' embrace of aspects of neoliberal policies does not necessarily reflect a complete rejection of the ideas of social democracy or redistribution that have characterized Black politics historically. As demonstrated by the Black education reformers in this book, Black responses to corporate school reform and privatization measures are also based in histories that preceded the so-called neoliberal moment.[12] When Black parents send their children to charter schools or Black education reformers fight to operate charter schools, they are not simply colluding with the corporatist order, but responding to the historic denial of quality education for Black children and a lack of Black community control of urban public schools. In this sense, a focus on neoliberalism can both powerfully articulate shifting political and economic dynamics and erase histories of Black struggles for racial justice. Nonetheless, corporatist reform policies have contributed greatly to the social dislocation of Black students, Black educators, and Black neighborhoods.

REARTICULATIONS OF BLACK DISPOSABILITY AND DISPLACEMENT

The number and the percentage of Black teachers in CPS have declined dramatically in the twenty-first century. In 1996 roughly 43 percent of CPS teachers were Black. By the 2016–17 school year, Black teachers made up only 22 percent of the CPS teaching force. This is particularly striking in Chicago, because Black teachers made huge inroads into the teaching force after the protests of the 1960s, unlike in other cities with large school systems, such as New York City. Black teachers are more likely to work in predominantly Black schools, the same schools that are disproportionately being closed or "turned around." When Black schools are closed, Black students lose neighborhood schools and Black teachers lose their jobs. Of the fifty schools closed in 2013, more than 70 percent had majority-Black teacher and student populations.[13]

School closings devastated already struggling Black neighborhoods where Black teachers lived and taught—neighborhoods like Auburn Gresham, Grand Crossing, Grand Boulevard, Englewood, South Shore, and Austin. It is not a coincidence that the Black neighborhoods where schools were closed also suffered from other forms of systemic disinvestment and inequality: foreclosed homes, commercial flight, mass incarceration, and a lack of access to grocery stores. These patterns of disinvestment and abandonment, exacerbated by school closings, are a far greater threat than gentrification to many Black communities. Understanding this history is even more urgent given renewed national political attacks on public sector employees more generally, which have had a disproportionately negative impact on African Americans.[14]

The further tiering of public schools has also negatively affected Black students. In September 2009, the consent decree that had been in place since 1980 and compelled CPS to create a desegregation plan for selective enrollment schools was overturned. Requiring a suspension of disbelief, officials determined that the "remnants of past discrimination" were no longer operative in CPS. Like many other districts around the country, Chicago replaced policies that explicitly considered race in student assignments with policies that attempted to use socioeconomic status as a proxy for race after the U.S.

Supreme Court restricted the use of race in determining public school attendance in 2007.[15] One parent and education activist lamented that the most elite selective enrollment schools in Chicago have become "gated communities for children of privilege." In the time since race was eliminated as a category of consideration in selective enrollment admissions, the percentage of White students increased at several of the most elite selective enrollment high schools in the city. For example, at Walter Payton College Preparatory High School, the percentage of White freshmen increased from 29 percent in 2008 to 45 percent in 2013—well above the 35 percent White student enrollment limit imposed under the 1980 desegregation consent decree—while the percentage of Black freshmen decreased from 37 percent in 2008 to 17 percent in 2013. These attendance rates are grossly out of proportion with the demographics of the school system overall. In 2013, White, Black, and Latinx students made up 9 percent, 40 percent, and 45 percent of the total CPS student population, respectively. By 2017, Black students accounted for only 11 percent of students at Payton. Despite claims to the contrary by CPS officials and the courts, the "remnants of past discrimination" are certainly still operative in contemporary CPS policies and in the extreme racial segregation of neighborhoods and schools in Chicago.[16]

Meanwhile, systemwide racial isolation, of Black students in particular, has continued to be a defining feature of CPS. Lifting the desegregation consent decree helped to facilitate the massive school closings in the 2010s, as the consent decree had prohibited closing schools if the closures would reduce racial integration. In the wake of the decree, schools became even more segregated.[17] Moreover, the persistent claim by CPS and city officials that they have simply inherited the historical problem of racial segregation is patently false. When Janice Jackson, whom Mayor Emanuel named CPS's chief education officer in 2015, stated that segregation is "part of the history of Chicago.... I don't think that's a CPS issue," she erased CPS's long history and continued practices of exacerbating residential segregation and colluding to maintain school segregation. Just as CPS and city leaders were rightly blamed for maintaining and exacerbating residential segregation in the 1950s and 1960s by gerrymandering attendance boundaries and building "Willis Wagons" to segregate Black students, they are now culpable for overseeing and supporting racially segregated charter schools, increasingly White elite selective enrollment schools, and the construction of multimillion-dollar annexes and new buildings for schools that disproportionately serve the relatively few White students in the school system.[18]

As has been the case historically, these privileges and disadvantages are structured by White supremacy, a racial and economic order that systematically privileges White students and families and disadvantages Black and Latinx students and families. The intersection of race and class is key to the nature of persistent inequality. As president of the CTU, Karen Lewis explained in a 2013 message to CPS teachers: "If the status quo is maintained, our children and our members will never be winners because the game is rigged against us. Control lies in the hands of an ideologue [Mayor Rahm Emanuel] who amplifies a class divide—children of the elite are given a full, rich curriculum that allows them to explore, create and imagine, while the children of the poor and those who choose publicly funded public education are given the drudgery of test prep. Children of the elite are given a curriculum that prepares them to rule, while our children are given a curriculum that prepares them to be greeters at Wal-Mart." Education scholar Pauline Lipman goes further in arguing that the current stratification within public schools also mirrors the labor demands of the twenty-first-century economic order: elite public high schools provide a small number of rigorous, resource-robust educational opportunities to prepare a smaller class of "high-paid knowledge" workers, while a larger number of under-resourced neighborhood schools and "no excuses" charter schools focus on the "basic skills," "ability to follow directions," and "accommodating disposition toward work" required for employment in the expanding pool of low-wage and temporary service sector jobs. This is clearly not the desire of the vast majority of teachers, principals, parents, and students in lower-performing neighborhood schools, who want and work very hard for better outcomes for students but are hindered by inequitable resources and an unjust system.[19]

Long-standing funding inequities at the state and city levels also continue to exacerbate racial and economic inequities in education. Despite the state of Illinois's constitutional mandate to serve as the primary provider of public education funds, the state has never provided the majority of local school districts' funds. Illinois regularly comes in last in the nation as the state with the most economically and racially inequitable school funding formula. CPS's majority-Black-and-Latinx, majority-low-income students have been hit hard by these disparities. In 2017, CPS students (85 percent of whom were Black and Latinx) accounted for 20 percent of the state's students but received only 15 percent of state funds, the rest of which went to the state's other districts, which served a student population that was 58 percent White. Within the city, CPS and city officials have also pursued racially discriminatory policies that maintain resource inequities between different CPS schools. In the 1980s, funds marked for "equal educational opportunity programs" often more generously supplemented magnet, selective enrollment, and specialty programs, instead of adequately serving their intended compensatory function at Black schools. Moreover, between 1995 and 2005, as Mayor Daley presided over charter school expansion and spending to build new selective enrollment schools, he also approved diverting local tax funds earmarked for teachers' pensions to cover CPS's operating costs. This further plummeted CPS into debt. Beyond government funds, parents at the most elite CPS schools in the city—with disproportionately more White and economically advantaged students than the rest of the school system—raise millions of dollars in "Friends of" nonprofits to garner additional teachers, aides, programs, and resources for their schools.[20]

Elected officials and corporate reformers often comment that we can't keep "throwing money at the problem" in public schools. This is an anachronistic critique because CPS schools generally, and Black schools specifically, have never received racially equitable resources and funding. The many reforms documented in this book—for desegregation, community control, local school councils—tied these demands to increased and equitable funding for schools. While elements of these demands were implemented to some degree, if only temporarily—as in increased parental involvement/control in schools, marginal desegregation via magnet schools, and decentralization of power to the school level—the accompanying demands for increased and equitable funding for schools to meet the needs of students were never adequately met at the local, state, or federal level. Many of these proposed reforms could have worked, but not without the necessary funding. Ultimately, a stark reordering of our political priorities and a dramatic, progressive economic redistribution for schools, and our society at large, are necessary to provide Black students with an equitable, robust education.

Meanwhile on the contrary, education, perhaps more than any other part of the public sector, has laid bare the convergence of Democrats and Republicans in support of a neoliberal agenda. Before the vote to confirm President Donald Trump's nominee for U.S. secretary of education, Betsy DeVos, Senate Democrats made impassioned speeches on the floor of the Senate chamber in opposition to her nomination. To delay the confirmation vote, senators stood one by one and spoke all night about the virtues and necessity of high-quality, universally accessible public schools for the benefit of our most vulnerable students, the economy, civil society, and U.S. democracy. This was not without irony. Many of the Trump administration's K–12 education policies are but a more extreme extension of the market-based policies developed under Democrats in Chicago and amplified nationally by Democrats in the Clinton and Obama administrations that have eroded support for public schools. DeVos's advocacy for siphoning public monies to fund for-profit and religious schools may be more extreme than some Democrats' previous proposals. But despite the Democrats' lip service to the value and virtues of public education, since the 1990s they have often collaborated with Republicans to support corporate education reform policies and "school choice" measures that privatize public K–12 education. DeVos and the Trump administration aspired to knock down a door that had been steadily pushed more ajar by Democrats for years. The focus on "choice" and the needs of individual students deflected attention and resources away from efforts aimed at righting the historic systemic inequities that Black education reformers have struggled against for decades. Choice policies have failed to address problems of institutional racism in education that relegate African American students as a group to separate and unequal schools.[21]

In Chicago, it has been clear for some time that the emperor has no clothes. In this virtually one-party city, establishment Democratic leaders and their party organization have been the antagonists of movements for racial and economic justice in the city for most of the last eighty years. Chicago's rich organizing history is also formidable. Parents, teachers, and community groups from Black and Latinx urban neighborhoods continue to be on the front lines of opposition to austerity measures and the neoliberalization of public education, employing elements of the philosophies and tactics of earlier Black education struggles. Like earlier movements, these efforts generated national models for struggles against racist austerity policies.

"STAND UP AND FIGHT BACK!": AN OTHERWISE POLITICS

"When public education is under attack . . . what do we do? Stand up and fight back!" Since 2010, the CTU has been at the forefront of the fight against the politics of austerity. In the 2000s, the emergent Caucus of Rank-and-File Educators within the CTU, initially organized by White leftist teachers, participated in citywide progressive coalitions and organized alongside parent and community groups across the city that were pushing back against school closings, the proliferation of charter schools, and issues related to racial and economic inequality that impacted CPS families, the majority of which were low-income Black and Latinx families. Many of the people and neighborhood groups that the Caucus of Rank-and-File Educators partnered with had deep roots in earlier struggles against racial and educational inequities, including organizers in the Kenwood-Oakland Community Organization, PURE, Blocks Together, the Pilsen Alliance, and Designs for Change. Black and Latinx parents and community groups were among the first to fight back against school closings, with rank-and-file educators later joining these struggles. In 2010, CTU members voted to replace the by-then complacent CTU leadership with Karen Lewis and the other members of the Caucus of Rank-and-File Educators. This signaled a renewed commitment to the type of community organizing forged by Lillie Peoples and other Black educators during the 1960s and 1970s. The insurgency of the Caucus of Rank-and-File Educators developed from the ground up with teachers, parents, and community members working together. Teachers were once again organizing in the communities where their students lived, fighting back against city education reform plans that disproportionately impacted Black communities. They struggled for increased funding and resources for traditional public schools and against the broader policies and economic and social forces that supported disinvestment in Black and Latinx communities more broadly.[22]

The groundswell of community support that teachers received during the 2012 CTU strike was a culmination of several years of organizing by community organizations and CTU members in Chicago's Black and Latinx communities. During the strike, Chicago teachers negotiated issues of wages and compensation, but they also raised issues that were fundamental to any serious effort to transform public education and improve the quality of education for all children: smaller class sizes; reinstatement of the arts, physical education, and world language; adequate wraparound support services and professionals in all schools; and improved school facilities, technological resources, and instructional supplies. Karen Lewis understood the CTU's struggle as part of a global struggle: "People across the globe took note of our struggle because so many have lost faith that the voices of teachers, paraprofessionals and clinicians could be heard over the clamorous din of billionaire hedge fund operators, education dilettantes and misguided education missionaries. The conversation about the conditions in which many of our children live and learn was revived. . . . Those who claim we use poverty as an excuse make excuses for not challenging poverty. Those who have willfully or ignorantly supported policies that de-stabilize communities have been called to the carpet."[23] This vision of quality education and a more equitable distribution of resources is strikingly similar to the demands made by desegregation protesters, community control advocates, and organizations of Black teachers during the 1960s and 1970s.

A new generation of Black activist teachers emerged out of the extremely racially and economically diverse group that supported the strike. Brandon Johnson and Tara Stamps were part of this new generation of Black teacher activists, but their activism also developed in relation to Black political struggles of the past. Tara's mother, Marion Stamps, was a longtime public housing activist in Cabrini-Green whose community organizing efforts contributed to the election of Harold Washington. As a teacher, Tara Stamps worked at Jenner Elementary in the same neighborhood where she was raised and organized teachers, parents, and community members to keep Jenner Elementary open during the rash of school closings in 2013. Stamps mentored Brandon Johnson when he taught at Jenner. Johnson also learned about the struggles of previous generations of Black teachers from Dr. Grady Jordan, a retired teacher who was a member of the Black Teachers Caucus in the 1960s and mentored Johnson. For Johnson, these were formative relationships: "Understanding that struggle made the current fight that much more real. To be honest with you, I think it's where I find strength. . . . I feel like there's too much to protect of what we once had, and there's so much more to gain." Informed by this history, Johnson argues that Karen Lewis is "the embodiment of the Black political consciousness for this country" in the context of a longer tradition of Black women leaders, akin to "Nancy P. Jefferson or Marion Stamps and Ida B. Wells, Fannie Lou Hamer. Highly intelligent, highly gifted people. Extremely swift in their ability to think and process and purposeful agitation." Johnson helped to revive a new CTU Black Caucus and became a full-time CTU organizer the year before the 2012 strike. Building on their organizing work, both Stamps and Johnson have also run for local political office.[24]

Karen Lewis emerged as the face of the 2012 CTU strike and, for many, became a symbol of the possibility of a renewed progressive politics that centered on struggles for racial and economic justice. Many of her supporters anxiously anticipated the news that Lewis planned to challenge Rahm Emanuel as a candidate in the 2015 mayoral election. In early polling she was ahead of Emanuel. Unfortunately, she was diagnosed and treated for cancer just before the election and was unable to run. Jesús "Chuy" García accepted the endorsement of Lewis and the CTU, but he was unable to harness the charisma, accessible progressive politics, or community excitement (particularly in Chicago's Black communities) that Lewis had generated, leaving many to wonder what could have been. Despite this electoral setback and the tragedy of mass school closings, the joint organizing by parents, community groups, and the CTU destabilized and challenged what had become the accepted narrative of the necessity of corporate education reform and privatization. By way of example, in 2016 the *Chicago Reporter* revealed that the conservative Walton Family Foundation, which at one point spent more money funding charter schools in Chicago than anywhere else in the country because of its confidence in pro-charter mayor Emanuel, stopped funding charter schools in Chicago because local organizing had made the city a "hostile political climate" for charter school expansion.[25] As has been the case historically, Chicago continues to generate national models for Black organizing and grassroots politics.

Today, emergent movements are under way. As in previous eras, incidents of police brutality and state violence have been the catalyst for mass movements of Black people. When people exclaimed "Black Lives Matter" in the 2010s, they were also declaring that Black communities matter. Movements across the country have linked violent acts perpetrated on Black people, from police violence to the material violence of the low-wage service economy to the state violence of mass incarceration and poor-quality education.

Young people in particular are leading the way as organizers in intersectional struggles for racial and economic justice. In Chicago, Black and Latinx young people have developed a new set of organizations to support this work: the Black Youth Project 100 (BYP 100), Black Lives Matter Chicago, Let Us Breathe Collective, Voices of Youth in Chicago Education, Fearless Leading by the Youth (FLY), and Chicago Students Organizing to Save Our Schools. While many of these organizations are led by youth, they also have intergenerational dimensions. FLY was founded in 2007 by Black youth in Woodlawn organizing for improved conditions in the Cook County Juvenile Temporary Detention Center and later leading a coalition for a new level-one adult trauma center at the University of Chicago—TWO's foe and later collaborator. BYP 100 was founded in Chicago in 2013 from a national convening of young Black organizers brought together by University of Chicago professor and Black scholar-activist Cathy J. Cohen and galvanized by George Zimmerman's acquittal for killing Black teenager Trayvon Martin. BYP 100 now has multiple chapters and has waged campaigns for investments in quality childcare and public schools and against the school-to-prison pipeline as part of its "Agenda to Build Black Futures." Chicago Students Organizing to Save Our Schools is an organization led by Black and Latinx CPS students who have worked with the CTU and other community-based organizations to fight against school closings, including holding a citywide school boycott against the massive school closings in 2013.[26]

While many of these organizations may now invoke or be understood to be under the umbrella of #BlackLivesMatter, they all pre-dated the 2014–15 surge in Black uprisings and protest movements nationally. Many of the people involved in these groups cut their teeth and were politicized in youth, student, and education-related activism and engaged in multi-issue collaborative and coalitional organizing. While there is no straight line to be drawn between earlier movements for racial justice and the movements emerging today, many of the activists in these efforts make explicit connections between their movements and past struggles for racial justice. These contemporary movements force us to reconsider the multiple ideologies and strategies of Black organizers during the late twentieth century. Despite the impression that the late twentieth century was a period of demobilization when Black activism languished, Black people continued to organize, particularly at the local level. Their efforts served as examples to activists who would come later, planting the seeds for the political movements that would sprout during the early twenty-first century.

"Black Lives Matter" is an educational demand alongside other demands (for reparations, self-determination, and economic justice, and against state and gender-based violence, criminalization, and incarceration, among other things). Several dozen Black-led organizations from around the country created and endorsed the national policy platform of the Movement for Black Lives. Released in the summer of 2016, around the time of the Democratic National Convention, the platform included demands for "an end to the privatization of education and real community control by parents, students, and community members including Democratic School Board and Community Control Curriculum, Hiring/Firing, and Discipline policies." Education also figured prominently in organizers' "invest-divest" model, which included demands for "investments in the education, health and safety of Black people, instead of investments in the criminalizing, caging, and harming of Black people." Black women, like those in the education struggles documented in this book, have historically played central roles in Black freedom struggles. However, in contrast to previous generations, Black women, and queer Black women in particular, have more regularly served as the public faces and spokespersons of #BlackLivesMatter era organizing. This is not only a representational politics but also an intersectional politics that intentionally "elevat[es] the experiences and leadership of the most marginalized Black people, including but not limited to those who are women, queer, trans, femmes, gender nonconforming, Muslim, formerly and currently incarcerated, cash poor and working class, disabled, undocumented, and immigrant" to the center of organizing efforts. For education, this articulation includes "a constitutional right at the state and federal level to a fully-funded education which includes a clear articulation of the right to: a free education for all, special protections for queer and trans students, wrap around services, social workers, free health services (including reproductive body autonomy), a curriculum that acknowledges and addresses students' material and cultural needs, physical activity and recreation, high quality food, free daycare, and freedom from unwarranted search, seizure or arrest." As previous generations of organizers, activists, and revolutionaries have, this movement implores us to fight for transformative public educational spaces and expanded robust state resources and to "demand the impossible."[27]

Contributing to this emergent national political movement, a predominantly Black group of parents and community members in Chicago launched a thirty-four-day hunger strike to reopen Walter H. Dyett High School in August 2015. Dyett was located in the historically Black Bronzeville community that had been ravaged by school closings during the 2000s and 2010s. Black mothers and grandmothers, LSC members, Bronzeville area teachers, and organizers with the Kenwood-Oakland Community Organization collaborated with education scholars from the University of Illinois at Chicago, the CTU, and faith and community leaders as part of the Coalition to Revitalize Dyett. This coalition put forth a plan to reopen Dyett as a high school focused on global leadership and green technology. The decision to hold a hunger strike was an extreme measure taken after years of negotiations over a plan for Dyett's future and consistent rebuffs from CPS leaders. While the hunger strikers' plan for a high school focused on green technology and global leadership was not implemented, the school was reopened as a neighborhood high school focused on the arts, a feat that would have been unthinkable without community pressure.[28]

In explaining why she participated in the hunger strike, Dr. Monique Redeaux-Smith, a veteran Black CPS teacher, echoed the work of Lillie Peoples and the teachers in Operation Breadbasket's Teachers' Division in making connections between the challenges facing Black students, Black teachers, and Black communities:

> I have often taught children in dilapidated buildings, with ancient heating and cooling systems, if they have air conditioning at all. I have seen public schools closed in historic numbers: shut down and "turned around" only to be worse than the "failing" schools they supposedly rehabilitated. I have seen experienced Black teachers—anchors in the community, mentors who showed me how to maintain my love and appreciation for children while at the same time working for a system that despises these children—pushed out, laid off, and shamed by an unfair and biased evaluation system that labels their many years of experience as "developing."
>
> I have seen politicians and businessmen use education as a "get-rich-quick" scheme. While teachers are held accountable for more but provided with fewer and fewer resources, these same millionaire politicians assert

that we haven't put enough "skin in the game" and should not only work tirelessly with underprivileged students for 30–40 years in the conditions mentioned above, but should do so only to look forward to living in poverty once we retire because they refuse to adequately fund our pensions.

But in these ten years I have also met extraordinary Black and Brown young people who demonstrate that resiliency is as inherent within them as their hair and eye color. Students that inspire me with their brilliance. Students who I shed tears of joy with as they invite me to their prom send-offs and college trunk parties, and too many that I shed tears of sorrow and regret over as they are taken from us too soon.

These are the reasons why I go hungry for Dyett. Because I refuse to accept that the current state of education is the best we can do. Because every child deserves a world class education in their neighborhood. Because every child should see themselves reflected in their teachers and in their curricula. Because our children of color should see that both their bodies and their lives matter; that their greatness is what will transform our society. Because teachers deserve to be treated as professionals with knowledge and expertise that is not only valued, but coveted, especially as their years of experience increase. Because parents and families deserve a space where they, too, are valued and respected as having knowledge and expertise that is needed in the classroom. I am an experienced Black teacher, a mother, a union activist, and a resident in the community of Dyett High School. This is why I go hungry for Dyett.[29]

As in earlier eras, the coalitions that have more recently formed to fight for racial, economic, and educational justice are not without their tensions, both interracial and intraracial: between young organizers and more established organizations and labor unions, between community groups with constituencies from different parts of the city, between activists and educators with different ideological approaches to organizing and different ideas about what are the most pressing issues facing marginalized communities. Nonetheless, Chicago has been on the front lines of building coalitions against austerity policies and for racial and economic justice. These coalitions are mobilizing massive public demonstrations, pushing for sustainable community-based schools and for the decriminalization of Black and Latinx youth in schools and communities, lobbying for an elected representative school board and funding equity, and redefining "sanctuary" schools as sanctuaries from persecution for undocumented students and from state-sanctioned racial violence against Black children, among other efforts.

The period after the national mass mobilizations of the Civil Rights Movement, urban uprisings, and Black Power Movement is often imagined as a new nadir, a low point in African American life. There is no doubt that the deteriorating conditions in Black urban communities were very real and linked to deindustrialization, disinvestment, and institutional racism that isolated poor African Americans in urban centers.[30] However, as this book argues, African Americans continued to organize for better housing, employment opportunities, and quality education in a range of grassroots, community-based, and racial uplift organizations.

These diverse groups did not a share a single ideology but espoused various versions of integrationist, uplift, nationalist, Black feminist, socialist, and community control ideologies. The work of translating these political ideologies into practice on the ground was never straightforward or easy. With every political turn and choice, there were new opportunities and constrained political possibilities. Within Chicago's political context these struggles were further suppressed by the political apparatus of the Chicago Democratic machine, which by the late 1960s had bound itself to a racial politics that was blatantly antagonistic to African Americans.

It is thus all the more impressive that Black Chicagoans with differing political interests and ideologies joined together in the campaign to elect Harold Washington as the first Black mayor of Chicago. Black Chicagoans with distinctly different political ideologies put aside the issues that divided them — or at least ignored them temporarily — in order to harness the collective political will necessary to achieve a common goal. This collective success, however, was achieved in the context of a political election. Once Washington began governing, the fissures amongst his Black supporters and interracial coalitions reemerged. After Washington's death, his reform coalition crumbled. Without his leadership, there was no organizational infrastructure or equally charismatic leader to step into his place. Intraracial and interracial political divisions and the moments, like Washington's election and administration, that had the power to transcend these ideological chasms indicate the potential force and tenuous nature of Black power and Black politics.

Beyond political strategies, Black education organizers of an earlier era provide a set of alternative visions of society: interracial visions, visions of community control, visions of African diasporic identities, visions of equitable distributions of resources, visions of control and power over one's labor, visions of liberation, and visions of interconnected institutions that affirm the lives of Black people. These alternative visions of society echo Ashon Crawley's call for "a return to Black radicality as the space and zone from which otherwise modalities of living can emerge." Crawley goes on: "That the demands of various organizations have come from a decentralized Black leadership is important given the ways the voices of Black folks are often drowned out of such conversations about possible otherwise ways to be in the world."[31] Black education reformers' alternative visions for society create an opportunity for us to imagine otherwise worlds as well.

ACKNOWLEDGMENTS

Scholarly life is often characterized as a cloistered-away, solitary pursuit. That has never been my experience. So many people have walked with me and supported this book with their time, energy, and love. My village is fierce and deep. First, I need to thank the dozens of educators, organizers, parents, students, and civic leaders who graciously shared their stories with me in formal interviews and informal conversations. This book is dedicated to you. I've had the privilege of conducting amazing oral histories for this project. In particular, I must acknowledge Lillie Peoples, Soyini Walton, Carol Lee, Hal Baron, Karen Lewis, and Aurelia Spurlark for engaging in multiple follow-up conversations and meetings and often allowing me access to their private personal papers and photographs. Unfortunately, Ms. Peoples and Mr. Baron passed away before this book was published, but I hope to have honored their dedication to their life's work in these pages. I could not have uncovered many parts of the history in this book without the generosity of my interviewees.

While the stories of Black education organizers have not always been adequately documented in official historical records, I have certainly also relied on many archives and rich manuscript collections. I am indebted to the archivists at the Chicago Board of Education, University of Chicago Special Collections, the Chicago Public Library's Harold Washington Archives and Collections, and the Chicago History Museum. I am particularly grateful for the extensive time, patience, and meticulous assistance offered by Beverly Cook and Beth Loch at the Vivian G. Harsh Research Collection of Afro-American History and Literature at the Carter G. Woodson branch of the Chicago Public Library, and by Valerie Harris, Roberta Dupuis-Devlin, and Miguel Vazquez at the University of Illinois at Chicago's Special Collections and Photo Services. I would also like to thank Debby Pope and the staff at the Chicago Teachers Union for allowing me access to their in-office materials before their formal collection was processed.

I have so appreciated the University of North Carolina Press's enthusiasm for, and dedication to, this book. I would like to thank series editors Rhonda Williams and Heather Ann Thompson for their support of the project and my anonymous readers for their thoughtful consideration of the manuscript and thorough feedback. I would particularly like to thank Brandon Proia for making this entire process pleasant and productive. Brandon's critical eye, poignant feedback, transparency, and candor helped me to produce a book of which I am truly proud.

I was fortunate to secure a number of grants and fellowships supporting this project over the last decade, including financial and professional development resources from the National Academy of Education, the Spencer Foundation, the UIC Institute for Research on Race and Public Policy (IRRPP), the Social Science Research Council, the Andrew W. Mellon Foundation, the American Council of Learned Societies, and the Ford Foundation. Thank you to all the fellowship administrators, and particularly Tracy Sikorski at UIC, for helping me to plan and to make the most of these funds.

In my academic work I have been guided, challenged, and supported by an amazing group of mentors and advisors. But for the Mellon Mays Undergraduate Fellowship (MMUF) program at the University of Pennsylvania, I would never have thought it possible to research and write a book or pursue a career as a professor. At Penn, Barbara Savage, Herman Beavers, Valerie Swain-Cade McCoullum, Erica Armstrong Dunbar, Madeleine López, Chad Williams, Karlene Burrell-Mcrae, Sean Vereen, Valerie De Cruz, and Erin Cross taught me what it meant to be a scholar and modeled how to occupy academic spaces while honoring and working to serve the many people who have been systemically excluded from these same spaces. As an undergraduate in the Summer Research Opportunities Program at the University of Chicago, Mae Ngai and Arissa Oh kindly guided me through my first real experience conducting archival research in this city, and Allen Bryson and Christopher Freeburg taught me that I could continue to work hard and play hard as a graduate student. I cannot thank my advisors Tom Holt, Adam Green, and Charles Payne enough for rigorously and compassionately training me in the craft of history and shepherding me through my graduate studies at the U of C. I had an opportunity to take classes with Jim Grossman, who has continued to be a great support to me professionally. I am grateful that Tracye Matthews, Waldo Johnson, Michael Dawson, Theresa Mah, and the staff at the Center for the Study of Race, Politics and Culture created an oasis from the angst of graduate school where I could be my whole self. In graduate school I was also privileged to find an incredibly supportive network of fierce women scholars who mentored me and demonstrated the praxis of feminism, including Cathy Cohen, Melissa Harris Perry, and Leora Auslander. Thank you to my MMUF graduate initiatives program mentors, Cally Waite, O. Hugo Benevides, Michelle Scott, and Jacqueline Lazú, who helped me to push through the challenges of research and writing with care and empathy. They have continued to be sources of encouragement as I wrote this book. I am a better historian, scholar, and person because of the brilliant people who trained me.

Since I earned my Ph.D., the professional network of mentors, colleagues, and institutional spaces that have embraced this project have been similarly exceptional. The staff at Northwestern University's Alice Kaplan Institute for the Humanities, where I was a postdoctoral fellow, provided me with the space and time to begin writing this book in earnest. My colleagues at Governors State University helped me to become a better teacher and better scholar of education. During this time, I particularly benefited from my conversations and writing sessions with Debbie James. At UIC, my colleagues at and beyond the institution have further encouraged my professional growth and propelled this book to completion. I would particularly like to acknowledge Barbara Ransby, Jennie Brier, Cedric Johnson, Michelle Boyd, and Martha Biondi, who took the time to read and/or talk through significant parts of and issues related to the manuscript. My UIC colleagues Cynthia Blair, Chris Boyer, Joaquín Chávez, Leon Fink, Laura Hostetler, Lynn Hudson, Robert Johnston, Mónica Jiménez, Sue Levine, Rama Mantena, Sekile Nzinga-Johnson, Jane Rhodes, Kevin Schultz, and Rachel Weber offered timely encouragement and guidance for navigating academic life and publishing. I'm also indebted to Beth Ritchie, Francesca Gaiba, Iván Arenas, Amanda Lewis, Jill Petty, and IRRPP staff for the financial and writing group support that helped to push this project along.

This is a book about education, and I have to thank my students and fellow educators for their support in bringing this project to fruition. For four years I worked as a part-time teacher and counselor at the UChicago Charter School Woodlawn Campus. There I was nurtured and mentored by my colleagues on the AS3 staff, a group of Black educators whose collective years of work in Chicago's schools greatly informed my approach to this project. Special thanks to my colleagues "Queen Mother" Victoria Woodley, Lolita Godbold, Nicole Buckner, Johnny Dorsey, Tiffany Ellis, Dion Steele, Nabiha Calcuttawala, Curtis Nash, Greg Ingleright, Elizabeth Whittaker, LaTasha McMillan, Rob Lane, and Cheryl Daniel-Dyer, and my principals Barbara Crock and Shayne Evans. In that time, I was also privileged to work with incredible students. I am certain that I learned more from them than I ever taught them. My teaching experiences have been similarly rich at Governors State and UIC, public institutions where I've had the privilege to teach and learn from many undergraduate and graduate students who aim to become teachers or advance their craft as teachers. I know that my own work is also stronger for having engaged with the work and activism of UIC graduate students, in particular Jennifer Ash, Prudence Browne, Louis Mercer, Adam Mertz, and Marie Rowley. Thank you also to my amazing graduate research assistants: Eliot Fackler, for his tireless and diligent editorial work and research support, and José Acosta-Córdova, for his dedication to the project and map and data expertise.

I am a social writer and need people around me when I write. Thank you to Kerry Ann Rockquemore and the National Center for Faculty Development and Diversity for inviting me to my first write-on-site and introducing me to new writing strategies, and to my long-term accountability partners Kimberly Blockett and Yolonda Wilson, who helped me push these pages out and became dear friends. I am also grateful for my write-on-site crew, organized by Marisha Humphries and Lorena Garcia, who literally sat next to me weekly as I wrote and finished this book. Thank you to Chavella Pittman, Twyla Blackmond Larnell, Lali Morales, Tasleem Padamsee, Darcy Leach, and Marisha for your feedback on chapters at our writing retreats. Thank you also for the support of my writing buddies at my local coffee shops, particularly LaTrice Davis at Sip & Savor and Isis Ferguson at Currency Exchange Café.

So many mentors, colleagues, and friends have impacted this work in a variety of ways. Thank you to James Anderson, Dionne Danns, V. P. Franklin, Crystal Sanders, Michelle Purdy, and Michael Hevel, whose work on the history of education has inspired my own and whose feedback has made my scholarship better. I am grateful to scholar and activist Fannie Rushing for letting me learn from her and welcoming me into her community of veteran civil rights organizers. I have also learned so much from my super-smart friends since our Penn days: Isis Semaj Hall, Nicole Fields, Chevon Walker, Arinze Onugha, Courtney Patterson, Samir Meghelli, Robeson Taj Frazier, and Tanji Gilliam. My U of C support system got me through graduate school: Janette Gayle, Jennifer Vanore, Jessica Neptune, Quincy Mills, Dave Ferguson, Laurence Ralph, Jessica Graham, Marcus Board, Ainsley LeSure, Marcelle Medford, and Kodi Roberts. My extended MMUF family, Janaka Lewis, Uri McMillan, Dennis Tyler, Alisha Gaines, Jessica Marie Johnson, Treva Lindsey, and Trimiko Melancon, was always there to encourage my work and me. Much love to Danielle Smith and the potluck crew. A special thanks goes to Keeanga-Yamahtta Taylor, whose friendship and poignant feedback kept my writing going and deeply influenced this book. I must also thank my friend, the gifted writer and editor Summer McDonald, for her feedback and many conversations that helped make this a better book. I am so grateful to Summer, Moya Bailey, and Ashon Crawley for being my sounding board and cherished confidants throughout this process. To my besties and day-one supporters, Jasmine Harris, Stephanie Allen, Nicole Beechum, Kafi Moragne-Patterson, and Michelle Russell, I love you. To my brilliant friend Jonathan Rosa, thank you for being with me since the beginning of this journey, reading and rereading so many drafts of this manuscript, picking me up off the floor, and going out to celebrate along the way.

I am filled with gratitude for my amazingly supportive family. To my aunts and uncles and cousins, thank you for always supporting me. Your pride in me was so sustaining. Christina and Keyandra, thank you for always encouraging me and being the sisters that I needed. Jonny, thank you for being a calming voice of reason. To my Bubbie, my soulmate, thank you for demonstrating what unconditional love and joy look like in a world that, at times, seems lacking in both. My parents remain my first and best teachers and my greatest cheerleaders. My mother's life work in public advocacy on issues of education and labor deeply impacted this book and my decision to become an educator. I am ever grateful for the love of African American history that my father imparted to me at a young age. I love my parents immensely, and their influence (and remote archival research assistance!) runs through these pages. Alex, you have been my rock now for half of my life. Your keen reading and feedback on almost every aspect of this book was indispensable. You took care of me, and our family, so that I could pursue this project. Words fail to express the depths of what you mean to me or how much I love and appreciate you. My babies Natalie and Julia were born in this beautiful and challenging city after I started writing this book, but they've impacted every page. They made this a better book, made me a better person, and remind me constantly why a better world is worth fighting for.

NOTES

Abbreviations in the Notes

Beadle Records	University of Chicago Office of the President, Beadle Administration Records, University of Chicago Special Collections
CBOE Archives	Chicago Board of Education Archives
CTU Archives	Chicago Teachers Union Archives
CUL Records	Chicago Urban League Records, University of Illinois at Chicago Special Collections and University Archives
Davis Papers	Allison Davis Papers, University of Chicago Special Collections
Levi Records	University of Chicago Office of the President, Levi Administration Records, University of Chicago Special Collections
Peoples Papers	Lillie Peoples Personal Papers, Private Collection
Walton Papers	Soyini Walton Personal Papers, Private Collection
Washington Papers	Harold Washington Papers, Special Collections, Harold Washington Library Center, Chicago Public Library
Wyatt Papers	Rev. Addie and Rev. Claude Wyatt Papers, Carter G. Woodson Regional Library, Vivian G. Harsh Research Collection of Afro-American History and Literature

Introduction

1. Noreen Ahmed-Ullah and Joel Hood, "Nearly 90 Percent of Teachers Vote to Authorize Strike," *Chicago Tribune*, June 11, 2012; "Chicago Teachers Union (CTU) Strike Bulletin." I use "Latinx" as a gender nonbinary term for people of Latin American descent in the United States.

2. Klein, *Shock Doctrine*, 7–18; McNally, *Global Slump*, 5–31; Sugrue, *Origins of the Urban Crisis*; Peck, *Constructions of Neoliberal Reason*, 4–8; Harvey, *Brief History of Neoliberalism*, 2–3, 65–69; Brenner and Theodore, "Cities and the Geography of 'Actually Existing Neoliberalism,'" 2–32; Lipman, *New Political Economy of Urban Education*.

3. Notably in this classic social science "urban crisis" and urban "underclass" literature, see Wilson, *Declining Significance of Race*; Wilson, *Truly Disadvantaged*; and Massey and Denton, *American Apartheid*. For historical accounts of the "urban crisis," "White flight," and racial realignments of metropolitan space, see Katz, "*Underclass*" *Debate*; Hirsch, *Making the Second Ghetto*; Sugrue, *Origins of the Urban Crisis*; Sugrue, "Crabgrass-Roots Politics"; Jackson, *Crabgrass Frontier*; Kusmer, "African Americans in the City since World War II"; Self, *American Babylon*; and Gillette, *Camden after the Fall*.

4. On the rise of the right, conservatism, and suburban politics, see MacLean, *Democ-*

racy in Chains; Lassiter, Silent Majority; McGirr, Suburban Warriors; Nicolaides, My Blue Heaven; Troy, Morning in America; Moreton, To Serve God and Wal-Mart; Kruse, One Nation under God; Nickerson, Mothers of Conservatism; Stein, Pivotal Decade; and Avila, Popular Culture in the Age of White Flight.

5. Theoharis and Woodard, Freedom North; Murch, Living for the City; Williams, Politics of Public Housing; Countryman, Up South; Dougherty, More Than One Struggle.

6. Raser, "Quality Education Is the Civil Rights Issue of Our Time"; Bush, "Education Is the Civil Rights Issue of Our Time"; Kevin Johnson, "Education Is Still the Civil Rights Issue of Our Time," Louisville Courier-Journal, May 15, 2014. For a critique of this claim, see Powell, "No, Education Isn't the Civil Rights Issue of Our Time," and Ravitch, "Why Education Is Not the Civil Rights Issue of Our Time."

7. Scott and Holme, "Political Economy of Market-Based Educational Policies"; Payne, So Much Reform, So Little Change; Dixson, "Democracy Now?"; Lipman, New Political Economy of Urban Education; Buras et al., Pedagogy, Policy, and the Privatized City. For books that center on an organizing approach, see Dougherty, More Than One Struggle, and Danns, Something Better for Our Children.

8. Boyd, Jim Crow Nostalgia; Pattillo, Black on the Block; Dawson, Not in Our Lifetimes; Smith, Racial Democracy and the Black Metropolis; Johnson, Revolutionaries to Race Leaders; Reed, Stirrings in the Jug.

9. Joseph, Black Power Movement, 3; Green, Battling the Plantation Mentality, 3, 9. Williams, From the Bullet to the Ballot, 1–4; Johnson, Revolutionaries to Race Leaders, xxiv–xxxvii; Joseph, Neighborhood Rebels, 1–9. On different interpretations of Black Power, see Theoharis and Woodard, Freedom North; Biondi, Black Revolution on Campus; Countryman, Up South; Williams, Politics of Public Housing; Valk, Radical Sisters; Self, American Babylon; Thompson, Whose Detroit?; Mantler, Power to the Poor; Woodard, Nation within a Nation; Van Deburg, New Day in Babylon; and Ture and Hamilton, Black Power.

10. Anderson and Pickering, Confronting the Color Line, 168–94; Abu-Lughod, Race, Space, and Riots in Chicago, New York, and Los Angeles, 82–95; Williams, From the Bullet to the Ballot, 42–51; Royko, Boss, 155–65; Hampton, "Two Societies"; Joseph, Waiting 'til the Midnight Hour, 226–27; Orleck and Hazirjian, War on Poverty, 2–17; Vinovskis, Birth of Head Start, 36–39, 79–80. For an example of how local residents used War on Poverty funds and programs in a different city, see Germany, New Orleans after the Promises.

11. Building on works that extend the analysis of U.S. urban history and Black protest movements beyond the 1960s, see, for example, Hall, "Long Civil Rights Movement and the Political Uses of the Past"; Williams, Politics of Public Housing; Countryman, Up South; Theoharis and Woodard, Freedom North; Kusmer and Trotter, African American Urban History since World War II; and Chappell, War on Welfare. For a challenge to the idea of the Long Civil Rights Movement—that also interrogates Black freedom struggles before and after the 1960s—see Cha-Jua and Lang, "'Long Movement' as Vampire."

12. Brown v. Board of Education 347 U.S. 483 (1954); Patterson, Brown v. Board of Education; Ogletree, All Deliberate Speed; Orfield and Eaton, Dismantling Desegregation; Orfield, Must We Bus?; Orfield and Lee, "Brown at 50."

13. Moss, Schooling Citizens; Perry, "Up From the Parched Earth," 11–13, 19; Anderson, Education of Blacks in the South.

14. A number of Black schools were also established before emancipation. Between

1914 and 1927, Black southerners raised over $3.5 million to match philanthropist Julius Rosenwald's funds and build 3,769 schools in southern Black communities. See Anderson, *Education of Blacks in the South*, 4–11, 156–62, 285.

15. Watkins, "Reclaiming Historical Visions of Quality Schooling."

16. For more on Black education and dignity, see Irby, "Dignity-Based Black Male Achievement."

17. Stier and Tienda, *Color of Opportunity*, 43–53; Christopher Manning, "African Americans," *Encyclopedia of Chicago*; Barrett, *Work and Community in the Jungle*; Simpson interview by Fannie Rushing; Simpson interview by author; Dominic Pacyga, "Union Stockyard," *Encyclopedia of Chicago*.

18. Lang, *Black America in the Shadow of the Sixties*, xii.

19. Johnson, *Revolutionaries to Race Leaders*, xxiii–xxiv.

20. Drake and Cayton, *Black Metropolis*; Spear, *Black Chicago*; Grossman, *Land of Hope*; Baldwin, *Chicago's New Negroes*; Black, *Bridges of Memory: Chicago's First Wave of Black Migration*; Black, *Bridges Of Memory: Chicago's Second Wave of Black Migration*; Chatelain, *South Side Girls*. On migrant status and Black politics in a different city, see Murch, *Living for the City*.

21. Fraser and Gerstle, *Rise and Fall of the New Deal Order*; Cowie and Salvatore, "Long Exception"; Boyle, *Organized Labor and American Politics*; Battista, *Revival of Labor Liberalism*; O'Brien, *Workers' Paradox*; Freeman, *Working-Class New York*; Gross, *Broken Promise*; Davis, *Prisoners of the American Dream*.

22. Guinier, "From Racial Liberalism to Racial Literacy"; Scott, "Postwar Pluralism"; Scott, *Contempt and Pity*; Gordon, *From Power to Prejudice*, 1–25; Heclo, "1960s Civics"; Perlstein, *Justice, Justice*, 7–9; Biondi, *To Stand and Fight*, 137–90; Self, *American Babylon*, 52–58; Sugrue, "Crabgrass-Roots Politics."

23. Harris, *Price of the Ticket*, 36–45.

24. Grimshaw, *Bitter Fruit*.

25. Ibid.; Rivlin, *Fire on the Prairie*; Travis, "Harold," the People's Mayor; Anderson and Pickering, *Confronting the Color Line*.

26. Troy, *Morning in America*; Helgeson, *Crucibles of Black Empowerment*.

27. Osman, "Decade of the Neighborhood"; Pattillo, "Everyday Politics of School Choice in the Black Community"; Stulberg, *Race, Schools, and Hope*; Ravitch, *Reign of Error*, 15; Scott and Holme, "Political Economy of Market-Based Educational Policies"; Lipman, *New Political Economy of Urban Education*; Fabricant and Fine, *Charter Schools and the Corporate Makeover of Public Education*.

28. Collaborative for Equity and Justice in Education, "Research"; Chicago Public Schools: Renaissance 2010, "About Us."

29. Harris, *Price of the Ticket*, 3–45.

Chapter 1

1. Simpson interview by Fannie Rushing; Simpson interview by author; James R. Grossman, "Great Migration," *Encyclopedia of Chicago*.

2. Cutler, Glaeser, and Vigdor, "Rise and Decline of the American Ghetto," 472–73; Grossman, *Land of Hope*; Spear, *Black Chicago*; Hirsch, *Making the Second Ghetto*; Seligman, *Block by Block*; Anderson and Pickering, *Confronting the Color Line*.

3. Here I am using Earl Lewis's idea of congregation (*In Their Own Interests*, 90–96): the ways that African Americans reframed the structural limitations of segregation to claim space and create a relatively autonomous institutional and cultural life within Black communities. On migration and the culture of Black Chicago, see Baldwin, *Chicago's New Negroes*.

4. Simpson interview by Fannie Rushing; Simpson interview by author.

5. Historically Black high schools like Paul Laurence Dunbar in Washington, D.C., Frederick Douglass High School in Baltimore, Maryland, Crispus Attucks High School in Indianapolis, Indiana, and Howard High School in Wilmington, Delaware, were opened explicitly to serve Black students. Unlike many of these schools, which had been designed as segregated schools for Black students, when Phillips opened in 1904, it initially served the predominantly White students who lived near the school. As the Great Migration brought thousands of Black families into the neighborhoods surrounding Phillips, the community and the school's student population became all Black. See Simpson interview by Fannie Rushing; Simpson interview by author; Sufiya Abdur-Rahman, "Phillips High School Is Cradle of History: School of Legends May Be Landmark," *Chicago Tribune*, December 15, 2002; Stewart, *First Class*; "Crispus Attucks High School"; "Frederick Douglass High School"; and "History of Howard High School, Wilmington, Delaware."

6. Cobble, *Other Women's Movement*, 78–82; Christopher Manning, "African Americans," *Encyclopedia of Chicago*; Barrett, *Work and Community in the Jungle*; Fehn, "African-American Women and the Struggle for Equality," 47; Walker-McWilliams, *Reverend Addie Wyatt*.

7. Simpson interview by Fannie Rushing; Simpson interview by author; Fehn, "African-American Women and the Struggle for Equality," 47–51; Cobble, *Other Women's Movement*, 78–82.

8. Grimshaw, *Bitter Fruit*, 17–23; Cobble, *Other Women's Movement*, 78–82; Simpson interview by Fannie Rushing; Simpson interview by author.

9. Clinton E. Stockwell, "Englewood," *Encyclopedia of Chicago*.

10. Simpson interview by author; "'Politics' Charges Fly on 'Warehouse School': Classroom Empty, Church School Full as Parents Boycott," *Chicago Daily Defender*, February 2, 1963; Shipps, *School Reform, Corporate Style*, 65.

11. Simpson interview by author; "'Politics' Charges Fly on 'Warehouse School': Classroom Empty, Church School Full as Parents Boycott," *Chicago Daily Defender*, February 2, 1963; Simpson interview by Fannie Rushing.

12. Simpson interview by author.

13. "White Backlash," *Chicago Daily Defender*, October 15, 1966.

14. Bell, *Silent Covenants*, 4–10, 181–89; Payne, "'Whole United States Is Southern!'"

15. Orfield, "Growth of Segregation"; Orfield, *Must We Bus?*; Orfield and Lee, "*Brown* at 50."

16. Danns, *Desegregating Chicago's Public Schools*, 9; Danns, "Northern Desegregation," 79–82; Gadsden, *Between North and South*, 2–7, 195–96, 217–18.

17. Danns, *Desegregating Chicago's Public Schools*, 173–74; Danns, "Northern Desegregation," 79–82; Gadsden, *Between North and South*, 2–7, 195–96, 217–18; Ogletree, *All Deliberate Speed*; Orfield, *Must We Bus?*; Patterson, *Brown v. Board of Education*.

18. Payne, "'Whole United States Is Southern!,'" 89–91.

19. Patterson, *Brown v. Board of Education*, xxvi.

20. Langston Hughes, "The Dilemma of the Negro Teacher Facing Desegregation," *Chicago Defender*, October 1, 1955; "Negro Schools to Survive Desegregation: To Be Permanent, Patterson Says," *Chicago Daily Defender*, November 30, 1957; Fairclough, *Better Day Coming*. Payne ("'Whole United States Is Southern!,'" 89–91) notes that W. E. B. Du Bois's essays in the 1930s advocating for the development of race-based institutions contributed to his ouster from the NAACP, which embraced the fight for integration as a core component of its legal strategy.

21. Homel, "Politics of Public Education"; Homel, *Down from Equality*.

22. Anderson and Pickering, *Confronting the Color Line*, 46–55, 76–77; Mary E. H. Mark, "Parent Decries Conditions of Chicago Schools," *Chicago Defender*, July 2, 1938; Shipps, *School Reform, Corporate Style*, 65. At times Black communities' concerns over education took a back seat to concerns over employment and housing. Homel ("Politics of Public Education," 183, 191) notes that during the Depression era, direct-action protests around issues of education were rarer than prominent protests around issues of employment, such as the "Don't Spend Your Money Where You Can't Work" campaign.

23. Grimshaw, *Bitter Fruit*, 3–29; Peterson, *School Politics, Chicago Style*, 8–19.

24. Grimshaw, *Bitter Fruit*, 3–29; Peterson, *School Politics, Chicago Style*, 8–19.

25. Peterson, *School Politics, Chicago Style*, 3–17, 79–92.

26. During Willis's tenure as superintendent, over 200 schools were built or expanded. Under his administration, teachers' salaries increased, rewards and incentives for teachers with advanced levels of education were implemented, and the number of professional support staff—including nurses and psychologists—within the school system doubled. See Rury, "Race, Space, and the Politics of Chicago Public Schools," 124–32; Anderson and Pickering, *Confronting the Color Line*, 76–77; and Shipps, *School Reform, Corporate Style*, 69–70.

27. Rury, "Race, Space, and the Politics of Chicago Public Schools," 124–26; Anderson and Pickering, *Confronting the Color Line*, 46–49, 76–77; Homel, "Politics of Public Education," 183, 191.

28. Hickrod, Wallis, Hubbard, and Elder, "Brief History of K–12 Finance in Illinois"; CPS Annual Financial Report 1964, box Chicago Board of Education Finance, Annual Finance Reports 1937, 1939, 1940, 1943, 1947, 1957–1959, 1964, folder 1964, CBOE Archives.

29. Rury, "Race, Space, and the Politics of Chicago Public Schools," 126–27; Havighurst and Chicago Board of Education, *Public Schools of Chicago*.

30. Rury, "Race, Space, and the Politics of Chicago Public Schools," 127–30.

31. Danns, *Something Better for Our Children*, 26–30; "Willis Wagon Foe Is Vocal in Bias Fight," *Chicago Daily Defender*, September 4, 1963; "Hit 'Willis Wagons' in Englewood Community," *Chicago Daily Defender*, July 29, 1963; Simpson interview by Fannie Rushing; Simpson interview by author.

32. After an initial success in convincing the board to meet with CORE members and discuss their demands—negotiated by the Urban League, CORE, and board president Clair Roddewig—little changed and a wall was built, known as the "Willis Wall," at the Board of Education to prevent future sit-ins. See Danns, *Something Better for Our Children*, 29–30.

33. "Hit 'Willis Wagons' in Englewood Community," *Chicago Daily Defender*, July 29,

1963; Simpson interview by Fannie Rushing; Simpson interview by author; "Promise 3 More Weeks of Action at 73rd-Lowe," *Chicago Daily Defender*, August 15, 1963.

34. In the 2016 presidential primary race, this fifty-year-old Chicago neighborhood protest gained national media attention when a photograph surfaced of Democratic presidential candidate Bernie Sanders, at the time a student at the University of Chicago and a CORE activist, being arrested for his participation in the protest. See "'Fire Ben Willis,' Leader Demands," *Chicago Daily Defender*, August 21, 1963; "Hit 'Willis Wagons' in Englewood Community," *Chicago Daily Defender*, July 29, 1963; Simpson interview by Fannie Rushing; Simpson interview by author; "Promise 3 More Weeks of Action at 73rd-Lowe," *Chicago Daily Defender*, August 15, 1963; and Jeff Nichols, "The Untold School Segregation Story behind Bernie Sanders's 1963 Arrest," *Chicago Reader*, March 1, 2016.

35. Grimshaw, *Bitter Fruit*, 17–23; "Daley Flares at Picketing of Officials: Rips Integration Demonstrators," *Chicago Tribune*, August 17, 1963; Danns, *Something Better for Our Children*, 1, 26–30.

36. "School Pickets Stop: Leader, Daley Confer," *Chicago Tribune*, August 21, 1963; "'Fire Ben Willis,' Leader Demands," *Chicago Daily Defender*, August 21, 1963; "Promise 3 More Weeks of Action at 73rd-Lowe," *Chicago Daily Defender*, August 15, 1963; "Hit 'Willis Wagons' in Englewood Community," *Chicago Daily Defender*, July 29, 1963; Danns, *Something Better for Our Children*, 1, 26–30; Simpson interview by Fannie Rushing; Simpson interview by author.

37. CCCO was formally organized in 1961. The coalition eventually included around fifty official participating groups, including TWO, the Negro American Labor Council, interracial religious councils, Teachers for Integrated Schools, and the Chicago affiliates of the NAACP, SNCC, CORE, and other group. See Danns, *Something Better for Our Children*, 37–41; Anderson and Pickering, *Confronting the Color Line*; Simpson interview by Fannie Rushing; and Simpson interview by author.

38. Robnett, "African-American Women in the Civil Rights Movement, 1954–1965"; Sanders, *Chance for Change*, 80–92.

39. Danns, *Something Better for Our Children*, 34–35; Anderson and Pickering, *Confronting the Color Line*, 118–21; "Timeline."

40. "Minutes of Exploratory Conference of Persons Interested in National School Boycott," box 3, folder 7: Schools Boycott Research Materials, 1964–68, super series 1: Chicago Area Friends of SNCC (CAFSNCC), Chicago SNCC History Project, Carter G. Woodson Regional Library, Vivian G. Harsh Research Collection of Afro-American History and Literature; Anderson and Pickering, *Confronting the Color Line*, 118–21; Taylor, *Knocking at Our Own Door*, 6, 129–31; "Timeline."

41. Danns, *Something Better for Our Children*, 50.

42. Simpson interview by author; Quinn, Dickson, and Matthews, *'63 Boycott*; Simpson interview by Fannie Rushing.

43. As quoted in Danns, *Desegregating Chicago's Public Schools*, 1.

44. Danns, *Something Better for Our Children*, 50–54.

45. Shipps, *School Reform, Corporate Style*, 69–70, 175.

46. Nationally, civil rights and Black labor leader Bayard Rustin also remained committed to the principles of integration and promoted these ideals in New York City into the 1980s in his work with labor organizations. See Bayard Rustin, "Integration & Edu-

cation: 25 Years after Brown," *Los Angeles Sentinel*, May 24, 1979, and Perlstein, *Justice, Justice*, 81–96.

47. Williams's activism was in the context of more than six major race riots that broke out in Chicago between 1945 and 1954. These conflicts included prolonged violent struggles that lasted for months, as White residents fiercely opposed Blacks moving into their communities by organizing violent mobs—at times including as many as 10,000 White residents—to oppose perceived Black encroachment. See Weidner, "Debating the Future of Chicago's Youth," 82–87; Strickland, *History of the Chicago Urban League*, 155–61, 172–74, 180–97; and Green, *Selling the Race*.

48. "The Purposes and Goals of School Desegregation: A Position Statement to the City-wide Advisory Committee," October 1977, series II, box 261, folder 2620, CUL Records.

49. Reed, *Not Alms, but Opportunity*, 191–94; Pattillo, *Black on the Block*, 118–23.

50. Reed, *Not Alms, but Opportunity*, 5–7, 191–94; Pattillo, *Black on the Block*, 118–23; Burkholder, *Color in the Classroom*, 171–76. Scott ("Postwar Pluralism," 69–82) argues that the *Brown* decision, in particular, set the stage for struggles for multicultural education and pluralism in schools premised on a therapeutic understanding of race relations.

51. Strickland, *History of the Chicago Urban League*, 241.

52. Ibid., 222–23.

53. Ibid., 240; Sanders, *Chance for Change*, 80–91.

54. Chuck Stone, "The Rout of Civil Rights in Chicago: A Times to Re-Assess and Re-Group," *Chicago Daily Defender*, May 4, 1964; Anderson and Pickering, *Confronting the Color Line*, 291; Rivlin, *Fire on the Prairie*, 23–35; Simpson interview by author.

55. Speech by Edwin C. Berry at Baha'i Intercontinental Conference, October 7, 1967, series II, box, 277, folder 2733, CUL Records.

56. Remarks by Edwin C. "Bill" Berry at the Retreat of Operation PUSH, September 4, 1975, box 151, folder 11, Wyatt Papers.

57. Speech by Edwin C. Berry at Baha'i Intercontinental Conference, October 7, 1967, series II, box, 277, folder 2733, CUL Records.

58. Strickland, *History of the Chicago Urban League*, 229.

59. Gibson and Jung, "Historical Census Statistics on Population Totals by Race"; Fish, *Black Power/White Control*, 12; Seligman, *Block by Block*, 3–6, 213–15; Hirsch, *Making the Second Ghetto*, 212–58; Roger Biles, "Daley's Chicago," *Encyclopedia of Chicago*; Ann Durkin Keating, "Bungalow Belt," *Encyclopedia of Chicago*; Robin Einhorn, "Political Culture," *Encyclopedia of Chicago*; John Rury, "School Desegregation," *Encyclopedia of Chicago*.

60. "Unrealistic Plans for the Schools," *Chicago Tribune*, December 18, 1967, 22; Chicago Urban League Research Department, "Plan for a System of Educational Parks in Chicago," December 5, 1967, series II, box 74, folder 850, CUL Records; Chicago Public Schools, *Racial/Ethnic Survey—Students* (1980); Robin Einhorn, "Political Culture," *Encyclopedia of Chicago*; John Rury, "School Desegregation," *Encyclopedia of Chicago*.

61. "A Roundup: What Negros Are Thinking," *Chicago Daily Defender*, February 11, 1967.

62. Simpson interview by author.

63. Today these neighborhoods are known locally as Beverly and Morgan Park, respectively. However, in the materials produced by the organization at the time, the area today called Beverly is referred to consistently as "Beverly Hills."

64. While ESAA monies primarily funded local education agencies, the CUL received a portion of the 8 percent of ESAA funds in each state that were earmarked for nonprofit group projects in support of local education activities. In the 1970s, the CUL's ESAA Project received these federal funds, while CPS was denied ESAA funds for violating federal standards by failing to desegregate the teaching staff in its schools. See "Interracial/Intercultural Communications: A Media for Mobility, Change and Stability," July 11, 1973, series II, box 257, folder 2584, CUL Records.

65. Ibid.

66. "ESAA News," February 1974, series II, box 257, folder 2584, CUL Records; "ESAA News," July 1974, June 1975, and November 1975, series II, box 257, folder 2588, CUL Records; interdepartmental correspondence and attachments from Charles E. Johnson, ESAA Coordinator, February 4, 1975, series II, box 258, folder 2591, CUL Records.

67. Theoharis, "'We Saved the City,'" 61–62, 76–82; Formisano, Boston Against Busing, 1–2; "Desegregation Advisory Coalition Planning Meeting," December 1, 1976, series II, box 261, folder 2616, CUL Records.

68. The coalition was convened as a joint effort between the CUL, the CUL ESAA Project, and Aspira, Inc., of Illinois. This interracial group initially included CUL members and several representatives of the Beverly Hills–Morgan Park neighborhood organizations involved with the ESAA Project, including representatives of the Morgan Park Civic League, Vanderpoel Improvement Association, ESAA organizers, the Beverly–Morgan Park Council on Human Relations, and Concerned Parents of Morgan Park. Additional coalition members representing the Latinx community included ASPIRA, Inc.; the Latino Institute; and El Centro de La Casa. Representatives of neighborhood groups and nonprofits included Ada S. McKinley, Citizens Schools Committee, Hyde Park Kenwood Community Council, Organization of the North East, American Friends Service, Center for New Schools, Chicago Committee on Human Relations, and other concerned individuals. See Meg O'Connor, "Citizens Form Coalition to Aid City Desegregation Planning," Chicago Tribune, March 21, 1977, as well as "Desegregation Advisory Coalition Planning Meeting," December 1, 1976; "Steering Committee Meeting on Chicago Public School Desegregation," December 7, 1976; "Attendance at Desegregation Planning Meeting Chicago Circle Campus," December 1, 1976; and "Roster of Members of the Citizens Coalition on Desegregation," [December 1976], all series II, box 261, folder 2616, CUL Records.

69. Between 1975 and 1979, the U.S. Office of Education withheld federal ESAA funds from Chicago schools because of a lack of compliance with federal mandates to desegregate the teaching staff and inadequate services for students classified as "non-English speaking." At the state level, the Illinois State Board of Education put Chicago schools on probation and mandated that the city create a student desegregation plan in 1976. See Hess, "Renegotiating a Multicultural Society," 136, and "Desegregation Advisory Coalition Planning Meeting," December 1, 1976, series II, box 261, folder 2616, CUL Records.

70. Hess, "Renegotiating a Multicultural Society," 136; "Desegregation Advisory Coalition Planning Meeting," December 1, 1976, series II, box 261, folder 2616, CUL Records; Danns, Desegregating Chicago's Public Schools, 97–98; Meg O'Connor, "Citizens Form Coalition to Aid City Desegregation Planning," Chicago Tribune, March 21, 1977.

71. The implementation of "Access to Excellence" failed to meet the guidelines for

desegregation set forth by the state, and in 1979 federal authorities stepped in, effectively ending an era of state pressure to desegregate Chicago Public Schools. See Hess, "Renegotiating a Multicultural Society," 136; "School Desegregation Proposal," [1978], series II, box 261, folder 2620, CUL Records; and letter to John D. Carey from James W. Compton, April 16, 1979, series II, box 268, folder 2659, CUL Records.

72. Orfield, *Must We Bus?*

73. Danns, *Desegregating Chicago's Public Schools*, 19–27.

74. Ibid., 21–32.

75. "Busing Zealots," *Chicago Tribune*, January 11, 1968.

76. "Both Friends, Foes of Busing Unhappy at School Board Vote," *Chicago Tribune*, February 29, 1968.

77. "Catholic Interracial Council Backs Proposed Busing Plan," *Chicago Daily Defender*, February 3, 1968.

78. Ibid.; Casey Banas, "Pupil Bus Plan Delayed: Board Acts on Protests by Parents, Public Hearings to Be Called," *Chicago Tribune*, January 11, 1968.

79. "Cody for Busing," *Chicago Daily Defender*, January 29, 1968; "Chicago's 'Little Rock' Still Rocking," *Chicago Daily Defender*, February 10, 1968.

80. Danns, *Desegregating Chicago's Public Schools*, 42–50; Peter Negronda, "Year-Old Busing Plan Achieves Integration, Little Else," *Chicago Tribune*, March 9, 1969, 8.

81. Danns, *Desegregating Chicago's Public Schools*, 42–46.

82. Casey Banas, "Find City School Reading Level Low," *Chicago Tribune*, October 8, 1967.

83. Simpson interview by author; Wacquant and Wilson, "Cost of Racial and Class Exclusion in the Inner City," 13; Parks, "Revisiting Shibboleths of Race and Urban Economy," 125.

84. "Young Proposes Meaningful Action to Halt Poverty," *Chicago Daily Defender*, March 1, 1966.

85. "Moynihan Report Racial Tract, Says James Farmer," *Chicago Daily Defender*, December 20, 1965.

86. Danns, *Something Better for Our Children*, 66–71.

87. Betty Washington, "No Retreat: Dr. Redmond," *Chicago Daily Defender*, August 26, 1967, 1.

88. Mrs. Chatman Wailes, quoted in Danns, *Desegregating Chicago's Public Schools*, 36; Chicago Board of Education, "Transcript of Hearings at South Shore High School," February 5, 1968, 3, 4, Cyrus Hall Adams III Papers, box 35-4, Chicago History Museum.

89. Danns, *Desegregating Chicago's Public Schools*, 39.

90. Danns, *Something Better for Our Children*, 66–71.

91. Simpson interview by author.

Chapter 2

1. Sizemore, *Walking in Circles*, 9–28; "Barbara Sizemore, National Visionary"; Chase and Chase interview by author.

2. Sizemore, *Walking in Circles*, 27–32, 40.

3. Ibid., 27–42; Chicago Public Schools, *Racial/Ethnic Survey—Students* (1964); Chicago

Board of Education, "Head Count" Report, October 22, 1963, and CPS, September 1963 Facilities Inventory, in folder Aug.–Oct. 1963, box 1, Cyrus Hall Adams III Papers, Chicago History Museum; Illinois Department of Public Instruction, *Directory of Illinois Schools*.

4. Danns, *Something Better for Our Children*, 37–41; Anderson and Pickering, *Confronting the Color Line*, 2, 82–102; "Timeline"; "School-by-School Story of Boycott," *Chicago Daily Defender*, October 23, 1963.

5. Students above age five were divided into skill-level-based teaching groups— "lanes" A, B, C, and D—by content area. For example, all students over age five reading at level B in the primary grade were taught together in the same teaching group, regardless of age. The percentage of students deemed "ready to read" on the Metropolitan Readiness Test jumped from 23 percent to 47 percent within one year. See Sizemore, *Walking in Circles*, 42–43.

6. Ibid., 114.

7. Sizemore's children were excluded from activities and opportunities at integrated Evanston schools. See ibid., 43–47; "Sizemore Outlines City Desegregation Plan," *University Times*, 15 November 1979, Personal File: Sizemore, Barbara, University of Pittsburgh Archives Personal Files, University of Pittsburgh Archives & Special Collections; and Barbara Sizemore, "An Uncle Tom?," *Chicago Daily Defender*, August 11, 1970, 13.

8. In the early to mid-1960s, established civil rights groups in Chicago—including TWO, CCCO, and the CUL—were promoting desegregation as the solution to problems of racial inequality in education and other institutions. King lived in an apartment near Dvorak in 1966 when he led civil rights protests in Chicago. See Sizemore, *Walking in Circles*, 43–44; Danns, *Something Better for Our Children*, 20–54; and Anderson and Pickering, *Confronting the Color Line*, 2, 85–102, 105–26.

9. Fish, *Black Power/White Control*, 175–76.

10. Barbara A. Sizemore, "Making the Schools a Vehicle for Cultural Pluralism," [1971?], 16, box 64, folder 1, Sol Tax Papers, University of Chicago Special Collections.

11. Bell, *Silent Covenants*, 4–10, 181–89; Dougherty, *More Than One Struggle*, 173–78; Edmonds, "Effective Schools for the Urban Poor," 15–24; Henderson et al., "High-Quality Schooling for African American Students," 181–82; Taylor, *Knocking at Our Own Door*, 172.

12. Henderson et al., "High-Quality Schooling for African American Students"; Bell, *Silent Covenants*.

13. Williamson, "Community Control with a Black Nationalist Twist," 138, 152.

14. Coleman et al., *Equality of Educational Opportunity*; "Education: Is Minority Child Still Shut Out?," *Chicago Defender*, September 22, 1966; Payne, *So Much Reform, So Little Change*, 110; Sizemore, *Walking in Circles*, 86–87.

15. Coleman et al., *Equality of Educational Opportunity*, 20.

16. "Education: Is Minority Child Still Shut Out?," *Chicago Defender*, September 22, 1966.

17. Coleman maintained that the socioeconomic status of the fellow students of poor students was more important to their academic success than other educational interventions. See Coleman et al., *Equality of Educational Opportunity*, 22, 28; "Education: Is Minority Child Still Shut Out?," *Chicago Defender*, September 22, 1966; Schrag, "Why Our Schools Have Failed," 310–20; Kent, "Coleman Report," 83–88; Lee, "Historical Evolution of Risk and Equity," 66–69; "Johnson Years"; Bullard and Taylor, *Keepers of the Dream*, 423; and Sizemore, *Walking in Circles*, 88.

18. Schrag, "Why Our Schools Have Failed," 309–13.

19. Henderson et al., "High-Quality Schooling for African American Students," 170; Lee, "Historical Evolution of Risk and Equity," 66–69.

20. Henderson et al., "High-Quality Schooling for African American Students," 170; Lee, "Historical Evolution of Risk and Equity," 66–69; Coleman et al., *Equality of Educational Opportunity*, 22.

21. "Education: Is Minority Child Still Shut Out?," *Chicago Defender*, September 22, 1966; Rickford, "Integration, Black Nationalism, and Radical Democratic Transformation," 302; Williamson, "Community Control with a Black Nationalist Twist," 143–48; Dougherty, *More Than One Struggle*, 170–78; Shujaa and Afrik, "School Desegregation," 254–56.

22. Todd-Breland, "Control and Independence." For more on Ocean Hill–Brownsville and community control and civil rights in New York City, see Podair, *Strike That Changed New York*; Perlstein, *Justice, Justice*; Taylor, *Knocking at Our Own Door*; Taylor, *Civil Rights in New York City*; Gordon, *Why They Couldn't Wait*; Gittell and Berube, *Local Control in Education*; Kahlenberg, *Tough Liberal*; and Taylor, *Reds at the Blackboard*.

23. Todd-Breland, "Barbara Sizemore and the Politics of Black Educational Achievement"; Montgomery, "Our Changing School and Community," 273; Campbell, "Black Teacher and Black Power," 23–24; Frank Kent interview with Norma Jean Anderson, "Message to the Establishment," 64.

24. Fish, *Black Power/White Control*, 189–90.

25. Willis, "'Let Me In, I Have the Right to Be Here'"; Hale, "'Student as a Force for Social Change'"; Tag Archive for "SCLC," *Publishing the Long Civil Rights Movement*.

26. Abu-Lughod, *Race, Space, and Riots*, 3–7; Anderson and Pickering, *Confronting the Color Line*, 333–34; Seligman, "'But Burn—No,'" 230–32.

27. During the summer of 1966, urban uprisings broke out in Chicago in response to police violence in the Puerto Rican community near Division Street on the near Northwest Side and in the Black community near Roosevelt Road on the West Side. Mayor Richard J. Daley sent in National Guard troops to put down the Black uprising on the West Side. In 1968, there was not a concentrated uprising or similarly extensive property damage on the South Side. Scholars often attribute this difference to the historically older network of Black institutions on the South Side and the work of TWO and youth gangs like the Blackstone Rangers that helped to ease tensions on the streets in the wake of King's murder. See Anderson and Pickering, *Confronting the Color Line*, 168–94; Abu-Lughod, *Race, Space, and Riots*, 82–95; Williams, *From the Bullet to the Ballot*, 42–51; Seligman, *Block by Block*, 218–20; Hirsch, *Making the Second Ghetto*, 257; Royko, *Boss*, 155–65; Hampton, "Two Societies"; "Student Reactions Mixed over King's Death: Prayers, Plans, and Riots Are Outlets for Grief," *Chicago Daily Defender*, April 8, 1968, 16; Pacyga, *Chicago*, 354; and "West Madison Street, 1968," *Encyclopedia of Chicago*.

28. Williams, *From the Bullet to the Ballot*, 42–51; Hampton, "Two Societies"; Royko, *Boss*, 162–65; Seligman, "'But Burn—No.'"

29. Williams, *From the Bullet to the Ballot*, 42–51; Hampton, "Two Societies"; Royko, *Boss*, 162–65; Seligman, *Block by Block*, 218–20; Pacyga, *Chicago*, 354; "West Madison Street, 1968," *Encyclopedia of Chicago*; Seligman, "'But Burn—No,'" 234–35.

30. African Americans also participated in the protests during the Democratic Na-

tional Convention, including national affiliates and Illinois members of the Black Panther Party, members of the Blackstone Rangers, and comedian and activist Dick Gregory. In addition to protesting the war, Black protesters drew attention to police brutality, racial inequality, and persistent poverty in U.S. cities. See Williams, *From the Bullet to the Ballot*, 103–7; Simpson interview by Fannie Rushing; Alk, *American Revolution II*; and Sarah S. Marcus, "The Whole World Is Watching," *Encyclopedia of Chicago*.

31. Black students also organized at individual schools. Between 1965 and 1968, Black students like Clarence James and Patricia Smith at Marshall High School on the West Side organized Black student groups to protest against overcrowding, inadequate supplies, and racist teachers. Black students also held sit-ins, walkouts, and rallies at dozens of other schools across the city and rallied to support teachers who were fired for supporting civil rights activities. See Danns, "Chicago's High School Students' Movement for Quality Public Education," 138–44; Danns, *Something Better for Our Children*, 74–88; Donald Mosby, "Black Students Plan Big Walkout Today: Fifth Week of School Turmoil Here," *Chicago Daily Defender*, October 14, 1968; Faith C. Christmas, "35,000 Stage Peaceful School Walkout: Student Protesters Seek More Black Influence Here," *Chicago Daily Defender*, October 15, 1968; and Faith C. Christmas, "700 Teachers Join Second Boycott," *Chicago Daily Defender*, October 22, 1968.

32. Williams, *From the Bullet to the Ballot*, 64–80; Danns, *Something Better for Our Children*, 74–88; Biondi, *Black Revolution on Campus*, 79–113.

33. In March 1968, Chicano students in Los Angeles staged a series of mass walkouts or "blowouts" in response to the poor quality of education provided for Chicano students in public schools. Black students at Jefferson High School in South Los Angeles also walked out of school around the same time. As in Chicago, participants in the Los Angeles blowouts drew on support from Chicano teachers and community groups. As with many activist groups of the era in Chicago, protesting Black and Latinx students were closely monitored by Chicago's "Red Squad" in coordination with FBI surveillance of "subversive" groups. See Tejada, "Genealogies of the Student 'Blowouts' of 1968"; Delgado Bernal, "Grassroots Leadership Reconceptualized," 120; Theoharis, "'W-A-L-K-O-U-T!'"; Augustus Hawkins, "Inside Government: The Agonies of Social Change," *Los Angeles Sentinel*, March 21, 1968; Chicago Public Schools, *Racial/Ethnic Survey—Students* (1968); Danns, *Something Better for Our Children*, 75; and Alanis, "Harrison High School Walkouts of 1968," 103–22.

34. Students protested in the 1970s at Bowen High School and Gage Park High School—schools located in communities where Black students were entering previously all-White schools and facing violent backlash from White parents and local community residents. See Williams, *From the Bullet to the Ballot*, 54–61, 69–75.

35. Faith C. Christmas, "Student Leader Ridicules League Seminar," *Chicago Daily Defender*, December 19, 1968, 12; Community Seminar on Local Control of Schools (1968), series I, box 9, folder 156, CUL Records.

36. Danns, *Something Better for Our Children*, 74–88; Faith C. Christmas, "700 Teachers Join Second Boycott," *Chicago Daily Defender*, October 22, 1968.

37. Speakers included Dr. Preston Wilcox, Rev. Herbert Oliver, Ken Haskins, and Albert Vann. See Doris E. Saunders, "Confetti," *Chicago Daily Defender*, November 12, 1968.

38. Dougherty, *More Than One Struggle*, 173–78; Bell, *Silent Covenants*, 4–10, 181–89;

Arnez, "Implementation of Desegregation as a Discriminatory Process"; Edmonds, "Effective Schools for the Urban Poor"; Perlstein, *Justice, Justice,* 114–15, 119–21; Shujaa, *Too Much Schooling, Too Little Education*; Shujaa, *Beyond Desegregation*; Gittell and Hevesi, *Politics of Urban Education*; Cronin, *Control of Urban Schools*; Ornstein, *Metropolitan Schools*; Altshuler, *Community Control*.

39. In 1965, the heavily Democratic U.S. Congress passed the ESEA, which included funding for economically disadvantaged students, instructional materials for schools, the creation of educational research laboratories, state departments of education, and services to supplement traditional school systems. See Vinovskis, *Birth of Head Start*, 36–39, 79–80; CPS Annual Financial Report 1964, box Chicago Board of Education Finance, Annual Finance Reports 1937, 1939, 1940, 1943, 1947, 1957–1959, 1964, folder 1964, CBOE Archives; Chicago Public Schools Facts and Figures 1963, box Board of Education Finance, Facts and Figures, folder 1961–1963, CBOE Archives; and Chicago Public Schools Facts and Figures, September 1968, box Chicago Board of Education Finance, Facts and Figures, folder 1968–1969, CBOE Archives.

40. Brazier, *Black Self-Determination*, 11, 25; Fish, *Black Power/White Control*, 12; Lloyd General, "Fight New Land Grab for Seminary in Hyde Park Area," *Chicago Defender*, July 20, 1963; Madalene Chafin, "Urban Renewal Bars Negroes in $$ Development," *Chicago Defender*, December 28, 1963; Arnold R. Hirsch, "Urban Renewal," *Encyclopedia of Chicago*.

41. Brazier, *Black Self-Determination*, 10, 24–25; Amanda Seligman, "Woodlawn," *Encyclopedia of Chicago*.

42. Beginning in 1958, co-pastors Dr. Charles Leber and Dr. Ulysses Blakeley of First Presbyterian Church, Father Martin Farrell of Holy Cross Roman Catholic Church, and Rev. Kenneth Profrock of Immanuel Lutheran Church began meeting regularly with public officials, civic leaders, local community groups, and representatives of the University of Chicago to try to create solutions to the many problems facing Woodlawn. Frustrated with the limited capacity of existing organizations and the inaction of public officials, these clergy members formed the Woodlawn Pastors' Alliance and planned to develop a new, stronger community organization. The early funding for the Woodlawn Pastors' Alliance community organizing work came from a $50,000 donation from the Catholic Church, a $69,000 contribution from the Schwartzhaupt Foundation, and $21,000 from the First Presbyterian Church. Alinsky, a prominent community organizer, and the Industrial Areas Foundation had successfully helped to organize other Chicago communities, notably in the Back-of-the-Yards neighborhood. In January 1961, facilitated by foundation organizers, the Woodlawn Pastors' Alliance and community organizations officially formed the Temporary Woodlawn Organization—eventually changing "Temporary" to "The" but maintaining the same acronym, TWO. Individuals participated in the organization through their membership in TWO-member organizations. Voting membership in TWO was limited to local civic community organizations in Woodlawn. TWO organized a mass march of 1,000 local residents down 63rd Street protesting exploitative local business practices by White merchants. This demonstration of the power to mobilize mass community support was coupled with forums to publicly shame duplicitous merchants and the creation of a code of ethics for Woodlawn businesses. These multipronged organizing efforts and attacks on community issues became a hallmark of TWO's organizing style and brand of protest politics. More importantly, these efforts

produced results, as residents witnessed decreases in dishonest business practices. Early successes like these helped TWO win the allegiance of Woodlawn residents. These efforts increased organizational membership—at one point including upward of 100 local organizations and numerous block clubs. See Brazier, *Black Self-Determination*, 23–28, 30–32, 38–39, 42–43, 53, and Fish, *Black Power/White Control*, 13–16, 46–47.

43. There were many contentious standoffs between the University of Chicago and local organizers in Woodlawn. In the summer of 1960, the University of Chicago proposed expanding the campus south into the northernmost section of the Woodlawn neighborhood, requiring clearance of a one-block-by-one-mile section of residential land. The relationship between the university and Woodlawn residents was exacerbated further when the university built a barbed wire fence along a section of the southern edge of the campus to create a border between the increasingly Black Woodlawn community and the university's campus. See Fish, *Black Power/White Control*, 4, and Brazier, *Black Self-Determination*, 50–58.

44. The mayor was also pushed to step in because the city stood to lose as much as $14 million in federal funds if the South Campus project did not get off the ground with approval by community members and the university. TWO created a community development corporation to develop the low-income housing on Cottage Grove Avenue. The South Campus agreement did, however, bring closure to an episode of great conflict between TWO and the University of Chicago and ushered in a period of more cooperative interactions between the two parties. See Brazier, *Black Self-Determination*, 51–58.

45. Fish, *Black Power/White Control*, 4.

46. Brazier, *Black Self-Determination*, 11–13, 19.

47. The Unity Plan would have the benefits of smaller school communities with more personalized relationships between teachers and students, individual counseling, and more effective discipline, while also reaping the benefits of the larger educational park: a diverse student population, specialty classes, the cost of expensive facilities shared amongst the four embedded schools, a well-equipped library to be shared amongst the schools, and efficiently shared food preparation. See "Proposal for Expansion of Hyde Park High School into Secondary Educational Park: An Outline," August 10, 1965, box 86, folder 2, Beadle Records; "Unrealistic Plans for the Schools," *Chicago Tribune*, December 18, 1967, 22; and Chicago Urban League Research Department, "Plan for a System of Educational Parks in Chicago," December 5, 1967, series II, box 74, folder 850, CUL Records. For more on education parks, see Erickson, "Desegregation's Architects."

48. "Proposal for Expansion of Hyde Park High School into Secondary Educational Park: An Outline," August 10, 1965, box 86, folder 2, Beadle Records; "Unrealistic Plans for the Schools," *Chicago Tribune*, December 18, 1967, 22; Chicago Urban League Research Department, "Plan for a System of Educational Parks in Chicago," December 5, 1967, series II, box 74, folder 850, CUL Records; "4 Groups to Eye 'Education Park,'" *Chicago Defender*, February 1, 1966; Fish, *Black Power/White Control*, 90.

49. The White student population at Hyde Park High School was not declining numerically, but the Black population was increasing rapidly, causing the percentage of White students to decrease precipitously. The elementary school population in Hyde Park–Kenwood was approximately 30 percent White and 70 percent African American. In response to pressure from the HPKCC and other proponents of building a new

high school, Superintendent Willis proposed a site for a new high school in the Hyde Park community adjacent to integrated Murray Elementary School at 5335 S. Kenwood. Led by CCCO, TWO, and the Murray PTA, approximately 200 Black, White, and Asian American parents picketed in front of Murray school in opposition to Willis's plan and proposed location for the new school. See "Proposal for Expansion of Hyde Park High School into Secondary Educational Park: An Outline," August 10, 1965, box 86, folder 2, Beadle Records; Hirsch, *Making the Second Ghetto*, 157–70; "Editorial: Integration Is Necessary," *Hyde Park Herald*, June 30, 1965, 4; "Hyde Park–Kenwood Community Conference Statement on High School Facilities," June 7, 1965, box 86, folder 2, Beadle Records; Fish, *Black Power/White Control*, 90; and "Southsiders Picket a School Project," *Chicago Daily Defender*, September 22, 1965, 1.

50. "TWO Raps Ben's Hyde Park Plan," *Chicago Daily Defender*, September 11, 1965, 5; Casey Banas, "Board to Air Cut in Kenwood High Plans," *Chicago Tribune*, October 25, 1966.

51. Fish, *Black Power/White Control*, 92–93, 214–15; Louise Ryan, "New High School for Hyde Park," *Hyde Park Herald*, February 2, 1966, 1; Casey Banas, "Board to Air Cut in Kenwood High Plans," *Chicago Tribune*, October 25, 1966.

52. Brazier to delegates meeting, January 9, 1967, as quoted in Fish, *Black Power/White Control*, 176.

53. Brazier, *Black Self-Determination*, 17–18.

54. "New School Facilities Will Open Next Week," *Chicago Tribune*, September 4, 1966, R2; "Proposal for Expansion of Hyde Park High School into Secondary Educational Park: An Outline," August 10, 1965, and "Hyde Park-Kenwood Community Conference Statement on High School Facilities," June 7, 1965, in folder 2, box 86, Beadle Records; Fish, *Black Power/White Control*, 90–93, 214–15; Sizemore, *Walking in Circles*, 47–50; "Willis Tells of Gains at Forrestville: Classrooms for 2,500 Being Added," *Chicago Tribune*, April 6, 1966, B6; Sam Washington, "Forrestville: Turmoil Brews in School," *Chicago Defender*, December 3, 1966, 1–2. Many of the students attending Forrestville lived in nearby public housing projects and overcrowded apartments and had to traverse the intersections of different gang territories to get to school. The planning for a new school site for Forrestville dovetailed with the controversy over the establishment of the new Kenwood High School.

55. "New School Facilities Will Open Next Week," *Chicago Tribune*, September 4, 1966, R2; "Willis Tells of Gains at Forrestville: Classrooms for 2,500 Being Added," *Chicago Tribune*, April 6, 1966, B6; Sam Washington, "Forrestville: Turmoil Brews in School," *Chicago Daily Defender*, December 3, 1966, 1–2; "Proposal for Expansion of Hyde Park High School into Secondary Educational Park: An Outline," August 10, 1965, and "Hyde Park–Kenwood Community Conference Statement on High School Facilities," June 7, 1965, in folder 2, box 86, Beadle Records; Fish, *Black Power/White Control*, 90–93, 214–15; Sizemore, *Walking in Circles*, 47–50; Williamson, "Community Control with a Black Nationalist Twist," 143–48; Shujaa and Afrik, "School Desegregation," 254–56.

56. Sizemore, *Walking in Circles*, 47–50; "Willis Tells of Gains at Forrestville: Classrooms for 2,500 Being Added," *Chicago Tribune*, April 6, 1966, B6; Sam Washington, "Forrestville: Turmoil Brews in School," *Chicago Daily Defender*, December 3, 1966, 1–2.

57. Sizemore, *Walking in Circles*, 47–50; Williamson, "Community Control with a Black Nationalist Twist," 143–48; Dougherty, *More Than One Struggle*, 170–78; Shujaa and Afrik,

"School Desegregation," 254–56; Rachell, "Jitu Weusi Got Mad Soul"; Gittell and Berube, *Local Control in Education*, 1, 64; Podair, *Strike That Changed New York*, 4–8; Perlstein, *Justice, Justice*, 6–8.

58. At Forrestville, homeroom periods were extended to carry out programming that built a sense of community and family among students. Sizemore and assistant principal Anderson Thompson identified and called on students who were leaders of peer groups and gangs in the school and the neighborhood to mediate disputes. A group of Black male students, the "Magnificent Seven," became nationally renowned for reciting speeches by famous Black orators, including Frederick Douglass, Booker T. Washington, W. E. B. Du Bois, Marcus Garvey, Malcolm X, Martin Luther King Jr., and others. Today, educational professionals laud the types of practices that Sizemore implemented as culturally relevant pedagogy. See Sizemore, *Walking in Circles*, 47–50; "Forrestville Principals Gets Teacher OK," *Chicago Daily Defender*, December 14, 1966; and Barbara Sizemore, "An Uncle Tom?," *Chicago Daily Defender*, August 11, 1970. On culturally relevant pedagogy, see Ladson-Billings, "But That's Just Good Teaching!," 159–65; Ladson-Billings, *Dreamkeepers*; Lee, "Profile of an Independent Black Institution"; Lee, *Culture, Literacy, and Learning*; and Lee, "Centrality of Culture to the Scientific Study of Learning and Development."

59. Audrey Weaver, "Parallel Black Strategy," *Chicago Daily Defender*, August 10, 1968.

60. Faith C. Christmas, "700 Teachers Join Second Boycott," *Chicago Daily Defender*, October 22, 1968.

61. Brazier, *Black Self-Determination*, 10–11, 82–90; Fish, *Black Power/White Control*, 220–21.

62. Brazier, *Black Self-Determination*, 11, 17–18, 60–62; Sizemore, *Walking in Circles*, 57–58; Fish, *Black Power/White Control*, 179–80.

63. "Proposal for an Urban Education Laboratory," submitted to the U.S. Commissioner of Education, mimeographed (Committee on Urban Education, University of Chicago, October 15, 1965), 2, 6, 18, 29–30, 32, as quoted in Fish, *Black Power/White Control*, 178.

64. "Letter from Brazier to Dean Roald Campbell," on file at TWO, May 16, 1966, as quoted in Fish, *Black Power/White Control*, 179–80; Brazier, *Black Self-Determination*, 60; Sizemore, *Walking in Circles*, 58.

65. In denying the university's initial proposal for funding to support the educational research and development center, the U.S. Office of Education also questioned why the university felt it was necessary to establish its own independent school instead of conducting the proposed research within existing CPS schools in the Woodlawn community. This gave TWO leverage, because the university would have to involve it and CPS in order for the plan to move forward. See "Letter from Ward Mason to Dr. George Beadle," on file at WESP, June 3, 1966, as quoted in Fish, *Black Power/White Control*, 181–82.

66. Fish, *Black Power/White Control*, 182–90; Sizemore, *Walking in Circles*, 58; Brazier, *Black Self-Determination*, 60–64.

67. Brazier, *Black Self-Determination*, 61–62; Fish, *Black Power/White Control*, 180–90.

68. The Illinois School Code mandated that the Chicago Board of Education and the general superintendent administer all CPS schools. The language of the memorandum of agreement was drafted and redrafted several times until the Board of Education's legal council was satisfied that it did not usurp Board of Education power and TWO was satisfied that the agreement still granted the community more than just an advisory role in

the administration of the experimental project. The completed memorandum of agreement allowed the WCB to reapply to the U.S. Office of Education for funding for WESP, with evidence that all necessary parties were on board and that a structure of governance was in place. See Fish, *Black Power/White Control*, 192–96.

69. Sizemore, *Walking in Circles*, 57.

70. Ibid.

71. Fish, *Black Power/White Control*, 201–13.

72. Ibid., 115–74, 201–13; Brazier, *Black Self-Determination*, 82–125; Woodlawn Experimental Schools Project End of Project Report, June 1972, Davis Papers; Moore and Williams, *Almighty Black P Stone Nation*, 56–77, 103–28.

73. Community teachers and parents attended pedagogy workshops to learn how to teach basic reading skills, about ethnoliguistic approaches to teaching oral language, and about testing and screening children's sensory motor skills. See Fish, *Black Power/White Control*, 218, and Barbara A. Sizemore, "Making the Schools a Vehicle for Cultural Pluralism," [1971?], box 64, folder 1, Sol Tax Papers, University of Chicago Special Collections.

74. The meetings of the Black P Stone Nation were among the only other meetings in Woodlawn that drew more participants than WCB meetings. The Black P Stone Nation (also known at times as the Blackstone Rangers), an organization known alternatively as a youth organization or gang, was one of the groups that TWO worked with in the Youth Manpower Project that used antipoverty funds from the Office of Economic Opportunity. See Fish, *Black Power/White Control*, 218; Moore and Williams, *Almighty Black P Stone Nation*; Memorandum to Woodlawn Community Board Members, September 20, 1968, box 350, folder 4, Beadle Records; and Memorandum to Woodlawn Community Board Members, May 9, 1969, box 350, folder 5, Levi Records.

75. Memorandum to Woodlawn Community Board Members, May 9, 1969, box 350, folder 5, Levi Records; Fish, *Black Power/White Control*, 218–20.

76. Fish, *Black Power/White Control*, 190–91, 209; Woodlawn Experimental Schools Project End of Project Report, June 1972, Davis Papers.

77. In the CAPTS model, if parent councils and school senates came up with ideas for new programming or policies to implement in the schools, they would distribute the plan to one another to discuss and negotiate. The negotiated proposal would be passed on to the professional educational bureaucracy in the schools—teachers, counselors, administrators, WESP staff, etc.—to translate the plan into an educational program. The program would then be organized by the administrative staff into a proposal to be submitted to the WCB. If the WCB approved the proposal, and it did not infringe on the authority of the Chicago Board of Education, then the proposal would be passed back to the administrative staff, who would coordinate the new program, and to the professional bureaucracy, who would implement the program, and finally back to the CAPTS congress to evaluate the program. If the WCB rejected the proposal or the Chicago Board of Education vetoed the proposal, it would be sent back down to the CAPTS congress to start the process all over again. See Woodlawn Experimental Schools Project End of Project Report, June 1972, Davis Papers, and Sizemore, "Education for Liberation."

78. Fish, *Black Power/White Control*, 210–14; Memorandum to Woodlawn Community Board Members, May 9, 1969, box 350, folder 5, Levi Records.

79. Memorandum to Woodlawn Community Board Members, October 17, 1968, and November 6, 1968, both in box 350, folder 4, Beadle Records.

80. Fish, *Black Power/White Control*, 211–12.

81. As among the few Black women principals in CPS, Kolheim and Sizemore knew each other before WESP and had a great deal of respect for each other. Kolheim was a former chair of the NAACP's schools committee and had spoken out powerfully against Willis Wagons and inequality in CPS. Sizemore supported the hiring of Kolheim as principal of Hyde Park High School. See "Principal Blasts Supt. Willis for Racism in Chicago Schools," *Chicago Daily Defender*, October 14, 1963; Fish, *Black Power/White Control*, 227–29; and Sizemore, *Walking in Circles*, 59–62.

82. Fish, *Black Power/White Control*, 226–27; Faith C. Christmas, "Blasts U.S. School Order," *Chicago Daily Defender*, September 29, 1970, 2; "Charge Board Killing Black School Project," *Chicago Daily Defender*, October 17, 1970; Danns, *Desegregating Chicago's Public Schools*.

83. Fish, *Black Power/White Control*, 292–304; "McNeil Ruffled: TWO Convention Guests Speechless," *Chicago Daily Defender*, May 3, 1972.

84. Fish, *Black Power/White Control*, 292–310; "McNeil Ruffled: TWO Convention Guests Speechless," *Chicago Daily Defender*, May 3, 1972.

85. Toni Anthony, "Arrest Nine Waller Students," *Chicago Daily Defender*, April 8, 1971, 1; Faith C. Christmas, "700 Teachers Join Second Boycott," *Chicago Daily Defender*, October 22, 1968.

86. Toni Anthony, "Arrest Nine Waller Students," *Chicago Daily Defender*, April 8, 1971; Faith C. Christmas, "700 Teachers Join Second Boycott," *Chicago Daily Defender*, October 22, 1968.

87. Fish, *Black Power/White Control*, 233, 294, 297–310; "McNeil Ruffled: TWO Convention Guests Speechless," *Chicago Daily Defender*, May 3, 1972; Toni Anthony, "TWO's McNeil Rips Anna Kolheim Foes," *Chicago Daily Defender*, May 22, 1971, 1.

88. "Charlie Cherokee Says," *Chicago Defender*, July 18, 1974.

89. Fish, *Black Power/White Control*, 198–201, 205–11; Sizemore, *Walking in Circles*, 64.

90. Fish, *Black Power/White Control*, 230; Brazier, *Black Self-Determination*, 62–63.

91. Sizemore, *Walking in Circles*, 64; Woodlawn Experimental Schools Project End of Project Report, June 1972, Davis Papers.

92. Woodlawn Experimental Schools Project End of Project Report, June 1972, Davis Papers.

93. Goldberger, "Karen Lewis, Street Fighter"; Biondi, *Black Revolution on Campus*.

Chapter 3

1. Walton interview by author, October 9, 2014.

2. Ibid.; Dennis McClendon, "Expressways," *Encyclopedia of Chicago*; Spatz, "Roads to Postwar Urbanism."

3. Walton interview by author, October 9, 2014.

4. During this period many Black cultural nationalists took on new names from African languages as a personal and political statement. While some still use the African names they took on in the 1960s and 1970s, others changed their names multiple times. It will be noted when an individual was referred to by multiple names in the course of this

research. Haki Madhubuti previously went by Don L. Lee but changed his name during the 1970s as a personal and political statement and still goes by this name. Some publications and speeches cited herein are under Don L. Lee; others, Haki Madhubuti. In this text I will refer to him using his first and last name, Haki Madhubuti, or just Haki, rather than using only his last name, so as to limit confusion with Carol Lee, his wife, who also goes by Safisha Madhubuti.

5. Walton interview by author, October 9, 2014; Rickford, *We Are an African People*, 6, 16–17.

6. "New Concept Development Center Curriculum: Organization of Instruction," [1993], folder NCDC Curriculum, Walton Papers.

7. Williams, *From the Bullet to the Ballot*, 1–4; Johnson, *Revolutionaries to Race Leaders*, xxiv–xxxvii; Joseph, *Neighborhood Rebels*, 1–9; Rickford, *We Are an African People*, 129–30. On different interpretations of Black Power, see Theoharis and Woodard, *Freedom North*; Joseph, *Black Power Movement*; Countryman, *Up South*; Williams, *Politics of Public Housing*; Valk, *Radical Sisters*; Self, *American Babylon*; Thompson, *Whose Detroit?*; Woodard, *Nation within a Nation*; Marable, *Race, Reform, and Rebellion*; and Ture and Hamilton, *Black Power*.

8. Williams, *From the Bullet to the Ballot*, 42–74.

9. Lomotey and Brookins, "Independent Black Institutions," 166; Foster, "Historically Black Independent schools," 293–94.

10. Shujaa and Afrik, "School Desegregation," 265.

11. Foster, "Historically Black Independent schools," 293; Ratteray, "Search for Access and Content in the Education of African-Americans," 128–29, 131–33.

12. Anderson, *Education of Blacks in the South*, 2–3; Harrison, *Piney Woods School*; Hayes, "Very Meaning of Our Lives"; Slaughter and Johnson, "Introduction and Overview," 1–5; Kharem and Hayes, "Separation or Integration," 82; Ratteray and Shujaa, "Defining a Tradition," 184–87.

13. Perlstein, "Minds Stayed on Freedom," 55.

14. Williamson, "Community Control with a Black Nationalist Twist," 152–54; Hale, "'Student as a Force for Social Change.'"

15. Hayes, "Rise and Fall of a Black Private School," 201–20.

16. Born Carol Easton, she married Don L. Lee (later Haki Madhubuti), becoming Carol Lee. She also went by, and continues to go by, the names of Aminifu Safisha Laini and Safisha Madhubuti over the course of the period covered herein. In this text she will be referred to as Carol Lee, the name she presently uses professionally. In this text I will also use her first and last name together, Carol Lee, or just Carol, rather than only using her last name, so as to limit confusion with her husband, Haki Madhubuti, previously Don L. Lee.

17. Lee interview by author, March 11, 2009; Madhubuti interview by author; "TWP History"; "Meet the Founders."

18. Lee, *From Plan to Planet*, 9.

19. This trajectory is notably reflected in the artistic trajectory of Amiri Baraka (LeRoi Jones). See Smethurst, *Black Arts Movement*, 22–76, and Joseph, *Black Power Movement*, 121.

20. Haki was impressed by the Burroughses' commitment to creating independent Black institutions. Margaret Burroughs was an artist and author who was also the youngest board member of the South Side Community Arts Center, the oldest New Deal era

Works Progress Administration Black arts center in the country. Haki first met Brooks in 1967 at a creative writing class in Woodlawn that she was running for members of the Blackstone Rangers youth gang. Brooks embraced the younger artists of the Black Arts Movement. See Smethurst, *Black Arts Movement*, 196–97, 211–13, 228–30; Madhubuti, "About Us"; H. Madhubuti, *YellowBlack*; Madhubuti interview by author; and Walton interview by author, October 9, 2014.

21. Walton interview by author, November 23, 2009; Walton interview by author, October 9, 2014.

22. "Baraza Ya Kati," September 30, 1973, folder IPE, Walton Papers.

23. Woodard, *Nation within a Nation*, 67, 145–46, 168–83, 220.

24. Between 1966 and the early 1970s there was a series of Black Power conferences, developing into the Modern Black Convention Movement, which worked to articulate a common political agenda across Black ideological camps. See Johnson, *Revolutionaries to Race Leaders*, 85–130, 157–63; Woodard, *Nation within a Nation*; and Frazier, "Congress of African People."

25. Lee interview by author, March 11, 2009.

26. Taylor, *From #BlackLivesMatter to Black Liberation*, 36–55; Rotella, *October Cities*, 4–7; Fish, *Black Power/White Control*, 242; Pritchett, "Which Urban Crisis?"; D. Bradford Hunt, "Model Cities," *Encyclopedia of Chicago*.

27. Rickford, *We Are an African People*, 2; Pritchett, "Which Urban Crisis?"

28. Lee, *From Plan to Planet*, 41, 45.

29. Identity, Purpose, and Direction were also key concepts in Kawaida, the philosophy and ideology of the US Organization and Maulana Karenga on which much of the value system upheld by IPE was based. See Ibid., 33.

30. Ibid., 30–40.

31. Maulana Karenga was also known as Ron Karenga. See Brown, *Fighting for US*, 33–36, 163.

32. Lee, *From Plan to Planet*, 80.

33. Brown, *Fighting for US*, 68–69.

34. Lee, *From Plan to Planet*, 79–83; Walton interview by author, October 9, 2014; Lee interview by author, March 11, 2009, and June 13, 2017.

35. Third World Press published historical works about precolonial Africa and colonialism, including works by John Henrik Clarke and Chancellor Williams. Works by these authors were also used in IPE study sessions. See Kelley, *Freedom Dreams*, 15 (quote), 13–35; Moses, *Afrotopia*; Connolly, "How 'Black Panther' Taps into 500 Years of History"; Walton interview by author, October 9, 2014; Lee interview by author, March 11, 2009, and June 13, 2017; and Madhubuti interview by author.

36. This smaller group of women and men included the head, Mwalimu (Haki Madhubuti), and three high-ranking representatives, each from the Baraza Wanamume (men's council) and Idara Kwa Utu Uke (women's council). Departments, programs, and groups therein included a community support group, a community advisory council, and administrative services. Administrative services were divided into sections of political, social, economic, community, and educational services. Each section included additional subdepartments and programs. See "IPE Organizational Chart" and "Reach Out and Teach—Pull In Those Reached," folder IPE, Walton Papers.

37. In 1973 this group included Carol Lee, Haki Madhubuti, Johari Amini (Jewel C. Latimore), Saundra Malone (Kimya Maunda Moyo), and Kofi Moyo (Lloyd Sanders), among others. See Baraza Ya Kati Meeting Minutes, September 23, 1973, and "Reach Out and Teach—Pull In Those Reached," folder IPE, Walton Papers.

38. Those who could not meet all of these requirements could still serve as IPE volunteers. Payroll was administered on a biweekly basis, and employees had to fill out time sheets. After working for IPE for six months, staff members would receive a half-day sick day each month. After one year, staff members would receive one week of vacation time. At NCDC, students were off during federal holidays, but staff came to work for professional development. "Employment Practices," "Organization Policies and Guidelines," and "New Concept Handbook, 1978," 11, folder IPE, Walton Papers; Lee, "Profile of an Independent Black Institution," 164; "Institute of Positive Education Staff/Volunteers," [1973], folder IPE, Walton Papers.

39. Baraza Ya Kati Meeting Minutes, September 30, 1973, folder IPE, Walton Papers.

40. Lee, From Plan to Planet, 30–45, 79–83.

41. Letter from Phyllis K. Franklin, October 15, 1973, folder IPE, Walton Papers.

42. Letter from Waminifu, [1973], folder IPE, Walton Papers.

43. Rickford, We Are an African People, 153–56; Taylor, Promise of Patriarchy.

44. Rickford, We Are an African People, 153–56; Walton interview by author, October 9, 2014.

45. Rickford, We Are an African People, 153–56; Walton interview by author, October 9, 2014; Lee interview by author, June 13, 2017.

46. Walton interview by author, October 9, 2014; "Socialisation of Women," folder IPE, Walton Papers.

47. "Socialisation of Women" and IPE press release, August 11, 1976, folder IPE, Walton Papers; Lee interview by author, March 11, 2009.

48. Mwalimu Don L. Lee, "Ujamaa Codes, 1973," folder IPE, Walton Papers.

49. Jawanza Kunjufu, "Staff Concerns Memo," and Jabari Mahiri, "A Modest Proposal (III)," folder IPE, Walton Papers; Walton interview by author, October 9, 2014.

50. Haki Madhubuti, "A Proposal for Development, March 1977," folder IPE, Walton Papers; Lee interview by author, March 11, 2009.

51. Initially called the New Concept School, within the first few years the name was changed to the New Concept Development Center.

52. "New Concept School Pamphlet," [1972], folder IPE, Walton Papers; Lee, "Profile of an Independent Black Institution," 163; Lee interview by author, March 11, 2009; "New Concept Handbook, 1978," 12, 20, folder IPE, Walton Papers.

53. Lee interview by author, March 11, 2009; "New Concept Handbook, 1978," 12, 20, folder IPE, Walton Papers; Lee, "Profile of an Independent Black Institution," 165–73; Rickford, We Are an African People, 153–56.

54. As in the way that historian Barbara Ransby discusses Eslanda Robeson's marriage to Paul Robeson (Ransby, Eslanda, 5–6), Carol Lee's marriage to a prominent male artist gave her access to circles she may not have had otherwise. However, she used that platform to "amplify her own creative voice" and "promote her vision for a different kind of world" in NCDC (Madhubuti interview by author).

55. "New Concept Handbook, 1978," 19, folder IPE, Walton Papers.

56. Ibid.; Lee interview by author, March 11, 2009; "New Concept Handbook, 1978," 12, 20, folder IPE, Walton Papers; Lee, "Profile of an Independent Black Institution," 165–73; Rickford, *We Are an African People*, 153–56.

57. "New Concept Handbook, 1978," 6, folder IPE, Walton Papers.

58. Ibid., 4–6.

59. In another lesson, young students studied a copy of the image of the Talasimu (a visual representation of Kawaida philosophy with triangles, stars, cords, and other symbols representing specific aspects of Kawaida beliefs). The students were reminded from a previous lesson that the Talasimu was a whole and were asked to identify the multiple parts (or subsets) of the whole that make up the Talasimu. The teacher then modeled how to ask questions about the Talasimu by asking the students a series of questions: What did each part or set of shapes represent? Who created the Talasimu? Why was it created? The students, in turn, generated their own who, what, when, where, and how questions about aspects of the Talasimu that they still did not understand. NCDC teachers were able to build on students' ability to comprehend concepts (in this example, sets and subsets, parts and a whole) and the skill of developing questions that they saw as important in applying to any text or material, while also indoctrinating the students in the ways of the Nguzo Saba and Kawaida teachings. The curriculum used these techniques to teach venn diagrams, vocabulary, music analysis, memorization, Black history, concentration, and inferences. See "Reading Development," folder Language Arts, Walton Papers.

60. Texts used by NCDC for six- to ten-year-olds included *Children of Afrika Coloring Book* in English and Kiswahili; *Our Nation Reader*, by the Nation of Islam; *Country of the Black People*, by Corene Casselle; *I Want to Be*, by Pat and Dexter Oliver; *African Frame of Reference*, by Johari M. Amini; *Destruction of Black Civilization*, by Chancellor Williams; *From Plan to Planet*, by Haki Madhubuti; and *Unity in the Black Community*, by Lerone Bennett. See "Reading Development" and "Language Arts Basic Texts List," folder Language Arts, Walton Papers.

61. "Tri-Continental Antiquity," folder Social Studies, Walton Papers; Lee interview by author, March 11, 2009, and June 13, 2017; Lee, "Profile of an Independent Black Institution," 163–68.

62. Hannibal Tirus Afrik, "Science for Black Survival" [1977], folder Science Curr., Walton Papers; Danns, "Chicago Teacher Reform Efforts and the Politics of Educational Change," 179–80, 188–94; Lee, "Profile of an Independent Black Institution," 168–71; "Science for Nation Building Science Fair" [1977], folder Science Curr., Walton Papers; Lee interview by author, March 11, 2009.

63. While some of the original CIBI institutions eventually closed, NCDC is still in operation today. See Shujaa and Afrik, "School Desegregation," 254; Lee interview by author, March 11, 2009; and Hayes," Rise and Fall of a Black Private School," 203.

64. Lee, "Comment," 93; Stulberg, *Race, Schools, and Hope*, 58–59, 68–69.

65. Pattillo-McCoy, "Limits of Out-Migration for the Black Middle Class"; Parks, "Revisiting Shibboleths of Race and Urban Economy"; Katz, Stern, and Fader, "New African American Inequality"; Wacquant and Wilson, "Cost of Racial and Class Exclusion in the Inner City," 14.

66. Wacquant and Wilson, "Cost of Racial and Class Exclusion in the Inner City," 12, 21.

67. Letter from Haki Madhubuti to Staff, November 28, 1977; NCDC Administrative

Report, November 7, 1977; and NCDC General Report Staff Meeting, October 17, 1977, folder IPE, Walton Papers; Stulberg, *Race, Schools, and Hope*, 68–69.

68. Stulberg, *Race, Schools, and Hope*, 68–69; Staff Study Session Notes, October 24, 1977, folder IPE, and NCDC 1982/1983 Parent Roster, folder NCDC History, Walton Papers.

69. Letter from Foluke, January 5, 1978, folder IPE, Walton Papers; Walton interview by author, October 9, 2014.

70. Letter from Haki Madhubuti to Staff, November 28, 1977; NCDC Administrative Report, November 7, 1977; and NCDC General Report Staff Meeting, October 17, 1977, folder IPE, Walton Papers.

71. Staff Study Session Notes, October 24, 1977, folder IPE, Walton Papers.

72. Letter from Haki Madhubuti to Staff, November 28, 1977; NCDC General Report Staff Meeting, October 17, 1977; and "New Concept Handbook, 1978," 21, folder IPE, Walton Papers; NCDC 1982/1983 Parent Roster, 1982, folder NCDC History, Walton Papers.

73. Johnson, *Revolutionaries to Race Leaders*, 159–61; Rickford, *We Are an African People*, 132–33; "Reach Out and Teach—Pull In Those Reached," folder IPE, Walton Papers.

74. Walton interview by author, October 9, 2014.

75. Ibid.

76. Lee, *From Plan to Planet*, 83.

77. Lee interview by author, March 11, 2009; Haki Madhubuti, "A Proposal for Development, March 1977," folder IPE, Walton Papers; Stulberg, *Race, Schools, and Hope*, 66–67.

78. Lee interview by author, March 11, 2009; Stulberg, *Race, Schools, and Hope*, 66–67.

79. Lee interview by author, March 11, 2009, and June 13, 2017.

80. Ibid.; Walton interview by author, October 9, 2014.

81. Madhubuti interview by author; Madhubuti, "Enemy"; Madhubuti, "Latest Purge"; Brown, *Fighting for US*; Woodard, *Nation within a Nation*.

82. S. Madhubuti, "Forward," in Sizemore, *Walking in Circles*, ix–xvii; Lee interview by author, June 13, 2017; Walton interview by author, October 9, 2014.

83. Lee, "Profile of an Independent Black Institution," 174; Walton interview by author, October 9, 2014; Lee interview by author, June 13, 2017.

84. Ladson-Billings, "But That's Just Good Teaching!"; Ladson-Billings, *Dreamkeepers*; Lee, "Profile of an Independent Black Institution"; Lee, *Culture, Literacy, and Learning*; Lee, "Centrality of Culture to the Scientific Study of Learning and Development"; Lee, "Comment."

Chapter 4

1. Peoples interview by author, December 2, 2014.

2. Ibid. On the experiences of Black migrant girls, see Chatelain, *South Side Girls*.

3. Peoples interview by author, December 2, 2014.

4. Ibid.; Chicago Public Schools, *Racial/Ethnic Survey—Students* (1968); Chicago Public Schools, *Racial/Ethnic Survey—Staff* (1968).

5. "Operation Breadbasket"; Peoples interview by author, December 2, 2014.

6. Danns, *Desegregating Chicago's Public Schools*, 60–61; Becker, "Schools and Systems of

Social Status"; Becker, "Career of the Chicago Public School Teacher"; Chicago Public Schools, *Racial/Ethnic Survey—Students* (1968); Chicago Public Schools, *Racial/Ethnic Survey—Staff* (1968).

7. Chicago Public Schools, *Racial/Ethnic Survey—Staff* (1984).

8. On African Americans in the public sector, see Parks, "Revisiting Shibboleths of Race and Urban Economy," and Katz, Stern, and Fader, "New African American Inequality." On the impact of deindustrialization on Black communities, see Sugrue, *Origins of the Urban Crisis*; Gillette, *Camden after the Fall*; Katz, *"Underclass" Debate*; Wilson, *Declining Significance of Race*; Wilson, *Truly Disadvantaged*; and Self, *American Babylon*.

9. Black teachers were active in many groups, including CCCO, the Association of Afro-American Educators, the Black Teachers' Caucus, Concerned FTBs, Teachers for Integrated Schools, Teachers' Committee for Quality Education, the Negro American Labor Council, the NAACP, and the Congress of Racial Equality. Many of these organizations were led by Black teachers and former teachers, including Al Raby, Mattie Hopkins, Carl Lewis, Lois Ricks, Lillie Peoples, Lois Saunders, Elsie Tucker, Bobby Wright, Hannibal Afrik (Harold Charles), James McQuirter, Harold Pates, David Harrison, and Timuel Black. See Danns, *Something Better for Our Children*, 74–88, 105–6, and Peoples, "Black Teacher Organizations in the Black Power Movement."

10. House, *Jesse Jackson and the Politics of Charisma*, 8–12; "Operation Breadbasket."

11. Peoples interview by author, December 2, 2014.

12. Peoples, "Black Teacher Organizations in the Black Power Movement," 24; Mattie Hopkins Funeral Service Program [July 1988], Peoples Papers; Patrick Reardon, "City School Board's Mattie Hopkins," *Chicago Tribune*, July 19, 1988; Peoples interview by author, December 2, 2014.

13. Peoples, "Black Teacher Organizations in the Black Power Movement," 24; Mattie Hopkins Funeral Service Program [July 1988], Peoples Papers; Patrick Reardon, "City School Board's Mattie Hopkins," *Chicago Tribune*, July 19, 1988; Peoples interview by author, December 2, 2014.

14. Dixson, "'Let's Do This!'"; Beauboeuf-Lafontant, "Womanist Lessons for Reinventing Teaching"; Beauboeuf-Lafontant, "Womanist Experience of Caring"; Walker, *Their Highest Potential*; Alridge et al., "Teachers in the Movement"; Peoples interview by author, December 2, 2014, and March 9, 2017.

15. Before becoming a teacher, Afrik was a biochemistry researcher at the University of Illinois at Chicago. He felt compelled to become a full-time teacher after attending the 1963 March on Washington and interacting with Black high school students who had received inadequate science training in CPS. See Peoples, "Black Teacher Organizations in the Black Power Movement"; "CCCO Going into Politics," *Chicago Defender*, May 23, 1964; Danns, "Chicago Teacher Reform Efforts and the Politics of Educational Change," 185–92; Danns, *Something Better for Our Children*, 93–113; Lyons, *Teachers and Reform*, 159–60; Peoples interview by author, December 2, 2014; Faith C. Christmas, "700 Teachers Join Second Boycott," *Chicago Daily Defender*, October 22, 1968.

16. Harold Charles, "Position Paper: The Leadership Crisis in the Chicago teachers Union," May 13, 1969, box 149, folder 149-7, Wyatt Papers; "Breadbasket Teachers Division against Teachers' Strike," January 12, 1971, box 149, folder 149-10, Wyatt Papers;

Peoples interview by author, December 2, 2014, and March 9, 2017; Lee interview by author, June 13, 2017.

17. Harold Charles, "Position Paper: The Leadership Crisis in the Chicago teachers Union," May 13, 1969, box 149, folder 149-7, Wyatt Papers; "Breadbasket Teachers Division against Teachers' Strike," January 12, 1971, box 149, folder 149-10, Wyatt Papers; Peoples, "Black Teacher Organizations in the Black Power Movement"; Danns, "Chicago Teacher Reform Efforts and the Politics of Educational Change," 185–92; Danns, *Something Better for Our Children*, 93–113; Lyons, *Teachers and Reform*, 159–60; Peoples interview by author, December 2, 2014.

18. Danns, *Something Better for Our Children*, 110–12; Lyons, *Teachers and Reform*, 150–53, 160–63; Heise, "John M. Fewkes, 91, Teachers Union Founder," *Chicago Tribune*, July 25, 1992.

19. "Press Time Bulletin," *Chicago Union Teacher*, October 1968, CTU Archives; "Urges Action to Cope with School Furor: Union Asks Redmond to Clarify Policy," *Chicago Tribune*, October 12, 1968; Danns, *Something Better for Our Children*, 110–12; Lyons, *Teachers and Reform*, 150–53, 160–63.

20. Letter to the Editor, *Chicago Union Teacher*, January 1969, CTU Archives; Danns, *Something Better for Our Children*, 110–12; Lyons, *Teachers and Reform*, 150–53, 160–63.

21. Lyons, *Teachers and Reform*, 3.

22. Ibid., 163–67; Shipps, *School Reform, Corporate Style*, 62–64. Also see Kahlenberg, *Tough Liberal*.

23. Shipps, *School Reform, Corporate Style*, 61–63; Lyons, *Teachers and Reform*, 1–2, 163–70.

24. Shipps, *School Reform, Corporate Style*, 61–63; Lyons, *Teachers and Reform*, 1–2, 163–70; Faith C. Christmas, "Black Poll Is Strike Key," *Chicago Daily Defender*, August 20, 1969.

25. Chicago Public Schools, *Racial/Ethnic Survey—Staff* (1969); Chicago Public Schools, *Racial/Ethnic Survey—Students* (1969); Lyons, *Teachers and Reform*, 15–17; Worrill interview by author.

26. Black Teachers Caucus, Letter to the Editor, *Chicago Union Teacher*, November 1968, CTU Archives; Landwermeyer, "Teacher Unionism—Chicago Style," 443–46; Danns, *Something Better for Our Children*, 94–95, 111–12; Lyons, *Teachers and Reform*, 185–88; Peoples interview by author, December 2, 2014, and March 9, 2017.

27. Black Teachers Caucus, Letter to the Editor, *Chicago Union Teacher*, October 1968, CTU Archives.

28. Black Teachers Caucus, Letter to the Editor, *Chicago Union Teacher*, November 1968, CTU Archives.

29. "School Boycott Leaders Threaten Drastic Action," *Chicago Daily Defender*, October 31, 1968; Lyons, *Teachers and Reform*, 185–88; Peoples interview by author, December 2, 2014.

30. Faith C. Christmas, "Speeches Probe 'Waste of Time': Teacher Wright 'Could Care Less,'" *Chicago Daily Defender*, December 23, 1968; Faith C. Christmas, "Witnesses Testify at Hearing on Bias," *Chicago Daily Defender*, December 3, 1968; Peoples interview by author, December 2, 2014.

31. Black Teachers Caucus, Letter to the Editor, November 1968, and October 1968, CTU Archives; Landwermeyer, "Teacher Unionism—Chicago Style," 443–46; Danns,

Something Better for Our Children, 94–95, 111–12; Lyons, *Teachers and Reform*, 185–88; Black interview by author; Peoples interview by author, December 2, 2014.

32. As Black Teachers Caucus vice president Robert Mason explained, he loved the CTU "enough to criticize it fundamentally" and believed that Black teachers would be the "ultimate salvation of Chicago Public Schools." See Landwermeyer, "Teacher Unionism—Chicago Style," 443–46; Danns, *Something Better for Our* Children, 94–95, 111–12; Lyons, *Teachers and Reform*, 185–88; Black interview by author; Peoples interview by author, December 2, 2014.

33. Robnett, "African-American Women in the Civil Rights Movement, 1954–1965"; Black Teachers Caucus, Letter to the Editor, November 1968, CTU Archives; Landwermeyer, "Teacher Unionism—Chicago Style," 443–46; Danns, *Something Better for Our Children*, 94–95, 111–12; Lyons, *Teachers and Reform*, 185–88; Black interview by author; Peoples interview by author, March 9, 2017, and December 2, 2014.

34. Collins, *"Ethnically Qualified,"* 4–10, 44–45, 66–96; Landwermeyer, "Teacher Unionism—Chicago Style," 443–46; Danns, *Something Better for Our Children*, 94–95, 111–12; Lyons, *Teachers and Reform*, 175–79, 185–88; Black interview by author; Peoples interview by author, December 2, 2014; Worrill interview by author.

35. Collins, *"Ethnically Qualified,"* 4–10, 44–45, 66–96; Rury, "Race, Space, and the Politics of Chicago Public Schools," 124–26; Anderson and Pickering, *Confronting the Color Line,* 77; Landwermeyer, "Teacher Unionism—Chicago Style," 443–46; Danns, *Something Better for Our Children,* 94–95, 111–12; Lyons, *Teachers and Reform*, 175–79, 185–88; Black interview by author; Peoples interview by author, December 2, 2014; Worrill interview by author.

36. Interview with Grady Jordan, as quoted in Lyons, *Teachers and Reform,* 178.

37. Faith C. Christmas, "Black Teachers Label Their Union 'Racist,'" *Chicago Daily Defender,* January 9, 1969; Landwermeyer, "Teacher Unionism—Chicago Style," 443–46; Danns, *Something Better for Our Children,* 94–95, 111–12; Lyons, *Teachers and Reform*, 175–76, 185–88; Black interview by author; Peoples interview by author, December 2, 2014; Worrill interview by author.

38. "Beware of False Leaders," editorial, *Chicago Union Teacher,* October 1967, CTU Archives; Lyons, *Teachers and Reform*, 171, 176–79, 190–92; Danns, *Something Better for Our Children,* 107–12; Worrill interview by author; Peoples, "Black Teacher Organizations in the Black Power Movement," 20.

39. Black Teachers Caucus, Letter to the Editor, *Chicago Union Teacher,* October 1968, CTU Archives; Landwermeyer, "Teacher Unionism—Chicago Style," 443–46; Danns, *Something Better for Our Children,* 94–95; Lyons, *Teachers and Reform*, 185–88, 200–201; Black interview by author; Peoples interview by author, December 2, 2014.

40. "Teachers to 'Work' in Strike," *Chicago Daily Defender,* May 17, 1969; Landwermeyer, "Teacher Unionism—Chicago Style," 440–43; Lyons, *Teachers and Reform*, 171, 198–202; Danns, *Something Better for Our Children,* 112; Worrill interview by author; Peoples interview by author, December 2, 2014; Teachers' Division Operation Breadbasket Newsletter, May 18, 1969, Peoples Papers; Podair, *Strike That Changed New York,* 153–82; Perrillo, *Uncivil Rights,* 128–29, 136.

41. Faith C. Christmas, "Education Budget Cuts Threaten 1,900 Black Teachers: Figure Could Be Doubled," *Chicago Daily Defender,* April 26, 1969.

42. Landwermeyer, "Teacher Unionism—Chicago Style," 440–43; Lyons, *Teachers and*

Reform, 171, 198–202; Danns, *Something Better for Our Children*, 112; Worrill interview by author; Peoples interview by author, December 2, 2014; Teachers' Division Operation Breadbasket Newsletter, May 18, 1969, Peoples Papers.

43. Teachers' Division Operation Breadbasket Newsletters, May 27, June 1, September 17, 1969, Peoples Papers; Landwermeyer, "Teacher Unionism—Chicago Style," 445–46.

44. Danns, *Desegregating Chicago's Public Schools*, 57–89.

45. The 1969 report did not include extensive data for support and clerical staff to allow for a direct comparison with the 1979 data. See Chicago Public Schools, *Racial/Ethnic Survey—Staff* (1969); Chicago Public Schools, *Racial/Ethnic Survey—Staff* (1978); Chicago Public Schools, *Racial/Ethnic Survey—Staff* (1979).

46. The definition of "pupil services" has changed over time and now often specifically refers to support staff working with special education students. The broader definition that encompasses various categories of school aides is still used as well. In some districts, these workers constitute as much as a third of the district's employees. See Chicago Public Schools, *Racial/Ethnic Survey—Staff* (1979); Chicago Public Schools, *Racial/Ethnic Survey—Students* (1979); and Michelle C. Russell, text message to author, December 18, 2014.

47. "Operation Breadbasket—Teachers Division Position Paper on the Public School Security Manual," [1969], Peoples Papers.

48. Kafka, *History of "Zero Tolerance,"* 7–10, 120–23; Lyons, *Teachers and Reform*, 144–45, 153–54, 176; "Operation Breadbasket—Teachers Division Position Paper on the Public School Security Manual," [1969], Peoples Papers; "Union Demands More Security in Schools," *Chicago Union Teacher*, October 1969, CTU Archives.

49. Barbara Amazaki, "O.K. to Train Veterans as Teachers," *Chicago Tribune*, September 5, 1968; "Redmond Asks for 'Dr. King' School Name: He Also Proposes New Teacher Corps," *Chicago Tribune*, August 27, 1968; telegram to Elliott Richardson, Secretary of HEW: Position Paper—Teachers Corps: Teachers Division Operation Breadbasket, [n.d.], Peoples Papers; "Board Seeking 400 Negroes to Teach Here: Received $150,000 in Training Grants," *Chicago Tribune*, December 12, 1968; Faith C. Christmas, "Black Teachers Label Their Union 'Racist,'" *Chicago Daily Defender*, January 9, 1969; Peoples interview by author, December 2, 2014.

50. Danns, *Desegregating Chicago's Public Schools*, 8; Hirsch, *Making the Second Ghetto*, 17.

51. Efforts to desegregate teaching staff progressed from school-based efforts of the late 1950s to citywide boycotts and protests in the 1960s and continued endeavors to desegregate schools via legal means at the state and federal levels, culminating in a 1980 federal desegregation consent decree. See Danns, *Desegregating Chicago's Public Schools*, 66–67, and Danns, "Northern Desegregation," 90.

52. Danns, "Northern Desegregation," 90; Peoples interview by author, December 2, 2014; Danns, *Desegregating Chicago's Public Schools*, 74.

53. Danns, *Desegregating Chicago's Public Schools*, 69; "Public Statement," August 4, 1969, Peoples Papers; Peoples interview by author, December 2, 2014.

54. Becker, "Career of the Chicago Public School Teacher," 472; "Public Statement," August 4, 1969, Peoples Papers; Peoples interview by author, December 2, 2014.

55. "Public Statement," August 4, 1969, Peoples Papers; Peoples interview by author, December 2, 2014.

56. Faith C. Christmas, "Teachers Fear Ouster Plot," *Chicago Daily Defender*, October 22, 1969; Peoples interview by author, December 2, 2014.

57. Hirsch, "Massive Resistance in the Urban North."

58. "Public Statement," August 4, 1969, Peoples Papers; Peoples interview by author, December 2, 2014.

59. Danns, *Desegregating Chicago's Public Schools*, 69–77.

60. In addition to the segregation of the CPS faculty, ESAA funds were denied because by 1975 CPS had not developed an adequate approach to bilingual education and, later, because it had not adequately desegregated the CPS student population. See Danns, "Northern Desegregation," 90; Hess, "Renegotiating a Multicultural Society," 136; "Desegregation Advisory Coalition Planning Meeting," December 1, 1976, series II, box 261, folder 2616, CUL Records.

61. "Union Members Speak Their Minds," *Chicago Union Teacher*, April 1977, CTU Archives.

62. Dorothy Collin, "Fear Hits a Homer in Bogan Schools," *Chicago Tribune*, June 19, 1977, 25; Danns, *Desegregating Chicago's Public Schools*, 83–87.

63. Danns, *Desegregating Chicago's Public Schools*, 83–87; "Integration Protest: 90% Boycott of Bogan Bias Transfer Plans," *Chicago Tribune*, June 15, 1977, B8; Chicago Public Schools, *Racial/Ethnic Survey—Students* (1977); Daniel Fegan, Letter to the Editor, *Chicago Union Teacher*, November 1976, CTU Archives.

64. Danns, *Desegregating Chicago's Public Schools*, 83–87; Peoples interview by author, December 2, 2014.

65. "2 Educators Rap Busing Edict," *Chicago Daily Defender*, April 21, 1971; Fish, *Black Power/White Control*, 226–27; Faith C. Christmas, "Blasts U.S. School Order," *Chicago Daily Defender*, September 29, 1970, 2; "Charge Board Killing Black School Project," *Chicago Daily Defender*, October 17, 1970.

66. David Rosenbaum, "U.S. and Chicago Sign Accord for Schools," *New York Times*, October 13, 1977.

67. Chicago Public Schools, *Racial/Ethnic Survey—Staff* (1969); Chicago Public Schools, *Racial/Ethnic Survey—Staff* (1977); Chicago Public Schools, *Racial/Ethnic Survey—Staff* (1984).

68. "CTU Receives Civil Rights Citation," *Chicago Union Teacher*, December 1973, CTU Archives; Lyons, *Teachers and Reform*, 201–4; Jacquelyn Heard, "Union Leader Jacqueline Vaughn," *Chicago Tribune*, January 23, 1994; "History of JBV"; "Jacqueline B. Vaughn."

69. Peoples interview by author, December 2, 2014.

70. The 1987 report was the first report I found that included separate data about women and men by racial group. See Chicago Public Schools, *Racial/Ethnic Survey—Staff* (1987).

71. Peoples interview by author, December 2, 2014, and March 9, 2017.

72. "Breadbasket Teachers Division against Teachers' Strike," January 12, 1971, box 149, folder 149-10, Wyatt Papers.

73. In 1973 "reestablish[ing] traditional alliances between our movements, such as the labor movement," was one of PUSH's internal "program mandates." The CTU and other unions were honored at PUSH events and made donations to PUSH to support its Coalition for Jobs and Economic Justice. This coalition focused on creating jobs, job

training, fighting hunger, halting rising food costs, tax reform, and a reallocation of defense and military spending to address domestic needs. See Peoples interview by author, December 2, 2014, and March 9, 2017; in the Wyatt Papers, box 151, see "Operation PUSH Program Mandates for 1973," folder 4; "Hi-Lites of P.U.S.H. Activities: The First 365 Days," folder 3; "Labor Participation in 1973 PUSH 'Family Affair' at McCormick Place," May 18, 1973, folder 5; "This Is Operation PUSH," brochure, 1975, folder 9; and "September 8th Set as Mobilization Date for Jobs and Economic Justice," July 27, 1973, and Spring Offensive Labor Coalition Receipt Book, folder 6.

74. Chicago African-American Teachers Association, "The 60's—Chicago Educators of Action! Where Are They Now?," *Newsletter* 9, no. 1 (Spring ed., 1974): 3, Chicago History Museum.

75. Peoples interview by author, December 2, 2014.

76. Shipps, *School Reform, Corporate Style*, 89–99.

77. Ibid., 75–85.

78. Parks, "Revisiting Shibboleths of Race and Urban Economy," 110–22.

79. "Raby and the CTU," editorial, *Chicago Union Teacher*, October 1972, CTU Archives; Black Caucus, *The Alternative* 1, no. 1 (September 1974), United Teachers of Chicago, Peoples Papers; Peoples interview by author, December 2, 2014, and March 9, 2017.

80. Black Caucus, *The Alternative* 1, no. 1 (September 1974), United Teachers of Chicago, Peoples Papers.

81. Peoples interview by author, December 2, 2014, and March 9, 2017; Sizemore, *Abashing Anomaly*; Arnez, "Selected Black Female Superintendents of Public School Systems"; Edmonds, "Effective Schools for the Urban Poor."

82. Stokes, "New Black Dimension in Our Society."

83. Campbell, "The Difference," from Afro-American Teachers *Forum* 2 (1968), as quoted in Wright, *What Black Educators Are Saying*, 25–26.

84. Peoples interview by author, December 2, 2014; United States House of Representatives, "Metcalfe, Ralph Harold."

85. Chicago Public School Facts and Figures 1971–1972, Annual Financial Report 1982, box Chicago Board of Education Finance, Annual Financial Reports, folder Annual Financial Report 1982, CBOE Archives; Facts of the Chicago Public Schools 1987–88 School Year, box Chicago Board of Education Finance, Facts and Figures, folder 1987–1988, CBOE Archives; Ravitch, *Death and Life of the Great American School System*, 23–30.

86. Lyons, *Teachers and Reform*, 204.

87. Peoples interview by author, December 2, 2014.

88. Ibid.; Walker, *Their Highest Potential*; Walker, *Hello Professor*.

Chapter 5

1. Johnson, *Revolutionaries to Race Leaders*, xxix.

2. Rivlin, *Fire on the Prairie*, 27–31; Steve Bogira, "How Many Chicago Mayors Have Graduated from a Chicago Public High School?," *Chicago Reader*, January 6, 2015.

3. Friesema, "Black Control of Central Cities"; Kraus and Swanstrom, "Minority Mayors and the Hollow-Prize Problem."

4. Ravitch, *Death and Life of the Great American School System*, 23–30; "National Commission on Excellence in Education Publishes Report—Feds Say 'Offer More but We Won't Pay!,'" *Chicago Union Teacher*, May 1983, CTU Archives.

5. Harris, *Price of the Ticket*, 144.

6. Taylor, *From #BlackLivesMatter to Black Liberation*, 78–100; Harris, *Price of the Ticket*, 44–52, 144; Thompson, *Double Trouble*, 1–17; Moore, *Carl B. Stokes and the Rise of Black Political Power*, 5–8.

7. "SOCDS Census Data."

8. Grimshaw, *Bitter Fruit*, 3–29, 19–25, 115–19, 125–27; Williams, *From the Bullet to the Ballot*.

9. Fernández, *Brown in the Windy City*, 3–5; Gibson and Jung, "Historical Census Statistics on Population Totals by Race."

10. Grimshaw, *Bitter Fruit*, 21–23, 164–66.

11. Harold Washington served as a precinct captain under Third Ward alderman and committeeman Ralph Metcalfe. Daley perceived Washington as a man who would be loyal to him and the machine. Washington's refusal to tolerate racially motivated interpersonal attacks ultimately cost him his favored position with Daley. For example, during his stint as a city lawyer, Washington was involved in a racially charged public argument with a fellow city lawyer who was White. Word of this argument spread all the way to the mayor's office, and Daley sent a Black woman lawyer to counsel Washington to avoid public disputes and ignore perceived racial slights from his colleagues. See Rivlin, *Fire on the Prairie*, 42–49.

12. Carl, "Harold Washington and Chicago's Schools," 318–22.

13. Ibid.

14. Harold Washington as quoted in Travis, *"Harold," the People's Mayor*, 80.

15. Grimshaw, *Bitter Fruit*, 5–6; Ture and Hamilton, *Black Power*, 46–47; Johnson, *Revolutionaries to Race Leaders*, xxiii; Taylor, *From #BlackLivesMatter to Black Liberation*, 75–106.

16. Pushed by community activists and the changing politics of Chicago's Black communities, former Daley loyalist Congressman Ralph Metcalfe, whom Washington had previously worked under, defected from the machine. See Grimshaw, *Bitter Fruit*, 136–38; Peoples interview by author, December 2, 2014; Rivlin, *Fire on the Prairie*, 57; Peterson, *School Politics, Chicago Style*, 35–36; Travis, *"Harold," the People's Mayor*, 111–12.

17. Rivlin, *Fire on the Prairie*, 58–60; Committee on House Administration of the U.S. House of Representatives, *Black Americans in Congress, 1870–2007*, 524–28; Carl, "Harold Washington and Chicago's Schools," 326; Travis, *"Harold," the People's Mayor*, 111–12, 135–38.

18. Although Byrne had previously worked for Mayor Daley, Bilandic was seen as a final vestige of the Richard J. Daley machine. Many also credited Byrne's Black support to Bilandic's mishandling of a massive snowstorm in the winter of 1979, when CTA trains were directed to bypass stations in Black neighborhoods to more efficiently deliver White riders to and from the downtown business district, causing Black residents to wait for hours in the snow for trains. See Travis, *Autobiography of Black Politics*, 529–34; Grimshaw, *Bitter Fruit*, 145–58; and Colby and Green, "Byrne's Victory," *Illinois Issues*, May 1979.

19. Shipps, *School Reform, Corporate Style*, 91–102; Mirel, "School Reform, Chicago Style," 124–25; Civic Federation, "School Finance Authority."

20. Shipps, *School Reform, Corporate Style*, 91–102; Mirel, "School Reform, Chicago Style," 124–25; Civic Federation, "School Finance Authority."

21. Klein, *Shock Doctrine*, 6–22; Shipps, *School Reform, Corporate Style*, 91–102; Mirel, "School Reform, Chicago Style," 124–25; Chicago Public Schools, *Racial/Ethnic Survey—Students* (1979); Chicago Public Schools, *Racial/Ethnic Survey—Students* (1981).

22. Rivlin, *Fire on the Prairie*, 23–35, 37; Harris, *Price of the Ticket*, 41–45; Worrill interview by author; Travis, *Autobiography of Black Politics*, 547.

23. Robert Davis and William Juneau, "Suit Filed to Keep Ayers off Chicago School Board," *Chicago Tribune*, April 19, 1980, S1; Rivlin, *Fire on the Prairie*, 35; Harris, *Price of the Ticket*, 41–45; Worrill interview by author.

24. Travis, *Autobiography of Black Politics*, 533–37; Alkalimat and Gills, *Harold Washington and the Crisis of Black Power in Chicago*, 99; Shipps, *School Reform, Corporate Style*, 75–82, 97–99; Robert Davis and William Juneau, "Suit Filed to Keep Ayers off Chicago School Board," *Chicago Tribune*, April 19, 1980; Worrill interview by author; Robert Davis, "Smith, Byrne Make Peace at Brief Meeting," *Chicago Tribune*, May 21, 1980.

25. "Welcome Dr. Love!," Citizens Schools Committee Report 4, 3 (1981), Chicago History Museum; Shipps, *School Reform, Corporate Style*, 107.

26. Travis, *Autobiography of Black Politics*, 533–37; Alkalimat and Gills, *Harold Washington and the Crisis of Black Power in Chicago*, 99; Mirel, "School Reform, Chicago Style," 125–26.

27. Travis, *Autobiography of Black Politics*, 536.

28. Alkalimat and Gills, *Harold Washington and the Crisis of Black Power in Chicago*, 27–29, 99; Williams, *From the Bullet to the Ballot*, 194–99.

29. Williams, *From the Bullet to the Ballot*, 125–66, 196–99.

30. Travis, *Autobiography of Black Politics*, 547; Rivlin, *Fire on the Prairie*, 23–35, 37, 148; Harris, *Price of the Ticket*, 41–45; Worrill interview by author.

31. Travis, *Autobiography of Black Politics*, 548, 554, 558.

32. Alkalimat and Gills, *Harold Washington and the Crisis of Black Power in Chicago*, 41–42; Rivlin, *Fire on the Prairie*, 37; Grimshaw, *Bitter Fruit*, 163.

33. Córdova, "Harold Washington and the Rise of Latino Electoral Politics in Chicago"; Fernández, *Brown in the Windy City*, 207–10.

34. Córdova, "Harold Washington and the Rise of Latino Electoral Politics in Chicago," 36–39; Williams, *From the Bullet to the Ballot*, 195–99.

35. Alkalimat and Gills, *Harold Washington and the Crisis of Black Power in Chicago*, 63; Grimshaw, *Bitter Fruit*, 171–73; Rivlin, *Fire on the Prairie*, 128–29; Peoples interview by author, December 2, 2014; Black Caucus, *The Alternative* 1, no. 1 (September 1974), United Teachers of Chicago, Peoples Papers.

36. Carl, "Harold Washington and Chicago's Schools," 326; Peoples interview by author, December 2, 2014, and March 9, 2017; Walton interview by author, October 9, 2014.

37. The Task Force was initially organized by a group including Lu Palmer and led by co-chairs Conrad Worrill, chairman of the Chicago chapter of the National Black United Front, and Robert Starks, a Black nationalist academic. Renault Robinson, Washington's original campaign manager, was also active in the group, which was initially intended to create the institutional infrastructure necessary to create a Black independent political organization, the Black equivalent of the predominantly White liberal reform-centered group the Independent Voters of Illinois. According to Worrill, this never materialized

in part due to a lack of organization and infighting within the Task Force. Another contributing factor was the singular focus of the Task Force on electing Harold Washington, a charismatic leader, rather than on building the institutional structure of a political organization. See Rivlin, *Fire on the Prairie*, 129–40; Alkalimat and Gills, *Harold Washington and the Crisis of Black Power in Chicago*, 63–67; Worrill interview by author; and Grimshaw, *Bitter Fruit*, 151.

38. Grimshaw, *Bitter Fruit*, 174; Rivlin, *Fire on the Prairie*, 138–39; Worrill interview by author.

39. Grimshaw, *Bitter Fruit*, 178; Alkalimat and Gills, *Harold Washington and the Crisis of Black Power in Chicago*, 73, 102–6.

40. Letter from Leon Finney to Albert Raby, February 23, 1983, Staff Series, Individual Files/Al Raby, box 3, folder 10, Washington Papers.

41. Rast, "Manufacturing Industrial Decline."

42. Reed, "Black Urban Regime," 160–62; Arena, *Driven from New Orleans*, xxiii–xxv; Reed, "Black Urban Administrators."

43. Anderson and Pickering, *Confronting the Color Line*, 120; Chicago Public Schools, *Racial/Ethnic Survey—Students* (1983); Carl, "Harold Washington and Chicago's Schools," 315–16; John Rury, "School Desegregation," *Encyclopedia of Chicago*; Gibson and Jung, "Historical Census Statistics on Population Totals by Race."

44. Travis, *"Harold," the People's Mayor*, 211–19, 243–54; Grimshaw, *Bitter Fruit*, 189; Carl, "Harold Washington and Chicago's Schools," 329–31.

45. Travis, *"Harold," the People's Mayor*, 211–19.

46. Edward Vrdolyak as quoted in Travis, *"Harold," the People's Mayor*, 176–77.

47. Travis, *"Harold," the People's Mayor*, 211–19, 243–54; Grimshaw, *Bitter Fruit*, 189; Córdova, "Harold Washington and the Rise of Latino Electoral Politics in Chicago," 41–47.

48. Travis, *"Harold," the People's Mayor*, 211–19, 243–54; Grimshaw, *Bitter Fruit*, 189.

49. Carl, "Harold Washington and Chicago's Schools," 330–31.

50. National Commission on Excellence in Education, *Nation at Risk*; Ravitch, *Death and Life of the Great American School System*, 23–30; Hawkins, "Becoming Preeminent in Education"; Spencer Rich, "'Safety Net' Strands Thinner under Reagan," *Washington Post*, November 27, 1988.

51. Chicago Public School Facts and Figures 1971–1972, Annual Financial Report 1982, box Chicago Board of Education, Finance Annual Financial Reports, folder Annual Financial Report 1982, CBOE Archives; Facts of the Chicago Public Schools 1987–88 School Year, box Chicago Board of Education Finance, Facts and Figures, folder 1987–1988, CBOE Archives; Ravitch, *Death and Life of the Great American School System*, 23–30; National Commission on Excellence in Education, *Nation at Risk*.

52. "Vaughn Testifies before Congress: 'Make an Investment in Education in Our Nation's Future,'" *Chicago Union Teacher*, January 1987, CTU Archives.

53. O'Connell, *School Reform, Chicago Style*, 1–13; Jacqueline Vaughn, "Tell Legislators You Support Increased School Funding before June 30," *Chicago Union Teacher*, June 1987, CTU Archives; "Setting New Courses" and "Union Starts Down Road to Renewing Profession," *Chicago Union Teacher*, January 1985, CTU Archives; "We Choose Education Reform over Decline and Business as Usual," *Chicago Union Teacher*, February 1988, CTU Archives.

54. R. C. Longworth, "Chicago: City on the Brink: 'How Much Time Do We Have? . . .

No Time'" *Chicago Tribune*, May 10, 1981; R. C. Longworth, "City Needs Jobs, Jobs, Jobs," *Chicago Tribune*, April 25, 1983.

55. Rast, "Manufacturing Industrial Decline"; Wacquant and Wilson, "Cost of Racial and Class Exclusion in the Inner City," 13; Rich, *Black Mayors and School Politics*, 182–84; Doussard, Peck, and Theodore, "After Deindustrialization."

56. Rich, *Black Mayors and School Politics*, 182–83; Carl, "Harold Washington and Chicago's Schools," 330–31; "Executive Summary of Education and Unemployment in Chicago: A Briefing Paper for the Mayor's Education Summit," draft version, October 21, 1986, Education Summit, box 31, folder 23, Washington Papers.

57. "Proposed Revised Mission Statement, Mayor's Education Summit," [November 1987], Education Oversight Committee, box 30, folder 29, Washington Papers.

58. Travis, *"Harold," the People's Mayor*, 163–63; Carl, "Harold Washington and Chicago's Schools," 331–32; "Learning Works in Chicago Summary," [1986], Community Services Series, box 30, folder 32, Washington Papers.

59. "Passport to Excellence: A Two-Pronged Approach," [1987?], Community Services Series, box 31, folder 15, Washington Papers; Minutes Community Support Work Group, November 10, 1986, Community Services Series, box 31, folder 14, Washington Papers.

60. Education Summit Steering Committee, November 18, 1986, Community Services Series, box 31, folder 3, Washington Papers.

61. Breakfast with School Improvement Representatives Minutes, January 22, 1987, Community Services Series, box 31, folder 8, Washington Papers; Grimshaw, *Bitter Fruit*, 189–94; Córdova, "Harold Washington and the Rise of Latino Electoral Politics in Chicago," 47–48.

62. Carl, "Harold Washington and Chicago's Schools," 332–33.

63. Willmott interview by author; letter from Peter Willmott to Members of Hiring Compact Delegation, August 3, 1987, Community Services Series, box 30, folder 19, Washington Papers; Casey Banas, "Byrd Labels 'Learn-Earn' Proposal Unfair to Schools," *Chicago Tribune*, November 11, 1987; Carl, "Harold Washington and Chicago's Schools," 333.

64. Letter from Peter Willmott to Members of Hiring Compact Delegation, August 3, 1987, Community Services Series, box 30, folder 19, Washington Papers; Carl, "Harold Washington and Chicago's Schools," 333; Willmott interview by author.

65. Shipps, *School Reform, Corporate Style*, 16–33, 94–95, 110–11; Carl, "Harold Washington and Chicago's Schools," 331–32; "Learning Works in Chicago Summary," [1986], Community Services Series, box 30, folder 32, Washington Papers; Breakfast with School Improvement Representatives Minutes, January 22, 1987, Community Services Series, box 31, folder 8, Washington Papers.

66. Bendick, "Privatizing the Delivery of Social Welfare Services"; Tingle, "Privatization and the Reagan Administration."

67. As quoted from the 1988 budget in Tingle, "Privatization and the Reagan Administration," 230.

68. "Welcome Dr. Love!," Citizens Schools Committee Report 4, 3 (1981), Chicago History Museum; Shipps, *School Reform, Corporate Style*, 101–5; Ravitch, *Death and Life of the Great American School System*, 23–30.

69. "Vaughn Testifies before Congress: 'Make an Investment in Education in Our Na-

tion's Future,'" *Chicago Union Teacher*, January 1987, CTU Archives; Hawkins, "Becoming Preeminent in Education," n. 64.

70. Carl, "Harold Washington and Chicago's Schools," 334–35; Ayers and Klonsky, "Navigating a Restless Sea," 10; "Welcome Dr. Love!," Citizens Schools Committee Report 4, 3 (1981), Chicago History Museum.

71. Carl, "Harold Washington and Chicago's Schools," 335–36; Ayers and Klonsky, "Navigating a Restless Sea," 10–12; O'Connell, *School Reform, Chicago Style*, 3–4; "No Progress in School Strike Despite Pleading by Parents," *Chicago Tribune*, September 13, 1987; "Passport to Excellence: A Two-Pronged Approach," [1987?], Community Services Series, box 31, folder 15, Washington Papers; Minutes Community Support Work Group, November 10, 1986, Community Services Series, box 31, folder 14, Washington Papers; "The Strike Is Over: The Work Begins," October 3, 1987, Community Services Series, box 30, folder 3, Washington Papers.

72. Casey Banas, "Strike's Wake Leaves Winners and Losers," *Chicago Tribune*, October 5, 1987, 2.

73. Casey Banas and Cheryl Devall, "A 1st Step to Reform in Schools," *Chicago Tribune*, October 12, 1987, 1.

74. "Proposed Revised Mission Statement, Mayor's Education Summit," [November 1987], Education Oversight Committee, box 30, folder 29, Washington Papers; City of Chicago, *Mayor's Education Summit*, 3; Carl, "Harold Washington and Chicago's Schools," 338.

75. O'Connell, *School Reform, Chicago Style*, 11–12; Melvin Holli, "A Watershed in Chicago's History," *Chicago Tribune*, December 7, 1987; Chicago Public Schools, *Racial/Ethnic Survey—Students* (1987); George, Dilts, Yang, Wasserman, and Clary, *Chicago Children and Youth*.

76. Jack Houston, "Mayor: We'll Clean Up Schools, He Answers Education Secretary's Criticism of Chicago," *Chicago Tribune*, November 8, 1987; "PCC Guiding Principles for School Reform and Schedule for Community Forums," November 7, 1987, Community Services Series, box 31, folder 24, Washington Papers; O'Connell, *School Reform, Chicago Style*, 11–12; Carl, "Harold Washington and Chicago's Schools," 335–39; Baron interview by author.

77. Casey Banas, "Chicago's Schools Hit as Worst," *Chicago Tribune*, November 7, 1987; "Schools in Chicago Are Called the Worst by Education Chief," *New York Times*, November 7, 1987; letter from Jacqueline Vaughn to Secretary Bennett, *Chicago Union Teacher*, March 1988, CTU Archives.

78. Jack Houston, "Mayor: We'll Clean Up Schools, He Answers Education Secretary's Criticism of Chicago," *Chicago Tribune*, November 8, 1987.

79. Baron interview by author.

80. O'Connell, *School Reform, Chicago Style*, 11–16; Carl, "Harold Washington and Chicago's Schools," 341; Worrill interview by author.

81. O'Connell, *School Reform, Chicago Style*, 11–16; Carl, "Harold Washington and Chicago's Schools," 341; Worrill interview by author.

82. Willmott interview by author; O'Connell, *School Reform, Chicago Style*, 12–15.

83. Willmott interview by author; O'Connell, *School Reform, Chicago Style*, 12–15.

84. O'Connell, *School Reform, Chicago Style*, 12–15.

85. Ibid., 12–18.

86. Corretta McFerren as quoted in *The Neighborhood Works*, December 1987, as quoted in O'Connell, *School Reform, Chicago Style*, 16.

87. Ture And Hamilton, *Black Power*, 46–47; Johnson, *Revolutionaries to Race Leaders*, xxiii; Taylor, *From #BlackLivesMatter to Black Liberation*, 75–106.

88. O'Connell, *School Reform, Chicago Style*, 12; Carl, "Harold Washington and Chicago's Schools," 338–40; Worrill interview by author. The Center for Inner City Studies allowed the PCC to use its facilities to hold meetings and work with the consultants.

89. Elizabeth Hinton et al., "Did Blacks Really Endorse the 1994 Crime Bill?," *New York Times*, April 13, 2016.

90. Karen Thomas, "Parents Make Push for Schools," *Chicago Tribune*, January 24, 1988; O'Connell, *School Reform, Chicago Style*, 12.

91. Carl, "Harold Washington and Chicago's Schools," 340; O'Connell, *School Reform, Chicago Style*, 15–18; Worrill interview by author; Baron interview by author.

92. O'Connell, *School Reform, Chicago Style*, 15–18; Worrill interview by author; Baron interview by author.

93. Carl, "Harold Washington and Chicago's Schools," 340–41; Willmott interview by author.

94. Shipps, *School Reform, Corporate Style*, xii, 107; Sizemore, *Walking in Circles*, 64, 93–96; Carl, "Harold Washington and Chicago's Schools," 340–41; Lee interview by author, March 11, 2009; Worrill interview by author.

95. Lewis and Nakagawa, *Race and Education Reform in the American Metropolis*, 7.

96. Sizemore, *Walking in Circles*, 64, 93–96; Carl, "Harold Washington and Chicago's Schools," 340–41; Willmott interview by author.

97. Worrill interview by author.

98. Karanja interview by author, March 27, 2017.

99. Taylor, *From #BlackLivesMatter to Black Liberation*, 78–106.

100. Doussard, Peck, and Theodore, "After Deindustrialization," 185, 188, 201; Rich, *Black Mayors and School Politics*, 182–84.

101. Rich, *Black Mayors and School Politics*, 155.

102. Isabel Wilkerson, "Chicago Picks Chief for New School Plan," *New York Times*, October 16, 1989.

Chapter 6

1. Sara Spurlark Obituary; Lee Botts, "Kenwood Boycott Issues Unclear, Adults Organize Student Meeting," *Hyde Park Herald*, October 23, 1968.

2. Ayers and Klonsky, "Navigating a Restless Sea," 15; Chicago Public Schools, "About Us"; "Neoliberalism Is a Political Project"; Klein, *Shock Doctrine*, 9–22; Brewer, "21st-Century Capitalism, Austerity, and Black Economic Dispossession"; Lydon, "Noam Chomsky."

3. Ayers and Klonsky, "Navigating a Restless Sea," 15; "Neoliberalism Is a Political Project"; Klein, *Shock Doctrine*, 9–22.

4. O'Connell, "School Reform, Chicago Style," 27–29; Sara L. Spurlark, "Commission Gave Mayor Excellent Board Choices," *Catalyst*, May 1990, 20; Isabel Wilkerson, "Chicago Picks Chief for New School Plan," *New York Times*, October 16, 1989.

5. Poinsett, "School Reform, Black Leaders"; O'Connell, "School Reform, Chicago Style," 27–29.

6. Poinsett, "School Reform, Black Leaders."

7. Ayers and Klonsky, "Navigating a Restless Sea," 15; Poinsett, "Council Chairperson Sees New Leaders Emerging."

8. Poinsett, "School Reform, Black Leaders"; O'Connell, "School Reform, Chicago Style," 27–29; Ayers and Klonsky, "Navigating a Restless Sea," 15.

9. Poinsett, "School Reform, Black Leaders."

10. Ibid.

11. Grimshaw, *Bitter Fruit*, 171–72, 181–82, 197–209; Gibson and Jung, "Historical Census Statistics on Population Totals by Race."

12. Grimshaw, *Bitter Fruit*, 171–72, 181–82, 197–209; Shipps, *School Reform, Corporate Style*, 133–35.

13. Ayers and Klonsky, "Navigating a Restless Sea," 15; O'Connell, "School Reform, Chicago Style," 27–29; Willmott interview by author.

14. Poinsett, "School Reform, Black Leaders"; Ayers and Klonsky, "Navigating a Restless Sea," 15.

15. Poinsett, "School Reform, Black Leaders."

16. Shipps, *School Reform, Corporate Style*, 147–56; Thomas Hardy and Robert Davis, "Edgar Won't Bail Out City Schools," *Chicago Tribune*, January 20, 1995.

17. Shipps, *School Reform, Corporate Style*, 147–56; Civic Federation, "School Finance Authority."

18. Harold Howe, "Teaching as a Business and Desire," *Chicago Union Teacher*, September 1966, CTU Archives.

19. As quoted in Haney, "1995 Chicago School Reform Amendatory Act and the CPS CEO," 73; Shipps, *School Reform, Corporate Style*, 147–56; Don Terry, "In A G.O.P. World, a Democrat Rules Chicago," *New York Times*, April 1, 1995.

20. Ayers and Klonsky, "Navigating a Restless Sea"; Shipps, *School Reform, Corporate Style*, 147–59; "Meet Paul Vallas."

21. Hess, "Community Participation or Control?," 221; Shipps, *School Reform, Corporate Style*, 135, 154–56, 203–4; Haney, "1995 Chicago School Reform Amendatory Act and the CPS CEO"; "President Hails Chicago Schools: Reform Efforts Cited as Model," *Chicago Sun-Times*, October 29, 1997; "President William Jefferson Clinton State of the Union Address"; "Text of President Clinton's 1998 State of the Union Address."

22. Shipps, *School Reform, Corporate Style*, 134–36; Mahtesian, "Taking Chicago Private."

23. Ayers and Klonsky, "Navigating a Restless Sea," 15; Shipps, *School Reform, Corporate Style*, 150–59; Chicago Public Schools, *Racial/Ethnic Survey—Staff* (1989); "District Teacher Demographics By Ethnicity (2007–16)."

24. May interview by author; Heath interview by author; Shipps, *School Reform, Corporate Style*, 154–61; Thomas C. Reece, "President's Message to the Members," *Chicago Union Teacher*, June 1995, CTU Archives; "A Settlement That Puts Schools First: Daley's Board Defends Us against Republican Intentions," *Chicago Union Teacher*, September 1995, CTU Archives.

25. Shipps, *School Reform, Corporate Style*, 154–59, 203–4; "A Settlement That Puts Schools First: Daley's Board Defends Us against Republican Intentions," *Chicago Union*

Teacher, September 1995, CTU Archives; Haney, "1995 Chicago School Reform Amendatory Act and the CPS CEO," 108–38; "Chico, Vallas Impress House," *Chicago Union Teacher*, December 1995, CTU Archives; de la Torre et al., *Changes in Student Populations and Teacher Workforce in Low-Performing Chicago Schools Targeted for Reform*.

26. Peoples interview by author, December 2, 2014, and March 9, 2017; Landwermeyer, "Teacher Unionism—Chicago Style," 440–43; Lyons, *Teachers and Reform*, 171, 198–202. Danns, *Something Better for Our Children*, 112; Worrill interview by author; Teachers' Division Operation Breadbasket Newsletter, May 18, 1969, Peoples Papers.

27. Dawson, *Not in Our Lifetimes*, 104.

28. Cavounidis and Lang, "Discrimination and Worker Evaluation"; Kahrl, "Capitalizing on the Urban Fiscal Crisis"; Pattillo, "Black Middle-Class Neighborhoods"; Parks, "Revisiting Shibboleths of Race and Urban Economy." For more on race, gender, and precarity, see Butler, *Precarious Life*; Butler, *Frames of War*; Nyong'o, "Situating Precarity between the Body and the Commons"; and Ridout and Schneider, "Precarity and Performance."

29. Peoples interview by author, December 2, 2014.

30. Shipps, *School Reform, Corporate Style*, 107, 154–56; Leslie T. Fenwick in Valerie Strauss, "Ed School Dean: Urban School Reform Is Really about Land Development (not Kids)," *Washington Post*, May 28, 2013.

31. "History of the Effective Schools Movement."

32. Henderson et al., "High-Quality Schooling for African American Students," 170, 181–82; "History of the Effective Schools Movement."

33. Edmonds, "Effective Schools for the Urban Poor," 15–24.

34. In 1973 Sizemore was hired as the superintendent of Washington, D.C., Public Schools, becoming the first Black woman to lead a public school system in a major U.S. city. In 1977 she was hired as a researcher and professor at the University of Pittsburgh. In this post, Sizemore studied high-performing Black schools in a project funded by the National Institute of Education. Sizemore returned to Chicago and became dean of DePaul University's School of Education in 1992. See Sizemore, *Walking in Circles*, 82, 203–10, 248–54; Arnez, "Selected Black Female Superintendents of Public School Systems," 311; Berry, "Twentieth-Century Black Women in Education," 291; Sizemore, "Pitfalls and Promises," 269–88; Lamb, "Barbara Sizemore Dies; D.C. Superintendent," *Washington Post*, July 28, 2004, B6; and Chase and Chase interview by author.

35. Henderson et al., "High-Quality Schooling for African American Students," 171–72; Saunders and Saunders, "W. Edward Deming, Quality Analysis, and Total Behavior Management"; Watson, "Integrating Lean Manufacturing with Technology," 50–52.

36. Henderson et al., "High-Quality Schooling for African American Students," 171–73; "Correlates of Effective Schools 1989–Present"; Bullard and Taylor, *Keepers of the Dream*, 16–18.

37. Edmonds et al., "Search for Effective Schools"; Edmonds and Frederiksen, "Search for Effective Schools."

38. Bullard and Taylor, *Keepers of the Dream*, 16–18; Henderson et al., "High-Quality Schooling for African American Students," 171–73.

39. Sizemore, "Pitfalls and Promises," 287–88.

40. "Welcome Dr. Love!," Citizens Schools Committee Report 4, 3 (1981), Chicago

History Museum; Shipps, *School Reform, Corporate Style*, 101–5; Todd interview by author; Henderson et al., "High-Quality Schooling for African American Students," 171–73.

41. "History of the Effective Schools Movement"; O'Connell, "School Reform, Chicago Style," 13; press statement by Carol Long, Chicago Schoolwatch, November 6, 1985, Education: Board of Education, box 30, folder 11, Washington Papers; Shipps, *School Reform, Corporate Style*, 140–41, 192–94.

42. "University of Chicago Launches Urban Education Institute"; Shipps, *School Reform, Corporate Style*, 140–41, 193–94; "Bryk, Anthony S."; Lenz interview by Tony Sarabia; Thomas Reece, "President's Message to the Members," *Chicago Union Teacher*, November 1995, CTU Archives.

43. Shipps, *School Reform, Chicago Style*, 140–41, 193–94; Poinsett, "School Reform, Black Leaders"; "Sara Spurlark, 1923–2012," *Chicago Tribune*, February 21, 2012; Hassrick, Raudenbush, and Rosen, *Ambitious Elementary School*, 40–45, nn. 3–5, 188–90.

44. Sizemore, *Walking in Circles*, 203–10.

45. Kent, "Coleman Report," 83–88; Bullard and Taylor, *Keepers of the Dream*, 17.

46. Goldring and Smrekar, "Magnet Schools," 13; West, "Desegregation Tool That Backfired," 2568–69; Ravitch, *Death and Life of the Great American School System*, 116.

47. Goldring and Smrekar, "Magnet Schools," 13; West, "Desegregation Tool That Backfired," 2568–69; Ravitch, *Death and Life of the Great American School System*, 116; "Brief History of Magnet Schools."

48. "Magnet Schools—Elementary"; Danns, *Desegregating Chicago's Public Schools*, 109–17; Baron, *Metro*; "A Magnet Is a School," *Chicago Union Teacher*, March 1973, CTU Archives; "Disney Magnet School Accepting Applications," *Chicago Tribune*, October 19, 1969; "Magnet Schools Garner Plaudits," *Chicago Tribune*, March 6, 1977; "Groups Charge Civil Rights Violations in Magnet Schools," *Chicago Tribune*, March 8, 1970.

49. "Disney Magnet School Accepting Applications," *Chicago Tribune*, October 19, 1969; "Magnet Schools Garner Plaudits," *Chicago Tribune*, March 6, 1977; "Groups Charge Civil Rights Violations in Magnet Schools," *Chicago Tribune*, March 8, 1970.

50. Danns, *Desegregating Chicago's Public Schools*, 109–17; letter to John D. Carey from James W. Compton, April 16, 1979, series II, box 268, folder 2659, CUL Records; "A Magnet Is a School," *Chicago Union Teacher*, March 1973, CTU Archives; "Magnet Schools Garner Plaudits," *Chicago Tribune*, March 6, 1977.

51. Ravitch, *Death and Life of the Great American School System*, 114–18.

52. Danns, *Desegregating Chicago's Public Schools*, 109–17; Russom, "Obama's Neoliberal Agenda for Public Education," 117; "School Competition," *Chicago Union Teacher*, March 1967, CTU Archives; "U.S. Chamber Received Report Urging Education Help for Poor," *Washington Post, Times Herald*, December 25, 1966.

53. "Voucher System Can End American Public Education" and "Education Committee Hears the Performance Contract Story," *Chicago Union Teacher*, December 1970, CTU Archives; "Tuition Tax Credits Must Be Defeated," *Chicago Union Teacher*, April 1978; Stulberg, *Race, Schools, and Hope*, 81–83; William K. Stevens, "Education Voucher Plan Is Making Slow Progress," *New York Times*, July 2, 1971; Christopher Jencks, "Private Schools for Black Children," *New York Times*, November 3, 1968; Christopher Jencks, "A Reappraisal of the Most Controversial Educational Document of Our Time," *New York Times*, August 10, 1969.

54. "Voucher System Can End American Public Education" and "Education Commit-

tee Hears the Performance Contract Story," *Chicago Union Teacher*, December 1970, CTU Archives; "Tuition Tax Credits Must Be Defeated," *Chicago Union Teacher*, April 1978; Stulberg, *Race, Schools, and Hope*, 81–83; William K. Stevens, "Education Voucher Plan Is Making Slow Progress," *New York Times*, July 2, 1971.

55. Klein, *Shock Doctrine*, 6–22.

56. Danns, *Desegregating Chicago's Public Schools*, 109–17; letter to John D. Carey from James W. Compton, April 16, 1979, series II, box 268, folder 2659, CUL Records; Russom, "Obama's Neoliberal Agenda for Public Education," 117; Stulberg, *Race, Schools, and Hope*, 85.

57. Stulberg, *Race, Schools, and Hope*, 72–92.

58. Fuller, *No Struggle, No Progress*, 11, 201–7; Dougherty, *More Than One Struggle*, 173–93; Sanchez, "Lessons on Race and Vouchers from Milwaukee"; Stulberg, *Race, Schools, and Hope*, 72–92.

59. Fuller, *No Struggle, No Progress*, 11, 201–7; Russom, "Obama's Neoliberal Agenda for Public Education," 117; Stulberg, *Race, Schools, and Hope*, 72–92; Sanchez, "Lessons on Race and Vouchers from Milwaukee"; Scott and Holme, "Political Economy of Market-Based Educational Policies."

60. Danns, *Desegregating Chicago's Public Schools*, 109–17; letter to John D. Carey from James W. Compton, April 16, 1979, series II, box 268, folder 2659, CUL Records; VanTassel-Baska, "History of Urban Gifted Education"; Kryczka, "Selective Renewal"; "Chicago's Reaction to 'Access,'" *Illinois Issues*, September 1978.

61. "A Magnet Is a School," *Chicago Union Teacher*, March 1973, CTU Archives; Danns, *Desegregating Chicago's Public Schools*, 109–17; letter to John D. Carey from James W. Compton, April 16, 1979, series II, box 268, folder 2659, CUL Records; address given by Edwin C. Berry in Springfield, Illinois, June 24, 1969, series II, box, 277, folder 2733, CUL Records.

62. Astin, "Educational 'Choice'"; Taylor, *From #BlackLivesMatter to Black Liberation*, 75–82.

63. Kocoras, Consent Decree Memorandum Opinion.

64. Chicago Public Schools, *Racial/Ethnic Survey—Students* (1980).

65. Danns, *Desegregating Chicago's Public Schools*, 124.

66. Chicago Board of Education, *Comprehensive Student Assignment Plan*, 137.

67. Shipps, *School Reform, Corporate Style*, 157; Astin, "Educational 'Choice.'"

68. Casey Banas, "10 Chicago Public Schools That Come Up Winners," *Chicago Tribune*, November 8, 1980; "City/Suburbs: Principals Not Looking Forward to Fall Dialogue," *Chicago Tribune*, July 1, 1983; Astin, "Educational 'Choice'"; Karen M. Thomas, "Parents Vote for Local School Control," *Chicago Tribune*, January 21, 1988, 6; Tzeggai, *Defining Racial Equity in Chicago's Segregated Schools*.

69. Lipman, *New Political Economy of Urban Education*, 121.

70. Kahlenberg, "Charter School Idea Turns 20"; Ravitch, *Death and Life of the Great American School System*, 122–27; Podair, *Strike That Changed New York*; Perlstein, *Justice, Justice*; Lewis, *New York City Public Schools from Brownsville to Bloomberg*.

71. Kahlenberg, "Charter School Idea Turns 20"; Ravitch, *Death and Life of the Great American School System*, 122–27; "A Magnet Is a School."

72. Ravitch, *Death and Life of the Great American School System*, 122–27; Stulberg, *Race, Schools, and Hope*, 96; Hale, "Making of the New Democrats."

73. Rooks, *Cutting School*; Shipps, *School Reform, Corporate Style*, 107, 154–56; Leslie T. Fenwick in Valerie Strauss, "Ed School Dean: Urban School Reform Is Really about Land Development (not Kids)," *Washington Post*, May 28, 2013; Kahlenberg, "Charter School Idea Turns 20"; Ravitch, *Death and Life of the Great American School System*, 122–27.

74. Kahlenberg, "Charter School Idea Turns 20"; Steve Kerch, "Trying to Turn City Schools from Issues into Assets," *Chicago Tribune*, February 2, 1997; Jane Adler, "Class Struggles, Developers and Educators Join Forces to Open Good Public Schools That Will Keep Middle-Class Families in the City," *Chicago Tribune*, February 2, 1997.

75. Betty Shabazz International Charter School, "About Us"; Lee interview by author, March 11, 2009.

76. Lee interview by author, March 11, 2009, and June 13, 2017.

77. Lee, "Profile of an Independent Black Institution," 174, 175; Lee interview by author, March 11, 2009, and June 13, 2017.

78. Lee interview by author, March 11, 2009, and June 13, 2017; Stulberg, *Race, Schools, and Hope*, 97.

79. Madhubuti interview by author; Madhubuti, "Enemy"; Madhubuti, "Latest Purge"; Brown, *Fighting for US*; Woodard, *Nation within a Nation*.

80. Lipman, *New Political Economy of Urban Education*, 121–29; Shipps, *School Reform, Corporate Style*, 164–67.

81. Simpson interview by Fannie Rushing; Simpson interview by author; Peoples interview by author, December 2, 2014.

82. Dobbie and Fryer, "Charter Schools and Labor Market Outcomes"; Institute on Metropolitan Opportunity, *Charter Schools in Chicago*; Farmer, Baber, and Poulos, "Closed by Choice"; Lipman, *New Political Economy of Urban Education*.

83. Brazier, *Black Self-Determination*, 11.

84. Apostolic became a megachurch with thousands of members at the corner of 63rd Street and Dorchester Ave. See Apostolic Church of God, "Pastor Emeritus"; "Bishop Arthur Brazier Biography"; and Fish, *Black Power/White Control*, 292–304.

85. Antonio Olivo, "Questions Raised about Leon Finney Jr.'s Woodlawn Organization," *Chicago Tribune*, January 6, 2012; Joel Kaplan and Stanely Ziemba, "Possible HUD Violations by CHA's Finney," *Chicago Tribune*, May 20, 1987; "$1.5 Billion Pot Brims with Secretive Pork; Illinois' Top Lawmakers Guard Fund Despite Budget Cuts," *Chicago Tribune*, February 3, 2002; Apostolic Church of God, "Pastor Emeritus"; Fish, *Black Power/White Control*, 292–304; Worrill interview by author; Karanja interview by author.

86. Brazier, *Black Self-Determination*, 12.

87. Gilmore, "In the Shadow of the Shadow State"; Arena, *Driven from New Orleans*, xix.

88. Arena, *Driven from New Orleans*, xviii–xix; Gilmore, "In the Shadow of the Shadow State."

89. Gilmore, "In the Shadow of the Shadow State"; Arena, *Driven from New Orleans*, xviii–xix.

90. The author worked at UChicago Charter School Woodlawn Campus from 2006 to 2010 as a part-time social studies instructor and college counselor. See Hassrick, Raudenbush, and Rosen, *Ambitious Elementary School*, 50–60.

91. Sam Cholke, "Woodlawn Faced with Big Empty School after U. of C. Charter Moves," *DNAinfo Chicago*, January 12, 2017; City of Chicago, "Land Sale Will Support New

University of Chicago Charter School in Woodlawn"; "UChicago Celebrates Ground-breaking for New Charter School in Woodlawn"; "U of C Gets $1 Land Deal for Charter School"; Allison Matyus, "U. of C. Presents Development Plans for South of 61st Street," *Hyde Park Herald*, May 26, 2016.

92. Payne, *So Much Reform, So Little Change*, 61–65; Ayers and Klonsky, "Navigating a Restless Sea," 15; Ravitch, *Reign of Error*, 14–16; Astin, "Educational 'Choice,'" 259; Scott, "Rosa Parks Moment?"; Pattillo, "Everyday Politics of School Choice in the Black Community"; Stulberg, *Race, Schools, and Hope*; Lipman, *New Political Economy of Urban Education*; Fabricant and Fine, *Charter Schools and the Corporate Makeover of Public Education*.

93. Thomas H. Reece, "President's Message to the Members," *Chicago Union Teacher*, March 1995, CTU Archives.

94. Barbara A. Sizemore, "Making the Schools a Vehicle for Cultural Pluralism," [1971?], 16, box 64, folder 1, Sol Tax Papers, University of Chicago Special Collections.

95. Payne, *So Much Reform, So Little Change*, 61–65; Pattillo, "Everyday Politics of School Choice in the Black Community"; Stulberg, *Race, Schools, and Hope*; Ravitch, *Reign of Error*, 15; Lipman, *New Political Economy of Urban Education*.

96. Scott, "Rosa Parks Moment?"; Astin, "Educational 'Choice,'" 259; Pattillo, "Everyday Politics of School Choice in the Black Community"; Stulberg, *Race, Schools, and Hope*.

97. Kantor and Lowe, "From New Deal to No Deal," 483.

98. Madhubuti interview by author.

Epilogue

1. Lewis interview by author; Goldberger, "Karen Lewis, Street Fighter"; Danns, "Black Student Empowerment and Chicago."

2. Lewis interview by author.

3. Originally a neighborhood school, Forrestville High School was renamed for Martin Luther King Jr. In the late 1960s. Barbara Sizemore implemented community-engaged culturally responsive practices as principal of Forrestville. See Lewis interview by author.

4. Rhodes, *Education in Politics*, 174–78; Ravitch, *Reign of Error*, 15; Lipman, *New Political Economy of Urban Education*, 60–61; Fabricant and Fine, *Charter Schools and the Corporate Makeover of Public Education*.

5. Researchers and journalists had differing accounts of the actual number of schools that were "closed," referencing 49 or 50, depending on how they interpreted a school building where the high school was closed but not the elementary school in the same building and various forms of co-location and consolidation. See "CPS Closings: Board Votes to Close 50 Chicago Schools," *DNAinfo Chicago*, May 22, 2013; Vevea, "CPS Board Votes to Close 50 Schools"; Collaborative for Equity and Justice in Education, "Research"; Chicago Public Schools: Renaissance 2010, "About Us."

6. Ravitch, "Futility of Closing Schools in Chicago."

7. Hirsch, *Making the Second Ghetto*; Venkatesh, *American Project*; Linda Lutton, Becky Vevea, and Sarah Karp, "Map: 40 Percent of Closed Schools Now Privately Run," *Catalyst Chicago*, January 15, 2013; Farmer, Baber, and Poulos, "Closed by Choice"; Jankov and Caref, "Segregation and Inequality in Chicago Public Schools"; Lipman, "Landscape of Education 'Reform' in Chicago."

8. Scott, "Politics of Venture Philanthropy in Charter School Policy and Advocacy"; Lipman, *New Political Economy of Urban Education*, 104–10; Buras et al., *Pedagogy, Policy, and the Privatized City*; Ravitch, *Reign of Error*; Jankov and Caref, "Segregation and Inequality in Chicago Public Schools."

9. Dawson and Francis, "Black Politics and the Neoliberal Racial Order"; Dawson, *Not in Our Lifetimes*, 92–98, 103–4; Taylor, *From #BlackLivesMatter to Black Liberation*, 106.

10. Richard Fausset and Alan Blinder, "Atlanta School Workers Sentenced in Test Score Cheating Case," *New York Times*, April 14, 2015; Sarah Karp and Melissa Sanchez, "Feds Investigating $20 Million SUPES Contract, Byrd-Bennett Ties," *Catalyst Chicago*, April 15, 2015; "Byrd-Bennett Sobs While Trying to Explain Corruption, Gets 4½ Years in Prison," *Chicago Tribune*, April 28, 2017.

11. Connolly, *World More Concrete*, 275.

12. Perlstein, *Justice, Justice*, 152; Dawson, *Not in Our Lifetimes*, 92–98, 103–4.

13. Chicago Public Schools, "Stats and Facts"; Brandon Johnson, "Disappearing Acts: The Decline of Black Teachers," *Austin Weekly News*, January 30, 2013; Jankov and Caref, "Segregation and Inequality in Chicago Public Schools"; Peoples interview by author, December 2, 2014, and March 9, 2017.

14. Brandon Johnson, "Disappearing Acts: The Decline of Black Teachers," *Austin Weekly News*, January 30, 2013; Jankov and Caref, "Segregation and Inequality in Chicago Public Schools"; Peoples interview by author, December 2, 2014, and March 9, 2017.

15. After *Parents Involved in Community Schools Inc. v. Seattle School District* and *Meredith v. Jefferson County (Ky.) Board of Education*, many school districts began using socioeconomic class as a stand-in for race in order to retain some semblance of racial integration in public schools. In Chicago, the board put in place a system that considered five socio-economic characteristics by census tract: (1) median family income, (2) percentage of single-family homes, (3) percentage of homes where English is not the first language, (4) percentage of homes occupied by the homeowner, and (5) level of adult education attainment. A sixth characteristic was the achievement scores from area schools. Based on this information, each census tract is classified into one of four tiers. For selective enrollment high schools, 30 percent of the student body is selected strictly based on which applicants, regardless of tier, scored highest on testing and academic criteria. The remaining applicants to the school are ranked based on testing and academic criteria within their tier. An equal number of students from each of these remaining tiers are invited to attend the school, unless there are not enough eligible applicants in any given tier, in which case an even number of students from the remaining tiers with eligible applicants are invited to attend the school. Different combinations and weighting of testing, socioeconomic status, proximity to schools, and sibling attendance policies were put in place for magnet schools and other specialty programs as well. See Chicago Public Schools, "Adopt a New Admissions Policy for Magnet, Selective Enrollment and Other Options for Knowledge Schools and Programs, 2011"; Chicago Public Schools, "News and Announcements"; "CPS Must Show It Still Values Racial Diversity," *Chicago Sun-Times*, October 2, 2009; "Divided Court Limits Use of Race by School Districts," *Washington Post*, June 29, 2007; and Tzeggai, *Defining Racial Equity in Chicago's Segregated Schools*.

16. "Whites Getting More Spots at Top Chicago Public High Schools," *Chicago Sun-Times*, April 28, 2014; "Minority Student Enrollment Declining in CPS Elite Schools," *ABC7*

Chicago, July 15, 2014; Chicago Public Schools, *Racial/Ethnic Survey, 2013–2014 School Year;* "Payton HS."

17. "CPS Officials Defend Diversity of Selective-Enrollment High Schools," CBS Chicago, July 15, 2014; "Elite CPS High Schools Need to Reconsider Race as Factor," editorial, *Chicago Sun-Times,* July 20, 2014; Maureen Kelleher, "Rocky Start for Renaissance," *Catalyst Chicago,* October 2004.

18. Sarah Karp and Becky Vevea, "How Chicago School Construction Furthers Race and Class Segregation," WBEZ, July 7, 2016; Jankov and Caref, "Segregation and Inequality in Chicago Public Schools."

19. Lipman, "Education and the New Urban Workforce in a Global City"; Karen Lewis, "The President's Message," *Chicago Union Teacher,* May 2013, CTU Archives.

20. A new state school funding formula was passed in the summer of 2017, but it still remains to be seen how it will impact CPS's long-term funding prospects. See Hickrod, Wallis, Hubbard, and Elder, "Brief History of K–12 Finance in Illinois"; Phil Kadnor, "Illinois Schools Have Biggest Funding Gap in Country," *Chicago Tribune,* March 26, 2015; Tzeggai, *Defining Racial Equity in Chicago's Segregated Schools;* Heather Cherone and Erica Damarest, "CPS Sues State of Illinois: City Kids at 'Back of Bus' in Funding," *DNAinfo Chicago,* February 14, 2017; Maureen Kelleher, "Roots of the Chicago Teacher Pension Crisis," *Chicago Reporter,* July 2, 2015; and Joel Hood, "CPS Wades into Debate over Charities Subsidizing Public Schools," *Chicago Tribune,* April 16, 2011.

21. Scott, "Rosa Parks Moment?"; Russom, "Obama's Neoliberal Agenda for Public Education."

22. Uetricht, *Strike for America.*

23. Karen Lewis, "President's Message," *Chicago Union Teacher,* September/October 2012, CTU Archives.

24. In 2015, Tara Stamps ran for alderman, as the CTU worked to transition its community organizing efforts into electoral politics. Although she did not win, Stamps was a competitive candidate and forced a runoff election. Johnson won the March 2018 Democratic primary for Cook County commissioner. See "Tara Stamps" and Johnson interview by author.

25. "Walton Family Stops Funding Chicago Charters," *Chicago Reporter,* April 22, 2016; Lipman, "Landscape of Education 'Reform' in Chicago."

26. "May 20th Boycott—Chicago Students Organizing to Save Our Schools"; "Black Youth Project History"; Austin Brown, "Growing Pains for Woodlawn Park," *South Side Weekly,* April 12, 2016.

27. Movement for Black Lives, *Vision for Black Lives;* Claire Bushey, "The Rumble and the Reversal," pt. 1, *Crain's Chicago Business;* STOP Chicago, "Youth Justice Program"; Taylor, *From #BlackLivesMatter to Black Liberation,* 163–67; Ayers, *Demand the Impossible.*

28. Jeanette Taylor-Ramann, "Why I'm Hunger Striking for Dyett High School," *Chicago Reporter,* August 24, 2015; Redeaux-Smith, "Why I Go Hungry for Dyett"; Ewing, "Shuttered Schools in the Black Metropolis."

29. Redeaux-Smith, "Why I Go Hungry for Dyett."

30. Wilson, *Declining Significance of Race;* Wilson, *Truly Disadvantaged;* Massey and Denton, *American Apartheid;* Katz, "Underclass" Debate.

31. Crawley, "Otherwise Movements."

BIBLIOGRAPHY

Manuscript Collections

Chicago, Ill.
  Chicago Board of Education Archives
      Chicago Board of Education Annual Financial Reports
      Chicago Board of Education Facts and Figures
      Chicago Public Schools, *Racial/Ethnic Surveys*
  Chicago History Museum
      Cyrus Hall Adams III Papers
      Chicago African-American Teachers Association *Newsletter*
      Citizens Schools Committee Records
  Chicago Teachers Union Archives
      Chicago Union Teacher
  Lillie Peoples Personal Papers, Private Collection
  University of Chicago Special Collections
      Allison Davis Papers
      Sol Tax Papers
      University of Chicago Office of the President, Beadle Administration Records
      University of Chicago Office of the President, Levi Administration Records
  University of Illinois at Chicago Special Collections and University Archives
      Chicago Urban League Records
      James S. Parker Collection
  Soyini Walton Personal Papers, Private Collection
  Harold Washington Library Center, Chicago Public Library
      Municipal Reference Collection
          Chicago Public Schools, *Racial/Ethnic Surveys*
      Special Collections
          Harold Washington Papers
  Carter G. Woodson Regional Library, Vivian G. Harsh Research Collection of
          Afro-American History and Literature
      Chicago SNCC History Project
      Rev. Addie and Rev. Claude Wyatt Papers
Pittsburgh, Pa.
  University of Pittsburgh Archives & Special Collections
      University Archives Personal Files

Newspapers and Magazines

Catalyst Chicago

Chicago Daily Defender

Chicago Defender

Chicago Reader

Chicago Reporter

Chicago Sun-Times

Chicago Tribune

Chicago Union Teacher

Crain's Chicago Business

DNAinfo Chicago

Huffington Post

Hyde Park Herald

Illinois Issues

Los Angeles Sentinel

Louisville Courier-Journal

New York Times

South Side Weekly

Washington Post

Oral History Interviews by Author

Baron, Harold "Hal." Audio recording. Chicago, Ill., November 12, 2013.

Black, Timuel. Chicago, Ill., November 19, 2007.

Bracey, John H. Audio recording. Chicago, Ill., June 15, 2015.

Chase, Kymara, and Kafi Chase. Audio recording. Evanston, Ill., February 15, 2013.

Evans, Shayne. Audio recording. Chicago, Ill., August 3, 2017.

Heath, Howard. Audio recording. Chicago, Ill., March 10, 2017.

Howze, Tamanika. Phone interview. Pittsburgh, Pa., January 23, 2013.

Johnson, Brandon. Audio recording. Chicago, Ill., October 15, 2014.

Karanja, Sokoni. Chicago, Ill., February 9, 2009, and audio recording. March 27, 2017.

Knazze, Patricia. Audio recording. Chicago, Ill., March 23, 2017.

Lee, Carol. Audio recording. Chicago, Ill., March 11, 2009, and phone interview, June 13, 2017.

Lewis, Karen G. J. Audio recording. Chicago, Ill., March 7, 2017.

Madhubuti, Haki. Audio recording. Chicago, Ill., November 23, 2010.

May, Audrey. Audio recording. Chicago, Ill., February 6, 2017.

Moore, Sonjanita. L. Audio recording. Chicago, Ill., July 31, 2017.

Owens, Roxanne. Audio recording. Chicago, Ill., May 17, 2013.

Peoples, Lillie. Audio recordings. Chicago, Ill., December 2, 2014, and March 9, 2017.

Simpson, Rosie. Audio recording. Chicago, Ill., June 18, 2014.

Spurlark, Aurelia L. Audio recording. Chicago, Ill., September 8, 2017.

Todd, Saralee. Phone interview. January 2, 2013.

Vinson, Tammie. Audio recording. Chicago, Ill., June 8, 2017.

Walton, Soyini. Audio recordings. Chicago, Ill., November 23, 2009, and October 9, 2014.

Williams, Rufus. Audio recording. Chicago, Ill., April 5, 2017.

Willmott, Peter. Audio recording. Chicago, Ill., December 7, 2009.

Wilson, Roberta. Audio recording. Chicago, Ill., June 14, 2017.

Worrill, Conrad. Audio recording. Chicago, Ill., May 28, 2010.

Other Oral Histories and Interviews

Lenz, Linda. Interview by Tony Sarabia, *The Morning Shift*, 91.5 WBEZ FM, April 20, 2015.

Simpson, Rosie. Interview by Fannie Rushing. Video recording, May 19, 2009. Video-cassette, box 18, folder 15, Super Series 3, Chicago SNCC History Project, Vivian G. Harsh Research Collection of Afro-American History and Literature, Carter G. Woodson Regional Library.

Films

Alk, Howard. *American Revolution II: Riots to Revolution, Chicago in 1968.* 1969; reissued, Chicago: Facts Video, 2007.

Hampton, Henry. "Two Societies (1965–1968)." *Eyes on the Prize: America's Civil Rights Movement.* Directed by Sheila Curran Bernard and Samuel D. Pollard. DVD. Boston: Blackside, Inc., PBS Home Video, 1990, 2007.

Quinn, Gordon, Rachel Dickson, and Tracye Matthews. *'63 Boycott.* Chicago: Kartemquin Films, 2017. http://63boycott.kartemquin.com/about-the-film/.

Government Documents

Brown v. Board of Education 347 U.S. 483 (1954).

Bush, Esther L. "Education Is the Civil Rights Issue of Our Time." February 27, 2013. https://obamawhitehouse.archives.gov/blog/2013/02/27/education-civil-rights-issue-our-time.

Chicago Board of Education. *Comprehensive Student Assignment Plan, 1982.* Chicago: Chicago Board of Education, 1982.

Chicago Public Schools. "Adopt a New Admissions Policy for Magnet, Selective Enrollment and Other Options for Knowledge Schools and Programs, 2011." http://www.cpsoae.org/ourpages/auto/2011/9/14/15383328/Admissions%20Policy%20for%20Magnet_%20Selective_%20other%20options%20Schools%20and%20Programs.pdf. Accessed August 24, 2011.

Chicago Public Schools. "News and Announcements." Office of Access and Enrollment. 2011. http://www.cpsoae.org/apps/news/show_news.jsp?REC_ID=184188&id=0. Accessed June 17, 2012.

Chicago Public Schools. *Racial/Ethnic Survey — Students.* Chicago: Chicago Board of Education, 1964.

———. *Racial/Ethnic Survey — Staff.* Chicago: Chicago Board of Education, 1968.

———. *Racial/Ethnic Survey — Students.* Chicago: Chicago Board of Education, 1968.

———. *Racial/Ethnic Survey — Staff.* Chicago: Chicago Board of Education, 1969.

———. *Racial/Ethnic Survey — Students.* Chicago: Chicago Board of Education, 1969.

———. *Racial/Ethnic Survey — Staff.* Chicago: Chicago Board of Education, 1977.

———. *Racial/Ethnic Survey — Students.* Chicago: Chicago Board of Education, 1977.

———. *Racial/Ethnic Survey — Staff.* Chicago: Chicago Board of Education, 1978.

———. *Racial/Ethnic Survey — Staff.* Chicago: Chicago Board of Education, 1979.

———. *Racial/Ethnic Survey — Students.* Chicago: Chicago Board of Education, 1979.

————. *Racial/Ethnic Survey—Students*. Chicago: Chicago Board of Education, 1980.

————. *Racial/Ethnic Survey—Students*. Chicago: Chicago Board of Education, 1981.

————. *Racial/Ethnic Survey—Students*. Chicago: Chicago Board of Education, 1983.

————. *Racial/Ethnic Survey—Staff*. Chicago: Chicago Board of Education, 1984.

————. *Racial/Ethnic Survey—Staff*. Chicago: Chicago Board of Education, 1987.

————. *Racial/Ethnic Survey—Students*. Chicago: Chicago Board of Education, 1987.

————. *Racial/Ethnic Survey—Students*. Chicago: Chicago Board of Education, 1989.

————. *Racial/Ethnic Survey, 2013–2014 School Year*. http://www.cps.edu/SchoolData/Pages/SchoolData.aspx. Accessed September 2, 2014.

City of Chicago. "Land Sale Will Support New University of Chicago Charter School in Woodlawn." February 10, 2016. https://www.cityofchicago.org/city/en/depts/dcd/provdrs/ec_dev/news/2016/january/land-sale-would-support-new-university-of-chicago-charter-school.html.

City of Chicago. *The Mayor's Education Summit: An Agenda for the Reform of Chicago Public Schools*. Chicago: City of Chicago, 1988.

Coleman, James S., Ernest Q. Campbell, Carol J. Hobson, James McPartland, Alexander M. Mood, Frederic D. Weinfeld, and Robert L. York. *Equality of Educational Opportunity*. Summary Report. Washington, D.C.: Government Printing Office, 1966.

Committee on House Administration of the U.S. House of Representatives. *Black Americans in Congress, 1870–2007*. Washington, D.C.: Government Printing Office, 2008. https://www.gpo.gov/fdsys/pkg/GPO-CDOC-108hdoc224/pdf/GPO-CDOC-108hdoc224.pdf. Accessed December 10, 2017.

de la Torre, Marisa, et al. *Changes in Student Populations and Teacher Workforce in Low-Performing Chicago Schools Targeted for Reform*. Issues & Answers Report, REL 2012, No. 1231. Washington, D.C.: U.S. Department of Education, Institute of Education Sciences, National Center for Education Evaluation and Regional Assistance, Regional Educational Laboratory Midwest, April 2012. http://files.eric.ed.gov/fulltext/ED531351.pdf.

Edmonds, Ronald R., and John R. Frederiksen. *Search for Effective Schools: The Identification and Analysis of City Schools That Are Instructionally Effective for Poor Children*. Education Resources Information Center, 1979. ERIC Number ED170396. http://files.eric.ed.gov/fulltext/ED170396.pdf. Accessed December 9, 2017.

Edmonds, Ronald R., et al. *Search for Effective Schools: The Identification and Analysis of City Schools That Are Instructionally Effective for Poor Children*. Education Resources Information Center, 1977. ERIC Number ED142610. http://files.eric.ed.gov/fulltext/ED142610.pdf. Accessed December 9, 2017.

Gibson, Campbell, and Kay Jung. Illinois—Race and Hispanic Origin for Selected Large Cities and Other Places. "Historical Census Statistics on Population Totals by Race, 1790 to 1990, and by Hispanic Origin, 1970 to 1990, for Large Cities and Other Urban Places in the United States." Population Division Working Paper No. 76, U.S. Census Bureau, February 2005. https://www.census.gov/population/www/documentation/twps0076/twps0076.html. Accessed April 1, 2017.

Havighurst, Robert James, and Chicago Board of Education. *The Public Schools of Chicago: A Survey for the Board of Education of the City of Chicago*. Chicago: Board of Education of the City of Chicago, 1964.

Bibliography

Illinois Department of Public Instruction. *Directory of Illinois Schools, 1965–1966.* Spring-field, Ill., 1966.

Kocoras, Charles P. Consent Decree Memorandum Opinion. *United States v. Board of Education of the City of Chicago* 80 C 5124 (D.C. Ill. 2009).

National Commission on Excellence in Education. *A Nation at Risk: The Imperative for Educational Reform.* Washington, D.C.: United States Department of Education, 1983. https://www2.ed.gov/pubs/NatAtRisk/risk.html. Accessed December 10, 2017.

"Payton HS." http://schoolinfo.cps.edu/schoolprofile/schooldetails.aspx?SchoolId =609680. Accessed December 14, 2017.

"President William Jefferson Clinton State of the Union Address, January 19, 1999." https://clinton4.nara.gov/WH/New/html/19990119-2656.html. Accessed May 22, 2017.

"SOCDS Census Data: Output for Chicago City, IL." http://socds.huduser.org/Census /race.odb?msacitylist=1600.0*1700014000*1.0&metro=msa. Accessed December 18, 2014.

United States Census Bureau. "Illinois—Race and Hispanic Origin for Selected Large Cities and Other Places." https://www.census.gov/population/www/documentation /twps0076/ILtab.pdf. Accessed June 28, 2017.

United States House of Representatives. "Metcalf, Ralph Harold." http://history.house .gov/People/Detail?id=18169. Accessed December 19, 2014.

Internet-Accessed Sources

Alridge, Derrick P., et al. "Teachers in the Movement: A Civil Rights Oral History Project." http://curry.virginia.edu/research/projects/teachers-in-the-movement-a -civil-rights-oral-history-project. Accessed June 17, 2017.

Apostolic Church of God. "Pastor Emeritus." http://www.acog-chicago.org/index.php ?option=com_content&task=view&id=3&Itemid=35. Accessed May 1, 2010.

"Barbara Sizemore, National Visionary." Oral History Archive, National Visionary Leadership Project. http://www.visionaryproject.org/sizemorebarbara. Accessed February 16, 2013.

Baron, Paula, ed. *Metro: The Chicago Public High School for Metropolitan Studies, 1970–1991.* http://www.metrohschicago.com/book.pdf. Accessed May 11, 2017.

Betty Shabazz International Charter School. "About Us." http://bsics.net/aboutus.html. Accessed May 1, 2010.

"Bishop Arthur Brazier Biography." The History Makers. http://www.thehistorymakers .org/biography/bishop-arthur-brazier. Accessed December 10, 2017.

"Black Youth Project History." http://blackyouthproject.com/about-us/history/. Accessed June 15, 2017.

"A Brief History of Magnet Schools." Magnet Schools of America. http://www.magnet .edu/resources/msa-history. Accessed May 10, 2017.

"Bryk, Anthony S." Carnegie Foundation for the Advancement of Teaching. https:// www.carnegiefoundation.org/who-we-are/staff-directory/anthony-s-bryk/. Accessed May 9, 2017.

Cavounidis, Costas, and Kevin Lang. "Discrimination and Worker Evaluation." Working

Paper 21612. Cambridge, Mass: National Bureau of Economic Research, 2015. http://
www.nber.org.proxy.cc.uic.edu/papers/w21612.pdf. Accessed June 7, 2017.

Chicago Public Schools. "Stats and Facts." http://cps.edu/About_CPS/At-a-glance/Pages
/Stats_and_facts.aspxx. Accessed June 13, 2017.

Chicago Public Schools: Renaissance 2010. "About Us." http://www.ren2010.cps.k12.il
.us/. Accessed May 31, 2010.

"Chicago's Reaction to 'Access.'" *Illinois Issues*, September 1978. http://www.lib.niu.edu
/1979/ii790508.html.

"Chicago Teachers Union (CTU) Strike Bulletin: Recommended Strike Chants." https://
www.illinoispolicy.org/chicago-teachers-union-ctu-strike-bulletin-recommended
-strike-chants/. Accessed March 9, 2015.

The Civic Federation. "School Finance Authority: From Creation to Dissolution."
https://www.civicfed.org/civic-federation/blog/school-finance-authority-creation
-dissolution. Accessed March 29, 2017.

Colby, Peter W., and Paul Michael Green. "Byrne's Victory: True Grit and Heavy Snow."
Illinois Issues, May 1979. http://www.lib.niu.edu/1979/ii790508.html.

Collaborative for Equity and Justice in Education. "Research." http://ceje.uic.edu
/research/. Accessed December 18, 2014.

Connolly, N. D. B. "How 'Black Panther' Taps into 500 Years of History." *Hollywood Reporter*, February 16, 2018. https://www.hollywoodreporter.com/heat-vision/black
-panther-taps-500-years-history-1085334.

"Correlates of Effective Schools 1989–Present." Lake Forest College Archives and
Special Collections. http://www.lakeforest.edu/library/archives/effective-schools
/correlates.php. Accessed February 8, 2015.

Crawley, Ashon. "Otherwise Movements." *New Inquiry*, January 19, 2015. https://thenew
inquiry.com/otherwise-movements/.

"Crispus Attucks High School." National Park Service. http://www.nps.gov/nr/travel
/indianapolis/crispusattucks.htm. Accessed January 30, 2016.

"District Teacher Demographics by Ethnicity (2007–16)." City of Chicago SD 299
Teacher Profile. Illinois State Board of Education. https://www.illinoisreportcard
.com/District.aspx?source=teachers&source2=teacherdemographics&Districtid
=15016299025. Accessed June 22, 2017.

Encyclopedia of Chicago. http://www.encyclopedia.chicagohistory.org.

Farmer, Stephanie, Ashley Baber, and Chris Poulos. "Closed by Choice: The Spatial Relationship between Charter School Expansion, School Closures, and Fiscal Stress
in Chicago Public Schools." University of Illinois School of Labor and Employment
Relations, Labor Education Program, Project for Middle Class Renewal, March 20,
2017. https://www.roosevelt.edu/~/media/Files/pdfs/news/Closed-By-Choice.ashx
?la=en.

"Frederick Douglass High School: A Cherished Tradition since 1885." Baltimore City
Schools. http://www.baltimorecityschools.org/Page/27375. Accessed January 30,
2016.

Gilmore, Ruth Wilson. "In the Shadow of the Shadow State." *Scholar & Feminist Online* 13,
no. 2 (Spring 2016). http://sfonline.barnard.edu/navigating-neoliberalism-in-the

-academy-nonprofits-and-beyond/ruth-wilson-gilmore-in-the-shadow-of-the
-shadow-state/.

Goldberger, Ben. "Karen Lewis, Street Fighter." *Chicago Magazine*, October 2, 2012.
http://www.chicagomag.com/Chicago-Magazine/November-2012/Karen-Lewis
-Street-Fighter/index.php?cparticle=1&siarticle=0#artanc.

Hickrod, G. Alan, Karnes Wallis, Benjamin C. Hubbard, and David E. Elder. "A Brief
History of K–12 Finance in Illinois or 162 Years in Search of the Perfect Formula."
Center for the Study of Educational Finance, April 1987. https://education.illinois
state.edu/downloads/csep/series2.pdf. Accessed June 26, 2017.

"History of Howard High School, Wilmington, Delaware." Children & Youth in History,
George Mason University. http://chnm.gmu.edu/cyh/website-reviews/260. Accessed
January 30, 2016.

"History of JBV." Jacqueline B. Vaughn Graduate School for Teacher Leadership. http://
jbvedu.org/history%20of%20jbv.html. Accessed December 19, 2014.

"History of the Effective Schools Movement." Lake Forest College Archives and Special
Collections. http://www.lakeforest.edu/library/archives/effective-schools/Historyof
EffectiveSchools.php. Accessed April 16, 2015.

Institute on Metropolitan Opportunity. *Charter Schools in Chicago: No Model for Education
Reform.* Minneapolis: University of Minnesota Law School, October 2014. http://
www.law.umn.edu/sites/law.umn.edu/files/newsfiles/8a690b58/Chicago-Charters
-FINAL.pdf.

"Jacqueline B. Vaughn." Illinois Labor History. http://www.illinoislaborhistory.org
/articles/157-jacqueline-b-vaughn-.html. Accessed December 19, 2014.

"The Johnson Years: The Coleman Report—Equal Educational Opportunity." New
York State Archives. http://www.archives.nysed.gov/edpolicy/research/res_essay
_johnson_cole.shtml. Accessed February 8, 2015.

Kahlenberg, Richard. "The Charter School Idea Turns 20: A History of Evolution and
Role Reversals." *Education Week* 27, no. 29 (March 25, 2008). http://www.edweek.org
/ew/articles/2008/03/26/29kahlenberg_ep.h27.html.

Lydon, Christopher. "Noam Chomsky: Neoliberalism Is Destroying Our Democracy."
Nation, June 2, 2017. https://www.thenation.com/article/noam-chomsky-neoliberal
ism-destroying-democracy/.

Madhubuti, Haki. "About Us." http://www.sscartcenter.org/about.html. Accessed June
22, 2017.

"Magnet Schools—Elementary." Chicago Public Schools. http://www.cpsoae.org/apps
/pages/index.jsp?uREC_ID=72694&type=d. Accessed February 12, 2015.

"May 20th Boycott—Chicago Students Organizing to Save Our Schools." May 16 2013.
https://www.youtube.com/watch?v=ds8LApQ5Rrc. Accessed December 13, 2017.

"Meet Paul Vallas." https://www.quinnforillinois.com/00/meet-paul/. Accessed March
15, 2015.

"Meet the Founders." Institute of Positive Education, Inc. http://www.ipeclc.org/meet
-the-founders.html. Accessed June 22, 2017.

"Metcalfe, Ralph Harold." United States House of Representatives. http://history.house
.gov/People/Detail?id=18169. Accessed December 19, 2014.

The Movement for Black Lives. *A Vision for Black Lives: Policy Demands for Black Power, Freedom & Justice.* https://policy.m4bl.org/. Accessed June 15, 2017.

"Neoliberalism Is a Political Project: An Interview with David Harvey." *Jacobin*, July 23, 2016. https://www.jacobinmag.com/2016/07/david-harvey-neoliberalism -capitalism-labor-crisis-resistance/.

"Operation Breadbasket (1962–1972)." Martin Luther King Jr. and the Global Freedom Struggle. http://mlk-kpp01.stanford.edu/index.php/encyclopedia/ encyclopedia/enc _operation_breadbasket/. Accessed April 13, 2015.

Powell, Dave. "No, Education Isn't the Civil Rights Issue of Our Time." *Education Week*, May 15, 2017. http://www.edweek.org/ew/articles/2017/05/17/no-education-isnt -the-civil-rights-issue.html.

Publishing the Long Civil Rights Movement. https://lcrm.lib.unc.edu/blog/index.php/tag /sclc/. Accessed November 5, 2016.

Rachell, Lej. "Jitu Weusi Got Mad Soul." *Black Star News*, June 1, 2013. http://www.black starnews.com/ny-watch/news/jitu-weusi-got-mad-soul.html.

Raser, Tess. "Quality Education Is the Civil Rights Issue of Our Time." *Huffington Post*, May 11, 2014. http://www.huffingtonpost.com/tess-raser/quality-education-is-the -civil-rights-issue_b_4945511.html.

Ravitch, Diane. "The Futility of Closing Schools in Chicago." Diane Ravitch's Blog. March 21, 2013. http://dianeravitch.net/2013/03/21/the-futility-of-closing-schools -in-chicago/.

———. "Why Education Is Not the Civil Rights Issue of Our Time." *Education Week*, May 26, 2009. http://blogs.edweek.org/edweek/BridgingDifferences/2009/05/why _education_is_not_the_civil.html.

Redeaux-Smith, Monique. "Why I Go Hungry for Dyett." A Just Chicago. August 24, 2015. https://ajustchicago.org/2015/08/why-i-go-hungry-for-dyett/.

Sanchez, Claudio. "Lessons on Race and Vouchers from Milwaukee." National Public Radio. May 16, 2017. http://www.npr.org/sections/ed/2017/05/16/523612949/lessons -on-race-and-vouchers-from-milwaukee.

Sara Spurlark Obituary. "Present Tensed: Notes from the Now." February 25, 2012. https://shazrasul.wordpress.com/2012/02/25/sara-spurlark-1923-2012/. Accessed July 28, 2017.

"School Finance Authority: From Creation to Dissolution." The Civic Federation. May 19, 2010. https://www.civicfed.org/civic-federation/blog/school-finance-authority -creation-dissolution.

STOP Chicago. "Youth Justice Program." http://www.stopchicago.org/p/fly.html. Accessed June 15, 2017.

"Tara Stamps." Editorial Board Questionnaires. *Chicago Tribune.* http://elections.chicago tribune.com/candidates/tara-stamps/. Accessed April 22, 2015.

"Text of President Clinton's 1998 State of the Union Address, January 27, 1998." *Washington Post.* http://www.washingtonpost.com/wp-srv/politics/special/states/docs /sou98.htm. Accessed May 22, 2017.

"Timeline." University of Illinois at Chicago Special Collections. http://www.uic.edu /depts/lib/specialcoll/services/rjd/CULExhibit/Urban%20League%20Exhibit/Time line.htm. Accessed September 23, 2014.

"TWP History." http://www.thirdworldpressinc.com/history.php. Accessed May 23, 2010.

Tzeggai, Fithawee. *Defining Racial Equity in Chicago's Segregated Schools: The Complicated Legacy of Desegregation Reform for Urban Education Policy.* UC Berkeley: Institute for the Study of Societal Issues, April 25, 2016. http://escholarship.org/uc/item/8204p4f8. Accessed July 10, 2017.

"UChicago Celebrates Groundbreaking for New Charter School in Woodlawn." *UChicago News*, September 16, 2016. https://news.uchicago.edu/article/2016/09/15/uchicago -celebrates-groundbreaking-new-charter-school-woodlawn. Accessed May 22, 2017.

"The University of Chicago Launches Urban Education Institute; New Model Dedicated to Improving the Lives of Children in Urban America." June 3, 2008. http://news .uchicago.edu/article/2008/06/03/university-chicago-launches-urban-education -institute-new-model-dedicated-improvi. Accessed April 17, 2015.

"U of C Gets $1 Land Deal for Charter School." November 13, 2015. http://chigov.com /chicago/schools/u-of-c-woodlawn-charter-development. Accessed May 22, 2017.

Vevea, Becky. "CPS Board Votes to Close 50 Schools." WBEZ. May 22, 2013. https:// www.wbez.org/shows/wbez-news/cps-board-votes-to-close-50-schools/e7a8922a -8cc3-4ca9-b861-b9c1000928d8. Accessed July 10, 2017.

Published Articles and Books

Abu-Lughod, Janet L. *Race, Space, and Riots in Chicago, New York, and Los Angeles.* New York: Oxford University Press, 2007.

Alkalimat, Abdul, and Doug Gills. *Harold Washington and the Crisis of Black Power in Chicago: Mass Protest.* Chicago: Twenty-First Century Books and Publications, 1989.

Altshuler, Alan A. *Community Control: The Black Demand for Participation in Large Cities.* New York: Pegasus, 1970.

Anderson, Alan B., and George W. Pickering. *Confronting the Color Line: The Broken Promise of the Civil Rights Movement in Chicago.* Athens: University of Georgia Press, 1986.

Anderson, James D. *The Education of Blacks in the South, 1860–1935.* Chapel Hill: University of North Carolina Press, 1988.

Arena, John. *Driven from New Orleans: How Nonprofits Betray Public Housing and Promote Privatization.* Minneapolis: University of Minnesota Press, 2012.

Arnez, Nancy L. "Implementation of Desegregation as a Discriminatory Process." *Journal of Negro Education* 47 (Winter 1978): 28–45.

———. "Selected Black Female Superintendents of Public School Systems." *Journal of Negro Education* 51 (Summer 1982): 309–17.

Astin, Alexander W. "Educational 'Choice': Its Appeal May Be Illusory." *Sociology of Education* 65 (October 1992): 255–60.

Avila, Eric. *Popular Culture in the Age of White Flight: Fear and Fantasy in Suburban Los Angeles.* Berkeley: University of California Press, 2006.

Ayers, Bill. *Demand the Impossible: A Radical Manifesto.* Chicago: Haymarket Books, 2016.

Ayers, William, and Michael Klonsky. "Navigating a Restless Sea: The Continuing Struggle to Achieve a Decent Education for African American Youngsters in Chicago." *Journal of Negro Education* 63 (Winter 1994): 5–18.

Baldwin, Davarian L. *Chicago's New Negroes: Modernity, the Great Migration, and Black Urban Life*. Chapel Hill: University of North Carolina Press, 2007.

Barrett, James. *Work and Community in the Jungle: Chicago's Packinghouse Workers, 1894–1922*. Urbana: University of Illinois Press, 1987.

Battista, Andrew. *The Revival of Labor Liberalism*. Urbana: University of Illinois Press, 2008.

Beauboeuf-Lafontant, Tamara. "A Womanist Experience of Caring: Understanding the Pedagogy of Exemplary Black Women Teachers." *Urban Review* 34 (March 2002): 71–86.

———. "Womanist Lessons for Reinventing Teaching." *Journal of Teacher Education* 56 (November 2005): 436–45.

Becker, Howard S. "The Career of the Chicago Public School Teacher." *American Journal of Sociology* 57 (March 1952): 470–77.

———. "Schools and Systems of Social Status." *Phylon* 16, no. 2 (1955): 159–70.

Bell, Derrick. *Silent Covenants: Brown v. Board of Education and the Unfulfilled Hopes for Racial Reform*. New York: Oxford University Press, 2004.

Bendick, Marc, Jr. "Privatizing the Delivery of Social Welfare Services: An Idea to Be Taken Seriously." In *Privatization and the Welfare State*, edited by Sheila B. Kamerman and Alfred J. Kahn, 97–120. Princeton, N.J.: Princeton University Press, 1989.

Bernal, Dolores Delgado. "Grassroots Leadership Reconceptualized: Chicana Oral Histories of the East Los Angeles School Blowouts." *Frontiers: A Journal of Women Studies* 19, no. 2 (1998): 113–42.

Berry, Mary Frances. "Twentieth-Century Black Women in Education." *Journal of Negro Education* 51 (Summer 1982): 288–300.

Berta-Avila, Margarita, Anita Tijerina-Revilla, and Julie Figueroa, eds. *Marching Students: Chicana and Chicano Activism in Education, 1978–Present*. Reno: University of Nevada Press, 2011.

Biondi, Martha. *The Black Revolution on Campus*. Berkeley: University of California Press, 2012.

———. *To Stand and Fight: The Struggle for Civil Rights in Postwar New York City*. Cambridge, Mass.: Harvard University Press, 2003.

Black, Timuel D. *Bridges of Memory: Chicago's First Wave of Black Migration*. Evanston, Ill.: Northwestern University Press, 2003.

———. *Bridges of Memory: Chicago's Second Wave of Black Migration*. Evanston, Ill.: Northwestern University Press, 2007.

Boyd, Michelle R. *Jim Crow Nostalgia: Reconstructing Race in Bronzeville*. Minneapolis: University of Minnesota Press, 2008.

Boyle, Kevin, ed. *Organized Labor and American Politics, 1894–1994: The Labor-Liberal Alliance*. Albany: State University of New York Press, 1998.

Brazier, Arthur M. *Black Self-Determination: The Story of the Woodlawn Organization*. Grand Rapids, Mich.: Eerdmans, 1969.

Brenner, Neil, and Nik Theodore. "Cities and the Geography of 'Actually Existing Neoliberalism.'" In *Spaces of Neoliberalism: Urban Restructuring in North America and Western Europe*, edited by Neil Brenner and Nik Theodore, 2–32. Malden, Mass.: Blackwell, 2002.

Brewer, Rose M. "21st-Century Capitalism, Austerity, and Black Economic Dispossession." *Souls: A Critical Journal of Black Politics, Culture, and Society* 14 (2012): 227–39.

Brown, Scot. *Fighting for US: Maulana Karenga, the US Organization, and Black Cultural Nationalism*. New York: New York University Press, 2003.

Bullard, Pamela, and Barbara O. Taylor. *Keepers of the Dream: The Triumph of Effective Schools*. Chicago: Excelsior Foundation, 1994.

Buras, Kristen L., Jim Randels, Kalamu ya Salaam, and Students at the Center. *Pedagogy, Policy, and the Privatized City: Stories of Dispossession and Defiance from New Orleans*. New York: Columbia University Press, 2010.

Burkholder, Zoe. *Color in the Classroom: How American Schools Taught Race, 1900–1954*. New York: Oxford University Press, 2011.

Butler, Judith. *Frames of War: When Is Life Grievable?* New York: Verso, 2016.

———. *Precarious Life: The Powers of Mourning and Violence*. New York: Verso, 2003.

Campbell, Leslie J. "The Black Teacher and Black Power." 1967. In *What Black Educators Are Saying*, edited by Nathan Wright Jr., 23–24. New York: Hawthorne Books, 1970.

Carl, Jim. "Harold Washington and Chicago's Schools between Civil Rights and the Decline of the New Deal Consensus, 1955–1957." *History of Education Quarterly* 41 (Autumn 2001): 311–43.

Cha-Jua, Sundiata Keita, and Clarence Lang. "The 'Long Movement' as Vampire: Temporal and Spatial Fallacies in Recent Black Freedom Studies." *Journal of African American History* 92 (Spring 2007): 265–88.

Chappell, Marisa. *The War on Welfare: Family, Poverty, and Politics in Modern America*. Philadelphia: University of Pennsylvania Press, 2010.

Chatelain, Marcia. *South Side Girls: Growing Up in the Great Migration*. Durham, N.C.: Duke University Press, 2015.

Cobble, Dorothy Sue. *The Other Women's Movement: Workplace Justice and Social Rights in Modern America*. Princeton, N.J.: Princeton University Press, 2004.

Collins, Christina. *"Ethnically Qualified": Race, Merit, and the Selection of Urban Teachers, 1920–1980*. New York: Teachers College Press, 2011.

Connolly, N. D. B. *A World More Concrete: Real Estate and the Remaking of Jim Crow South Florida*. Chicago: University of Chicago Press, 2014.

Córdova, Teresa. "Harold Washington and the Rise of Latino Electoral Politics in Chicago." In *Chicano Politics and Society in the Late Twentieth Century*, edited by David Montejano, 31–57. Austin: University of Texas Press, 1999.

Countryman, Matthew J. *Up South: Civil Rights and Black Power in Philadelphia*. Philadelphia: University of Pennsylvania Press, 2006.

Cowie, Jefferson, and Nick Salvatore. "The Long Exception: Rethinking the Place of the New Deal in American History." *International Labor and Working-Class History* 74, no. 1 (2008): 3–32.

Cronin, Joseph M. *The Control of Urban Schools: Perspective on the Power of Educational Reformers*. New York: Free Press, 1973.

Cutler, David M., Edward L. Glaeser, and Jacob L. Vigdor. "The Rise and Decline of the American Ghetto." *Journal of Political Economy* 107 (June 1999): 455–506.

Danns, Dionne. "Black Student Empowerment and Chicago: School Reform Efforts in 1968." *Urban Education* 37, no. 5 (2002): 631–55.

———. "Chicago's High School Students' Movement for Quality Public Education, 1966–1971." Journal of African American History 88 (Spring 2003): 138–50.

———. "Chicago Teacher Reform Efforts and the Politics of Educational Change." In Black Protest Thought and Education, edited by William Henry Watkins, 179–96. New York: Peter Lang, 2005.

———. Desegregating Chicago's Public Schools: Policy Implementation, Politics, and Protest, 1965–1985. New York: Palgrave Macmillan, 2014.

———. "Northern Desegregation: A Tale of Two Cities." History of Education Quarterly 51 (February 2011): 77–104.

———. Something Better for Our Children: Black Organization in the Chicago Public Schools, 1963–1971. New York: Routledge, 2003.

Davis, Mike. Prisoners of the American Dream: Politics and Economy in the History of the US Working Class. London: Verso, 1986.

Dawson, Michael C. Not in Our Lifetimes: The Future of Black Politics. Chicago: University of Chicago Press, 2011.

Dawson, Michael C., and Megan Ming Francis. "Black Politics and the Neoliberal Racial Order." Public Culture 28, no. 1 (2016): 23–62.

Delgado Bernal, Dolores. "Grassroots Leadership Reconceptualized." Frontiers: A Journal of Women Studies 19, no. 2 (1998): 113–42.

Dixson, Adrienne D. "Democracy Now? Race, Education, and Black Self-Determination." Teachers College Record 113 (2011): 811–30.

———. "'Let's Do This!': Black Women Teachers' Politics and Pedagogy." Urban Education 38 (March 2003): 217–35.

Dougherty, Jack. More Than One Struggle: The Evolution of Black School Reform in Milwaukee. Chapel Hill: University of North Carolina Press, 2004.

Doussard, Marc, Jamie Peck, and Nik Theodore. "After Deindustrialization: Uneven Growth and Economic Inequality in 'Postindustrial' Chicago." Economic Geography 85 (April 2009): 183–207.

Drake, St. Clair, and Horace R. Cayton. Black Metropolis: A Study of Negro Life in a Northern City. Chicago: University of Chicago Press, 1945.

Edmonds, Ronald. "Effective Schools for the Urban Poor." Educational Leadership 37 (October 1979): 15–24.

Erickson, Ansley T. "Desegregation's Architects: Education Parks and the Spatial Ideology of Schooling." History of Education Quarterly 56 (November 2016): 560–89.

Fabricant, Michael, and Michelle Fine. Charter Schools and the Corporate Makeover of Public Education: What's at Stake? New York: Teachers College Press, 2012.

Fairclough, Adam. Better Day Coming: Blacks and Equality, 1890–2000. New York: Penguin, 2000.

Fehn, Bruce. "African-American Women and the Struggle for Equality in the Meatpacking Industry, 1940–1960." Journal of Women's History 10 (Spring 1998): 45–69.

Fernández, Lilia. Brown in the Windy City: Mexicans and Puerto Ricans in Postwar Chicago. Chicago: University of Chicago Press, 2012.

Fish, John Hall. Black Power/White Control: The Struggle of the Woodlawn Organization in Chicago. Princeton, N.J.: Princeton University Press, 1973.

Bibliography

Formisano, Ronald P. *Boston Against Busing: Race, Class, and Ethnicity in the 1960s and 1970s.* Chapel Hill: University of North Carolina Press, 2004.

Foster, Gail. "Historically Black Independent Schools." In *City Schools,* edited by Diane Ravich and Joseph Viteritti, 291–309. Baltimore: Johns Hopkins University Press, 2000.

Fraser, Steve, and Gary Gerstle, eds. *The Rise and Fall of the New Deal Order, 1930–1980.* Princeton, N.J.: Princeton University Press, 1989.

Frazier, Robeson Taj P. "The Congress of African People: Baraka, Brother Mao, and the Year of '74." *Souls: A Critical Journal of Black Politics, Culture, and Society* 8 (2006): 142–59.

Freeman, Joshua Benjamin. *Working-Class New York: Life and Labor since World War II.* New York: New Press, 2000.

Friesema, Paul H. "Black Control of Central Cities: The Hollow Prize." *Journal of the American Institute of Planners* 35 (1969): 75–79.

Fuller, Howard. *No Struggle, No Progress: A Warrior's Life from Black Power to Education Reform.* Milwaukee: Marquette University Press, 2014.

Gadsden, Brett. *Between North and South: Delaware, Desegregation, and the Myth of American Sectionalism.* Philadelphia: University of Pennsylvania Press, 2013.

George, Robert, John Dilts, Duck-Hye Yang, Miriam Wasserman, and Anne Clary. *Chicago Children and Youth, 1990–2010: Changing Population Trends and Their Implications for Services.* Chicago: Chapin Hall Center for Children at the University of Chicago, 2007.

Germany, Kent. *New Orleans after the Promises: Poverty, Citizenship, and the Search for the Great Society.* Athens: University of Georgia Press, 2007.

Gillette, Howard, Jr. *Camden after the Fall: Decline and Renewal in a Post-Industrial City.* Philadelphia: University of Pennsylvania Press, 2005.

Gittell, Marilyn, and Maurice R. Berube. *Local Control in Education: Three Demonstration School Districts in New York City.* New York: Praeger, 1972.

Gittell, Marilyn, and Alan G. Hevesi, eds. *The Politics of Urban Education.* New York: Praeger, 1969.

Goldring, Ellen, and Claire Smrekar. "Magnet Schools: Reform and Race in Urban Education." *Clearing House* 76 (September–October 2002): 13–15.

Goldring, Ellen, and Clair Smrekar. "Magnet Schools and the Pursuit of Racial Balance." *Education and Urban Society* 33, no. 1 (2000): 17–35.

Gordon, Jane Anna. *Why They Couldn't Wait: A Critique of the Black-Jewish Conflict over Community Control in the Ocean Hill–Brownsville Community, 1967–1971.* New York: Routledge, 2001.

Gordon, Leah. *From Power to Prejudice: The Rise of Racial Individualism in Midcentury America.* Chicago: University of Chicago Press, 2015.

Green, Adam. *Selling the Race: Culture, Community, and Black Chicago, 1940–1955.* Chicago: University of Chicago Press, 2007.

Green, Laurie Beth. *Battling the Plantation Mentality: Memphis and the Black Freedom Struggle.* Chapel Hill: University of North Carolina Press, 2007.

Grimshaw, William. *Bitter Fruit: Black Politics and the Chicago Machine, 1931–1991.* Chicago: University of Chicago Press, 1992.

Gross, James. *Broken Promise: The Subversion of U.S. Labor Relations.* Philadelphia: Temple University Press, 2014.

Grossman, James R. *Land of Hope: Chicago, Black Southerners, and the Great Migration.* Chicago: University of Chicago Press, 1989.

Guinier, Lani. "From Racial Liberalism to Racial Literacy: *Brown v. Board of Education* and the Interest-Divergence Dilemma." *Journal of American History* 91 (June 2004): 92–118.

Hale, Jon F. "The Making of the New Democrats." *Political Science Quarterly* 110 (Summer 1995): 207–32.

Hale, Jon N. "'The Student as a Force for Social Change': The Mississippi Freedom Schools and Student Engagement." *Journal of African American History* 96 (Summer 2011): 325–47.

Hall, Jacquelyn Dowd. "The Long Civil Rights Movement and the Political Uses of the Past." *Journal of American History* 91 (March 2005): 1233–63.

Harris, Frederick. *The Price of the Ticket: Barack Obama and the Rise and Decline of Black Politics.* New York: Oxford University Press, 2012.

Harrison, Alferdteen. *Piney Woods School: An Oral History.* Jackson: University Press of Mississippi, 1982.

Harvey, David. *A Brief History of Neoliberalism.* New York: Oxford University Press, 2005.

Hassrick, Elizabeth McGhee, Stephen W. Raudenbush, and Lisa Rosen. *The Ambitious Elementary School: Its Concept, Design, and Implications for Educational Equality.* Chicago: University of Chicago Press, 2017.

Hawkins, Augustus F. "Becoming Preeminent in Education: America's Greatest Challenge." *Harvard Journal of Law and Public Policy* 14 (1991): 367–96.

Hayes, Worth Kamili. "Rise and Fall of a Black Private School." In *Using Past as Prologue: Contemporary Perspectives on African American Educational History,* edited by Dionne Danns, Michelle A. Purdy, and Christopher M. Span, 201–20. Charlotte: Information Age Publishing, 2015.

———. "The Very Meaning of Our Lives: Howalton Day School and Black Chicago's Dual Educational Agenda, 1946–1985." *American Educational History Journal* 37, no. 1/2 (2010): 75–94.

Heclo, Hugh. "1960s Civics." In *The Great Society and the High Tide of Liberalism,* edited by Sidney M. Milkis and Jerome M. Mileur, 53–82. Amherst: University of Massachusetts Press, 2005.

Helgeson, Jeffrey. *Crucibles of Black Empowerment: Chicago's Neighborhood Politics from the New Deal to Harold Washington.* Chicago: University of Chicago Press, 2014.

Henderson, Ronald D., Nancy M. Greenberg, Jeffrey M. Schneider, Oscar Uribe Jr., and Richard R. Verdugo. "High-Quality Schooling for African American Students." In *Beyond Desegregation: The Politics of Quality in African American Schooling,* edited by Mwalimu J. Shujaa, 138–61. Thousand Oaks, Calif.: Corwin Press, 1996.

Herrick, Mary J. *The Chicago Schools: A Social and Political History.* Beverly Hills, Calif.: Sage Publications, 1971.

Hess, G. Alfred, Jr. "Community Participation or Control? From New York to Chicago." *Theory into Practice* 38 (Autumn 1999): 217–24.

———. "Renegotiating a Multicultural Society: Participation in Desegregation Planning in Chicago." *Journal of Negro Education* 53 (Spring 1984): 132–46.

Hirsch, Arnold R. *Making the Second Ghetto: Race and Housing in Chicago, 1940–1960.* New York: Cambridge University Press, 1983.

————. "Massive Resistance in the Urban North: Trumbull Park, Chicago, 1953–1966." *Journal of American History* 82 (September 1995): 522–50.

Homel, Michael. *Down From Equality: Black Chicagoans and the Public Schools, 1920–41.* Urbana: University of Illinois Press, 1984.

————. "The Politics of Public Education in Black Chicago, 1910–1941." *Journal of Negro Education* 45 (Spring 1976): 176–91.

House, Ernest R. *Jesse Jackson and the Politics of Charisma: The Rise and Fall of the PUSH/Excel Program.* Boulder, Colo.: Westview Press, 1988.

Jackson, Kenneth T. *Crabgrass Frontier: The Suburbanization of the United States.* New York: Oxford University Press, 1985.

Jankov, Pavlyn, and Carol Caref. "Segregation and Inequality in Chicago Public Schools, Transformed and Intensified under Corporate Education Reform." *Education Policy Analysis Archives* 25 (June 2017): 1–30.

Johnson, Cedric. *Revolutionaries to Race Leaders: Black Power and the Making of African American Politics.* Minneapolis: University of Minnesota Press, 2007.

Joseph, Peniel E. *The Black Power Movement: Rethinking the Civil Rights–Black Power Era.* New York: Routledge, 2006.

————. *Waiting 'til the Midnight Hour: A Narrative History of Black Power in America.* New York: Henry Holt, 2006.

————, ed. *Neighborhood Rebels: Black Power at the Local Level.* New York: Palgrave Macmillan, 2010.

Kafka, Judith. *The History of "Zero Tolerance" in American Public Schooling.* New York: Palgrave Macmillan, 2011.

Kahlenberg, Richard. *Tough Liberal: Albert Shanker and the Battles over Schools, Unions, Race, and Democracy.* New York: Columbia University Press, 2007.

Kahrl, Andrew W. "Capitalizing on the Urban Fiscal Crisis: Predatory Tax Buyers in 1970s Chicago." *Journal of Urban History* (May 2015): 1–20.

Kantor, Harvey, and Robert Lowe. "From New Deal to No Deal: No Child Left Behind and the Devolution of Responsibility for Equal Opportunity." *Harvard Educational Review* 76 (December 2006): 474–502.

Katz, Michael B., ed. *The "Underclass" Debate: Views from History.* Princeton, N.J.: Princeton University Press, 1993.

Katz, Michael B., Mark J. Stern, and Jamie J. Fader. "The New African American Inequality." *Journal of American History* 92 (June 2005): 75–108.

Kelley, Robin D. G. *Freedom Dreams: The Black Radical Imagination.* Boston: Beacon Press, 2002.

Kent, Frank. Interview with Norma Jean Anderson. "A Message to the Establishment." September 1969. In *What Black Educators Are Saying*, edited by Nathan Wright Jr., 63–78. New York: Hawthorne Books, 1970.

Kent, James K. "The Coleman Report: Opening Pandora's Box." In *The Politics of Urban Education*, edited by Marilyn Gittell and Alan G. Hevesi. New York: Praeger, 1969.

Kharem, Haroon, and Eileen M. Hayes. "Separation or Integration: Early Black Nationalism and the Education Critique." In *Black Protest Thought and Education*, edited by William H. Watkins, 67–88. New York: Peter Lang, 2005.

Klein, Naomi. *The Shock Doctrine: The Rise of Disaster Capitalism.* New York: Picador, 2007.

Kraus, Neil, and Todd Swanstrom. "Minority Mayors and the Hollow-Prize Problem." *Political Science and Politics* 34 (March 2001): 99–105.

Kruse, Kevin. *One Nation under God: How Corporate America Invented Christian America*. New York: Basic Books, 2015.

Kusmer, Kenneth L. "African Americans in the City since World War II: From the Industrial to the Post-Industrial Era." *Journal of Urban History* 21 (May 1995): 458–504.

Kusmer, Kenneth L., and Joe W. Trotter, eds. *African American Urban History since World War II*. Chicago: University of Chicago Press, 2009.

Ladson-Billings, Gloria. "But That's Just Good Teaching! The Case for Culturally Relevant Pedagogy." *Theory into Practice* 34 (Summer 1995): 159–65.

———. *The Dreamkeepers: Successful Teachers of African American Children*. San Francisco: Jossey Bass, 1994.

Lang, Clarence. *Black America in the Shadow of the Sixties: Notes on the Civil Rights Movement, Neoliberalism, and Politics*. Ann Arbor: University of Michigan Press, 2015.

Lassiter, Matthew D. *Silent Majority: Suburban Politics in the Sunbelt South*. Princeton, N.J.: Princeton University Press, 2006.

Lee, Carol D. "The Centrality of Culture to the Scientific Study of Learning and Development: How an Ecological Framework in Education Research Facilitates Civic Responsibility." *Education Researcher* 37 (June–July 2008): 267–79.

———. "Comment: Unpacking Culture, Teaching, and Learning: A Response to 'The Power of Pedagogy.'" In *Race and Education: The Roles of History and Society in Educating African American Students*, edited by William H. Watkins, James H. Lewis, and Victoria Chou, 89–99. Boston: Allyn and Bacon, 2001.

———. *Culture, Literacy, and Learning: Taking Bloom in the Midst of the Whirlwind*. New York: Teachers College Press, 2007.

———. "Historical Evolution of Risk and Equity: Interdisciplinary Issues and Critiques." *Review of Research in Education* 33 (March 2009): 63–100.

———. "Profile of an Independent Black Institution: African-Centered Education at Work." *Journal of Negro Education* 61 (Spring 1992): 160–77.

Lee, Don L. *From Plan to Planet: Life Studies: The Need for Afrikan Minds and Institutions*. Detroit: Broadside Press, 1973.

Lewis, Dan A., and Kathryn Nakagawa. *Race and Educational Reform in the American Metropolis: A Study of School Decentralization*. Albany: State University of New York Press, 1995.

Lewis, Earl. *In their Own Interests: Race, Class, and Power in Twentieth-Century Norfolk, Virginia*. Berkeley: University of California Press, 1993.

Lewis, Heather. *New York City Public Schools from Brownsville to Bloomberg: Community Control and Its Legacy*. New York: Teacher College Press, 2013.

Lipman, Pauline. "Education and the New Urban Workforce in a Global City." In *City Kids, City Schools: More Reports from the Front Row*, edited by William Ayers, Gloria Ladson-Billings, and Gregory Michie, 273–86. New York: New Press, 2008.

———. "The Landscape of Education 'Reform' in Chicago: Neoliberalism Meets a Grassroots Movement." *Education Policy Analysis Archives* (online) 25, no. 54 (June 5, 2017).

———. *The New Political Economy of Urban Education*. New York: Routledge, 2011.

Lomotey, Kofi, and Craig Brookins. "Independent Black Institutions: A Cultural Perspective." In *Visible Now: Blacks in Private Schools*, edited by Diana T. Slaughter and Deborah J. Johnson, 163–83. Westport, Conn.: Greenwood, 1988.

Lyons, John F. *Teachers and Reform: Chicago Public Education, 1929–1970.* Urbana: University of Illinois Press, 2008.

MacLean, Nancy. *Democracy in Chains: The Deep History of the Radical Right's Stealth Plan for America.* New York: Viking, 2017.

Madhubuti, Haki. "Enemy: From the White Left, White Right, and In-Between." *Black World* 23 (October 1974): 36–47.

———. "The Latest Purge: The Attack on Black Nationalism and Pan-Afrikanism by the New Left, the Sons and Daughters of the Old Left." *Black Scholar* 6 (September 1974): 43–56.

———. *YellowBlack: The First Twenty-One Years of a Poet's Life.* Chicago: Third World Press, 2006.

Mahtesian, Charles. "Taking Chicago Private: Under Richard M. Daley, the 'City That Works' Is Learning to Live with a Few Less Workers on the Public Payroll." *Governing Magazine* 7 (April 1994): 26–32.

Mantler, Gordon K. *Power to the Poor: Black-Brown Coalition and the Fight for Economic Justice, 1960–1974.* Chapel Hill: University of North Carolina Press, 2013.

Marable, Manning. *Race, Reform, and Rebellion: The Second Reconstruction and Beyond in Black America, 1945–2006.* 1984. Oxford: University Press of Mississippi, 2007.

Massey, Douglas, and Nancy Denton. *American Apartheid: Segregation and the Making of the Underclass.* Cambridge, Mass.: Harvard University Press, 1993.

McGirr, Lisa. *Suburban Warriors: The Origins of the New American Right.* Princeton, N.J.: Princeton University Press, 2001.

McNally, David. *Global Slump: The Economics and Politics of Crisis and Resistance.* Oakland, Calif.: PM Press, 2011.

Mirel, Jeffrey. "School Reform, Chicago Style: Educational Innovation in a Changing Urban Context, 1976–1991." *Urban Education* 28 (July 1993): 116–49.

Montgomery, M. Lee. "The Education of Black Children." In *What Black Educators Are Saying*, edited by Nathan Wright Jr., 48–52. New York: Hawthorne Books, 1970.

———. "Our Changing School and Community." In *What Black Educators Are Saying*, edited by Nathan Wright Jr., 272–77. New York: Hawthorne Books, 1970.

Moore, Leonard N. *Carl B. Stokes and the Rise of Black Political Power.* Urbana: University of Illinois Press, 2002.

Moore, Natalie Y. *The South Side: A Portrait of Chicago and American Segregation.* New York: St. Martin's Press, 2016.

Moore, Natalie Y., and Lance Williams. *The Almighty Black P Stone Nation: The Rise, Fall, and Resurgence of an American Gang.* Chicago: Chicago Review Press, 2011.

Moreton, Bethany. *To Serve God and Wal-Mart: The Making of Christian Free Enterprise.* Cambridge, Mass.: Harvard University Press, 2009.

Moses, Wilson Jeremiah. *Afrotopia: The Roots of African American Popular History.* New York: Cambridge University Press, 1998.

Moss, Hilary J. *Schooling Citizens: The Struggle for African American Education in Antebellum America.* Chicago: University of Chicago Press, 2009.

Murch, Donna Jean. *Living for the City: Migration, Education, and the Rise of the Black Panther Party in Oakland, California.* Chapel Hill: University of North Carolina Press, 2010.

Nickerson, Michelle M. *Mothers of Conservatism: Women and the Postwar Right.* Princeton, N.J.: Princeton University Press, 2012.

Nicolaides, Becky M. *My Blue Heaven: Life and Politics in the Working-Class Suburbs of Los Angeles, 1920–1965.* Chicago: University of Chicago Press, 2002.

Nyong'o, Tavia. "Situating Precarity between the Body and the Commons." *Women and Performance: A Journal of Feminist Theory* 24, no. 2 (2013): 157–61.

O'Brien, Ruth. *Workers' Paradox: The Republican Origins of New Deal Labor Policy, 1886–1935.* Chapel Hill: University of North Carolina Press, 1998.

O'Connell, Mary. "School Reform, Chicago Style: How Citizens Organized to Change Public Policy." In *The Neighborhood Works*, special issue. Chicago: Center for Neighborhood Technology, 1991.

Ogletree, Charles J. *All Deliberate Speed: Reflections on the First Half Century of Brown v. Board of Education.* New York: Norton, 2004.

Orfield, Gary. "The Growth of Segregation: African Americans, Latinos, and Unequal Education." In *Dismantling Desegregation: The Quiet Reversal of Brown v. Board of Education*, edited by Gary Orfield and Susan Eaton, 53–72. New York: New Press, 1996.

———. *Must We Bus? Segregated Schools and National Policy.* Washington, D.C.: Brookings Institution, 1978.

Orfield, Gary, and Chungmei Lee. "*Brown* at 50: King's Dream or *Plessy*'s Nightmare?" In *The Structure of Schooling: Readings in the Sociology of Education*, edited by Richard Arum and Irenee Beattie, 165–77. New York: McGraw-Hill Higher Education, 2000.

Orleck, Annelise, and Lisa Gayle Hazirjian, eds. *The War on Poverty: A New Grassroots History, 1964–1980.* Athens: University of Georgia Press, 2011.

Ornstein, Allan C. *Metropolitan Schools: Administrative Decentralization vs. Community Control.* Metuchen, N.J.: Scarecrow Press, 1974.

Osman, Suleiman. "Decade of the Neighborhood." In *Rightward Bound: Making America Conservative in the 1970s*, edited by Bruce J. Schulman and Julian E. Zelizer, 106–27. Cambridge, Mass.: Harvard University Press, 2008.

Pacyga, Dominic. *Chicago: A Biography.* Chicago: University of Chicago Press, 2009.

Parks, Virginia. "Revisiting Shibboleths of Race and Urban Economy: Black Employment in Manufacturing and the Public Sector Compared, Chicago, 1950–2000." *International Journal of Urban and Regional Research* 35 (January 2011): 110–29.

Patterson, James T. *Brown v. Board of Education: A Civil Rights Milestone and Its Troubled Legacy.* New York: Oxford University Press, 2001.

Pattillo, Mary. "Black Middle-Class Neighborhoods." *Annual Review of Sociology* 31 (August 2005): 305–29.

———. *Black on the Block: The Politics of Race and Class in the City.* Chicago: University of Chicago Press, 2007.

———. "Everyday Politics of School Choice in the Black Community." *DuBois Review* 12 (April 2015): 41–71.

Pattillo-McCoy, Mary. "The Limits of Out-Migration for the Black Middle Class." *Journal of Urban Affairs* 22 (September 2000): 225–41.

Payne, Charles M. *So Much Reform, So Little Change: The Persistence of Failure in Urban Schools.* Cambridge, Mass.: Harvard Education Press, 2008.

———. "'The Whole United States Is Southern!': *Brown v. Board* and the Mystification of Race." *Journal of American History* 91 (June 2004): 83–91.

Peck, Jamie. *Constructions of Neoliberal Reason.* New York: Oxford University Press, 2010.

Perlstein, Daniel. *Justice, Justice: School Politics and the Eclipse of Liberalism.* New York: Peter Lang, 2004.

———. "Minds Stayed on Freedom: Politics and Pedagogy in the African-American Freedom Struggle." *American Educational Research Journal* 39 (Summer 2002): 249–77.

Perrillo, Jonna. *Uncivil Rights: Teachers, Unions, and Race in the Battle for School Equality.* Chicago: University of Chicago Press, 2012.

Perry, Theresa. "Up From the Parched Earth: Toward a Theory of African-American Achievement." In *Young, Gifted, and Black: Promoting High Achievement among African American Students,* edited by Theresa Perry, Claude Steele, and Asa G. Hilliard, 1–10. Boston: Beacon Press, 2003.

Peterson, Paul E. *School Politics, Chicago Style.* Chicago: University of Chicago Press, 1976.

Podair, Jerald E. *The Strike That Changed New York: Blacks, Whites, and the Ocean Hill–Brownsville Crisis.* New Haven, Conn.: Yale University Press, 2002.

Poinsett, Alex. "Council Chairperson Sees New Leaders Emerging." *Catalyst: Voices of Chicago School Reform* 1 (May 1990): 8–9.

———. "School Reform, Black Leaders: Their Impact on Each Other." *Catalyst: Voices of Chicago School Reform* 1 (May 1990): 7–11, 43.

Pritchett, Wendell E. "Which Urban Crisis? Regionalism, Race, and Urban Policy, 1960–1974." *Journal of Urban History* 34 (January 2008): 266–86.

Ransby, Barbara. *Ella Baker and the Black Freedom Movement: A Radical Democratic Vision.* Chapel Hill: University of North Carolina Press, 2005.

———. *Eslanda: The Large and Unconventional Life of Mrs. Paul Robeson.* New Haven, Conn.: Yale University Press, 2013.

Rast, Joel. "Manufacturing Industrial Decline: The Politics of Economic Change in Chicago, 1955–1998." *Journal of Urban Affairs* 23 (April 2001): 175–90.

Ratteray, Joan Davis. "The Search for Access and Content in the Education of African-Americans." In *Too Much Schooling, Too Little Education: A Paradox of Black Life in White Societies,* edited by Mwalimu J. Shujaa, 123–42. Trenton, N.J.: Africa World Press, 1994.

Ratteray, Joan Davis, and Mwalimu J. Shujaa. "Defining a Tradition: Parental Choice in Independent Neighborhood Schools." In *Visible Now: Blacks in Private Schools,* edited by Diana T. Slaughter and Deborah J. Johnson, 184–98. Westport, Conn: Greenwood, 1988.

Ravitch, Diane. *The Death and Life of the Great American School System: How Testing and Choice Are Undermining Education.* New York: Basic Books, 2010.

———. *Reign of Error: The Hoax of the Privatization Movement and the Danger to America's Public Schools.* New York: Random House, 2013.

Reed, Adolph, Jr. "Black Urban Administrators." *Telos* 65 (September 1985): 47–58.

———. "The Black Urban Regime: Structural Origins and Constraints." In *Power, Community, and the City: Comparative Urban and Community Research,* vol. 1., edited by Michael Peter Smith, 138–89. New Brunswick, N.J.: Transaction Books, 1988.

———. *Stirrings in the Jug: Black Politics in the Post-Segregation Era*. Minneapolis: University of Minnesota Press, 1999.

Reed, Touré F. *Not Alms, but Opportunity: The Urban League and the Politics of Racial Uplift, 1910–1950*. Chapel Hill: University of North Carolina Press, 2008.

Rhodes, Jesse. *An Education in Politics: The Origins and Evolution of No Child Left Behind*. Ithaca, N.Y.: Cornell University Press, 2012.

Rich, Wilbur C. *Black Mayors and School Politics: The Failure of Reform in Detroit, Gary, and Newark*. New York: Garland, 1996.

Rickford, Russell. "Integration, Black Nationalism, and Radical Democratic Transformation in African American Philosophies of Education, 1965–1974." In *The New Black History: Revising the Second Reconstruction*, edited by Manning Marable and Elizabeth Kai Hinton, 287–317. New York: Macmillan, 2011.

———. *We Are an African People: Independent Education, Black Power, and the Radical Imagination*. New York: Oxford University Press, 2016.

Ridout, Nicholas, and Rebecca Schneider. "Precarity and Performance: An Introduction." *TDR* 56, no. 4 (2012): 5–9.

Rivlin, Gary. *Fire on the Prairie: Harold Washington, Chicago Politics, and the Roots of the Obama Presidency*. Philadelphia: Temple University Press, 2012.

Robnett, Belinda. "African-American Women in the Civil Rights Movement, 1954–1965: Gender, Leadership, and Micromobilization." *American Journal of Sociology* 101 (May 1996): 1661–93.

Rooks, Noliwe. *Cutting School: Privatization, Segregation, and the End of Public Education*. New York: New Press, 2017.

Rotella, Carlo. *October Cities: The Redevelopment of Urban Literature*. Berkeley, Calif.: University of California Press, 1998.

Royko, Mike. *Boss: Richard J. Daley of Chicago*. New York: Plume, 1971.

Rury, John L. "Race, Space, and the Politics of Chicago Public Schools: Benjamin Willis and the Tragedy of Urban Education." *History of Education Quarterly* 39 (Summer 1999): 117–42.

Russom, Gillian. "Obama's Neoliberal Agenda for Education." In *Education and Capitalism: Struggles for Learning and Liberation*, edited by Jeff Bale and Sarah Knopp, 109–34. Chicago: Haymarket Books, 2012.

Sanders, Crystal. *A Chance for Change: Head Start and Mississippi's Black Freedom Struggle*. Chapel Hill: University of North Carolina Press, 2016.

Saunders, Richard R., and Jay L. Saunders. "W. Edward Deming, Quality Analysis, and Total Behavior Management." *Behavior Analyst* 17 (Spring 1994): 115–35.

Schrag, Peter. "Why Our Schools Have Failed." In *The Politics of Urban Education*, edited by Marilyn Gittell and Alan G. Hevesi. New York: Praeger, 1969.

Scott, Daryl Michael. *Contempt and Pity: Social Policy and the Image of the Damaged Black Psyche, 1880–1996*. Chapel Hill: University of North Carolina Press, 1997.

———. "Postwar Pluralism, *Brown v. Board of Education*, and the Origins of Multicultural Education." *Journal of American History* 91 (June 2004): 69–82.

Scott, Janelle T. "The Politics of Venture Philanthropy in Charter School Policy and Advocacy." *Educational Policy* 23 (January 2009): 106–36.

———. "Rosa Parks Moment? School Choice and the Marketization of Civil Rights." *Critical Studies in Education* 54 (February 2013): 5–18.

Scott, Janelle T., and Jennifer Jellison Holme. "The Political Economy of Market-Based Educational Policies: Race and Reform in Urban School Districts, 1915 to 2016." *Review of Research in Education* 40 (March 2016): 250–97.

Self, Robert O. *American Babylon: Race and the Struggle for Postwar Oakland.* Princeton, N.J.: Princeton University Press, 2003.

Seligman, Amanda. *Block by Block: Neighborhoods and Public Policy on Chicago's West Side.* Chicago: University of Chicago Press, 2005.

———. "'But Burn—No': The Rest of the Crowd in Three Civil Disorders in 1960s Chicago." *Journal of Urban History* 37 (March 2011): 230–55.

Shipps, Dorothy. *School Reform, Corporate Style: Chicago, 1880–2000.* Lawrence: University Press of Kansas, 2006.

Shujaa, Mwalimu J., ed. *Beyond Desegregation: The Politics of Quality in African American Schooling.* Thousand Oaks, Calif.: Corwin Press, 1996.

———. *Too Much Schooling, Too Little Education: A Paradox of Black Life in White Societies.* Trenton, N.J.: Africa World Press, 1994.

Shujaa, Mwalimu J., and Hannibal T. Afrik. "School Desegregation, the Politics of Culture, and the Council of Independent Black Institutions." In *Beyond Desegregation: The Politics of Quality in African American Schooling,* edited by Mwalimu J. Shujaa, 253–68. Thousand Oaks, Calif.: Corwin Press, 1996.

Sizemore, Barbara A. *An Abashing Anomaly: The High Achieving Predominantly Black Elementary School.* Pittsburgh: University of Pittsburgh and National Institute of Education, 1983.

———. "Education for Liberation." *School Review* 81 (May 1973): 399–401.

———. "Pitfalls and Promises of Effective Schools Research." *Journal of Negro Education* 54 (Summer 1985): 269–88.

———. *Walking in Circles: The Black Struggle for School Reform.* Chicago: Third World Press, 2008.

Slaughter, Diana T., and Deborah J. Johnson. "Introduction and Overview." In *Visible Now: Blacks in Private Schools,* edited by Diana T. Slaughter and Deborah J. Johnson, 1–5. Westport, Conn.: Greenwood, 1988.

Smethurst, James Edward. *The Black Arts Movement: Literary Nationalism in the 1960s and 1970s.* Chapel Hill: University of North Carolina Press, 2005.

Smith, Preston H., II. *Racial Democracy and the Black Metropolis: Housing Policy in Postwar Chicago.* Minneapolis: University of Minnesota Press, 2012.

Smith, William David. "Test Validity, Reliability: The Effect of Tests Results on the Black Self-Concept and the Educational Curriculum." *Journal of Black Psychology* 1 (February 1975): 84–94.

Spear, Allan. *Black Chicago: The Making of a Negro Ghetto, 1890–1920.* Chicago: University of Chicago Press, 1967.

Stein, Judith. *Pivotal Decade: How the United States Traded Factories for Finance in the Seventies.* New Haven, Conn.: Yale University Press, 2010.

Stewart, Allison. *First Class: The Legacy of Dunbar, America's First Black Public High School.* Chicago: Chicago Review Press, 2015.

Stier, Haya, and Marta Tienda. *The Color of Opportunity: Pathways to Family, Welfare, and Work*. Chicago: University of Chicago Press, 2000.

Strickland, Arvah E. *History of the Chicago Urban League*. Urbana: University of Illinois Press, 1966.

Stokes, Olivia Pearl. "The New Black Dimension in Our Society." In *What Black Educators Are Saying*, edited by Nathan Wright Jr., 18–22. New York: Hawthorne Books, 1970.

Stulberg, Lisa M. *Race, Schools, and Hope: African Americans and School Choice after Brown*. New York: Columbia University Press, 2008.

Sugrue, Thomas J. "Crabgrass-Roots Politics: Race, Rights, and the Reaction against Liberalism in the Urban North, 1940–1964." *Journal of American History* 82, no. 2 (1995): 551–78.

———. *The Origins of the Urban Crisis: Race and Inequality in Postwar Detroit*. Princeton, N.J.: Princeton University Press, 1996.

Taylor, Clarence. *Knocking at Our Own Door: Milton A. Galamison and the Struggle to Integrate New York City Schools*. New York: Columbia University Press, 1997.

———. *Reds at the Blackboard: Communism, Civil Rights, and the New York City Teacher's Union*. New York: Columbia University Press, 2010.

———, ed. *Civil Rights in New York City: From World War II to the Giuliani Era*. New York: Fordham University Press, 2011.

Taylor, Keeanga-Yamahtta. *From #BlackLivesMatter to Black Liberation*. Chicago: Haymarket Books, 2016.

Taylor, Ula Yvette. *The Promise of Patriarchy: Women and the Nation of Islam*. Chapel Hill: University of North Carolina Press, 2017.

Tejada, Carlos. "Genealogies of the Student 'Blowouts' of 1968." In *Marching Students: Chicana and Chicano Activism in Education, 1968–Present*, edited by Margarita Berta-Avila, Anita Tijerina-Revilla, and Julie Figueroa, 9–42. Reno: University of Nevada Press, 2011.

Theoharis, Jeanne. "'W-A-L-K-O-U-T!': High School Students and the Development of Black Power in L.A." In *Neighborhood Rebels: Black Power at the Local Level*, edited by Peniel Joseph, 107–30. New York: Palgrave Macmillan, 2010.

———. "'We Saved the City': Black Struggles for Educational Equality in Boston, 1960–1976." *Radical History Review* 81, no. 1 (2001): 61–93.

Theoharis, Jeanne, and Komozi Woodard, eds. *Freedom North: Black Freedom Struggles outside the South, 1940–1980*. New York: Palgrave Macmillan, 2003.

Thompson, Heather Ann. *Whose Detroit? Politics, Labor, and Race in a Modern American City*. Ithaca, N.Y.: Cornell University Press, 2001.

Thompson, Philip, III. *Double Trouble: Black Mayors, Black Communities, and the Call for a Deep Democracy*. New York: Oxford University Press, 2006.

Tingle, Michel Laurie. "Privatization and the Reagan Administration: Ideology and Application." *Yale Law and Policy Review* 6 (1988): 229–57.

Todd-Breland, Elizabeth. "Barbara Sizemore and the Politics of Black Educational Achievement and Community Control, 1963–1975." *Journal of African American History* 100 (Fall 2015): 636–62.

———. "Control and Independence: Black Alternatives for Urban Education." In *Using Past as Prologue: Contemporary Perspectives on African American Educational History*, edited by Dionne Danns, Michelle A. Purdy, and Christopher M. Span, 253–74. Charlotte: Information Age Publishing, 2015.

Travis, Dempsey J. *An Autobiography of Black Politics*. Chicago: Urban Research Press, 1987.

———. *"Harold," the People's Mayor: An Authorized Biography of Mayor Harold Washington*. Chicago: Urban Research Press, 1989.

Troy, Gil. *Morning in America: How Ronald Reagan Invented the 1980s*. Princeton, N.J.: Princeton University Press, 2005.

Ture, Kwame, and Charles V. Hamilton. *Black Power: The Politics of Liberation in America*. 1967. New York: Vintage Books, 1992.

Uetricht, Micah. *Strike for America: Chicago Teachers against Austerity*. London: Verso, 2014.

Valk, Anne M. *Radical Sisters: Second Wave Feminism and Black Liberation in Washington, D.C.* Urbana: University of Illinois Press, 2008.

Van Deburg, William L. *New Day in Babylon: The Black Power Movement in American Culture, 1965–1975*. Chicago: University of Chicago Press, 1992.

VanTassel-Baska, Joyce. "The History of Urban Gifted Education." *Gifted Child Today* 33, no. 4 (Fall 2010): 18–27.

Venkatesh, Sudhir Alladi. *American Project: The Rise and Fall of a Modern Ghetto*. Cambridge, Mass.: Harvard University Press, 2000.

Vinovskis, Maris. *The Birth of Head Start: Preschool Education Policies in the Kennedy and Johnson Administrations*. Chicago: University of Chicago Press, 2005.

Wacquant, Loic J. D., and William Julius Wilson. "The Cost of Racial and Class Exclusion in the Inner City." *Annals of the American Academy of Political and Social Science* 501 (January 1989): 8–25.

Walker, Vanessa Siddle. *Hello Professor: A Black Principal and Professional Leadership in the Segregated South*. Chapel Hill: University of North Carolina Press, 2009.

———. *Their Highest Potential: An African American School Community in the Segregated South*. Chapel Hill: University of North Carolina Press, 1996.

Walker-McWilliams, Marcia. *Reverend Addie Wyatt: Faith and the Fight for Labor, Gender, and Racial Equality*. Urbana: University of Illinois Press, 2016.

Watkins, William H. "Reclaiming Historical Visions of Quality Schooling: The Legacy of Early 20th Century Black Intellectuals." In *Beyond Desegregation: The Politics of Quality in African American Schooling*, edited by Mwalimu J. Shujaa, 9–25. Thousand Oaks, Calif.: Corwin Press, 1996.

West, Kimberly C. "A Desegregation Tool That Backfired: Magnet School and Classroom Segregation." *Yale Law Journal* 103, no. 8 (June 1994): 2567–92.

Williams, Jakobi. *From the Bullet to the Ballot: The Illinois Chapter of the Black Panther Party and Racial Coalition Politics in Chicago*. Chapel Hill: University of North Carolina Press, 2013.

Williams, Rhonda. *The Politics of Public Housing: Black Women's Struggles against Urban Inequality*. New York: Oxford University Press, 2004.

Williamson, Joy. "Community Control with a Black Nationalist Twist: The Black Panther Party's Educational Programs." In *Black Protest Thought and Education*, edited by William H. Watkins, 137–58. New York: Peter Lang, 2005.

Willis, Vincent. "'Let Me In, I Have the Right to Be Here': Black Youth Struggle for Equal Education and Full Citizenship after the *Brown* Decision, 1954–1969." *Citizenship Teaching and Learning* 9 (December 2013): 53–70.

Wilson, William Julius. *The Declining Significance of Race: Blacks and Changing American Institutions.* Chicago: University of Chicago Press, 1978.

——. *The Truly Disadvantaged: The Inner City, the Underclass, and Public Policy.* Chicago: University of Chicago Press, 1987.

Woodard, Komozi. *A Nation within a Nation: Amiri Baraka (LeRoi Jones) and Black Power Politics.* Chapel Hill: University of North Carolina Press, 1999.

Wright, Nathan, Jr., ed. *What Black Educators Are Saying.* New York: Hawthorne Books, 1970.

Unpublished Sources

Alanis, Jaime. "The Harrison High School Walkouts of 1968: Struggle for Equal Schools and Chicanismo in Chicago." Ph.D. diss., University of Illinois, Urbana-Champaign, 2010.

Dobbie, Will S., and Roland G. Fryer Jr. "Charter Schools and Labor Market Outcomes." NBER Working Paper No. 22502, National Bureau of Economic Research, August 2016.

Ewing, Eve L. "Shuttered Schools in the Black Metropolis: Race, History, and Discourse on Chicago's South Side." Ph.D. diss., Harvard University, 2016.

Haney, LeViis A. "The 1995 Chicago School Reform Amendatory Act and the CPS CEO: A Historical Examination of the Administration of CEOs Paul Vallas and Arne Duncan." Ed.D. diss., Loyola University, Chicago, 2011.

Irby, Decoteau J. "Dignity-Based Black Male Achievement: What It Entails and Its Relevance for Social Justice Leadership." Paper delivered at Re-Imagining the Frontiers of Education: Leadership With/In Transnational & Transcultural Spaces, November 20–23, 2015, San Diego, Calif.

Kryczka, Nicholas. "Selective Renewal: Education Markets and Urban Renaissance in Post–Civil Rights Chicago" Ph.D. diss., University of Chicago, forthcoming.

Landwermeyer, Francis Michael. "Teacher Unionism—Chicago Style: A History of the Chicago Teachers Union, 1937–1972." Ph.D. diss., University of Chicago, 1978.

Peoples, Lillie. "Black Teacher Organizations in the Black Power Movement." Master's thesis, Northeastern Illinois University, 1980.

Russell, Michelle C. Text message to author. December 18, 2014.

Spatz, David A. "Roads to Postwar Urbanism: Expressway Building and the Transformation of Metropolitan Chicago, 1930–1975." Ph.D. diss., University of Chicago, 2010.

Watson, John L., Jr. "Integrating Lean Manufacturing with Technology: Analyzing the Effects of Organizational Performance in Terms of Quality, Cost, and Response Time." Ph.D. diss., Capella University, 2006.

Weidner, Catherine Sardo. "Debating the Future of Chicago's Youth: Black Professionals, Black Labor, and Educational Politics during the Civil Rights Era, 1950–1965." Ph.D. diss., Northwestern University, 1989.

INDEX

busing, 22, 38, 40–46, 64, 131, 147, 197, 202

BYP 100. *See* Black Youth Project 100

Byrd, Manford, Jr., 152, 158, 162–63, 169, 170, 174, 185

Byrne, Jane, 161, 274n18; appointments by, 151–52, 159; austerity embraced by, 150–51; education privatization and, 135, 150–51; as mayoral candidate (1979), 146, 150; as mayoral candidate (1983), 155–56, 158; as mayoral candidate (1987), 162

Campbell, Leslie (Jitu Weusi), 54, 85, 138

Campbell, Roald, 70

CAPTS. *See* Community, Administrators, Parents, Teachers, and Students

Carmichael, Stokely, 148, 170

Cartwright, Gene, 161

Catalyst (Lenz), 194

Catholic Interracial Council, 42

Caucus of Rank-and-File Educators, 220, 229, 230

Crawley, Ashon, 236–37

CBUC. *See* Chicago Black United Communities

CCCO. *See* Coordinating Council of Community Organizations

Center for Education Reform, 205

Center for Inner City Studies, 68–69, 87, 171

Center for School Improvement (Center for Urban School Improvement), 179, 194, 195, 213

Centers for New Horizons, 86

certification. *See* teacher certification

Charles, Harold (Hannibal Afrik), 85, 101, 116, 118, 139, 165, 268n9

charter schools, 6, 12, 14, 107–8, 177, 180, 191, 200–201, 203, 220, 228; Black enrollment in, 13, 209, 224–25; IPE's operation of, 107, 108, 206–8, 217, 223; opposition to and criticism of, 209, 215–16, 217, 231–32; origins and expectations of, 204–10; school clos-

ings and, 221–22; University of Chicago's operation of, 80, 213–15

Chein, Isidor, 32

Chicago Black United Communities (CBUC), 151–55

Chicago Black United Front, 155

Chicago Commercial Club, 31, 150, 203, 222

Chicago Defender, 23, 24, 44, 69, 77

Chicago Democratic machine (Cook County Democratic Party): Black opposition to, 55, 121, 138, 145–48, 149–50, 168; Blacks marginalized and antagonized by, 9–10, 25, 121, 148, 157–58, 170, 222, 236; constituencies of, 9–10, 25, 35, 121, 145, 184; and Latinx antimachine politics, 154; operations and power of, 25, 31, 90, 157–58, 170, 173, 174, 218, 220. *See also* Daley, Richard J.; patronage

Chicago Freedom Movement, 28, 33, 49

Chicago Housing Authority, 211. *See also* public housing; Plan for Transformation

Chicago Learning Works Compact, 162–63, 164, 166, 175

Chicago Metropolitan (Metro) High School, 197

Chicago Panel on Public School Policy and Finance, 182, 194

Chicago Partnership for Education Progress, 162–63

Chicago School Finance Authority, 135, 150–51, 152, 163, 168–69, 179, 186

Chicago School Reform Act (1988), 13, 194, 204; Black perspectives on, 171–73, 174, 175, 182–84; decentralization effected by, 172–73, 175, 183; LSCs created by, 172, 174, 181–82; partial rollback of, 186; White liberal support for, 171, 177, 182, 195

Chicago School Reform Amendatory Act (1995), 185

Chicago School Reform Movement, 79, 139; coalitions and conflict within,

Index

Index

Mahiri, Jabari, 97
Malcolm X, 88, 94
Malcolm X College (Crane Junior College), 57
Malone, Saundra (Kimya Mainda Moyo), 265n37
manufacturing, 7, 42, 43–44, 136, 160
March on Washington for Jobs and Freedom, 29
Martin, Trayvon, 232
Marxism, 84, 89, 107
Mary McLeod Bethune Teacher Training Institute, 207–8
Mason, Robert, 270n32
May Elementary School, 41
McCallie, Franklin, 39
McClelland, Lelia, 72
McCurties, Samuel, 39
McFerren, Coretta, 169–70, 171, 183
McGee, Robert, 61
McLawler, Jewel C. (Jewel C. Latimore; Johari Amini), 87, 100
McNeil, E. Duke, 75–76, 77
McQuirter, James, 124, 268n9
meatpacking, 21, 43
Melnick, Curtis, 70, 76
merit pay, 186
Metcalfe, Ralph, 138, 274n11, 274n16
Mexican Americans, 57–58, 146, 154
Milliken v. Bradley (1974), 23–24
Milwaukee, 200
Mississippi, 55, 86
Model Cities, 106
Modern Black Convention Movement, 264n24
Montessori, Maria, 101
Montgomery, M. Lee, 54
Moore, Don, 171, 182, 194
Morgan Park, 37–39, 47
Morgan Park High School, 133, 203
Mount Greenwood, 197
Movement for Black Lives, 233
Moynihan, Daniel Patrick, 43
Moynihan Report (*The Negro Family*; 1965), 10, 43–44, 52, 105

Moyo, Kofi (Lloyd Sanders), 265n37
Muhammad Speaks, 100

NAACP. *See* National Association for the Advancement of Colored People
National Advisory Commission on Civil Disorders (Kerner Commission), 55
National Association for the Advancement of Colored People (NAACP), 9, 21, 24, 26, 29, 219, 250n37, 268n9
National Association of African-American Educators, 54
National Education Association, 137, 194
National Teacher Corps, 128
Nation at Risk, A, 144, 159, 193, 199
Nation of Islam, 86, 100
NCDC. *See* New Concept Development Center
Negro American Labor Council, 250n37, 268n9
Negro Family, The (Moynihan Report; 1965), 10, 43–44, 52, 105
neighborhood schools, 11, 13, 19, 26, 41, 42, 45, 53, 61, 109, 131, 180, 197, 202, 209, 221, 225, 227
neoliberalism, 2, 5, 13–14, 180–81, 191, 207–8, 222; bipartisan support for, 212, 228; Black support for, 220, 223–25; community-based politics vs., 15, 217, 220, 229–30, 231–32; public-private partnerships linked to, 60. *See also* accountability; corporatism; privatization
Newark, N.J., 35, 55, 89, 95–96, 145
New Concept Development Center (NCDC), 81, 83, 85, 87, 94, 97–109, 206–7, 208; curriculum and pedagogy of, 87, 98–102, 108–9, 266nn59–60
New Deal, 9, 10, 211
New Orleans, 102, 212
New York City, 54, 85, 123–24, 225
Nguzo Saba (Seven Principles), 91–92, 94, 98, 100, 137
Nixon, Richard, 198

Made in the USA
Columbia, SC
11 September 2020